Mikoyan-Gure
MiG-17

The Soviet Union's Jet Fighter of the Fifties

Yefim Gordon

Mikoyan-Gurevich MiG-17
The Soviet Union's Jet Fighter of the Fifties
© 2002 Yefim Gordon
ISBN 1 85780 107 5

Published by Midland Publishing
4 Watling Drive, Hinckley, LE10 3EY, England
Tel: 01455 254 490   Fax: 01455 254 495
E-mail: midlandbooks@compuserve.com

Midland Publishing is an imprint of
Ian Allan Publishing Ltd

Worldwide distribution (except North America):
Midland Counties Publications
4 Watling Drive, Hinckley, LE10 3EY, England
Telephone: 01455 254 450   Fax: 01455 233 737
E-mail: midlandbooks@compuserve.com
www.midlandcountiessuperstore.com

North American trade distribution:
Specialty Press Publishers & Wholesalers Inc.
11605 Kost Dam Road, North Branch, MN 55056
Tel: 651 583 3239   Fax: 651 583 2023
Toll free telephone: 800 895 4585

Design concept and layout
© 2002 Midland Publishing and
Stephen Thompson Associates

Printed in England by
Ian Allan Printing Ltd
Riverdene Business Park, Molesey Road,
Hersham, Surrey, KT12 4RG

Contents

Introduction: Genealogy 3

Chapters
   1 Building a Better Fighter 5
   2 The MiG-17 Family 10
   3 Foreign Production 44
   4 The MiG-17 in Action 59
   5 MiG-17 Operators Worldwide 74
   6 The MiG-17 in Detail 108

End notes 111

MiG-17 in Colour 113

MiG-17 Family Drawings 132

Title page: **This late production MiG-17 *Fresco-A*
with 0.88m² airbrakes is a gate guard at one of
the Russian Air Force's fighter bases.**

Below: **01 Blue, an early MiG-17 *Fresco-A* with
0.5m² airbrakes, is preserved in the museum of
the Russian Air Defence Force's 148th Combat
and Conversion Training Centre at Savostleyka
AB. Very few examples of the original production
version survive.** Both Yefim Gordon archive

Genealogy

The design bureau led by Artyom Ivanovich Mikoyan and Mikhail Iosifovich Gurevich, aka OKB-155[1] or MMZ[2] 'Zenit' (Zenith), had established itself as a 'fighter maker' prior to the Second World War. Its first products to enter production and service – the MiG-1 and MiG-3 high-altitude interceptors – were built on a small scale and overshadowed by the tactical fighters developed by the Yakovlev and Lavochkin bureaux, as these were built in in much greater numbers to suit the needs of the time.

When Soviet aviation entered the jet age, however, the Mikoyan/Gurevich OKB was at the forefront. At first, like the other Soviet fighter design bureaux, OKB-155 tried jet boosters and rocket motors at first; unlike the other design bureaux, however, these were 'clean sheet of paper' designs, not adaptations of production models. The I-250[3] (manufacturer's designation *izdeliye* N)[4] mixed-power fighter was brought out in 1945. It featured a VRDK 'pseudo-turbojet engine' (*vozdooshno-reaktivnyy dvigatel', kompressornyy*) in the tail, the axial compressor being driven via an extension shaft by a Klimov VK-107R 12-cylinder liquid-cooled piston engine which also drove a regular airscrew. This was followed in 1946 by the I-270 (*izdeliye* Zh) interceptor powered by a twin-chamber liquid-fuel rocket motor. However, even as design work on these aircraft progressed the design team realised that pure jet aircraft were the way to go.

Initially known as the I-300 (manufacturer's designation *izdeliye* F) and later as the MiG-9 (NATO reporting name *Fargo*), the Mikoyan OKB's first jet fighter made its maiden flight on 24th April 1946 – the first flight of a jet-powered aircraft in the Soviet Union. It was powered by two RD-20 engines, Soviet copies of the German BMW 003 turbojet. This was a forced measure intended to save time; true enough, the Soviet aircraft industry was already working on indigenous turbojet engines, but then the West already had put jet fighters into squadron service. Catching up with the West in this respect was a priority task which could not wait until the Soviet jet engines were brought up to scratch.

In its production form (I-301/*izdeliye* FS) the MiG-9 became the first 'real' jet fighter to enter service with the Soviet Air Force (VVS – *Voyenno-vozdooshnyye seely*). In this context 'real' means that, as far as the VVS was concerned, Yakovlev's first jet fighter – the Yak-15 *Feather* (which entered flight test on the same day as the I-300) – was no more than a sort of conversion trainer to ease the transition from piston-engined fighters to jets due to its rather disappointing performance. Other contemporary Soviet jet fighters created by Aleksandr S Yakovlev's OKB-115, Semyon A Lavochkin's OKB-301, Pavel O Sukhoi's OKB-51 and Semyon M Alekseyev's OKB-21 fared even worse, reaching only the prototype stage. The MiG-9 was also the first Soviet jet fighter to achieve export status, a small number of these machines being delivered to the People's Republic of China. Yet once again the MiG-9 was a rather obscure type built in limited numbers.

The next type developed by OKB-155, however, was so successful that it brought Mikoyan world fame (or notoriety, depending on which side of the Iron Curtain you were on), becoming for many years a symbol of *the Soviet Threat*. Powered by a 2,270-kgp (5,004-lbst) Rolls-Royce Nene I turbojet, the first prototype of the I-310 (*izdeliye* S) light tactical fighter made its first flight on December 30, 1947. After some minor redesign the aircraft entered production and service with the Soviet Air Force in 1948 as the MiG-15 *Fagot-A* (*izdeliye* SV) with the RD-45F, a licence-built version of the Nene II.[5]

In its day the MiG-15 was a high-performance aircraft, with good maneuverability and an excellent rate of climb. It was heavily armed, with two 23-mm (.90 calibre) Nudel'man/Sooranov NS-23KM cannons to port and one 37-mm (1.45 calibre) Nudel'man N-37 cannon to starboard. Though having a fairly low rate of fire, they packed a tremendous punch and were very lethal, especially for slow and ponderous bombers which could not get out of the way quickly. Ingeniously, the cannons and their ammunition boxes were neatly mounted on a single tray under the cockpit. This tray could be winched down quickly by means of a hand crank and four pulleys for reloading and maintenance, reducing turnaround time dramatically. As a bonus, this arrangement placed the cannon muzzles well aft of the air intake lip, preventing blast gas ingestion and engine surge. The engineers obviously learned from experience with the MiG-9 where the protruding cannons, one of which was mounted in the intake splitter, caused the engines to flame out when they were fired.

The fighter evolved into several versions, the best-known of which were the MiG-15*bis Fagot-B* (*izdeliye* SD) tactical fighter powered by a 2,700-kgp (5,952-lbst) VK-1 turbojet[6] and the UTI-MiG-15 *Midget* advanced trainer (I-312, *izdeliye* ST-1 and ST-2). Over the years the design was progressively improved; for instance, on the MiG-15*bis* the NS-23KMs with a 550-rpm rate of fire soon gave way to Nudel'-man/Rikhter NR-23 cannons of identical calibre which offered a much higher rate of fire (850 rounds per minute) for virtually no increase in weight, and more effective airbrakes were introduced. The fighter proved to be quite versatile, serving such roles as ground attack (fighter-bomber), tactical photo reconnaissance, long-range escort and even target towing, to say nothing of the numerous weapons and avionics testbeds and other research and development versions.

The MiG-15 was built in huge numbers at nine (!) factories in the Soviet Union, as well as under licence in China, Czechoslovakia and Poland; Soviet production alone totalled no fewer than 13,131 copies! The aircraft was so successful that it paved the way for Mikoyan (and generally Soviet) fighter design for the next decade.

The *Fagot* was to have a long service career both at home and abroad, participating in quite a few conflicts around the world, the best-known of which is undoubtedly the Korean War of 1950-53. The MiG-15 also saw a lot of action in the Middle East – and on home ground, intercepting and destroying Western spyplanes which intruded into Soviet airspace quite frequently during the 1950s and 1960s.

The MiG's combat debut in Korea was a rude shock to the Western world; when the fighter had made its first public appearance at Moscow's Tushino airfield in August 1948, Western experts dismissed it as 'Russian, ergo substandard', and there was hell to pay for this approach. Early straight-wing jet fighters like the Lockheed P-80 Shooting Star, Republic F-84 Thunderjet and Gloster Meteor F.8 stood virtually no chances against the 'MiG Menace'; it was not until the MiG-15's nearest Western equivalent, the North American F-86 Sabre, arrived on the scene that things began to change. (Like the MiG-15, the F-86 also took to the air in 1947 (on 1st October), entered production in 1948 and was built by the thousand in its home countries and abroad.) Even so, the MiG and the Sabre were quite a match for each other when flown by experienced pilots; a lot depended on tactics, experience and the pilots' personal qualities. This was shown to good effect by the famous test pilot Charles 'Chuck' Yeager who evaluated a MiG-15*bis* captured in Korea.

According to USAF specialists, the MiG-15 was a well-built and reliable combat aircraft but with no finesse such as special fuel, new structural materials or other innovations. Western experts noted that the aircraft was lighter than contemporary swept-wing fighters (35% lighter than the F-86F and 47% lighter than the Hawker Hunter). They liked the neat weapons arrangement and ease of engine change but criticized the MiG's oversized inlet, low rate of fire and lack of a gun ranging radar which reduced the chances of a 'kill'.

The MiG-15 soon earned a good reputation for rugged simplicity, reliability, ease of maintenance and the ability to take a lot of punishment – all invaluable qualities in a war. The nickname bestowed on it by its pilots and ground crews, *samolyot-soldaht* ('soldier aircraft'), has to be regarded as the ultimate praise.

Still, people are never quite happy with what they have. Faced with the need to counter the threat posed by new fighter jets under development in the USA and their NATO allies, the Soviet Air Force demanded higher performance. This could be achieved by developing an all-new fighter or by redesigning the existing MiG-15 (installing a more powerful engine,

increasing wing sweep to increase speed etc). The Mikoyan OKB chose both ways. The second, evolutionary approach produced the fighter which is the subject of this book – the MiG-17; a fighter which equalled the fame of its predecessor and saw no less action than the MiG-15

Acknowledgements

The author wishes to express his gratitude to the following persons who have contributed to the making of this book:

First of all, as usual, I would like to thank the translator, Dmitriy S Komissarov, without whose work and assistance the book would never have appeared.

Also, my thanks go to Nigel Eastaway, one of the leaders of the Russian Aviation Research Trust, who provided a lot of valuable information on Chinese licence-built MiGs, and Helmut Walther and Keith Dexter who supplied photos which would otherwise hardly be obtainable.

Below: **This MiG-17 *Fresco*-A, a gate guard at one of the Russian Air Force's fighter bases, graphically shows the scimitar wing shape.**

Russian Language and Transliteration

The Russian language is phonetic – pronounced as written, or 'as seen'. Translating into English gives rise to many problems and the vast majority of these arise because English is not a straightforward language, with many pitfalls of pronunciation!

Accordingly, Russian words must be translated through into a *phonetic* form of English and this can lead to different ways of helping the reader pronounce what he sees. Every effort has been made to standardise this, but inevitably variations will occur. While reading from source to source this might seem confusing and/or inaccurate but it is the name as *pronounced* that is the constancy, not the *spelling* of that pronunciation!

The 20th letter of the Russian (Cyrillic) alphabet looks very much like a 'Y' but is pronounced as a 'U' as in the word 'rule'.

Another example is the train of thought that Russian words ending in 'y' are perhaps better spelt out as 'yi' to underline the pronunciation, but it is felt that most Western speakers would have problems getting their tongues around this!

This is a good example of the sort of problem that some Western sources have suffered from in the past (and occasionally even today) when they make the mental leap about what they see approximating to an English letter.

Chapter One

Building a Better Fighter

The MiG-17's descent is patently obvious in these views; it was not for nothing the aircraft was known as MiG-15bis 45°. Another early designation was I-330. Mikoyan OKB

I-330 (MiG-15bis 45°) experimental fighter (izdeliye SI)

The success of the MiG-15 convinced OKB-155 leaders Artyom I Mikoyan and Mikhail I Gurevich that the evolutionary approach they had taken with this fighter was a good one. Now OKB-155 began the next stage in the evolution of the *Fagot*, mating the fuselage, tail unit and VK-1 turbojet of the MiG-15bis with new wings swept back 45° at quarter-chord instead of 35°. This promised an improvement in performance at the expense of minimum changes in design and manufacturing technology.

Besides, the Soviet leaders, including the omnipotent Iosif V Stalin, also favoured the evolutionary approach. The other Soviet fighter makers – the Yakovlev and Lavochkin design bureaux – repeatedly approached the government, proposing new fighter types, but Stalin's reaction was invariably the same: 'We've got a good fighter, the MiG-15, and there's no point in developing new fighters in the near future. Let's concentrate on upgrading the MiG...'

Hence in early 1949 the Council of Ministers issued a directive tasking the Mikoyan OKB with the development of an improved MiG-15 in two basic versions – a 'normal' tactical fighter

and a radar-equipped all-weather interceptor (which is described separately). Continuing the line of fighter-type service designations, the directive referred to the new fighter as the I-330 – a designation that was hardly used at all.

The redesigned wings were the principal new feature of the I-330. Since the aircraft was based on the *Fagot-B*, the day fighter version received the manufacturer's designation *izdeliye* SI, the I probably standing for *izmenyonnoye* (altered). Unsurprisingly, it was also known initially as the MiG-15bis 45° or MiG-15bis 'strela 45' (pronounced *strelah* – lit. 'arrow 45'); the latter appellation was technical slang, since the Russian term for wing sweep is *strelovidnost'*.

The SI (MiG-15bis 45°) was not the first Soviet aircraft to have 45° wing sweep; this distinction belonged to the Lavochkin La-176 experimental fighter, a spinoff of the La-15 *Fantail* which entered flight test in September 1948. (The La-176 also gained the distinction of being the first Soviet aircraft to break the sound barrier, reaching Mach 1.02 in a shallow dive on 26th December 1948 with I Ye Fyodorov at the controls and later also in horizontal flight at the hands of Fyodorov and O V Sokolovskiy.)

Such wings were also being tested by TsAGI (*Tsentrahl'nyy aero- i ghidrodinameecheskiy institoot* – Central Aerodynamics & Hydrodynamics Institute named after Nikolay Ye Zhukovskiy) at the time, using wind tunnel

These views of the MiG-17 first prototype (SI-1) clearly show the new sharply-swept wings with a cranked leading edge and additional boundary layer fences. Mikoyan OKB

models and gliding models. Additional data had been obtained with the B-5 rocket-powered transonic research aircraft developed by Matus Ruvimovich Bisnovat and the DFS 346 rocket-powered Mach 2.5 research aircraft which was captured in almost complete condition by the end of the war and tested in the USSR.[1]

Mikoyan engineers went one step further than the others in choosing wing planform. The SI's wings had a scimitar shape, although nowhere nearly as pronounced as on the Handley Page HP.80 Victor bomber. Sweep at quarter-chord was 45° on the inboard half-span and 42° outboard (leading-edge sweep was 49° and 45° 30' respectively). This was done both for aerodynamic balancing purposes (to reduce the danger of tip stall) and to ensure maximum commonality with the MiG-15 (the root rib/fuselage attachment points were the same on the MiG-15 and the SI). The kink in the trailing edge at the root became more pronounced than on the MiG-15 and the unswept portion of the trailing edge adjacent to the fuselage was much bigger.

Wing area was increased from the MiG-15's 20.6m² (221.5ft²) to 22.6m² (243.0ft²) and anhedral from 2° to 3°; incidence remained unchanged at 1°. The wings utilised new airfoils (TsAGI S-12S at the root and TsAGI SR-11 at the tip). Aspect ratio and wing taper were

lower than on the MiG-15 (4.08 and 1.23 versus 4.85 and 1.61 respectively), while mean aerodynamic chord was increased from 2.12m (6ft 11½in) to 2.19m (7ft 2¼in).

The wingtips were more rounded than the MiG-15's; an extra pair of boundary layer fences was fitted on the inner wings to limit spanwise flow, increasing the total number to six, and the wing/fuselage joint carefully faired at the trailing edge. These measures were aimed at improving the aircraft's lift-to-drag ratio. The ailerons had internal aerodynamic balances and the port one incorporated a trim tab. Finally, the wing structure was stiffened by using thicker skins. Mikoyan had learned their lesson with the MiG-15 which had a tendency to drop a wing at high speed, called *val'ozhka* in Russian and caused caused by torsional stiffness asymmetry in the port and starboard wings. The problem was a result of the learning curve during initial production; a lengthy 'anti-*val'ozhka*' research programme had to be undertaken to cure it.

The forward fuselage up to the fuselage break point (frame 13) was identical to that of the MiG-15*bis*. The aft fuselage was new, being 900mm (2ft 11in) longer; total fuselage length was 8.805m (28ft 11in). Originally the airbrakes were only a little larger than on early *Fagot-Bs*, with an area of 0.522m² (5.61ft²) each;[2] maximum deflection was 50° versus 55° on the MiG-15.

The airbrakes were rectangular and placed low on the aft fuselage sides some way ahead of the engine nozzle. They were to function primarily as dive brakes during bombing (Soviet pilots fighting in Korea noted that the *Fagot-A/B*'s airbrakes were of little use during air-to-air combat).

Vertical tail area was enlarged slightly from 4.0m² (43.0ft²) to 4.26m² (45.8ft²) but fin leading-edge sweep remained unchanged at 55° 41'. The horizontal tail, however, was new, with 45° leading-edge sweep instead of 40°, a span of 3.18m (10ft 5¼in) and an area of 3.1m² (33.3ft²) versus 3.0m² (32.25ft²). A small ventral fin with an integral tail bumper was added to improve directional stability. The airframe made large-scale use of the new V95 aluminium alloy.

There were no major changes to the control system as compared to the MiG-15*bis*. The control surfaces were actuated by push-pull rods and the ailerons were powered, with a single B-7 hydraulic actuator installed in the cockpit immediately aft of the ejection seat, just like on the updated first production MiG-15 (construction number 101003) used for development purposes and on the MiG-15*bis*P (*izdeliye* SP-1) experimental interceptor[3] – a much-modified *Fagot-A* (c/n 102005)[4] equipped with the Toriy (Thorium) radar. In the course of the flight tests the shape of the elevator leading edges was changed from elliptical to circular.

Two rubber fuel cells holding 1,250 litres and 150 litres (275 and 33 Imperial gallons) were located in the centre fuselage and installed via special access hatches; total fuel capacity, including the engine feeder tank, was 1,412 litres (310.64 Imperial gallons). The fuel cells were positioned in such a way that fuel burnoff did not affect CG position. There were provisions for two 400-litre (88 Imperial gallons) drop tanks.

The SI's armament was almost identical to that of the MiG-15*bis*, consisting of one N-37 cannon with 40 rounds and two NR-23s with 80rpg. The heavy cannons were intended primarily for destroying American heavy bombers. For strike missions the wing hardpoints could be used for carrying 100-kg or 250-kg (220-lb or 551-lb) bombs. As on the *Fagot*, there was an S-13 gun camera on the intake upper lip and provisions for an AFA-I reconnaissance camera (*aerofotoapparaht* – aerial camera) in the forward fuselage. The pilot was protected by two 10mm (0.39in) armour plates up front, a 10mm armored headrest and a 60mm (2.36in) bulletproof windscreen.

The avionics suite was identical to that of the MiG-15*bis* – an RSIU-3 Klyon (Maple) UHF radio (RSI-6M receiver and RSI-6K transmitter), an SRO-1 Bariy-M (Barium-M) identification friend-or-foe (IFF) transponder, an RPKO-10M direction finder and an OSP-48 instrumental landing system (ILS).[5] The latter comprised an ARK-5 Amur (a river in the Soviet Far East; pronounced like the French word *amour*) automatic direction finder, an RV-2 Kristall (Crystal) low-range radio altimeter and an MRP-48 Dyatel (Woodpecker) marker beacon receiver.[6] The ground part of the system included two range beacons, three marker beacons, communications radios and an HF or VHF radio direction finder to facilitate approach and landing in bad weather. The ILS was fairly simple and had few components, which rendered the ground part suitable for use on *ad hoc* tactical airfields (in truck-mounted form). Electric equipment was powered by a 3-kilowatt GS-3000 starter-generator and a 12A-30 DC battery.

As a result of these changes the SI's lift/drag ratio deteriorated to 13.6 (compared to the *Fagot-A*'s 13.9). Hence, with an equal fuel load, the aircraft had 35km (18.9nm) shorter range than the *Fagot-B*.

In early 1949 the Mikoyan OKB's experimental shop (MMZ No155) began construction of two SI prototypes followed shortly afterwards by a third aircraft in SP-2 interceptor configuration (see next chapter). Designated SI-1, the first prototype of the day fighter version was completed in July 1949. However, the process of refining it and applying the finishing touches dragged on for several months and it was not until December that the aircraft was trucked to Mikoyan's flight test facility at the Flight Research Institute (LII – **Lyot***no-is***sle***dovatel'skiy insti***toot**) in Zhukovskiy near Moscow.[7]

I T Ivaschchenko (Hero of the Soviet Union) was assigned project test pilot. He was one of the first four Soviet pilots to gain the HSU title, receiving it for his contribution to jet aircraft development in the USSR. Among other things, he was actively involved in the MiG-15's trials, notably in ejection seat tests, and knew many of the quirks of the early jets; thus, the SI-1 was in good hands. A F Toorchkov was the engineer in charge of the test programme.

The VK-1 turbojet fitted to the SI-1 turned out to be defective, and the first flight did not take place until 14th January 1950. At an early stage of the initial flight test programme Ivaschchenko reported that the aircraft was some 40km/h (21.62kts) faster than the production *Fagot-B*. A lot of refinements was made to the prototype in the course of the manufacturer's flight tests (eg, various joints were carefully sealed to reduce drag, increasing top speed still further). On 1st February the SI-1 reached 1,114km/h (602.16kts) at 2,200m (7,218ft); top speed at 10,200m (33,464ft) was 1,077km/h (582.16kts) or Mach 1.0. The SI was superior to the production MiG-15*bis* in almost every aspect of basic performance.

The concluding stage of the manufacturer's trials involved several sessions of aerobatics, since aerobatics in fast jets were still almost untrodden ground at the time. On 17th March 1950 Ivaschchenko took off on yet another test flight. Having climbed to 11,000m (36,089ft)

First prototype's performance specifications	Manufactuer's estimates	Test results
Top speed, km/h (kts):		
at S/L	1,152 (622.7)	n/a
at 2,000m (6,561ft)	n/a	1,112 (601.08)
at 2,200m (7,218ft)	n/a	1,114 (602.16)
at 5,000m (16,404ft)	1,162 (628.1)	1,110 (600.0)
at 10,000m (32,808ft)	1,116 (603.24)	1,050 (567.56)
at 10,200m (33,464ft)	n/a	1,077 (582.16)
Landing speed, km/h (kts)	159 (86)	n/a
Time to height, min:		
to 5,000m (16,404ft)	2.0	2.0
to 10,000m (32,808ft)	4.9	5.2
Rate of climb, m/sec (ft/min):		
at S/L	51.3 (10,100)	48.0 (9,450)
at 5,000m (16,404ft)	35.5 (7,000)	33.5 (6,600)
at 10,000m (32,808ft)	22.5 (4,430)	18.6 (3,660)
Service ceiling, m (ft)	16,000 (52,493)	15,600 (51,181)
Turning time at 1,000m (3,280ft), sec	23	n/a
Range at 10,000m (32,808ft), km (nm):		
on internal fuel only	1,200 (648) *	1,062 (574) †
with drop tanks	1,570 (848) *	n/a
Endurance in cruise at 10,000m (32,808ft), hrs:		
on internal fuel only	1.60 *	n/a
with drop tanks	2.17 *	n/a
Maximum endurance, hrs:		
on internal fuel only	1.88	n/a
with drop tanks	2.54	n/a
Take-off run, m (ft)	500 (1,640)	n/a
Landing run, m (ft)	650 (2,132)	n/a

* at 740km/h (400kts); † at 900km/h (486.5kts)

and completed the day's programme, he reported that the aircraft was behaving as usual and began his descent. At 5,000m (16,404ft) the SI-1 suddenly entered a steep dive and crashed, killing the pilot.

The aircraft had hit the ground at enormous speed, disintegrating utterly and digging a large crater. Disaster had struck so suddenly that even Ivaschchenko, a highly experienced pilot, had no time to contact the tower, and the wreckage told very little about the cause of the crash. Whatever had killed Ivaschchenko could only be discovered by continuing the flight tests. The first prototype's performance is indicated in the table above. Some of the SI-1's characteristics remained undetermined, as measurements had not been taken before the crash.

Even before Ivaschchenko's accident Artyom I Mikoyan had asked Gheorgiy A Sedov, a test pilot with the Air Force Research Institute (NII VVS – *Na***oochno-is***sle***dovatel'skiy insti***toot** *voyen***no-vozdoosh***nykh* **see***l*), to work for OKB-155. Sedov had been at odds with the institute's leadership for some time, and he willingly accepted the offer. In March 1950 Sedov resumed the flight test programme with the second prototype designated SI-2 which had been completed at MMZ No155 early in the year.

According to OKB documents dated 14th March 1950 the SI-2 had an empty weight of 3,646kg (8,038 lb), a normal all-up weight of 5,050kg (11,133 lb) and a maximum all-up weight (AUW) of 5,480kg (12,081 lb). The internal fuel

load was 1,200kg (2,645.5 lb), increasing to 1,600kg (3,527 lb) with drop tanks; normal payload was 1,404kg (3,095 lb) and maximum payload with drop tanks 1,834kg (4,043 lb). Thus, despite the extensive structural changes, the SI-2 was only marginally heavier than the production MiG-15*bis* (the *Fagot-B* had an empty weight of 3,651kg/8,049 lb and a normal AUW of 5,044kg/11,120 lb). The second prototype's payload/take-off weight ratio was 27.8%, wing loading was 223kg/m^2 (1,084 lbft^2) and thrust loading 1.87kg/kgp (lb/lbst).

Trials of the SI-2 continued throughout 1950. Construction of the next two tactical fighter prototypes designated SI-01 and SI-02 did not begin until January 1951. Actually these were pre-production aircraft; they were manufactured to Mikoyan OKB specifications by the Gor'kiy aircraft factory No21 named after Sergo Ordzhonikidze.[8] The SI-01 and SI-02 were built under the in-house product code 'izdeliye 54' and had a complete avionics and equipment package. Thus the MiG-15*bis* 45° – which was to be redesignated yet – beat the MiG-15*bis*R (the tactical photo reconnaissance version of the *Fagot-B*) to the Gor'kiy production line, which is why the latter aircraft was given a higher product code, 'izdeliye 55'.

The second pre-production aircraft (SI-02) laid down on 15th January was completed within a month and rolled out on 16th February *ahead of the first aircraft*. Interestingly, despite the 'new-build' c/n 54210102, it carried a serial which did not match, 671 Red, revealing that the aircraft had been built using the forward fuselage of a MiG-15*bis* with the construction number 53210671![9] The SI-02 was then dismantled and delivered to LII by land, becoming the third MiG-15*bis* 45° to fly.

(Speaking of serials, in the early 1950s Soviet fighters had three- or four-digit *serial numbers*. These allowed more or less positive identification, since they tied in with the aircraft's construction number – usually the last one or two digits of the batch number plus the number of the aircraft in the batch.

In 1955, however, the VVS switched (probably for security reasons) to the current system of two-digit *tactical codes* which, as a rule, are simply the aircraft's number in the unit operating it, making positive identification impossible. Three- or four-digit tactical codes are rare and are usually worn by development aircraft only, in which case they still tie in with the c/n or fuselage number (manufacturer's line number). On military *transport* aircraft, however, three-digit tactical codes are usually the last three of the former civil registration; many Soviet/Russian Air Force transports were, and still are, quasi-civilian. At the same time the star insignia on the aft fuselage were deleted, remaining on the wings and vertical tail only.)

Some design flaws became apparent even as the second prototype (SI-2) was undergoing manufacturer's tests. In one of the flights Gheorgiy A Sedov almost duplicated the circumstances in which Ivaschchenko had lost his life. As soon as the aircraft passed 1,000km/h (540.54kts), tailplane flutter began. Reacting instantly, Sedov throttled back and hauled back on the stick, trying to put the aircraft into a climb and stop the vibration. He was a split second too late – the elevators failed; the outer ends were torn off symmetrically, only some 40% of the original area remaining. Using only engine power to balance the aircraft, Sedov managed to make a safe landing.

'I was prepared for this, – Sedov recalled, – because we knew that the horizontal tail had disintegrated at 1,020 to 1,040km/h [551.35 to 562.16kts] on the first prototype. It had nothing to do with quick reaction. The attitude was normal when it all happened, the aircraft was actually beginning to pitch up a little. I tried a little elevator input and felt the aircraft respond. Well, there was a danger that the remaining elevator area might not be enough during approach when speed was low, but I made it; the prototype was saved.'

The cause of the flutter was discovered and it became clear that it was tailplane flutter and structural failure that killed Ivaschchenko. Apart from that, Sedov reported aileron reversal at high speeds caused by insufficient wing tor-

Top and above: **The second prototype, the SI-2 (671 Red), was rebuilt from a MiG-15*bis* in order to quickly replace the crashed SI-1.** Mikoyan OKB

Bottom: **This view of the SI-2 illustrates the deployed flaps and airbrakes.** Mikoyan OKB

Photographs on the opposite page:

Serialled '01 Red', the SI-01 (c/n 54210101) was the first pre-production aircraft rolled out in May 1951. Mikoyan OKB

Probably the same aircraft at a later date. The red fin cap and the Gor'kiy aircraft factory badge on the nose are gone. Mikoyan OKB

sional stiffness. These and other reasons necessitated a pause in the flights so that the aircraft could be repaired and the tail redesigned.

Testing resumed with the suitably modified SI-02 in the spring of 1951. After making a total of 44 flights under the manufacturer's test programme the aircraft was handed over to NII VVS for State acceptance (ie, certification) trials in April 1951. Stage 1 of the trials ended on 1st July 1951; the SI-02 was flown by L M Koovshinov, Yuriy A Antipov, V S Kotlov and other NII VVS test pilots. The State Commission's report drawn up after Stage 1 said that generally the aircraft met the Air Force's requirements and the manufacturer's specifications were largely confirmed. Shortcomings noted at this stage included an awkwardly positioned pitot. Originally it was located approximately at mid-span, MiG-15 style. As a result, drop tanks could not be carried because interference from them affected the pitot and the airspeed indicator gave incorrect readings.

Most of the deficiencies discovered during Stage 1 of the State acceptance trials were quickly corrected. Thus Stage 2 began just ten days later, on 10th July and was completed on 8th August. The SI-02's top speed and rate of climb at various altitudes as measured during State acceptance trials are listed in the table on the right.

As the table shows, the SI-02's rate of climb was almost on target. Deceleration time from Vmax to 0.7 Vmax was 17 seconds. Handling characteristics were very similar to the production MiG-15bis, except for marginally worse horizontal manoeuvrability. Field performance also deteriorated slightly, but this was deemed unimportant, since the aircraft could still operate from the same runways as the MiG-15. The table below illustrates the SI-02's range and endurance data.

The State Commission's report after Stage 2 read as follows:

'The modified MiG-15bis with 45° wing sweep and new tail unit has the following advantages over the production MiG-15 (sic):

1. Top speed is 46 to 56km/h (24.8 to 30.3kts) higher;
2. The Mach limit is raised from 0.92 to 1.08;
3. Climb time to 10,000m (32,808ft) is reduced by 20 to 30 seconds.

The MiG-15bis 45° is recommended for production.'

Range & Endurance data	'Clean'	Drop tanks
Normal take-off weight, kg (lb)	5,212 (11,490)	5,930 (13,073)
Fuel capacity, litres (Imp gals)	1,410 (310.2)	2,205 (485.1)
Cruise altitude, m (ft)	12,000 (39,370)	12,000 (39,370)
Fuel consumption, litres/km (gallons/nm)	0.83 (0.338)	0.91 (0.37)
Fuel consumption, litres/hr (gallons/hr)	685 (150.7)	750 (165)
Maximum range, km (nm)	1,295 (700)	2,150 (1,162)
Endurance	1 hr 40 min	2 hr 42 min

Nevertheless, one of the SI-02's major deficiencies – excessive shell scatter and hence poor accuracy when the NR-23 cannons were fired – remained. This problem also affected the MiG-15bis and was caused by insufficiently rigid cannon mounts.

At this stage someone apparently decided that the changes introduced on the MiG-15bis 45° were serious enough to warrant a new service designation. During the State acceptance trials the aircraft received the designation under which it would gain fame – MiG-17.

The rollout of the fourth development aircraft – that is, the first pre-production aircraft (SI-01, c/n 54210101) was delayed until May 1951. Unlike the SI-02, this aircraft was quite logically serialled '01 Red', so the 'donor' (if any) cannot be traced. Manufacturer's tests began on 1st June and were duly completed on 23rd June. After completing a brief spinning trials programme at the hands of G A Sedov in August the SI-01 was transferred to NII VVS on 28th August. There, additional spinning trials were held by L M Koovshinov between 11th September and 10th October. Test pilots noted that the MiG-17's spinning characteristics were similar to those of the Fagot-B and Midget; the aircraft flipped into an inverted spin only if the pilot made serious errors in spin recovery. The bottom line was that '...spinning and spin recovery on the MiG-17 are simpler and safer than on the MiG-15'.

Altitude, m (ft)	Top speed, km/h (kts)	Mach number	Rate of climb, m/sec (ft/min)	Time to height, min
S/L	n/a	n/a	48.0 (9,450)	n/a
1,000 (3,280)	n/a	n/a	45.4 (8,940)	0.3
2,000 (6,561)	1,114 (602.16)	0.931	42.9 (8,444)	0.7
3,000 (9,842)	1,110 (600.0)	0.941	40.3 (7,933)	1.0
4,000 (13,123)	1,106 (597.83)	0.948	34.8 (6,850)	1.6
5,000 (16,404)	1,100 (594.59)	0.955	35.3 (6,950)	2.0
6,000 (19,685)	1,092 (590.27)	0.960	32.7 (6,440)	2.5
7,000 (22,966)	1,082 (584.86)	0.964	30.1 (5,925)	3.0
8,000 (26,246)	1,071 (587.92)	0.967	27.7 (5,452)	3.6
9,000 (29,527)	1,059 (572.43)	0.970	25.5 (5,020)	4.2
10,000 (32,808)	1,046 (565.4)	0.992	22.5 (4,430)	4.9
11,000 (36,089)	1,033 (558.37)	0.972	20.2 (3,976)	5.7
12,000 (39,370)	1,027 (555.13)	0.967	15.6 (3,070)	6.7
13,000 (42,651)	n/a	n/a	11.2 (2,204)	7.9
14,000 (45,931)	n/a	n/a	6.9 (1,358)	9.7
15,000 (49,212)	n/a	n/a	2.6 (512)	13.5

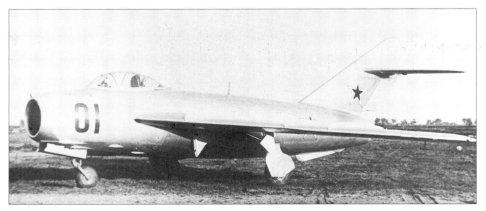

Chapter Two

The MiG-17 Family

MiG-17 *Fresco-A* tactical fighter
(*izdeliye* SI; izdeliye 54, *izdeliye* 40)

In typically Soviet fashion, the aircraft was ordered into production even before it had completed its trials programme. Pursuant to a Council of Ministers directive dated 25th August 1951 and Ministry of Aircraft Industry (MAP – *Ministerstvo aviatseeonnoy promyshlennosti*) order No 851 issued on 1st September 1951 at least six factories were to build the MiG-17. In reality, however, the type was built by five plants, all of which had built the *Fagot* – No 1 in Kuybyshev (starting in late 1951), No 21 in Gor'kiy, No 31 in Tbilisi (February 1953), No 126 in Komsomol'sk-on-Amur (late 1952) and No 153 in Novosibirsk; plant No 292 in Saratov, also a one-time MiG-15 manufacturer, never started MiG-17 production. As noted earlier, in Gor'kiy the MiG-17 was known as *izdeliye* 54; somewhat surprisingly, the product code in Kuybyshev was *izdeliye* 40, which is lower than the MiG-15's (*izdeliye* 50).

Unlike its predecessor which had started its service career with an elite fighter unit at Kubinka airbase near Moscow, the MiG-17 passed its service trials down south on the Black Sea. A fighter regiment based at Krymskaya AB on the Crimea peninsula was the first unit to operate the type. Production MiG-17s delivered to first-line units had slightly lower performance than the SI-01 and SI-02. Maximum speed at 2,000m (6,561ft) was 1,094km/h (591.35kts);

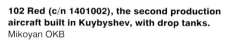

102 Red (c/n 1401002), the second production aircraft built in Kuybyshev, with drop tanks.
Mikoyan OKB

Seen sometime before 1955, four Gor'kiy-built late-production MiG-17s of the Naval air arm (c/ns 54210607, 5421060, 54210632 and 54210629) make an unusual formation with four MiG-15*bis Fagot-B*s from the same unit. The aircraft are carrying early-model slipper tanks. Yefim Gordon archive

Opposite page:

Two late-production *Fresco-A*s with post-1955 tactical codes and late-model 400-litre (88 Imperial gallon) drop tanks stream contrails across the sky. Yefim Gordon archive

the aircraft climbed to 5,000m (16,404ft) and 10,000m (32,808ft) in 2.5 and 6.6 minutes respectively, and the service ceiling was 14,500m (47,572ft).

Range was 1,290km (697nm) on internal fuel, increasing to 2,060km (1,113nm) with two 400-litre (88 Imperial gallons) drop tanks. Speaking of which, the original slipper tanks similar to those used on the MiG-15 soon gave way to cylindrical tanks with stabilising fins which were carried on three short struts (two in V fashion at the front and one at the rear). Early production MiG-17s had an empty weight of 3,800kg (8,377 lb) and an MTOW of 6,070kg (13,381 lb).

The MiG-17 became a worthy successor to the MiG-15 and MiG-15*bis*, replacing the *Fagot* in first-line service in the VVS and later in the air forces of the Soviet Union's Warsaw Pact satellites. Like the MiG-15, it was built under licence in Poland (foreign production is described separately). The new fighter received the ASCC reporting name *Fresco*; later, when other versions of the MiG-17 became known in the West, this was changed to *Fresco-A*.

The MiG-17 was very much a 'pilot's airplane' and capable of performing highly complex aerobatics; however, pilots noted that somewhat bigger control inputs were required than on the MiG-15. Acceleration after take-off was slightly better and the airbrakes enabled wingovers to be performed throughout the speed range and at altitudes up to 14,000m (45,931ft). The MiG-17 was rock-steady at high altitude and could make turns with only a minor loss of altitude even at its service ceiling. Dead-stick gliding speed, however, was higher than the *Fagot-B*'s, being 270 to 280km/h (145.95 to 151.35kts).

Various improvements were progressively introduced, such as an extra seat belt allowing the pilot to sit tighter during sharp turns and a second canopy jettison/ejection handle on the left armrest of the ejection seat (like on the MiG-15, originally the seat could be fired with the right hand only). Starting in late 1953, all MiG-17s were equipped with a new ejection seat designed in house. The seat featured a retractable visor protecting the pilot's face, leg restraints to prevent injury by the slipstream and stabilising surfaces which deployed after ejection to stop the seat from tumbling head over heels.

Mikoyan engineers also worked on improving rearward vision, designing a one-piece blown canopy without the rear transverse frame member characteristic of the MiG-15. This was not incorporated on production aircraft; later, however, production MiG-17s were fitted with rear-view periscopes.

Airbrake efficiency was soon found to be inadequate and the design was changed several times until the airbrakes were satisfactory (see section below on MiG-17 airbrake tests). The new airbrakes had an area of 0.88m^2 (9.46ft^2) and a pronounced trapezoidal shape, with a prominent teardrop fairing over the

actuator right in the middle of each airbrake panel. The latter was due to the fact that the airbrakes were located farther aft and the fuselage was too narrow at this point to house the actuators internally. Maximum deflection was increased to 55°.

MiG-17s with the redesigned airbrakes began rolling off the assembly lines in September 1952 – ie, at the same time when enlarged airbrakes were introduced on the MiG-15*bis*. The whole affair was perfectly logical; after all, the *Fagot-B* and the *Fresco* were developed almost in parallel and suffered from the same problems – and so the cure was the same, too.

Other changes introduced in 1952 included carefully sealed safety valves in the fuel tank pressurization system which ensured stable fuel delivery throughout the speed range. The FS-155 landing/taxi light in the air intake splitter was replaced by a retractable LFSV-45 light in the port wing root, just like on the MiG-15*bis*. A new PL-3A pitot was installed on the starboard wingtip and thus did not conflict with the drop tanks.

The avionics suite was also upgraded. An ASP-3N automatic gunsight (*avtomateech-eskiy strelkovyy preetsel*) was introduced at the same time as on the MiG-15*bis*. Later, the *Fresco* received the Sirena-2 radar homing and warning system (initially referred to as a 'tail protection device') with characteristic antennas

on the fin/stabilizer fairing and the wing leading edges and wingtips to give 360° coverage. Early-production MiG-17s had an AGK-476 artificial horizon usually fitted to bombers and transports – simply because there was no other model available. However, this model was totally unsuited for fighters and could not function during violent manoeuvres with large bank angles. Hence a new AGI-1 artificial horizon specially developed for fighters (*aviagorizont istrebeetel'nyy*) was tested almost simultaneously on the *Fagot* and the *Fresco* at NII VVS in 1953 and fitted to production MiG-17s, starting the following year.

The *Fresco* had self-contained engine starting capability from the outset (on the *Fagot* it was only introduced on late batches of the MiG-15*bis*). Of course, the engine could still be started in the usual way, using ground power sources.

The changes, however, were not limited to hardware – tactics changed, too, and new roles were sought. Among other things the VVS regarded the MiG-17 as an escort fighter, even conducting a special test programme to determine its combat radius. The results are given in the table at the top of the following page.

As noted earlier, the MiG-17 could also fill the strike role. In this case two 50-kg (110-lb) or 100-kg (220-lb) bombs were carried under the wings on D4-50 shackles.

MiG-17A *Fresco-A* tactical fighter

Late-production MiG-17s were powered by the VK-1A turbojet. While having an identical thrust rating (2,700kgp/5,925 lbst), the VK-1A had a much longer service life and was more refined technologically than the original VK-1. Aircraft powered by the VK-1A were designated MiG-17A.

MiG-17 *Fresco-A* development aircraft with modified airbrakes

In 1952 the Mikoyan OKB undertook a research programme in order to determine the optimum shape and area of the MiG-17's airbrakes. The objective was maximum airbrake efficiency at top speed and in a vertical dive from the aircraft's service ceiling. Two early-production *Fresco-As* were used to test five consecutive airbrake versions and the programme proceeded quickly.

The first aircraft (identity unknown) had the airbrakes installed in the usual position at frame 28; four versions were tested. On the other fighter (114 Red, c/n 54210114) tested in July 1952 the airbrakes were mounted immediately aft of the wing trailing edge between frames 18 and 22; in this location the airbrakes were found to have less effect on longitudinal stability when deployed. On 114 Red the airbrakes tapered *very* slightly towards the rear and the

final version had two prominent stiffening ribs. The first aft-mounted version was rejected as too inefficient both in level flight and in a dive, and versions 2 and 3 because stick forces with the airbrakes deployed were too high, but the next one (No 5) was deemed satisfactory and recommended for production. As noted earlier, MiG-17s with enlarged trapezoidal airbrakes on the aft fuselage began rolling off the assembly lines in September 1952.

Bomber escort trials data	Tupolev Tu-16 *Badger-A*			Il'yushin IL-28 *Beagle*		
Cruising altitude, m (ft)	5,000 (16,404)	10,000 (32,808)	12,000 (39,370)	5,000 (16,404)	10,000 (32,808)	12,000 (39,370)
Combat radius						
on internal fuel, km (nm)	265 (143)	380 (205)	430 (232)	260 (140.5)	365 (197)	415 (224)
with drop tanks, km (nm)	455 (246)	660 (356)	745 (402)	445 (240.5)	650 (351)	725 (392)

Airbrake trials data	Area, m² (ft²)	Deflection angle	Location
Original production version	0.522 (5.61)	55°	Frame 28
Test version 1	0.766 (8.23)	55°	Frame 28
Test version 2	0.966 (10.38)	55°	Frame 28
Test version 3	0.94 (10.1)	55°	Frame 28
Test version 4 (114 Red)	0.83 (8.92)	60°	Frames 18 to 22
Test version 5 (accepted)	0.88 (9.46)	55°	Frame 28
Test version 6 (114 Red)	0.96 (10.32)	n/a	Frames 18 to 22
Test version 7 (114 Red)	1.0 (10.75)	n/a	Frames 18 to 22

Late-production MiG-17s, including a Novosibirsk-built example (28 Blue, c/n 1115328), sit on a tactical airfield covered with perforated steel plate (PSP). Both Yefim Gordon archive

Bottom right: **The lead aircraft and the right-hand wingman (at the left in the picture) are two of a number of *Fresco-As* with large airbrakes immediately aft of the wings; compare with the third aircraft, a standard early-production MiG-17 with 0.522m² airbrakes.** Sergey and Dmitriy Komissarov collection

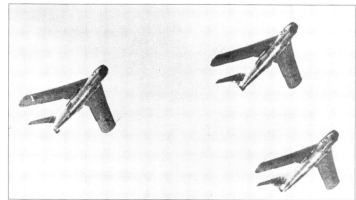

114 Red (c/n 54210114) was initially used to test new airbrake designs. Yefim Gordon archive

The SP-2 was equipped with a with a Korshoon radar, an improved version of the Toriy-A fitted to the SP-1, but had cleaner nose contours. Mikoyan OKB

Test results with the first of three forward-mounted versions (No 4) were inconclusive and no data are available as to the other two. Apparently, however, the final one was good enough, since a small batch of *Fresco-As* was built with airbrakes mounted immediately aft of the wings *à la* 114 Red. One such aircraft converted to fighter-bomber configuration was preserved at a pioneer camp near Rayki village about 40km (25 miles) east of Moscow at least until the late 1980s, wearing the (obviously bogus) tactical code '01 Red'.

As for 114 Red, when the test programme was over the aircraft was converted during 1952, becoming the *izdeliye* SG avionics test-bed described later in this chapter. Interestingly, it reverted to the original aft-mounted 0.522m² airbrakes in so doing!

MiG-17 (*izdeliye* SP-2) development aircraft

As noted earlier, the Council of Ministers directive concerning the MiG-15*bis* 45° ordered the development of an all-weather interceptor version in parallel with the basic day fighter. Designated *izdeliye* SP-2 by analogy with the MiG-15*bis*P (SP-1), the aircraft was equipped with a Korshoon (Kite, a bird of prey) single-antenna radar developed by NII-17[1] – an improved version of the Toriy-A radar fitted to the SP-1. Like the original Toriy, this radar lacked automatic target tracking capability, which was a major shortcoming; tracking had to be performed manually by the pilot, which increased pilot workload.

Development of the SI and the SP-2 proceeded in parallel, but construction of the latter aircraft began a little later; by January 1950 design was 75% complete and construction was 20% complete. The interceptor's wings, tail unit and aft fuselage were identical to those of the day fighter version. The forward fuselage was redesigned in a way similar to the SP-1, with a large bullet-shaped radome on the air intake upper lip. However, the radome was faired much more smoothly into the forward fuselage, not protruding above the circular cross-section of the nose, as on the SP-1. This was because forward fuselage and hence air intake diameter had been enlarged up to fuselage frame 3; actually the SP-2's nose shape was more similar to the experimental Mikoyan/Gurevich I-320 (*izdeliye* R) two-seat heavy interceptor than to the SP-1. The S-13 gun camera was moved to the starboard side of the air intake.

On the SP-1 the *Fagot-B*'s two NR-23 cannons had been deleted to save weight, leaving the aircraft with a single N-37D cannon. With the

SP-2, the engineers did exactly the opposite, deleting the N-37D and placing one NR-23 cannon on each side of the lower fuselage; the port and starboard cannons had an ammunition supply of 90 and 120 rounds respectively. The weapons were located sufficiently far apart and there was no need to redesign the nose gear unit, as had been the case with the predecessor. The aircraft had a PKI-1 collimator gunsight.

The canopy was modified, featuring a new lengthened windscreen accommodating the radar display; the rear fairing of the sliding portion was also modified. The bulletproof windshield was electrically de-iced by means of an AOS-81 automatic glazing de-icing unit (*avtomaht obogreva styokol*). The standard KP-14 oxygen apparatus (*kislorodnyy preebor*) gave way to a KP-18 unit with two spherical oxygen bottles holding 2 litres (0.44 Imperial gallons) each.

The capacity of the rear fuel cell was increased from 150 litres (33 Imperial gallons)

Yak-125 specifications	CofM directive	ADP specifications
Length overall	–	15.745m (51' 7.88")
Wing span	–	11.00m (36' 1.07")
Wing area, m² (ft²)	–	28.96 (311.39)
Empty weight, kg (lb)	4,985 (10,990)	n/a
Normal TOW, kg (lb)	9,500 to 10,000 (20,943 to 22,045)	8,750 (19,290)
Payload, kg (lb)	–	3,765 (8,300)
Fuel load, kg (lb)	–	3,500 (7,716)
Wing loading, kg/m² (lb/ft²)	–	310 (1,509.7)
Power loading, kg/kgp (lb/lbst)	–	2.2*
Top speed, km/h (kts):		
at 5,000 to 6,000m (16,404 to 19,685ft)	1,050 to 1,100 (567.56 to 594.59)	1,075 (581.08)†
at 10,000ft (32,808ft)	1,000 to 1,050 (540.54 to 567.56)	1,020 (551.35)
Landing speed, km/h (kts)	–	195 (105.4)
Climb time, min:		
to 5,000m (16,404ft)	–	2.0
to 10,000m (32,808ft)	5.0 (over the target)	4.1
Service ceiling, m (ft)	15,000 (49,212)	15,100 (49,540)
Range on internal fuel at 12,000 to 13,000m		
(39,370 to 42,651ft), km (nm)	4,000 (2,162)	4,088 (2,209)‡
Endurance on internal fuel		
at 12,000 to 13,000m, hours	5	5‡
Take-off run, m (ft)	–	900 (2,952)
Landing run, m (ft)	–	500 (1,640)

* Equals a thrust/weight ratio of 0.45; † at 5,000m (16,404ft); ‡ at 13,000m (42,651ft).

SP-2 performance	Manufacturer's estimates	Manufacturer's flight tests	State acceptance trials
Empty weight, kg (lb)	n/a	3,889/3,897 (8,573/8,591)*	3,873 (8,538)
Normal payload, kg (lb)	n/a	1,324 (2,919)	1,447 (3,190)
Max payload with drop tanks, kg (lb)	n/a	2,483 (5,474)	2,509 (5,531)
Normal fuel load, kg (lb)	n/a	1,247 (2,749)	1,260 (2,777)
Max fuel load with drop tanks, kg (lb)	n/a	2,243 (4,945)	2,260 (4,982)
Normal AUW, kg (lb)	n/a	5,313 (11,713)	5,320 (11,728)
MAUW with drop tanks, kg (lb)	n/a	6,380 (14,065)	6,382 (14,069)
Wing loading, kg/m² (lbft²)	n/a	235 (1,142)	236 (1,147)
Power loading, kg/kgp (lb./lbst)	n/a	1.97	1.97
Top speed, km/h (kts):			
at S/L	n/a	n/a	1,030 (556.75) †
at 3,000m (9,842ft)	1,112 (601.0)	n/a	1,109 (599.45)
at 5,000m (16,404ft)	1,094 (591.35)	n/a	1,097 (592.97)
at 10,000m (32,808ft)	1,047 (565.94)	1,042 (563.24)	1,046 (565.4)
at 12,000m (39,370ft)	n/a	1,022 (552.43)	n/a
Rate of climb, m/sec (ft/min):			
at S/L	50 (9,842)	n/a	47.1 (9,271)
at 5,000m (16,404ft)	35 (6,890)	n/a	33.8 (6,653)
at 10,000m (32,808ft)	20 (3,937)	n/a	20.6 (4,055)
Time to height, min:			
to 5,000m (16,404ft)	2.0	n/a	2.0
to 10,000m (32,808ft)	5.1	n/a	5.2
Service ceiling, m (ft)	15,400 (50,525)	15,600 (51,181)	15,200 (49,868)
Range on internal fuel only, km (nm):			
at 10,000m (32,808ft)	1,276 (689)	n/a	n/a
at 12,000m (39,370ft)	1,391 (752)	n/a	1,375 (743) ‡
Range with drop tanks, km (nm):			
at 12,000m 400-litre (88-gallon)	2,095 (1,132)	n/a	n/a
at 12,000m 600-litre (132-gallon)	2,520 (1,362)	2,500 (1,351)	2,510 (1,356)
Endurance on internal fuel only:			
at 10,000m (32,808ft)	1 hr 44 min	n/a	1 hr 47 min
at 12,000m (39,370ft)	2 hrs 04 min	n/a	n/a
Endurance with drop tanks:			
at 12,000m 600-litre (132-gallon)	n/a	n/a	3 hrs 11 min ‖
Max endurance at 12,000m (39,370ft):			
on internal fuel only	n/a	3 hrs 45 min	2 hrs 02 min §
600-litre (132 Imp gals) drop tanks	n/a	n/a	3 hrs 34 min ¶

* in 'clean' condition and with drop tanks respectively; † speed was limited up to 2,000m (6,561ft) because of the wing drop problem; ‡ at 824km/h (445.4kts); § at 578km/h (312.43kts); ¶ at 633km/h (342.16kts) with drop tanks and 580km/h (313.51kts) after jettisoning the tanks; ‖ at 807km/h (436.21kts) with drop tanks and 825km/h (445.94kts) after jettisoning the tanks.

to 250 litres (55 Imperial gallons).[2] Additionally, the SP-2 was to carry specially-developed 600-litre (132 Imperial gallons) drop tanks which were interchangeable with the standard 400-litre (88 Imperial gallons) model used on the MiG-17. The new tanks were carried on the same D4-50 shackles but necessitated some local reinforcement of the wing structure.

The airbrakes were programmed to deploy automatically when airspeed exceeded Mach 1.03 (to stop the aircraft from exceeding dynamic pressure limits) and retract automatically when airspeed dropped below Mach 0.97. They could also be operated manually, of course. The avionics fit was the same as on late-production *Fagot-Bs* (RSIU-3 VHF radio, OSP-48 ILS, SRO-1 Bariy-M IFF etc). A 6kW GS-6000 DC generator replaced the GS-3000 model which was standard on the MiG-17, and a separate SGS-7,5/3 AC generator powered the radar.

From March to 11th November 1951 the SP-2 underwent manufacturer's flight tests at the hands of Gheorgiy A Sedov, who also had to test-fly the SI day fighter version at the same time; S A Etchin was the engineer in charge of the test programme. Initially the aircraft flew *sans* radar; the Korshoon radar was installed at MMZ No155 between 11th and 25th October and radar performance tests began.

In mid-November the aircraft was transferred to NII VVS for State acceptance trials which lasted from 28th November to 29th December 1951. The SP-2 was flown by NII VVS and Air Defence Force (PVO – *Protivovozdooshnaya oborona*) pilots A P Sooproon, Yuriy A Antipov, Vasiliy G Ivanov, Ye I Dzyuba, Ye A Savitskiy and R N Sereda. A while earlier, in July and August 1951, the Korshoon radar had been tested on the I-320.

The SP-2's performance figures obtained during manufacturer's flight tests and State acceptance trials are given in the table above.

The State Commission's report said that the SP-2 met the performance target outlined in the Council of Ministers directive ordering its development; the interceptor's performance was almost identical to that of the standard MiG-17. However, the aircraft's combat potential was severely limited by the radar's complexity of operation – it was hard for one man to fly the aircraft and track the target at the same time. It was also difficult to estimate target range; finally, the radar was unreliable.

The Commission also noted that the airbrakes were inefficient, making it impossible to slow down quickly when closing in on the target, and that taxying and take-off with 600-litre drop tanks were extremely complicated, as the aircraft became heavy and sluggish.

As the Korshoon radar lacked auto-tracking capability and was not user-friendly, it was not recommended for production. On 24th May 1952 the Council of Ministers passed directive No 2460-933 ordering the MiG-17P interceptor (see below) into production and terminating the SP-2. However, the Mikoyan OKB put the aircraft to good use as an equipment testbed; for instance, in 1952 the SP-2 was used to test BU-1U irreversible hydraulic actuators in the pitch and roll channels.

MiG-17F *Fresco-C* tactical fighter (*izdeliye* SF)

As such, the VK-1 (VK-1A) centrifugal-flow turbojet powering the MiG-15*bis* and MiG-17 had no reserves for further uprating. Engine pressure ratio could not be increased since the airflow was split into nine flows for the individual combustion chambers, nor could turbine temperature be increased any further. Hence in 1949 the Central Institute of Aero Engines (TsIAM – *Tsentrahl'nyy institoot aviatseeonnovo motorostroyeniya*) and OKB-155 began investigating the possibility of uprating the VK-1 by means of afterburning.

Mikoyan engineers A I Komissarov and Gleb Ye Lozino-Lozinskiy designed the first Soviet afterburner with a stabilised flame front and enforced ignition. The unit consisted of a diffuser, the afterburner proper and a two-position ('bang-bang') axisymmetrical convergent-divergent nozzle; nozzle diameter was 540mm (21.3in) at full military power and 624mm (24.6in) in full afterburner. The main components of the afterburner were an annular V-section flame stabilizer and a fuel manifold with injectors. The afterburner was cooled by air bled from the inlet duct.

The afterburner was tested and perfected at TsIAM. Later it was mated to a production VK-1A turbojet; the resulting VK-1F completed bench tests in the summer of 1951. (In this case, unlike the RD-45F, the F **did** signify 'afterburning'.) During bench tests the engine was rated at 2,600kgp (5,732lbst) dry and 3,380kgp (7,451lbst) reheat, ie, about 25% more than the basic VK-1A.

The MiG-17 powered by the VK-1F engine received the manufacturer's designation '*izdeliye* SF' – ie, *izdeliye* S *s forsahzhem* (with afterburning). The prototype *izdeliye* SF was built by taking the forward fuselage of a Gor'kiy-

Above and right: **The MiG-17F prototype (SF) was converted from a MiG-15bis with the c/n 53210850, hence the serial '850 Red'.** Mikoyan OKB

Below right: **This view illustrates the variable-area nozzle of the VK-1F and the new larger airbrakes.** Mikoyan OKB

built MiG-15*bis* serialled 850 Red (c/n 53210850) and mating it with the wings, landing gear and some other components of the second pre-production MiG-17 (SI-02, 671 Red, c/n 54210102).[3] The rear fuselage was new, with structural changes to accommodate the afterburner. The fuel system was also modified, since fuel consumption and fuel flow increased sharply when the afterburner was ignited.

Outward recognition features of the SF were the abbreviated aft fuselage showing the convergent-divergent nozzle (the aircraft's length remained unchanged) and the redesigned airbrakes of reduced area (0.64m²/6.88ft²). These were located higher up on the fuselage sides immediately ahead of the engine nozzle and the actuator fairings were located ahead of the airbrake panels rather than in the middle of them.

Prototype construction began in March 1951 (some documents say May 1951) and the hybrid aircraft was rolled out on 20th September, still wearing the old serial '850 Red'. The manufacturer's flight tests were held at Kratovo right next to Zhukovskiy from 21st September to 1st November 1951. Actually the SF made its first flight on 29th September with Mikoyan test pilot A N Chernoboorov at the controls; the aircraft was also flown by G A Sedov and Konstantin Konstantinovich Kokkinaki, another famous Soviet test pilot.

On 31st January 1952 the aircraft was handed over to NII VVS for State acceptance trials which began on 16th February and were completed in June. Test pilots A G Solodovnikov and L M Koovshinov stated cracking Mach 1 in

a shallow dive right away, but going supersonic in the MiG-17 called for tremendous efforts. Solodovnikov, who eventually earned the Distinguished Test Pilot grade, recalled:

'The afterburner was quite well designed and improved the aircraft's performance a lot. For example, at full military power you could not get a climb rate better than 20m/sec [3,937ft/min]; in full afterburner it rose to 45m/sec [8,860ft/min]. The afterburner improved the aircraft's service ceiling and significantly enhanced vertical manoeuvrability in a dogfight.

Regrettably, the speed increase in horizontal flight when the afterburner was engaged proved to be small – in fact, at certain altitudes there was no improvement at all. What's more, the aircraft behaved strangely in transonic mode with the afterburner engaged. It looked like this. At the required altitude the aircraft accelerated to 1,080 to 1,100km/h [584 to 594kts], going absolutely level, and the afterburner was engaged. A couple of seconds later there was a slight jolt and a distinctive bubbling roar at the back told the pilot that lightup was OK. Next moment the pilot felt the aircraft being pushed forward by a tremendous force. The Mach meter needle crept towards 0.98 – and then, when Mach One was just a footstep away, the jet would suddenly try to climb of its own accord. The pilot would push the stick all the way forward, but still the aircraft kept climbing – there was not enough elevator authority to keep it in level flight with the 'burner on.

Test equipment readouts showed that stick forces reached 90kg [198 lb]! This phenomenon was most acute at altitudes up to 7,000m [22,965ft]; after that, the aircraft's tendency to climb decreased and above 10,000m [32,808ft] it could be countered even without pushing the stick all the way. The flight instruments also behaved rather strangely. For instance, the Mach meter would reach 0.98 and 'get stuck' at this reading for two or three seconds, then jump to 1.05. At the same time the altimeter reading would abruptly increase by 250 to 300m [820 to 984ft] and the climb/descent indicator needle would move sharply to 'climb', then return to the original position – even though the aircraft flew normally, with no signs of such wild bounds.

The aerodynamics experts told us that these funny readings were caused by the pitot tube which was not designed for supersonic speeds. Only later did we learn that the pitot was not to blame; this thing always happens when you break through the sound barrier.

In a steep dive we reached indicated airspeeds right up to Mach 1.25. At this point, however, the aircraft would start pulling out of the dive on its own, and there was no way we could make it go beyond Mach 1.25. Besides, flight recorder analysis revealed that the instruments tend to give exaggerated readings in a high-speed descent; the specialists claimed that true airspeed was actually *below* Mach 1. The conclusion was that an aircraft using this particular layout could not go supersonic, no matter how powerful an engine you put into it.

When the trials programme was almost completed, the final part was to test the afterburner's structural strength. This involved accelerating to topmost speed in full afterburner and then throttling back sharply to flight idle. At 1,150km/h [621kts] the pilot yanked the throttle all the way back – and suddenly an unexpectedly loud clattering noise began in the tail of the aircraft, as if someone was shaking a sheet of metal back there. Exhaust gas temperature started to grow alarmingly. Making a vigorous turn, the pilot advanced the throttle slowly and made for home.

The airfield was close, but the EGT indicator needle was already in the red and a smell of burnt kerosene filled the cockpit. Fearing a fire, the pilot shut down the engine and the cockpit became unusually quiet. After making a couple of turns for final approach he selected gear down and made a perfect dead-stick landing.

It transpired that when the engine was throttled back the afterburner chamber walls had caved in, coming apart at the seams; this reduced the jetpipe's cross-section considerably, causing the exhaust gas temperature to rise. Part of the exhaust gases escaping through the cracks found their way into the cockpit pressurization system, hence the smell in the cockpit. Some local reinforcement cured the problem and the afterburner worked reliably from then on.'

When the discovered defects had been eliminated, 850 Red was redelivered to NII VVS for renewed trials on 18th September 1952. In November, however, the aircraft went unserviceable again when the afterburner ignited uncommandedly as the engine was being ground-run, causing heat damage to the aft fuselage.

Performance comparison	MiG-17 (typical)	MiG-17F (c/n 0115302)
Powerplant	VK-1A	VK-1F
Rating, kgp (lbst)	2,700 (5,952)	2,600/3,380 (5,732/7,451) *
Thrust/weight ratio	0.51	0.487/0.633 *
Continuous operation at full military power, min	10	10/6 *
Wing area, m² (ft²)	22.6 (243.0)	22.6 (243.0)
Normal AUW, kg (lb):		
in 'clean' condition	5,254 (11,583)	5,324/5,340 (11,732/11,772) §
with drop tanks	6,018 (13,267)	6,048/6,064 (13,333/13,368) §
Fuel capacity, litres (Imperial gallons):		
in 'clean' condition	1,450 (319)	1,390/1,405 (305.8/309.1) §
with drop tanks	2,250 (495)	2,190/2,205 (481.8/485.1) §
Wing loading, kg/m² (lbft²)	234 (1,137)	236/240 (1,147/1,166) §
Top speed, km/h (kts):		
at 5,000m (16,404ft)	1,113 (601.62)	1,092/1,130 (590.27/610.8) *
at 10,000m (32,808ft)	1,050 (567.56)	1,048/1,071 (566.48/578.9) *
at 12,000m (39,370ft)	1,025 (554.0)	1,054 (569.72) †
at 14,000m (45,931ft)	n/a	1,040 (562.16) †
Max IAS, km/h (kts)	1,060 (572.97)	1,060 (572.97)
Mach limit	1.15	1.15
Landing speed, km/h (kts)	190 (102.7)	n/a
Rate of climb, m/sec (ft/min):		
at 5,000m (16,404ft)	33.1 (6,515)	65.0 (12,795) ‡
at 10,000m (32,808ft)	18.9 (3,720)	38.4 (7,560) ‡
at 14,000m (45,931ft)	4.7 (925)	17.2 (3,385) ‡
Time to height (in 'clean' condition), min:		
to 5,000m (16,404ft)	2.1	2.4/2.1 *
to 10,000m (32,808ft)	5.4	6.2/3.7 *
Effective time to height, min: †		
to 5,000m (16,404ft)	3.1	3.2
to 10,000m (32,808ft)	6.4	4.8
to 12,000m (39,370ft)	8.5	5.9
to 14,000m (45,931ft)	n/a	7.4
Service ceiling, m (ft)	15,100 (49,540)	15,100/16,470 (49,540/54,035) *
Acceleration from 700km/h (378.37kts)		
to 1,000km/h (540.54kts) at 10,000m (32,808ft), sec	100	63
Turning time at 10,000m (32,808ft), sec	62	54
Min turn radius at 12,000m (39,370ft), m (ft)	1,500 (4,921)	1,500 (4,921)
Range, km (nm):		
at 5,000m (16,404ft) on internal fuel only	775 (419)	730 (394)
at 10,000m (32,808ft) on internal fuel only	1,150 (621)	1,100 (594)
at 12,000m (39,370ft) on internal fuel only	1,320 (713)	1,240 (670)
at 5,000m with drop tanks	1,150 (621)	1,090 (589)
at 10,000m with drop tanks	1,715 (927)	1,650 (892)
at 12,000m with drop tanks	2,060 (1,113)	1,540 (832)
Endurance at 12,000m (39,370ft):		
on internal fuel only	1 hr 52 min	n/a
with drop tanks	2 hrs 55 min	n/a
Speed in max-range cruise, km/h (kts):		
at 5,000m (16,404ft) on internal fuel only	710 (383.78)	710 (383.78)
at 10,000m (32,808ft) on internal fuel only	790 (427.0)	789 (426.48)
at 5,000m with drop tanks	710 (383.78)	710 (383.78)
at 10,000m with drop tanks	790 (427.0)	789 (426.48)
Tu-16 bomber escorting radius, km (nm)	745 (403)	n/a
Take-off run, m (ft):		
with flaps down	600 (1,968)	n/a
with drop tanks	940 (3,084)	n/a
Landing run, m (ft):		
without brake parachute	925 (3,034)	n/a
with brake parachute	598 (1,962)	n/a
Landing distance, m (ft):		
without brake parachute	1,500 (4,921)	n/a
with brake parachute	1,170 (3,838)	n/a
Continuous firing time, sec	5.7	5.7

* at full military power/in full afterburner; † at full military power; ‡ in full afterburner; § different documents give different data

Despite these and other problems with the SF, the State Commission decided that the aircraft should be put into production and included into the VVS inventory under the designation MiG-17F. In speed, rate of climb and service ceiling the 'flamin' Fresco' surpassed not only its predecessor but also the best Western fighters in its class. At 12,000m (39,370ft), the prototype SF had a range of 1,160km (627nm), increasing to 1,940km (1,048nm) with drop tanks; endurance in these conditions was 1 hr 44 min and 2 hrs 52 min respectively. During the State acceptance trials the aircraft performed a lot of aerobatics with the afterburner engaged.

Since the prototype was damaged and unflyable, NII VVS obtained one of the first production MiG-17Fs built in Novosibirsk (102 Red, c/n 0115302)[4] for checkout trials. The aircraft passed them in late May 1952 with good results. The table opposite gives a performance comparison of the MiG-17 and the MiG-17F.

The MiG-17F entered mass production in Novosibirsk and Komsomol'sk-on-Amur in late 1952, attaining initial operational capability (IOC) in 1953. Service trials were again held at Krymskaya AB and went well; the service pilots were greatly impressed by the afterburning engine. Naturally, there were teething troubles which led to limits being imposed. On initial production VK-1Fs afterburner operation time was limited to 3 minutes at altitudes up to 7,000m (22,965ft) and 10 minutes above 7,000m. In the West the aircraft was codenamed Fresco-C.

The first two or three batches built in 1952 had the original 0.64m² airbrakes, but these were quickly found to be inadequate. NII VVS held a special test programme and airbrake area was increased *again* – this time to 0.97m² (10.43ft²). The new airbrakes introduced not later than Batch 4[5] had a distinctive pentagonal shape, and the actuator fairings were somewhat larger, too, suggesting that the actuators had been beefed up.

Production MiG-17Fs had high performance. Top speed in level flight at 3,000m (9,842ft) was 1,145km/h (618.9kts) and rate of climb at the same altitude was 75.8m/sec (14,921ft/min). The highest Mach number attained was 0.994 at 11,000m (36,089ft); thus, the Soviet Air Force now had a production fighter capable of almost supersonic speeds.

The armament comprised one N-37D cannon with 40 rounds and two NR-23s with 80rpg. Two 50-kg (110-lb), 100-kg (220-lb) or 250-kg

The MiG-17F's airbrakes deployed. Mikoyan OKB

A 400-litre standard drop tank under the port wing of a MiG-17F. Mikoyan OKB

A production MiG-17F taxies out for take-off. Yefim Gordon archive

The pilot of a *Fresco-C* gets ready for a sortie at dusk. Yefim Gordon archive

(551-lb) bombs could be carried on the wing hardpoints. Late-production MiG-17Fs could also carry four 190mm (7.48in) TRS-190 high-velocity aircraft rockets or two 212mm (8.34in) ARS-212 (aka S-21) HVARs[6] on underwing pylons. Alternatively, the aircraft could be armed with two folding-fin aircraft rocket (FFAR) pods. Usually the MiG-17F carried standard 400-litre (88 Imperial gallons) drop tanks; 600-litre (132 Imperial gallons) tanks were rarely used.

Even as the first production aircraft rolled off the line in 1952, the Mikoyan OKB made numerous detail improvements to the MiG-17F. A nozzle actuated by three hydraulic rams for greater reliability was introduced and the afterburner's cooling shroud was modified to reduce cooling air flow. Measures were taken to preclude take-off with the nozzle petals fully open. (Unlike today's fighters, the MiG-17F could not take off in full afterburner; the afterburner was only ignited at 3,000m/9,842ft.) The hydraulic system hoses connected to the airbrake actuators were protected from the hot air surrounding the afterburner and equipped with more reliable connectors.

From c/n 0415351 onwards all MiG-17Fs were equipped with the SRD-1 gun ranging radar (*samolyotnyy rahdiodal'nomer* – aircraft-mounted radio rangefinder) in a small strake-like fairing in front of the cockpit windshield (on the avionics bay cover). The final batches featured improved ejection seats (see *Fresco-A* section) and BU-1M irreversible hydraulic actuators in the pitch and roll channels. The actuators improved pitch control significantly, while the improvement in roll control was rather modest.

Updates were also made to aircraft in service. For instance, the fuel system was modified in early 1953 to ensure stable engine operation at negative G; six check valves enable the engine to run in afterburner mode in inverted flight for at least 15 seconds. For the first time on a Soviet fighter, a cooling turbine was introduced in the air conditioning system in November 1953 to improve working conditions for the pilot.

In 1953 test pilot P A Kaz'min tested the MiG-17F's stability and handling at supersonic speeds. He reported that 'at high Mach numbers the aircraft is like a stiff spring which is hard to bend in any direction… The aircraft becomes so steady that it is difficult to control in all three channels; this may significantly complicate manoeuvring in a dogfight… Some additional means of control are required for manoeuvring at supersonic speeds.'

Kaz'min had a point. At 11,000m (36,089ft) the stick force in Mach 0.98 cruise was about 5kg (11 lb), but it rose to 35kg (77 lb) at 5,000m (16,404ft). At higher speeds the increase in stick force was even more marked. The results of these tests were taken into account later when supersonic aircraft were designed.

As noted earlier, the MiG-17F was at least equal – and in some respects superior – to the best Western fighters of the time. Its closest counterpart was the Dassault Mystère IVA which first flew on 28th September 1952 – incidentally, with Constantin Rozanoff, a Frenchman of Russian descent, at the controls. The two fighters had a lot in common, differing mainly in wing design; the Mystère had low-set wings with less sweep and a thinner airfoil.

At normal TOW and maximum thrust (ie, in full afterburner) the MiG-17F and the Mystère IVA had a wing loading of 236.9kg/m² (1,151 lbft²) and 234kg/m² (1,137 lbft²) respectively; thrust/weight ratio at sea level was 0.486 and 0.6 respectively. The French fighter had a better rate of climb at S/L (45m/sec or 8,858ft/min versus 41.6m/sec or 8,189ft/min) because, unlike the MiG-17F, it could engage the afterburner on take-off. This advantage, however, was nullified above 3,000m (9,842ft), since at this altitude the *Fresco-C*'s rate of climb increased to 75.8m/sec (14,821ft/min).

It was the same story with speed. At S/L the Mystère was 60km/h (32.43kts) faster thanks to the afterburner, but this advantage was nullified at medium altitudes, and at 12,000m (39,370ft) the MiG was 70km/h (37.83kts) faster. The MiG-17F was quite manoeuvrable at medium altitudes; eg, at 5,400m (17,716ft) it could make a yo-yo in 45 seconds at full military power and in

38 seconds in full afterburner. The two aircraft first met in combat during the 1956 Suez Crisis; the result of an engagement between the MiG-17F and the Mystère IVA depended chiefly on the pilots' skill and tactics.

The MiG-17F joined the VVS inventory when the Korean War was still raging. Yet, even though this aircraft outperformed the F-86 (which was one of the world's best fighters) by a considerable margin, it never made it to that war; there are claims that Stalin personally vetoed the type's deployment to Korea. Like the basic *Fresco-A*, the MiG-17F was built under licence in China and Poland and evolved into several locally-designed versions in those countries as described in the next chapter.

MiG-17F with R-3S AAMs

Some MiG-17Fs exported in the 1960s were armed with R-3S (K-13A/NATO AA-2-2 *Advanced Atoll*) IR-homing air-to-air missiles (AAMs) at the customer's request. The R-3S was a reverse-engineered AIM-9 Sidewinder missile.

MiG-17R (*izdeliye* SR-2) experimental tactical reconnaissance aircraft

On 3rd August 1951 the Council of Ministers issued directive No 2817-1338 ordering the Mikoyan OKB to develop a tactical reconnaissance version of the MiG-17 equipped with a tilting camera installation and powered by the new and more powerful VK-5 afterburning turbojet; an MAP order to the same effect followed on 6th August. The same CofM directive tasked the Klimov OKB with the development of the said engine. Interestingly, the directive contained no target performance data for the aircraft.

Work in the Mikoyan and Klimov bureaux progressed almost as a neck-and-neck race. Klimov engineers tried two ways to gain the objective: an upgrade of the production VK-1F was begun in parallel with the development of

404 Red, the MiG-17R (SR-2) prototype.
Mikoyan OKB

the new engine. Prototypes of the new VK-5F and the upgraded VK-1SF were manufactured in 1952 but the test programme kept lagging behind schedule.

The Mikoyan OKB started work on the aircraft in November 1951. The general arrangement of the forward fuselage/camera installation was ready by the end of the month, and manufacturing drawings for the forward fuselage mockup were issued in December. A complete set of drawings for the aircraft was released in early 1952, and the prototype bearing the in-house designation 'izdeliye SR-2' (by analogy with the MiG-15bisR, or izdeliye SR) was completed in May. The aircraft was converted from a Gor'kiy-built Fresco-A (404 Red, c/n 54210404).

The VK-5F afterburning turbojet was rated at 3,000kgp (6,613 lbst) dry and 3,850kgp (8,487 lbst) reheat – an improvement of 400kgp (881 lbst) and 470kgp (1,036 lbst) respectively over the VK-1F – for no increase in weight; the external dimensions likewise remained unchanged. This undoubted achievement was made possible by the use of new heat-resistant alloys, a higher turbine temperature and more efficient cooling. (It should be noted that both development engines mentioned above had an identical specific fuel consumption which was 6% lower than the production VK-1F's, but the brand-new VK-5F was selected as the more promising engine.)

Though with considerable delay, a flight-cleared engine (interestingly, referred to in OKB documents as VK-5, not VK-5F) was installed in the SR-2 prototype. The new powerplant necessitated changes to the aft fuselage structure to accommodate the afterburner. Unlike the MiG-17F, the nozzle petals were not visible. The shape of the rear end of the fuselage was similar to the Fagot-B's but the kink was even more pronounced, resulting in a rather large 'visor' over the nozzle; this 'visor' possibly protected the lower part of the rudder from the afterburner flame. The engine had automatic afterburner controls as on the VK-1F and bleed valves preventing surge.

The other main new feature was the AFA-BA-40R camera installed aft of the nose gear unit on an AKAFU tilting mount for two-strip vertical photography. The camera could be adjusted on the ground for oblique photography at 30° to the surface of the ground, shooting to the left of the aircraft's flight path. Alternatively, an AFA-BA-21S wide-angle camera could be installed for single-strip low-altitude vertical photography. During take-off and landing the camera lens was protected by doors which opened automatically when the camera was 'fired'.

The instrument panel was redesigned to incorporate a camera control panel. The mission equipment also included an MAG-9 cockpit voice recorder for taping the pilot's observations as he flew over the target, thus saving him the trouble of making notes or memorizing what he had seen.

The N-37D cannon, being the heaviest one (103kg/227 lb), was deleted to make up for the weight penalty incurred by the camera installation. The two remaining NR-23s with 100rpg were installed on a new weapons pallet of riveted construction. Wing area was decreased slightly from 22.6m² (243.0ft²) to 22.22m² (238.9ft²). The airbrakes, on the other hand, were enlarged (again!) to 1.1m² (11.82ft²) to improve the aircraft's manoeuvrability; they were located between frames 19 to 23. The SR-2 also had powered elevators.

Changes to other systems and equipment included an improved ejection seat with visor and stabilising surfaces, a 6kW GSR-6000 generator to cater for the increased electric power consumption, and an Oozel (Knot) IFF interrogator. The radio, ILS and other avionics were identical to those of the production MiG-17.

Retaining the old serial '404 Red', the SR-2 was rolled out on 4th June 1952. However, the first flight (with A N Chernoboorov at the controls) did not take place until 3rd July because the engine proved to be defective and had to be replaced at the insistence of Vladimir Ya Klimov. The manufacturer's flight tests were rather lengthy, ending only in January 1954 because the engine still left a lot to be desired and required constant modifications; the SR-2 had three unscheduled engine changes in the course of the tests.

The manufacturer's tests proceeded in parallel with the State acceptance trials which began in July 1952 and were completed on 10th August 1954. At NII VVS the SR-2 was flown by Lt Col Stepan A Mikoyan, Lt Col P N Belyasnik, Col Yuriy A Antipov, Col L M Koovshinov, Lt Col Vasiliy G Ivanov, Maj A G Solodovnikov and Maj N I Korovooshkin. The VK-1SF and VK-5F engines passed their own State acceptance trials at the same time.

The performance of several PHOTINT aircraft tested at NII VVS is compared in the table on the following page.

The State Commission's report said that the SR-2 was by far superior to the IL-28R, Yak-125 and MiG-15bisR tactical PHOTINT aircraft in all performance aspects except range. The cameras and other mission equipment were used more efficiently than on the MiG-15bisR and conveniently located. However, cockpit visibility was inadequate; also, engine operation in full afterburner was only ten minutes.

Ironically, it was the engine that killed the SR-2's prospects. Even though the VK-1SF and the VK-5F both passed their State acceptance trials successfully, the requirements had changed by then and the two engines could not meet them. Therefore, the State Commission's report read:

'The SR-2 aircraft powered by the VK-5F engine has passed State acceptance trials satisfactorily.

1. Service introduction of the modified MiG-17R (ie, [samolyot-] razvedchik, reconnaissance aircraft – Auth.) powered by the VK-5F engine is inadvisable because its

performance is almost identical to that of the MiG-17F powered by the VK-1F engine.

2. The MiG-17R powered by the VK-1F engine and fitted with the same camera installation is hereby recommended for production.'

MiG-17R tactical reconnaissance aircraft (production version, *izdeliye* SR-2S)

In keeping with the State Commission's recommendations a tactical PHOTINT version of the *Fresco-C* was developed with the same mission equipment as the ill-starred SR-2. After being duly tested it entered small-scale production and service as the MiG-17R. This aircraft had the manufacturer's designation '*izdeliye* SR-2S', the suffix letter denoting *sereeynoye* (production, used attributively).

MiG-17 (*izdeliye* SI-O) development aircraft

In November 1952 the Mikoyan OKB developed modifications aimed at improving weapons reliability. To keep the cannons from freezing at low ambient temperatures an air duct was routed from the engine to the armament bay, allowing the latter to be heated by engine bleed air. A single late-production *Fresco-A* serialled 607 Red (c/n 54210607) was converted by the Mikoyan OKB branch office at the Gor'kiy aircraft factory, receiving the product code *izdeliye* SI-O;[7] the O stood for *obogrev* [*oroozhiya*] – weapons heating. The conversion was completed in early 1953 and the aircraft transferred to NII VVS for checkout trials.

MiG-17 (*izdeliye* SI-5) experimental fighter-bomber/weapons testbed

In the early 1950s the Soviet fighter design bureaux began attaching considerable attention to strike capability, especially to medium- and heavy-calibre unguided rockets. Numerous models of HVARs, launchers for same and bomb shackles were tested and the effect of rocket launches on drop tanks located alongside the launchers was investigated.

One of the aircraft used to test heavy unguided weapons was *izdeliye* SI-5, a production *Fresco-A* adapted to carry two 190mm TRS-190 HVARs or two 210mm (8.26in) S-21 HVARs. The TRS-190 rockets were carried in PU-O-46 launch tubes and resembled regular cannon shells. Instead of the usual stabilising fins they had two angled nozzles which caused it to rotate like a bullet, thus stabilising it. The S-21s were of more conventional design and were carried on PU-21 launch rails. The fighter's standard cannon armament was retained.

The SI-5 was equipped with a new ASP-5N gunsight linked to an SRD-1M (Radal'-M)[8] gun ranging radar; a PZV-5U control box was fitted when S-21 rockets were carried. The electric system included an MA-500 transformer associated with the rocket armament. Apart from the armament, the SI-5 could be identified by the non-standard canopy windshield; the bullet-proof windscreen was located further forward and there was an upper glazing panel in addition to the two curved sidelights. The canopy

Comparison of PHOTINT Aircraft tested at NII VVS

	SR-2 Manufacturers Estimates	SR-2 Manufacturers Flight Tests	SR-2 State Acceptance Trials	MiG-17F c/n 0115302 Checkout Tests	MiG-15bisR State Acceptance Trials	Yak-125* State Acceptance Trials
Wing area, m² (ft²)	22.22 (238.9)	22.22 (238.9)	22.22 (238.9)	22.6 (243.0)	20.6 (221.5)	28.98 (311.6)
Empty weight, kg (lb)	n/a	3,974 (8,761)	n/a	n/a	n/a	n/a
AUW, kg (lb):						
in 'clean' condition	5,245 (11,563)	5,348 (11,790)	5,330 (11,750)	5,324 (11,732)	5,050 (11,133)	9,177 (20,231)
with drop tanks	n/a	6,077 (13,397)	6,390 (14,087)	6,048 (13,333)	6,110 (13,470)	9,785 (21,571)
Wing loading, kg/m² (lbft²)	247 (1,200)	242 (1,176)	240 (1,166)	240 (1,166)	245 (1,190)	316.6 (1,538)
Power loading, kg/kgp (lb./lbst)	1.36/1.69	1.4	1.39	n/a	n/a	n/a
Fuel capacity, litres (Imp gals):						
in 'clean' condition	n/a	n/a	1,410 (310.2)	1,390 (305.81)	1,410 (310.2)	3,925 (863.5)
with drop tanks	n/a	n/a	2,605 (573.1)	2,190 (481.8)	2,620 (576.4)	4,600 (1,012)
Fuel capacity, kg (lb):						
in 'clean' condition	1,200 (2,645)	1,172 (2,584)	1,170 (2,579)	n/a	n/a	n/a
with drop tanks	1,864/2,196 (4,109/4,841) ‡	1,836 (4,047)	2,160 (4,762)	n/a	n/a	n/a
Top speed, km/h (kts):						
at 2,000m/6,561ft	n/a	n/a / 1,110 (n/a / 600.0)	n/a	n/a	n/a	n/a
at 5,000m/16,404ft	1,160/1,108 (627.0/598.9) †	1,130/1,092 (610.8/590.27)	1,138/1,068 (615.13/577.29) †	1,130/1,092 (610.8/590.27)	1,042 (563.24)	1,110 (600.0)
at 7,000m/22,965ft	n/a	1,110/1,086 (600.0./587.0)	n/a	n/a	n/a	n/a
at 10,000m/32,808ft	1,130/1,094 (610.8/591.35) †	1,071/1,048 (578.9/566.48) †	1,085/1,043 (586.48/563.78) †	1,071/1,048 (578.9/566.48) †	990 (535.13)	1,052 (568.64)
Max TAS, km/h (kts)	n/a	n/a	1,200 (648.64)	1,200 (648.64)	1,070 (578.37)	n/a
Mach limit	n/a	n/a	1.15	1.15	n/a	1.03
Service ceiling, m (ft)	17,000/16,000 (55,777/52,493) †	16,800/15,100 (55,118/49,540) †	17,400/15,200 (57,086/49,868) †	16,470/15,100 (54,035/49,540) †	15,700 (51,509)	14,900 (48,884)
Time to height, min:						
to 5,000m/16,404ft	0.81/1.7 †	2.6/3.0 †	1.5/3.35 †	2.1/2.4 †	2.1	3.3
to 10,000m/32,808ft	1.94/4.24 †	4.0/5.2 †	2.8/6.9 †	3.7/6.2 †	5.3	7.2
to 15,000m/49,212ft	4.23/10.6 †	n/a	n/a	n/a	n/a	–
Rate of climb, m/sec (ft/min):						
at S/L	n/a	n/a / 50.0 (n/a / 9,842) †	n/a	65.0 / n/a (12,795 / n/a) †	n/a	n/a
at 5,000m/16,404ft	n/a	83.5/33.8 (16,437/6,653) †	n/a	38.4 / n/a (7,560 / n/a) †	n/a	n/a
at 10,000m/32,808ft	n/a	51.6/18.2 (10,157/3,582) †	n/a	17.2 / n/a (3,385 / n/a) †	n/a	n/a
Range with drop tanks, km (nm):						
at 5,000m/16,404ft in place	n/a	n/a	1,100 (594)	1,090 (589)	1,410 (762)	n/a
at 10,000m/32,808ft jettisoned	2,085/2,460 (1,127/1,329) §	2,115 (1,143) **	2,150 (1,162)	n/a	2,560 (1,383)	3,040 (1,643)
Range on internal fuel only, km (nm):						
at 5,000m/16,404ft	n/a	n/a	680 (372)	730 (394)	830 (448)	1,570 (848)
at 12,000m/39,370ft	1,300/1,164 (702/629) ¶	1,134 (613)	1,120/1,270 (605/686) ‖	1,240 (670)	1,330 (719)	2,650 (1,432)
Endurance at 12,000m (39,370ft), hr, min:						
on internal fuel only	1:55/1:42 ¶	1:36	n/a	n/a	n/a	n/a
with drop tanks	2:00/3:32 §	2:54 **	n/a	n/a	n/a	n/a
Take-off run at full military power, m (ft)	n/a	n/a	910 (2,985)	n/a	805 (2,641)	850 (2,788)
T/O distance at full military power, m (ft)	n/a	n/a	1,850 (6,069)	n/a	2,020 (6,627)	2,170 (7,119)
Take-off run in full afterburner, m (ft)	n/a	n/a	675 (2,214)	n/a	n/a	n/a
T/O distance in full afterburner, m (ft)	n/a	n/a	1,490 (4,888)	n/a	n/a	n/a
Armament, cal x qty/ ammunition supply	2 x 23mm/160	2 x 23mm/200	2 x 23mm/200	1 x 37mm/40 2 x 23mm/160	1 x 37mm/40 1 x 23mm/80	1 x 23mm/80
Combat (recce) radius, km (nm):						
at 5,000m/16,404ft	n/a	n/a	430 (232)	–	500 (270)	645 (348)
at 10,000m/32,808ft	n/a	n/a	n/a	–	815 (440)	1,060 (573)
at 12,000m/39,370ft	n/a	n/a	320 (173)	–	n/a	n/a
at 13,000m/42,650ft	n/a	n/a	n/a	–	1,085 (586)	1,265 (683)
Photographed strip length, km (nm):						
to 1/4,000th scale	n/a	n/a	73 (39.45)	–	73 (39.45)	320 (173)
to 1/8,000th scale	n/a	n/a	146 (78.9)	–	146 (78.9)	640 (346)
to 1/12,000th scale	n/a	n/a	219 (118.3)	–	219 (118.3)	960 (519)

* The Yakovlev Yak-125 was an experimental reconnaissance version of the Yak-120 interceptor known in production form as the Yak-25 *Flashlight-A*; † in full afterburner/at full military power; ‡ with 400-litre (88 Imperial gallons)/600-litre (132 Imperial gallons) drop tanks; § at 12,000m (39,370ft) with 400-litre/600-litre drop tanks; ¶ at full military power only/using afterburner; ‖ at 12,000m (39,370ft)/14,000m (45,931ft); ** at 12,000m with 600-litre drop tanks.

design was similar to that of the I-1 (I-370) experimental fighter which was a sort of cross-breed between the MiG-17 and the MiG-19 *Farmer*.

Development began in August 1953; the completed aircraft was rolled out on 14th December. The gunsight and gun ranging radar were tested and refined by NII-2 and the Ministry of Defence Industry's Central Design Bureau No 589 (TsKB-589). Shortly afterwards the ASP-5N gunsight was removed for modifications by TsKB-589; the work was completed in April and the gunsight returned to Mikoyan on 26th April 1954 for re-installation. In late May the SI-5 commenced State acceptance trials, completing them satisfactorily in August.

Top right and right: **MiG-17 '114 Red' after conversion to the *izdeliye* SG avionics testbed with the ASP-4N Sneg gunsight and the SRD-3 Grad gun ranging radar.** Mikoyan OKB

Below left: **Close-up of the SG's forward fuselage with the avionics bay cover removed, showing the radome of the SRD-3 gun ranging radar.** Mikoyan OKB

Below right: **The ASP-4N gunsight required a new extended windshield (similar to that used later on the MiG-17P/PF) to accommodate it.** Mikoyan OKB

MiG-17F (*izdeliye* SI-7) experimental fighter-bomber/weapons testbed

A standard MiG-17F was modified in 1954 to test the ARS-70 Lastochka (Swallow) unguided rocket system. Two pods, each holding five 70mm (2.75in) ARS-70 FFARs, were carried on pylons installed between the main gear units and the regular drop tank hardpoints; two more pods could be carried on these hardpoints. Like the SI-5, this aircraft designated *izdeliye* SI-7 was equipped with an ASP-5N gunsight and an SRD-1M gun ranging radar. Since the ARS-70 was not cleared for production and service, all aircraft armed with these rockets (including the SI-7) did not progress beyond the trials stage.

MiG-17 (*izdeliye* SI-15) experimental fighter-bomber/weapons testbed

On 15th December 1951 the Council of Ministers issued a directive ordering a MiG-17 to be adapted for firing ARS-140-150 unguided rockets, followed by an MAP order to the same effect on 26th December. The aircraft was to begin trials in the first quarter of 1953.

The advanced development project was prepared by the Mikoyan OKB branch office at the Gor'kiy aircraft factory in 1952. Two MiG-17s (obviously Gor'kiy-built *Fresco-As*) were converted to test the new armament in 1953; the manufacturer's designation was *izdeliye* SI-15. Unfortunately, the identity of the aircraft is unknown.

MiG-17 (*izdeliye* SI-??) experimental fighter-bomber/weapons testbed

To meet a Soviet Navy requirement drawn up in March 1954, plant No 81 converted a late-production Novosibirsk-built MiG-17 1628 Red (c/n 1615328) for testing the B-374 missile system. The system was developed for use against enemy landing ships, other small vessels and surfaced submarines. It comprised two five-tube rocket pods; each pod held fifteen 85mm (3.34in) TRS-85 unguided rockets, three per tube. The pods were carried on pylons installed between the main gear units and the regular drop tank hardpoints. The rockets could be fired in single salvos or in ripples; if drop tanks were carried, these had to be jettisoned first.

005 Red (c/n 54211005), the SI-16 weapons testbed with two ORO-57 FFAR pods, was brought out in 1953. The pods could be carried simultaneously with 400-litre (88 Imperial gallon) slipper tanks. Mikoyan OKB

Manufacturer's flight tests took place during May and June 1955. After the deficiencies discovered at this stage had been corrected, the aircraft was handed over to Research Institute No 15 (the naval counterpart of NII VVS) for State acceptance trials which took place between 13th October 1955 and 16th June 1956. The initial verdict was that using TRS-85 rockets on the *Fresco* was advisable. The ultimate decision concerning the updating of in-service aircraft, however, was delayed until the trials had been completed. Further trials showed that the TRS-85 was directionally unstable when fired at high speeds; this could only be cured by a complete redesign of the weapon and the programme was abandoned.

MiG-17 (*izdeliye* SG) avionics testbed

On 6th October 1951 an F-86A-5-NA (49-1319/'FU-319') was shot down and captured almost intact in Korea. This prize proved invaluable for the Soviet aircraft industry, providing it with a wealth of information on the potential adversary's technologies and aircraft systems. Many equipment items from the Sabre were studied firsthand, tested, cop… sorry, *reverse-engineered* and put into production. This is how the ASP-4N Sneg (Snow) optical gunsight and the SRD-3 Grad (Hail; pronounced *grahd*) gun ranging radar, Soviet copies of the A-1C and the AN/APG-30 respectively, came into being. The ASP-4N could project the aiming reticle and target range data on the bulletproof windscreen, thus acting as a head-up display.

In mid-1952 the Mikoyan OKB developed a version of the MiG-17 equipped with the ASP-4N gunsight (in lieu of the standard ASP-3N) and the SRD-3 gun ranging radar. The aircraft was converted from the 14th production Gor'kiy-built *Fresco-A* (114 Red, c/n 54210114) previously used in an airbrake test programme (see above) and completed in October 1952, entering flight test early 1953. The manufacturer's designation was *izdeliye* SG – ie, *izdeliye* S [*s sistemoy*] *Grahd*.

The forward fuselage of the SG redesigned up to frame 4 was a curious blend of Sabre and MiG. The aircraft had the F-86's characteristic 'beak' of the gun ranging radar radome on the intake upper lip; this caused the S-13 gun camera to be relocated to the starboard side of the intake. However, the trademark dorsal avionics bay cover of the early MiGs (up to and including the MiG-21 *Fishbed*) and the standard palletised cannon armament were retained. The windshield was lengthened to accommodate the ASP-4N gunsight, featuring two curved sidelights and an upper glazing panel *à la* MiG-17P/PF, and the bulletproof windscreen was more sharply raked (30° instead of the usual 37°). The DC battery was relocated to the ventral fin to make room for the gun ranging radar and the instrument panel was suitably redesigned. The standard 3kW GSR-3000 generator was replaced by a 6kW GSR-6000 unit, and the RSIU-3 radio and the ARK-5 ADF were powered by a common MA-250 transformer.

In addition to the standard armament the aircraft carried two pods with eight 57mm (2.24in) ARS-57 FFARs each on short unswept pylons. Rocket launch was controlled from a panel in the cockpit and automatically disabled when the landing gear was down.

The conversion was completed on 28th October 1952. On 16th November upon completion of manufacturer's tests the aircraft was transferred to NII-17 for equipment tests. Meanwhile, a further two MiG-17s were built to *izdeliye* SG standard at the Gor'kiy aircraft factory. In the first six months of 1953 all three aircraft underwent State acceptance trials at NII VVS with the purpose of verifying the ASP-4N and the SRD-3. Both the gunsight and the gun ranging radar were recommended for production. However, the SRD-3 could not be brought up to scratch and was eventually discarded in favour of the more refined indigenous Kvant (Quantum) gun ranging radar which found widespread use on Soviet fighters. The Kvant was also installed on new-build MiG-17s and retrofitted to earlier *Frescos* in service.

MiG-17 (*izdeliye* SG-5) avionics testbed

Later, 114 Red was refitted with the ASP-5N gunsight, retaining the SRD-3 gun ranging radar; in this configuration the aircraft was known as *izdeliye* SG-5. Conversion work was completed in December 1953 and the aircraft commenced manufacturer's flight tests on 11th January 1954.

Once again the gunsight and gun ranging radar were tested by NII-2 and TsKB-589. Shortly afterwards the ASP-5N gunsight was removed for modifications and returned on 26th April 1954 for re-installation. On 12th May the SG-5 commenced State acceptance trials, passing them satisfactorily.

MiG-17 (*izdeliye* SI-16) experimental fighter-bomber/weapons testbed

On 27th May 1953 MAP issued an order concerning modification of a MiG-17 with two pylons for carrying two ORO-57 FFAR pods with eight ARS-57 rockets apiece; the aircraft was to begin trials in the fourth quarter of that year. The manufacturing drawings were completed by September and conversion work began on a Gor'kiy-built MiG-17 serialled 005 Red (c/n 54211005).

The pylons had a vertical leading edge and a raked trailing edge and were located just inboard of the drop tank hardpoints (400-litre slipper tanks could be carried). Both FFAR pods fired simultaneously and could be jettisoned in an emergency. The aircraft featured an AP-57 automatic gunsight.

Completion of the aircraft was delayed until January 1954 because plant No 598 was late in delivering the gunsight. Designated *izdeliye* SI-16, the aircraft entered flight test on 21st January; the manufacturer's flight tests consisted of two stages (airframe trials and rocket launches). On 27th March the SI-16 was delivered to NII VVS for State acceptance trials which were successfully completed in June and the FFAR pod installation was recommended for production.

MiG-17 (*izdeliye* SI-19) experimental fighter-bomber/weapons testbed

The same CofM directive of 15th December 1951 and MAP order of 26th December (see SI-15) stated that a MiG-17 was to be adapted for firing TRS-190 HVARs in ORO-190 launch tubes.[9] The aircraft was to commence State acceptance trials in August 1952.

All manufacturing drawings had been issued by June 1952. After that, the fourth Kuybyshev-built *Fresco-A* serialled 104 Red (c/n 1401004)[10] was fitted with two pylons in line with the innermost wing fences for carrying two ORO-190 launch tubes. The pylons were L-shaped, extending far beyond the wing leading edge. Alternatively, the rockets could be carried on special pylons installed at the regular drop tank hardpoints; these were similar to the ones fitted to the SI-16, with a vertical leading edge and a raked trailing edge. In this case the inboards pylons were removed.

The launch tubes were suspended on D3-40 shackles; they came in two sizes and the conical noses of the rockets protruded from the shorter version. The TRS-190 rockets were equipped with EV-51 impact/proximity fuses developed by NII-137, a division of the Ministry of Agricultural Machinery (! – *Auth.*). An AP-2R automatic sight was fitted for aiming the rockets.

Designated *izdeliye* SI-19, the aircraft was rolled out on 13 August 1952 and delivered to NII VVS after manufacturer's flight tests on 9th September. A G Solodovnikov flew the fighter at NII VVS.

Unbelievably, development of the TRS-190 with a high-explosive/fragmentation warhead was officially ordered *a year after the SI-19 flew* by CofM directive of 19th September 1953 and Ministry of Defence Industry (MOP – *Ministerstvo oboronnoy promyshlennosti*) order of 10th October 1953! The same directive and MAP order of 2nd October 1953 tasked Mikoyan with equipping the fighter with ORO-90 launch tubes, an AP-21 (AP-2R) gunsight and a PZV-52 fuse arming device;[11] the deadline for State acceptance trials was now the third quarter of 1953.

Even before that (on 12th August 1953) the SI-16 completed renewed manufacturer's tests. By 1st January 1954 it passed Stage 1 of the State acceptance trials. Stage 2 was held at the NII VVS shooting range and went smoothly. Still, like the previous aircraft armed with TRS-190 HVARs (the SI-5), the SI-16 did not enter service.

MiG-17 (*izdeliye* SI-21) experimental fighter-bomber

In July and August 1953 another MiG-17 (443 Red, c/n 54210443) was converted into an experimental fighter-bomber designated *izdeliye* SI-21; the designation referred to the AS-21 weapons system. The conversion was undertaken pursuant to an MAP order dated 15th July 1953.

Like the SI-19, the aircraft had two alternative pylon arrangements but was armed with ARS-212 HVARs on PU-21 launch rails attached on D4-50 shackles; the rockets were equipped with electric detonators.

Likewise, the aircraft was equipped with an AP-2R automatic sight 'linked to the landing gear retraction system' (*sic*)[12] which had two modes of operation for aiming either the cannons or the rockets (they could not be fired simultaneously). The outboard arrangement (when the launch rails were carried on the standard hardpoints) was broadly similar to the MiG-15*bis* (*izdeliye* SD-21).

The SI-21 passed its State acceptance trials successfully at the end of the year. On 11th May 1954 the Council of Ministers issued a directive, followed by an MAP order six days later. These documents ordered the aircraft into production at Tbilisi (starting in September) and Komsomol'sk-on-Amur (starting in October) as the MiG-17AS (see below).

MiG-17 (*izdeliye* SI-21M) experimental fighter-bomber

The CofM directive of 15th December 1951 and MAP order of 26th December mentioned earlier (see SI-15 and SI-19) concerned yet another weapons system – a MiG-17 armed with two ARS-212M Ovod (Gadfly) rockets. The aircraft was to commence State acceptance trials in the fourth quarter of 1952.

A set of manufacturing drawings was prepared by Mikoyan during October and November 1952 and shipped to the Gor'kiy aircraft factory. Conversion work started on two *Fresco-As* which received the designation '*izdeliye* SI-21M' (*modifitseerovannoye* – modified). One of them was serialled 421 Red (c/n 54210421). The aircraft carried the rockets on APU-5 launchers fitted to the drop tank hardpoints. The rockets were fired by pushing the cannon firing button after they had been armed. There is contradictory evidence regarding the aiming equipment: some documents state the aircraft had an AP-2R automatic sight while others say it had an ASP-5N sight and a Radal'-M gun ranging radar.

Conversion work lagged behind schedule because the aiming equipment was unavailable. Anyway, the SI-21M was shortlived. On 15th April 1953 the Council of Ministers issued a directive terminating the programme, followed on 8th May by an MAP order to the same effect. The first aircraft was by then in the middle of the manufacturer's flight tests and the second was not even completed.

MiG-17AS *Fresco-A/C* production fighter-bomber

In 1955 the Mikoyan OKB converted an early-production Novosibirsk-built MiG-17F (0124 Red, c/n 0115324) for checkout tests of the AS-21 weapons system. When the ARS-212 (S-21) HVAR entered production in the mid-50s, several batches of MiG-17As and MiG-17Fs were built with special reinforcement beams at the drop tank hardpoints to which PU-21 launchers could be attached. The launchers could also be installed between the drop tank hardpoints and the main gear units; in this case the drop tanks, if any, had to be jettisoned before the rockets could be fired. Aircraft thus modified, regardless of the original version, were designated MiG-17AS, the suffix letters referring to the AS-21 weapons system.

In the second half of 1955 all MiG-15*bis* and MiG-17 fighter-bombers with the AS-21 weapons system were progressively updated in service to preclude uncommanded launch of S-21 rockets (which happened from time to time before this update).

MiG-17 *Fresco-A* fighter-bomber conversion

A MiG-17 coded 15 Blue (ex-565 Red, c/n 54210565) was converted to fighter-bomber configuration at plant No 21 in Gor'kiy in early 1958, using drawings supplied by the Mikoyan OKB. Two BD3-56 pylons were fitted about

Top and above left: **The SI-19 weapons testbed (104 Red, c/n 1401004) with two TRS-190 HVARs in ORO-190 launch tubes. These were carried on special L-shaped pylons.** Mikoyan OKB

Above right and below: **The SI-19 in a different configuration with two straight pylons inboard of the drop tank hardpoints. ORO-190 launch tubes could be carried on these pylons without conflicting with the drop tanks. Unidentified streamlined pods, possibly with test instrumentation, are carried here.** Mikoyan OKB

halfway between the main gear units and the drop tank hardpoints. Installation of the pylons and associated equipment was easy and cheap.

The aircraft could carry three typical combinations of external stores: two 212mm (8.834in) two S-1-OF (aka TRS-212) rockets on ORO-212K launchers plus two 400-litre (88 Imperial gallons) drop tanks; two ORO-57K rocket pods with S-5M or S-5K FFARs plus two 400-litre (88 Imperial gallons) drop tanks; and two S-1-OF HVARs plus two 250-kg (551-lb) FAB-250 'iron bombs'. The cannon armament remained unchanged. The rockets and cannons were fired using the upper button and lower trigger on the stick respectively; all weapons were aimed using the standard ASP-3N gunsight.

Together with a similarly converted Novosibirsk-built MiG-15bis (24 Blue, ex-2811 Red, c/n 2815311) the aircraft went directly to NII VVS for trials which lasted from 4th March to 30th June 1959. The results were encouraging and the conversion was recommended for service.

MiG-17F (izdeliye SF-3) development aircraft

In an attempt to improve the Fresco's basic armament the Mikoyan OKB considered replacing the single N-37D and two NR-23s with a pair of new 30mm (1.18 calibre) Nudel'man/Rikhter NR-30 cannons (izdeliye 235P). A Council of Ministers directive to this effect was issued on 15th July 1954, followed by an MAP order to the same effect on 20th July: the aircraft was to commence trials in October.

Conversion work on a Novosibirsk-built MiG-17F serialled 0476 Red (c/n 0415376) started in July 1954. The two NR-30s were mounted on a new weapons pallet of riveted construction designed to fit the standard hoists. This necessitated changes to the forward fuselage up to frame 9. The cannons were installed in a staggered arrangement with the port cannon further forward.

Designated izdeliye SF-3, the aircraft had an ASP-5N-V3 gunsight[13] and a Radal'-M gun ranging radar, with appropriate changes to the instrument panel layout. The new gunsight necessitated the installation of a redesigned windshield similar to that of the SI-5 with the bulletproof windscreen further forward, an upper glazing panel and two sidelights. (This windshield design was borrowed from the MiG-17P/PF/PFU, which see.) The sliding part of the canopy was also new, more streamlined and with one-piece glazing à la Sabre (ie, without the aft transverse frame member).

The cockpit was equipped to use the VSS-04 pressure suit. The standard GSR-3000 generator was replaced by a GSR-6000 unit. The RSIU-3 radio and ARK-5 ADF now had a common aerial.

The SF-3 was completed on 29th October 1954. The manufacturer's flight tests lasted until late November; on 11th December the aircraft was transferred to NII VVS and passed its State acceptance trials with good results. The SF-3 as such was not recommended for production but the new cannon was; a Council of Ministers directive to this effect was passed on 9th May 1955.

MiG-17 (izdeliye SI-91) development aircraft

Another aircraft used by Mikoyan to test systems and equipment from the captured F-86A was izdeliye SI-91, a modified MiG-17 (identity unknown) fitted with the Sabre's automatic temperature and pressure control unit in the cockpit pressurization and air conditioning system. This unit automatically maintained cockpit air temperature at 16 to 25°C (60 to 77°F), saving the pilot the trouble of adjusting it manually. The system was tested successfully at up to 12,000m (39,370ft).

MiG-17 (izdeliye SN) development aircraft

Usually a fighter pilot had to take aim by pointing the whole aircraft, which took considerable time. In a dogfight, this put him at a disadvantage: he had to provide target lead by aiming at a point ahead of the target on its anticipated course. If the target was more agile than his own aircraft, the pilot had no choice but to break off the attack and start anew – and the few seconds lost in so doing could prove fatal. Conversely, on a fighter with movable armament the pilot could bring his guns to bear on the target much quicker and more accurately – even when pointing the aircraft itself was impossible. Ideally, this gave him first-shot, first-kill capability.

When the MiG-15 (izdeliye SU)[14] – a Fagot-A (935 Red, c/n 109035) fitted with the V-1-25-Sh-3 experimental weapons system – was tested and rejected in 1951, the Mikoyan OKB did not give up on the movable cannon idea. Two years later a late-production MiG-17 with 0.88m^2 airbrakes was converted into an experimental fighter designated izdeliye SN; it is not known what the N stands for.

Learning from their experience with the SU where the elevation angle was severely restricted by the cannons' location under the standard forward fuselage, Mikoyan engineers placed the cannons in the extreme nose. This necessitated a complete redesign of the entire forward and centre fuselage up to frame 13 (the fuselage break point). The single nose air intake was replaced by two small lateral intakes of elliptical section (with the large axis vertical) flanking the cockpit, beginning almost level with the windscreen's rear frame. The fuselage was area-ruled around the cockpit so that the intakes were semi-recessed in shallow troughs in the fuselage sides, in a manner similar to the Tu-16 bomber. The SN was the first Mikoyan aircraft with lateral intakes.

The extended and slightly drooped bullet-shaped nose changed the aircraft's silhouette completely, increasing overall length by 1.069m (3ft 6in). It terminated in a small radome housing an Aist (Stork; pronounced ah-ist) aiming radar[15] and an SRD-1M Radal'-M gun ranging radar; both were linked to an ASP-4NM optical gunsight for night/poor weather operations.

The canopy was all-new, being both larger in order to improve visibility and more streamlined. The bulletproof windshield was inclined 30° in connection with the use of the ASP-4NM gunsight. The instrument panel was also new. Fuel capacity was increased by 50 litres (11 Imperial gallons). The main gear units had new KT-23 wheels with more powerful brakes and the inboard main gear doors were redesigned to match the contour of the air intakes where they met the wings.

The main new feature, however, which caused all this massive redesign was of course the movable cannon installation developed under N I Volkov, the author of the MiG-15/MiG-17's unique weapons arrangement. The SV-25-MiG-17 cannon installation was intended primarily for strafing ground targets and comprised three 23mm Afanas'yev/Makarov AM-23 (aka TKB-495) cannons.[16] The brand-new AM-23's rate of fire was 1,250rpm – a world record for single-barrelled cannons at the time.

The cannons were mounted asymmetrically – two to port, one over the other, and one to starboard – and moved in vertical slits flanking the radome. The elevation angle was +27° 26'/-9° 28', compared to +11°/-7° for izdeliye SU. The pilot controlled cannon elevation by turning a knob on the throttle, just like on the SU; an electric motor moved the guns and the gunsight moved in concert. For reloading and maintenance the cannons were accessed via two detachable panels on the sides of the nose; these had a complex curvature, being convex at the front and concave at the rear.

The complete cannon installation weighed 469kg (1,033.95 lb), including 142.4kg (313.9 lb) for the elevating cannon mounts proper, 117kg (257.9 lb) for the three cannons and 139.7kg (304 lb) for the ammunition. The remaining 70kg (154 lb) are accounted for by various auxiliary equipment.

The unserialled izdeliye SN was completed on 20th July 1953 and test flown by Mikoyan test pilot Gheorgiy K Mosolov. State acceptance trials of the SV-25-MiG-17 cannon installation began on 15th February 1954. However, these were mostly held not on the SN but on an IL-28 bomber converted into a weapons testbed (the cannon installation replaced the navigator's glazing). NII VVS test pilots Yuriy A Antipov, A P Molotkov, N P Zakharov, Stepan A Mikoyan, V N Makhalin, A G Solodovnikov and Vasiliy G Ivanov made a total of 127 flights on this testbed.

As for the SN, the aircraft made 130 test flights at NII VVS but only 13 of them involved firing at ground targets; 15,000 rounds were expended during the State acceptance trials. The trials revealed a host of shortcomings; for example, when the cannons were angled up or down, firing all three cannons in bursts caused the aircraft to pitch down or up respectively. If the cannons were angled more than 10° up,

421 Red (c/n 54210421), the SI-21 weapons testbed of 1953 with ARS-212 HVARs on PU-21 launch rails. Mikoyan OKB

The MiG-17AS fighter-bomber had detachable pylons outboard of the drop tanks for carrying bombs and unguided rockets. Yefim Gordon archive

This MiG-17AS preserved in a pioneer camp near Moscow is one of a handful of *Fresco-A*s with airbrakes immediately aft of the wing trailing edge.

Close-up of the port wing pylon and airbrake of the preserved MiG-17AS; note the prominent stiffening ribs on the airbrake panel and the pylon nose fairing which is permanently attached to the wing. Both Sergey Komissarov

15 Blue (ex-565 Red, c/n 54210565) the prototype of the MiG-17 fighter-bomber conversion, seen during trials. Note the extra pylon and FFAR pod just inboard of the drop tank; the tanks had to be jettisoned before the rockets could be fired.

accurate shooting was out of the question; some means of compensating the recoil force was obviously needed. The message was clear: the advantages of the movable cannon armament could only be used if the installation was controlled automatically.

Some of the SN's deficiencies were caused by the heavily modified airframe. The lateral air intakes spaced wide apart had an adverse effect on engine operation (predictably so, since the Mikoyan OKB had no previous experience with this type of intakes – *Auth*.); the engine became prone to surge and less willing to start up in flight. Performance deteriorated somewhat in comparison with the standard *Fresco-A* because of the higher AUW and different aerodynamics. For instance, top speed was 60km/h (32.43kts) lower and service ceiling reduced by some 500m (1,640ft). The time required to reach 5,000m (16,404ft) and 10,000m (32,808ft) increased by 0.44 and 1.5 minutes respectively. But the bad news was the reduction in manoeuvrability; at 10,000m the aircraft's turning time was 77 seconds – ie, 15 seconds more than the standard MiG-17's!

'The SN was slightly inferior to the [production] MiG-17 as regards performance but superior in the use of its weapons, – A G Solodovnikov recalled. – In level flight it could destroy targets above its own flight level and attack ground targets while flying at low altitude – 100 to 200m [328 to 656ft] or less, depending on pilot skill. After the trials we recommended building a small batch of SNs, but the higher command had different views and the aircraft did not enter production.'

This second unsuccessful experiment with movable cannons located far from the aircraft's CG convinced the engineers that this was the wrong approach and the idea was not pursued.

The SF-3 development aircraft (c/n 0415376) featured a new armament (two 30mm NR-30 cannons) and an all-new canopy. Mikoyan OKB

MiG-17 (*izdeliye* SI-10) aerodynamics research aircraft

Benefiting from Korean War experience and studies of the captured F-86A, the Mikoyan OKB attempted to improve the *Fresco*'s manoeuvrability, stability at high angles of attack and field performance by means of effective high-lift devices.

To this end an early-production Gor'kiy-built MiG-17 with 0.522m² airbrakes serialled 214 Red (c/n 54210214) was converted into an aerodynamics research aircraft designated *izdeliye* SI-10.

The SI-10's wings were its main new feature. While retaining the standard basic structure and size, they had constant leading-edge sweep, lacking the MiG-17's characteristic kink at half-span. The wings were equipped with four-section automatic leading-edge slats occupying the outboard 67% of each half-span. The slats deflected 12°; each section moved on two guide rails made of Type 30KhGSA steel and the outer sections had black zebra-stripe markings applied for icing visualization during tests.

The standard flaps were replaced by Fowler flaps occupying the entire trailing edge between the ailerons and the fuselage. The flaps moved on four tracks each and had two settings, 16° for take-off and 25° for approach. For roll control the ailerons were assisted by

spoilers; these were located on the wing undersurface ahead of the flaps (!) and opened 55mm (2.16in) when aileron deflection exceeded 6°. Finally, the MiG-17's customary wing fences were deleted. In all other respects the SI-10 was a standard MiG-17 powered by a 2,700-kgp (5,952 lbst) VK-1A and armed with a single N-37D cannon and two NR-23s.

The new wings were designed in December 1952 according to TsAGI recommendations and manufactured at MMZ No155; the aircraft was completed in late 1954. The redesign incurred a sizeable weight penalty. The slats and flaps alone added 120kg (264.5 lb) to the aircraft's empty weight, the spoilers another 14kg (30.86 lb), and a 70-kg (154-lb) weight had to be installed in the forward fuselage to maintain CG position.

The SI-10 was completed on 10th November 1952; the maiden flight, however, was delayed until January 1953 because TsAGI took so long to prepare the report clearing the aircraft for flight tests. The manufacturer's flight tests were performed by Sultan Amet-Khan (LII) and OKB pilots Gheorgiy K Mosolov, Gheorgiy A Sedov and A N Chernoboorov between 17th February and 25th April 1953; Yuriy I Korolyov was the engineer in charge. They were part of a plan drawn up by MAP in order to eliminate the deficiencies of the SI-02 and SI-01 noted during State acceptance trials.

Left: *Izdeliye* SN was the Mikoyan OKB's second attempt to integrate elevating weapons and arguably the most radical modification of the MiG-17. This head-on view shows the semi-recessed lateral intakes to advantage.
Mikoyan OKB

Centre and bottom: The SN's extended nose terminating in a small radome and housing the movable cannons changed the MiG-17's silhouette considerably. Mikoyan OKB

In the fourth quarter of 1953 the standard horizontal tail was replaced variable-incidence stabilizers which could be adjusted from -5° to +3° for longitudinal trim. A BU-14 irreversible actuator was added in the pitch control circuit. This modification added another 28kg (61.72 lb) to the aircraft's empty weight. At this stage the aircraft was flown by Gheorgiy A Sedov.

In June and July 1955 the SI-10 passed its State acceptance trials which included a special spinning trials programme. The aircraft was flown by Stepan A Mikoyan, V N Makhalin, A P Molotkov and N I Korovin who logged a total of 32 hrs 10 min in 47 flights. The trials showed that the spoilers and the variable-incidence stabilizers improved manoeuvrability and handling considerably, especially at high speed and high altitude. Conversely, the automatic leading-edge slats, for all their extra weight,

gave no great improvement in manoeuvrability. Performance was very similar to that of the SI-02 pre-production aircraft. Hence the SI-10 remained a one-off.

MiG-17 control system testbeds
In 1952 an early-production MiG-17 was used to test a BU-1A hydraulic actuator in the elevator control circuit which reduced stick forces 3 times. The actuator was housed in the fin and accessed via a removable panel on the starboard side of the fin.

MiG-17 aerodynamics research aircraft
In 1952 another early-production MiG-17 was fitted with a redesigned fin swept back 55° at quarter-chord instead of 45° in an attempt to improve longitudinal stability. Thus this particular *Fresco-A* can be regarded as an aerodynamics research aircraft. Flight tests showed

that the idea was a good one; the new fin worked as it should, improving controllability at high Mach numbers.

MiG-17 RHAWS testbed (?)
One MiG-17 coded 32 Red featured non-standard probe-like excrescences on the intake upper lip (almost like a refuelling probe) and on top of the fin (facing aft). The aircraft was probably an avionics testbed for a radar warning and homing system.

MiG-17 brake parachute testbed (*izdeliye* SI-P)
A late-production Gor'kiy-built MiG-17 serialled 948 Red (c/n 54210948) was fitted experimentally with a 15m² (161ft²) PT-2165-51 brake parachute (*parashoot tormoznoy*) in similar fashion to the MiG-15bis (*izdeliye* SD-P) tested from May to July 1951. A brake parachute bay was located under the jetpipe between frames 27 to 30; the twin bay doors and the parachute release lock were actuated pneumatically. The ventral fin was enlarged, with a cutout in the middle where the bulged doors were located. The fuselage tail fairing was also recontoured and the tail bumper redesigned.

The modification was developed by the Mikoyan OKB branch office at the Gor'kiy aircraft factory in 1953. Designated *izdeliye* SI-P, the P standing for [*s tormoznym*] *parashootom* – with brake parachute, the aircraft passed State acceptance trials satisfactorily.

MiG-17 'false bomber target'

One late-production Gor'kiy-built MiG-17 (c/n 542112...; the last two digits have been obliterated) was used to simulate bombers for training air defence radar operators. To this end two large tetrahedral angle reflectors (so-called Luneberg lenses) were attached to the standard drop tanks in order to increase the aircraft's radar signature.

MiG-17P *Fresco-B* interceptor (*izdeliye* SP-6)

The Mikoyan OKB attached special importance to investigating the MiG-17's potential as a radar-equipped interceptor optimised for night and poor-weather operations. Hence in 1952 it began development of the MiG-17P (*perekhvaht*chik), aka *izdeliye* SP-6.

Below: **214 Red (c/n 54210214), the SI-10 aerodynamics research aircraft which served to investigate ways of improving the MiG-17's agility.** Mikoyan OKB

Bottom left: **Close-up of the SI-10's automatic leading-edge slats; note the black zebra-stripe markings applied for icing visualization during tests.** Mikoyan OKB

Bottom right: **The SI-10 also featured new Fowler flaps.** Mikoyan OKB

By then the Soviet fighter makers had several interceptor prototypes flying, but none of them had attained production status. The Yak-50 light interceptor – the first aircraft to bear this designation – entered flight test in 1949 and passed State acceptance trials in 1950.[17] It had wings swept back 45° at quarter-chord, cruciform tail surfaces, a single VK-1A turbojet, a bicycle landing gear and a Korshoon radar mounted in a similar way to the MiG-17 (*izdeliye* SP-2). The Yak-50 had outstanding performance, but some handling idiosyncrasies and the inadequate radar killed its chances. The La-200 twin-engined heavy interceptor which passed its trials satisfactorily in 1951 also fell victim to the Korshoon radar.

Conversely, the MiG-17 day fighter was by then in production at several aircraft factories, which meant an interceptor derivative could enter production without too much trouble. This, together with the general dearth of all-weather-capable interceptors, undoubtedly influenced the government's decision to launch production of the MiG-17P and the RP-1 Izumrood-1 (Emerald-1) radar.[18] (As far back as 24th May 1952, when the SP-6 was still unflown, the Council of Ministers had issued directive No 2460-933 ordering the aircraft and the RP-1 radar into production and ordering all further work on the Korshoon radar to be terminated.)

Development of the RP-1 had begun at NII-17 in 1948, mainly as an insurance policy in case the Toriy autonomous radar turned out to be a lemon (which it did). The Izumrood-1 was a twin-antenna radar, with separate search and tracking antennas. It provided target search, autotracking and attack in the fighter's forward hemisphere (in conjunction with the ASP-3N optical sight, later changed to the more advanced ASP-3NM) and identified the target in conjunction with the IFF system. The main advantage of the new radar was that it could be installed quite easily in a single-seat aircraft, since pilot workload was significantly lower than with the Toriy.

Designing the Izumrood took three years of hard work. It was a centimetre-waveband (S-band) radar with a 50 to 60kW transmitter, two aerials and two modes of operation: search and aiming (tracking). In search mode the radar had a 12-km (6.48nm) range[19] and a field of view of ±60° in azimuth and +26/-16° in elevation, scanning through the entire field of view in 1.33 sec. Tracking mode was switched on automatically when the target was in a 7° forward cone and at approximately 2km (1.08nm) range. At this range, autotracking accuracy was 1° and 150m (492ft).

The radar featured a cathode-ray tube (CRT) with a high retention (viewing) time enabling the pilot to observe multiple targets simultaneously; it also showed artificial horizon markers for attitude reference. The CRT was originally viewed through the ASP-3N sight by

The MiG-17P prototype. Yefim Gordon archive

This late-production MiG-17 has angle reflectors attached to the drop tanks in order to increase the signature. The aircraft was used to imitate bombers for training AD radar operators.
Yefim Gordon archive

means of mirrors, though on production aircraft equipped with the RP-1 it was a separate unit.

Interception was performed as follows. Assisted by ground control, the interceptor pilot entered the area where the intruder was supposed to be and switched on the radar, scanning the forward hemisphere in search mode. When the target was acquired the ASP-3N showed it as a blip of varying shape – 'T' if the target was above the fighter's flight level, 'inverted T' if it was below the fighter's flight level or '+' if it was on the same level. The pilot was to make sure he was on the same level with the target and close in on it so that the blip crossed the CRT's centreline, entering the radar's autotracking zone. Then the gunsight showed the target as a blip with wings (==O==), known in pilot slang as the *ptitsa* (bird), the wingspan depending on the target's range. When the range was right the computer gave the OK to fire. The radar not only indicated target range and position relative to the fighter but also target motion, enabling the pilot to make an attack manoeuvre and cut across the target's path. In visual meteorological conditions the pilot would switch off the radar and use the optical gunsight only.

The main challenge in fitting the RP-1 was in finding the best locations for the two antennas in the forward fuselage. At length, the engineers incorporated the search antenna into the air intake upper lip and the tracking antenna into the air intake splitter. Hence the S-13 gun camera had to be moved from its usual position on the intake upper lip to the starboard side. This arrangement with its characteristic twin radomes ('fat lip' and small bullet-shaped intake centrebody) became standard for all Mikoyan aircraft equipped with the Izumrood radar.

In 1950 the RP-1 was tested successfully on the MiG-15*bis*P (*izdeliye* SP-5) development aircraft, followed by more tests in various weather and climatic conditions on the UTI-MiG-15P (*izdeliye* ST-7/ST-8) radar trainer in 1953. These tests confirmed the Izumrood-1's high performance in comparison to contemporary Soviet airborne radars.

The forward fuselage was redesigned up to frame 9 and somewhat lengthened to accommodate the radar. The shape of the nose, especially of the search antenna radome ('fat lip'), was almost identical to that of the UTI-MiG-15P. The windshield was enlarged to accommodate

the gunsight and radar display, featuring a bullet-proof windscreen located further forward, an upper glazing panel and two sidelights. The instrument panel was suitably altered to incorporate the radar display with its long rubber sunblind; the latter was inevitably dubbed *sapog* (boot) in Air Force slang. Minor changes were made to the forward cockpit armour sheet located on frame 4 to fit the recontoured fuselage nose.

The aircraft had a new nose gear unit with a built-in nosewheel alignment mechanism located inside the oleo strut. Curiously, the nose gear could be extended independently in an emergency – presumably to protect the costly radar in a crash-landing, should the main gear fail to extend normally.

According to the project the SP-6 was to be based on the MiG-17F powered by the afterburning VK-1F but this was yet to change, as we shall see.

To make up for the weight of the radar and maintain CG position the N-37D cannon was replaced by a lighter NR-23; thus the SP-6 was armed with three NR-23s (two to port and one to starboard) with 100rpg. In overload condition the aircraft could carry two 250-kg (551-lb) bombs. Alternatively, 400-litre (88 Imperial gallons) drop tanks of either variety – slipper and non-slipper – could be carried. A BU-1U hydraulic actuator was provided in the aileron control circuit. A 6kW GSR-6000 generator was fitted to cater for the increased power consumption.

Five unserialled SP-6 prototypes were built in the summer of 1952. The first two were converted at MMZ No 155 from early-production

Fresco-As with 0.522m² airbrakes and the other three in Gor'kiy (with assistance from the local branch office of the Mikoyan OKB). All five aircraft were subsequently retrofitted with missile pylons and used in the development of the K-5 air-to-air missile (see next entry).

On 27th June 1953 the Council of Ministers issued directive No 1611-639 outlining the performance requirements for production aircraft. This was followed by MOP order No 471 to the same effect on 7th July ordering the SP-6 into production under the service designation MiG-17P. The interceptor was built in Gor'kiy and Tbilisi; the in-house product code at the former plant was either *izdeliye* 56 or *izdeliye* 57.

As noted earlier, the Mikoyan OKB envisaged the VK-1F engine for the MiG-17P. However, when production got under way the VK-1F was still in short supply. Also, air-to-air missiles were envisaged but their development turned out to be a lengthy process. Hence the first production interceptor version had to make do with cannons and the non-afterburning VK-1 or VK-1A.

Changes were introduced gradually. Some MiG-17Ps shared the armament of the *Fresco-A/C* (one N-37D cannon and two NR-23 cannons), others were armed with two or three NR-23s with up to 100rpg. If two NR-23s were fitted, the starboard cannon protruded while the port one was completely buried, just as on the SP-5. The earliest production aircraft even had the *Fresco-A*'s original 0.522m² airbrakes which were later superseded by the 0.88m² version. The ASP-3N gunsight fitted initially was later replaced by the intended ASP-3NM. All aircraft had self-contained engine starting capability and a 12SAM-25 battery. The avionics suite was standard, comprising the OSP-48 ILS, the SRO-1 Bariy-M IFF and the RSIU-3 UHF radio.

The MiG-17P became the first Soviet radar-equipped light interceptor to enter service. The type was operated by the Air Defence Force and the naval air arm. The NATO reporting name was *Fresco-B*; the MiG-17F which entered production and service ahead of the P was spotted at a later date, hence the later suffix to the name. The RP-1 radar also had a NATO code name, *Scan Odd*.

The MiG-17P's service introduction took a lot of effort, since there was as yet no proven method of training pilots in radar intercept techniques. The production RP-1 radar often did not wholly meet the stated performance figures. Theoretically it was to detect a bomber-type target such as a Tu-4 at up to 9.5km (5.13nm); in reality the detection range rarely exceeded 8km (4.32nm).

This late-production, Red coded, MiG-17 was an avionics testbed of unknown purpose, possibly for testing SHORAN equipment. Note the bullet fairings on the nose and tail and the flush antennas built into the fin.
Yefim Gordon archive

MiG-17P weapons testbed conversion (*izdeliye* SP-6 modified)

In the early 1950s the Soviet government issued a number of directives concerning the development of of air-to-air missiles and weapons systems built around them (putting it plainly, missile-armed interceptors). Several design bureaux were tasked with the development of AAMs, among them KB-1,[20] a division of the Ministry of Defence Industry, which began development of the K-5 missile.

(In passing, it may be noted that at the time KB-1 was headed by Sergey L Beria – the son of the infamous Lavrentiy P Beria, Stalin's feared Minister of the Interior. After Stalin's death in 1953 L P Beria was found guilty of high treason and executed, sharing the fate of many he had sent to death. Hence S L Beria was removed from office and replaced by K Patrookhin.)

One of the said directives issued on 26th November 1953 marked the birth of OKB-2 within the MAP framework; one of its principal tasks was AAM development. The bureau was led by Pyotr Dmitriyevich Grooshin, best known for his Sh-Tandem experimental tandem-wing attack aircraft of 1937. By November 1953 Grooshin had already gained some experience in the design of rocket weapons, having worked on the S-25 Berkoot (Golden Eagle) surface-to-air missile system at the Lavochkin OKB since 1951.[21]

The newly-established bureau took up residence at plant No 293 previously allocated to the defunct Bolkhovitinov OKB. Development of the K-5 AAM was transferred to OKB-2 – that is, except for the missile's radio command guidance system which remained the responsibility of KB-1. Two other bureaux, OKB-134 under I I Toropov and OKB-4 under Matus Ruvimovich Bisnovat, were also working in the same area.

Grooshin's OKB worked on three missiles at once (the K-5, K-6 and K-51), while the rival Toropov OKB developed the K-75 and K-7 AAMs and the Bisnovat OKB was busy with the K-8 missile.[22] On 30th December 1954 the Council of Ministers issued directive No 2543-1224 ordering these missile systems to be tested on interceptors. The corresponding MAP directive No 704 took a long time coming, appearing only on 5th November 1955. The 'missilization' programme was a monstrous research and development effort that required weapons, aircraft and avionics designers to work in close cooperation.

The Soviet Air Force and MAP had a hard time choosing the right aircraft for carrying the AAMs. Hence all four Soviet fighter makers were ordered to adapt their production and/or experimental fighters and present them for evaluation as missile platforms. Specifically, the Mikoyan OKB was to equip the MiG-17P and the *izdeliye* SM-7 interceptor prototype

Prototype Performance	Manufacturer's Flight Tests	CofM directive (target data for production aircraft)
Empty weight, kg (lb)	4,096 (9,030)	n/a
Normal AUW, kg (lb)	5,495 (12,114)	n/a
MAUW with 400-litre (88 Imp gal) drop tanks	6,215 (13,701)	n/a
Fuel load, kg (lb):		
internal fuel only	1,170 (2,579)	n/a
with 400-litre drop tanks	1,834 (4,043)	n/a
Payload, kg (lb):		
normal	1,139 (2,511)	n/a
max (with 400-litre drop tanks)	2,119 (4,671)	n/a
Normal wing loading, kg/m² (lbft²)	243 (1,181)	n/a
Normal power loading, kg/kgp (lb/lbst)	1.63	n/a
Top speed in full afterburner/ at full military power, km/h (kts):		
at 4,000m (13,123ft)	1,126/1,073 (608.64/580.0)	n/a
at 5,000m (16,404ft)	1,117/1,065 (603.78/575.67)	1,115/1,068 (602.7/577.29)
at 10,000m (32,808ft)	1,046/1,015 (565.4/548.64)	1,052/1,024 (568.64/553.51)
Time to height, min:		
to 5,000m (16,404ft)	2.5/2.8 *	n/a
to 10,000m (32,808ft)	4.3/7.2 *	4.5/7.6
to 14,000m (45,931ft)	7.7/15.3 *	n/a
Rate of climb, m/sec (ft/min):		
at S/L	34.0/34.0 (6,693/6,693)	n/a
at 5,000m (16,404ft)	61.0/24.8 (12,007/4,882) *	n/a
at 10,000m (32,808ft)	33.2/15.6 (6,535/3,070) *	n/a
at 14,000m (45,931ft)	10.8/2.5 (2,126/394) *	n/a
Service ceiling in full afterburner/ at full military power, m (ft)	15,700/14,700 (51,509/48,228) *	15,850/14,350 (52,001/47,080)
Range at 12,000m (39,370ft), km (nm):		
on internal fuel only	1,180 (638)	1,020/990 (551/535) †
with drop tank jettison	2,000 (1,081)	1,660/1,590 (897/859) †
with the drop tanks in place	1,812 (979)	n/a
Endurance at 12,000m (39,370ft), km (nm):		
on internal fuel only	1 hr 35 min	n/a
with drop tank jettison	2 hrs 31 min	n/a
with the drop tanks in place	2 hrs 20 min	n/a

* the afterburner was engaged at 4,000m (13,123ft); † at full military power/in full afterburner

(the future MiG-19P *Farmer-B*) with the K-5 weapons system and test them jointly with OKB-2.

In 1955 the K-5 AAM was put through its paces on a Yak-25M *Flashlight* interceptor converted into a weapons testbed and was recommended for production. The K-5 weapons system comprised the missiles proper, four APU-3 launch rails for same and the RP-5 Izumrood-2 radar suitably modified to act as a fire control radar. It was designed to destroy slow and sluggish targets – ie, heavy bombers such as the Boeing B-50, Convair B-36 Peacemaker and Boeing B-52 Stratofortress – in all weather conditions, day and night, at up to 3 to 3.5km (1.62 to 1.89nm) range. Installing this system on the MiG-17P could increase its combat potential appreciably.

The five prototypes of the MiG-17P were suitably converted into testbeds for the K-5. The APU-3 launch rails with D3-40 shackles were mounted on four pylons extending far beyond the wing leading edge between the inboard and centre wing fences, so that the aircraft could carry 400-litre (88 Imperial gallons) slipper tanks. The starboard NR-23 cannon was retained as a backup weapon, and the aircraft was equipped with an ASP-3NM gunsight.

After successfully passing manufacturer's tests and State acceptance trials the modified SP-6 was recommended for production. Actually it never entered production as such, but a missile-armed interceptor did enter service as described below (see MiG-17PFU).

MiG-17PF (early) *Fresco-D* interceptor (*izdeliye* SP-7; *izdeliye* 58)
When the MiG-17F entered mass production and sufficient VK-1F engines became available the new powerplant was finally fitted to the MiG-17P as well and the aircraft became the MiG-17PF, aka *izdeliye* SP-7. Its development was ordered by a Council of Ministers directive dated 24th May 1952 and an MAP order dated 2nd June; State acceptance trials were to begin in August.

The unserialled prototype was converted from the third Kuybyshev-built MiG-17 (c/n 1401003). Airframe construction was completed in mid-July 1952, but the rollout was delayed

until 4th August due to late delivery of the engine and radar. The aircraft made its maiden flight on 8th August with Gheorgiy A Sedov at the controls. NII-17 requested an extension of the manufacturer's test programme until mid-December because of development problems with the radar. The tests continued until 16th December (the test report was signed that day) and included 46 flights.

As compared to the basic *Fresco-A* the SP-7 had a 225kg (496 lb) higher AUW, reduced rate of climb, top speed and service ceiling; besides, the search antenna radome impaired visibility in the forward hemisphere. The prototype's performance as recorded during manufacturer's tests is indicated in the table on this page.

On 16th December the SP-7 was turned over to NII VVS for State acceptance trials which were successfully completed in May 1953.

The re-engined interceptor received the service designation MiG-17PF (*perekhvaht*chik *s forsahzhem*, interceptor with afterburning)[23] and the manufacturer's designation '*izdeliye* SP-7'; the in-house product code at the Gor'kiy factory was *izdeliye* 58. Apart from the powerplant and enlarged airbrakes, the MiG-17PF differed from the P in having a Sirena-2 RHAWS and an NI-50B navigation display (*navigat-seeonnyy indikahtor*).

The MiG-17PF showed a marked improvement over its predecessor in top speed and rate of climb. On the other hand, cruising speed and range deteriorated somewhat because of the higher AUW and because the engine's dry rating was 100kgp (220 lbst) lower. Top speed at 4,000m (13,123ft) was 1,121km/h (605.94kts), and service ceiling was 15,850m (52,001ft). The fighter could climb to 5,000m (16,404ft) and 10,000m (32,808ft) in 2.5 and 4.5 minutes respectively. Turning time increased to 85 seconds at full military power or 62 seconds in full afterburner and rate of climb at sea level dropped to 55m/sec (10,826ft/min).

Depending on armament fit and fuel quantity, take-off weight ranged from 5,340 to 5,550kg (11,772 to 12,235 lb) in 'clean' condition or from 6,069 to 6,280kg (13,379 to 13,844 lb) with 400-litre (88 Imperial gallons) drop tanks. In full 'burner the MiG-17PF became airborne in about 600m (1,968ft), and landing run with full flaps (60°) was 830m (2,723ft). In full 'burner the MiG-17PF became airborne in about 600m (1,968ft), and landing run with full flaps (60°) was 830m (2,723ft). Unstick speed in 'clean' condition and with drop tanks was 235km/h (127kts) and 250km/h (135kts) respectively.

The MiG-17PF's NATO code name was *Fresco-D*. The aircraft was manufactured under licence in China and Poland.

MiG-17PF (updated) (*izdeliye* SP-7F; *izdeliye* 58)
An improved version of the RP-1 Izumrood-1 radar was fitted to the MiG-17PF pursuant to a Council of Ministers directive dated 27th June 1953 and an MOP order dated 7th July. At the

same time the radar set modules were relocated to improve access during maintenance. The modified aircraft were given a separate manufacturer's designation, *izdeliye* SP-7F.

An unidentified *Fresco-D* fitted with the improved radar installation began State acceptance trials in January 1954. The trials went well and the modified RP-1 radar took over on the assembly lines, starting with Gor'kiy-built MiG-17PF '625 Red' (c/n 58210625).

MiG-17P (*izdeliye* SP-8) avionics testbed

In 1953 NII-17 developed the RP-5 Izumrood-2 radar. This was a derivative of the RP-1 with increased detection range (12km/6.48nm), higher resistance to jamming and a field of view of ±60° in azimuth and +26/-14° in elevation (some sources say +26/-16°). It was only logical that this radar should be fitted to the MiG-17PF. A Council of Ministers directive to this effect appeared on 9th August 1954, followed by an MAP order on 23rd August; the aircraft was to begin State acceptance trials in December 1954.

At the end of the year a very early MiG-17P with 0.522m² airbrakes and two NR-23s was converted into a testbed for the RP-5. Known in-house as *izdeliye* SP-8, the unserialled aircraft was also used, together with the SG-5 testbed, to evaluate the SRD-3 Grad gun ranging radar (which in this case was linked to the RP-5 radar).

MiG-17PF (late, *izdeliye* SP-8)

After successfully completing its trials the RP-5 Izumrood-2 radar was introduced on Tbilisi-built MiG-17PFs in December 1955, starting

Top right and right: **The SP-6 was effectively the prototype of the MiG-17PFU missile-armed interceptor. These views show clearly the four pylon-mounted missile rails and the late-model RP-5 radar.** Mikoyan OKB

Below: **The large centrebody radome of the SP-6 made a unique contrast with the small airbrakes of the early-production *Fresco-A* from which the aircraft was converted.** Mikoyan OKB

with Batch 10. Outwardly aircraft equipped with the RP-5 could be identified by the rather larger intake centrebody 'bullet', since the tracking antenna diameter was bigger, requiring the radome to be enlarged. Late-production *Fresco-D*s with the new radar likewise had the manufacturer's designation *izdeliye* SP-8.

MiG-17PFG *Fresco-D* interceptor

Production *Fresco-B*s were guided to their targets by ground controlled intercept (GCI) stations using target information from air defence radars. In the mid-50s a small number of MiG-17PFs was fitted with the Gorizont-1 command link system for GCI intercept. Such aircraft were designated MiG-17PFG (ie, MiG-17PF [*s sistemoy*] *Gorizont*).

MiG-17PF (*izdeliye* SP-9) weapons testbed

Mikoyan engineers tried using unguided rockets on interceptors as well as on tactical fighters. A Council of Ministers directive to this effect was issued on 19th September 1953, followed by an appropriate MAP order on 2nd October; the aircraft was to commence State acceptance trials in the third quarter of 1954.

On 26th November 1954 – rather later than anticipated – a production Gor'kiy-built MiG-17PF serialled 627 Red (c/n 58210627) was delivered to the Mikoyan experimental shop. Conversion work lasted all December and continued into January 1955; the resulting weapons testbed was designated *izdeliye* SP-9. The standard cannons were replaced by

209 Red (c/n 58210209), an early-production MiG-17PF with RP-1 Izumrood-1 radar, during manufacturer's flight tests. Yefim Gordon archive

A production MiG-17PF fitted with drop tanks. Yefim Gordon archive

Early-production *Fresco-D*s lined up at a PVO airbase. Yefim Gordon archive

a quartet of ARO-57-6 Vikhr' (Whirlwind) automatic rocket launchers, aka 3P-6-III;[24] these looked like outsize six-shooters with a long barrel and a revolving drum for six ARS-57 FFARs. The launchers were mounted symmetrically, two on each side, on a new weapons pallet with exhaust gas outlets at the back which was designed to work with the standard hoists. Thus the SP-9 was the nearest Soviet equivalent of the F-86D Sabre with its battery of Mighty Mouse FFARs.

Outwardly the installation looked like four ordinary heavy cannons, except that there were no spent case outlets where one would normally expect them to be. The barrels were recessed in deep narrow troughs and there were two large bulges on each side over the ammunition drums immediately aft of the nose gear unit. Additionally, four pods with eight ARS-57 FFARs each could be carried on the regular drop tank hardpoints and two streamlined pylons inboard of these. Alternatively, the SP-9 could carry two drop tanks and two FFAR pods with five 70mm ARS-70 Lastochka rockets each. The pods were attached on D3-40 shackles. Two podded cine cameras were installed under the wingtips to record rocket launches. The aircraft was tested from May to July 1955 but the results are not known.

MiG-17PF (*izdeliye* SP-10) weapons testbed
When the programme described above had been completed, MiG-17PF '627 Red' was converted again to test a new rapid-firing double-barrelled cannon. Two such cannons were mounted on a modified production MiG-17 weapons pallet. After this conversion the aircraft was redesignated *izdeliye* SP-10. The cannons could be fired either separately or simultaneously by means of several buttons on the stick. After being tested the new cannon was deemed substandard and did not enter production.

(Note: Some sources give a totally different story, claiming that the SP-10 was an avionics testbed for the Aist radar – the one fitted to the MiG-17/*izdeliye* SN – and was completed on 17th October 1954.)

MiG-17PF weapons testbed with K-13R (R-3S) AAMs
In keeping with a GKAT[25] and Air Force order signed on 21st January 1963 the Mikoyan OKB prepared a set of drawings for installation of two launch rails for K-13R (R-3S; NATO AA-2 *Atoll*) missiles on the MiG-17PF with appropriate changes to the electric system. A production MiG-17PF was fitted experimentally with these pylons at plant No 134 in the fourth quarter of 1963 and tested successfully in 1964.

MiG-17P (*izdeliye* SP-11) avionics testbed
A production *Fresco-B* was converted into a testbed for the experimental Vstrecha-1 (Rendezvous) aiming radar linked to an SRD-3 Grad

627 Red (c/n 58210627), the SP-9 weapons testbed. The bulges under the forward fuselage over the ZP-6-Sh Vikhr' automatic rocket launchers are well visible; note also the underwing ORO-57K FFAR pods. Mikoyan OKB

Close-up of the SP-9's weapons tray, showing the battery of rocket launchers. Mikoyan OKB

gun ranging radar and an ASP-4NM gunsight. Designated *izdeliye* SP-11, the aircraft also featured an SIV-52 infrared sight (*samolyotnyy infrakrahsnyy vizeer* – aircraft-mounted IR sight [developed in 1952] designed for night operations in clear weather only. The IR sight was mounted atop the instrument panel shroud and could slide back and forth along a special guide rail. In an emergency, to prevent pilot injury, it was retracted by a pneumatic actuator triggered by the ejection seat mechanism. The aircraft was completed on 5th December 1954.

MiG-17PFU *Fresco-E* interceptor mid-life update (*izdeliye* SP-15)
When the MiG-19P supersonic interceptor successfully completed its State acceptance trials

and entered production in 1955, MiG-17PF production began gradually winding down. Hence, when the Powers That Be contemplated introducing the K-5 (S-1-U) weapons system on the *Fresco-D* in service, it was found more advisable to retrofit it to existing aircraft with the original RP-1 radar than to build new ones. A Council of Ministers directive to this effect was issued on 30th December 1954, followed by an MAP order on 8th January 1955.

NII-17 under Viktor V Tikhomeerov was tasked with giving the RP-1 missile guidance capability. This upgrade programme was completed within a short period and the result was the RP-1-U, the suffix letter standing for *oopravleniye* [*snaryadami*] – missile control or guidance. Similarly, MiG-17PFs retrofitted with the K-5 weapons system and the upgraded radar received the designation MiG-17PFU. The NATO reporting name was *Fresco-E*. Conversion work was undertaken at the Gor'kiy aircraft factory in 1956; a total of 40 *Fresco-Ds* was upgraded.

Before entering service the upgrade was tested by the Mikoyan OKB on a prototype known in-house as *izdeliye* SP-15. Like the SP-6, the MiG-17PFU had four pylons for carrying RS-1-U missiles, as the K-5 AAM was known in production form (NATO code name AA-1 *Alkali*).[26] Apart from the powerplant, airbrakes and radar type, the 'production' version also differed from the SP-6 in lacking cannon armament.

The RS-1-U had semi-active radar homing (SARH). When the aircraft came within autotracking range of the target and got a lock-on, the pilot took aim by placing the reticle of the ASP-3NM gunsight over the target blip on the radar display and fired a missile. For a second the RS-1-U flew in autostabilization mode, then entered the radar beam and became controllable, following the beam's equisignal line. If the missile strayed from this line the control system deflected the rudders and made course corrections. 13 to 23 seconds after launch the missile's self-destructor detonated the warhead. By the time the solid rocket motor burned out the missile was travelling at 800m/sec (2,880km/h or 1,556kts); maximum launch range was 3km (1.62nm).

However, even though the S-1-U weapons system became operational ahead of other Soviet AAMs, it no longer met the growing requirements. Hence the MiG-17PFU found only limited use. Still, the type soldiered on with the PVO for a long time; in addition to its primary role, it was used as a trainer for MiG-19PM *Farmer-D* pilots in the late 1950s.

MiG-17PF (*izdeliye* SP-16) avionics/ weapons testbed

Two production MiG-17PFs were converted to testbeds for the ShM-60 radar jointly with KB-1. The aircraft were armed with K-5M (RS-2-U; likewise code-named AA-1 *Alkali*) AAMs developed for the MiG-19PM and thus effectively converted to MiG-17PFUs. Known as *izdeliye* SP-16, these aircraft successfully passed manufacturer's trials in October 1957; the objective was to test the new radar's and missiles' suitability for the new MiG-21 *Fishbed* fighter.

MiG-17PF avionics testbed with Globus-2 system

A production MiG-17PF was used as a testbed (no separate '*izdeliye* SP-something-or-other' designation is known) for the Globus-2 system. A DDV-1 aerial was mounted on the fin and two identical aerials were installed on the search antenna radome.

MiG-17PF avionics testbed with Yupiter FLIR

In 1956 a production MiG-17PF was used as a testbed for the Yupiter (Jupiter) forward-looking infra-red (FLIR) sensor (once again, no separate designation is known). The FLIR weighed 16kg (35 lb) and was installed in place of the tracking antenna radome. The same aircraft was previously used to test the similarly located Aist radar (see note in ST-10 entry).

MiG-17PF weapons testbed

In keeping with an MAP/VVS decision made on 21st January 1963 a single MiG-17PF was fitted with pylons for testing the K-13A (R-3S) AAM. As noted earlier, this was a copy of the AIM-9 Sidewinder and the reverse-engineering effort was undertaken by Toropov's OKB-134. The missile was tested successfully in 1964 and entered production, becoming the principal weapon of the MiG-21F *Fishbed-A*.

MiG-17K (MiG-17SDK) missile guidance system testbed (*izdeliye* SDK or SDK-5)

In the late 1940s and early 1950s, a part of the Mikoyan bureau's efforts was directed at the development of unmanned aerial vehicles. A section of the OKB led by Aleksandr Yakovlevich Bereznyak was tasked with designing air-to-surface missiles for Tupolev long-range strategic bombers and anti-shipping strike aircraft. The Bereznyak group was subsequently transformed into a separate design bureau; it gave the VVS and the AV-MF numerous cruise missiles which were the main weapon of Soviet bombers.

The first of these cruise missiles was the KS-1[27] (NATO AS-1 *Kennel*) which looked like a scaled-down MiG-15*bis*P (*izdeliye* SP-1) interceptor minus cockpit canopy. It was carried initially by the Tu-4KS and then by the Tu-16KS *Badger-B* equipped with the Kobal't-N search/ target illumination radar. A major issue during

Left: **A technician inspects the RS-1-US missiles of a production MiG-17PFU on a winter night.** Yefim Gordon archive

Top: **A cockpit check before a night sortie.** Yefim Gordon archive

Above: **A ground crewman waves goodbye as a *Fresco-E* prepares to taxi out.** Yefim Gordon archive

its development was the testing of its guidance system. The general problem with missiles is that test launches result in the destruction of the prototypes and thus do not provide as much information for their further refinement as in the case of aircraft. The obvious solution was to use a piloted analogue which could be landed safely, allowing test data to be analysed.

The KS-1's guidance system was initially tested on two Lisunov Li-2 *Cab* transports converted into avionics testbeds, then on the MiG-9L (*izdeliye* FK) of 1949 – a much-modified production *Fargo* (*izdeliye* FS) with numerous antennas and a second cockpit for the radar operator.[28] The next step was the development of the MiG-17K or MiG-17SDK missile imitator (*samolyot-dooblyor Komety* – 'doubler aircraft', ie, analogue, of the Comet missile).[29] The manufacturer's designation was *izdeliye* SDK-5, though some documents contain the abbreviated form '*izdeliye* SDK'.

The aircraft had a K-1M guidance radar installed in a large bullet-shaped radome on the air intake upper lip protruding perceptibly above the nose contour, and the S-13 gun camera was relocated to the starboard side of the intake. Thus the shape of the forward fuselage was almost identical to that of the SP-1, except that the radome extended even further ahead of the intake. A small cigar-shaped fairing installed on top of the fin housed an aft-looking antenna for receiving mid-course guidance signals from the mother aircraft. The armament was deleted to make room for the autopilot and there was a flat-bottomed fairing offset to port under the centre fuselage over test equipment. Several MiG-17s were converted to *izdeliye* SDK-5 standard; known serials are 06 Red (c/n 54211006?) and 007 Red (c/n 54211007).

The trials technique was as follows. The MiG-17SDK was suspended under the wing of a bomber by means of a lug on the centre fuselage, just like a real missile; the aircraft took off and proceeded to the target area. The crew completed all preparations for missile launch as if they were working with the real thing, with the exception of engine starting which was performed by the SDK's pilot. Having located the target, the navigator/radar operator switched the Kobal't-N radar to auto-tracking mode; after making sure he had a good lock-on he gave the OK to start the engine. The MiG-17SDK then fell away from the bomber and was guided to the target by signals from the bomber and then by its own K-1M radar at the terminal guidance phase; the pilot sat back and did not touch the

controls. If all went well and the imitator stayed on its intended course, the pilot took over at 500 to 600m (0.27 to 0.32nm) from the target and brought the aircraft home where test equipment readouts would be analysed.

Later still, the Mikoyan OKB built several *izdeliye* K imitator aircraft which were piloted versions of the actual KS-1 with a bicycle landing gear and a cockpit instead of the explosive charge. This was the final step towards 'the real McCoy'. (On reflection, had Western experts been aware of *izdeliye* K's existence, they would undoubtedly have decided the crazy Russians were developing suicide bombs!)

The KS-1 cruise missile passed its State acceptance trials successfully between July 1952 and January 1953 and was included into the VVS and AV-MF inventory. After that, the MiG-17SDK imitator aircraft were used for further refinement of the missile. Pursuant to the Soviet Navy HQ's directive No 53280 issued on 30th August 1955 the 124th TBAP DD was formed in the Black Sea Fleet's air arm.[30] The unit operated twelve Tu-4KS missile strike aircraft and several support aircraft, including two MiG-17SDKs. MiG-17SDK operations continued in the Black Sea Fleet and the North Fleet at least until 1958 along with practice launches of KS-1 missiles; for instance, 77 imitator flights were made between 1955 and 1958 in the North Fleet alone.

MiG-17K (MiG-17SDK) missile guidance system testbed (*izdeliye* SDK-5TG)

One MiG-17 was similarly converted to a missile imitator with a different guidance system. The K-1M guidance radar was replaced by a Sputnik-2 infra-red seeker head linked to an S-3 flight control system; hence the aircraft was designated *izdeliye* SDK-5TG, the TG standing for *teplovaya golovka* [*samonavedeniya*] – IR homing system. The conversion was performed by plant No 256 in 1958.

MiG-17K (MiG-17SDK) missile guidance system testbed (*izdeliye* SDK-7 & SDK-7A)

Three more MiG-17s were converted to KS-1 missile imitator aircraft for the Air Force during 1953 and 1954, plus a fourth aircraft for the Navy during July and August 1954; these aircraft were known as *izdeliye* SDK-7. Four more conversions were undertaken in the first quarter of 1956; designated *izdeliye* SDK-7A, all four aircraft were delivered to the Air Force between February and June 1956. This version probably differed from the original SDK-5 in having a different control system.

MiG-17K (MiG-17SDK) missile guidance system testbed (*izdeliye* SDK-7TG)

This was an IR-homing derivative of the SDK-7. Like the SDK-5TG, it featured a Sputnik-2 infra-red seeker head but a K-1M guidance radar was also fitted. The conversion was performed by plant No 256 in December 1957.

MiG-17K (MiG-17SDK) missile guidance system testbed (*izdeliye* SDK-15)

A single MiG-17 was converted for testing the guidance system of the P-15 maritime cruise missile. The conversion was performed by plant No 256 in 1957 for KB-1.

MiG-17 refuelling system testbed

A single *Fresco-A* coded 153 Red was fitted experimentally with a fixed refuelling probe on the air intake upper lip. Sadly, no information is available on the tests carried out by this aircraft.

MiG-17 testbeds/research aircraft at LII

The Flight Research Institute (LII) had several late-production MiG-17 *Fresco-As* converted into systems testbeds. One of them, 611 Blue (c/n 54210611), had a small teardrop fairing above the port airbrake and a long slender pitot on the intake upper lip. The type of equipment tested on this aircraft is unknown.

Two other aircraft were used for aerodynamics research. The first, a Kuybyshev-built MiG-17 coded 638 Blue (c/n 1406038), had bulbous fairings on the wingtips, a massive vertical frame with eight pitot heads (the thing looked every bit like a garden rake!) carried on a strut ahead of the port stabilizer, a long pitot on the intake upper lip and a cine camera faired into the aft portion of the cockpit canopy. Black stripes were painted on the port wing upper surface, possibly for icing visualization. The other, a Gor'kiy-built aircraft (813 Blue, c/n 54210813), had the entire starboard wing covered in wool tufts and an identical cine camera installation, suggesting a modified airfoil.

Additionally, LII used a MiG-17 erected vertically to investigate the peculiarities of jet engine operation in the vertical position (ie, in a vertical climb) and the impact of jet exhaust on dirt and concrete landing strips as part of vertical take-off and landing (VTOL) technology research.

Another MiG-17 was used by LII for an aero-medical experiment to investigate the effect of altitude on the precision of the pilot's actions.

LL-MiG-17 reaction control testbed

As Aram Nazarovich Rafaelyants developed his *Toorbolyot* VTOL technology demonstrator vehicle – the Soviet answer to the Rolls-Royce Thrust Measuring Rig ('Flying Bedstead') which first flew in 1957 – LII tested the efficiency of wingtip reaction control jets, or 'jet ailerons', on a modified *Fresco-A* designated LL-MiG-17. The work proceeded in 1956-59 under the supervision of V V Matveyev. Engineer Ye N Toropchenko and test pilots Yakov I Vernikov and Sergey N Anokhin were involved with the LL-MiG-17, while engineers A I Kvashnin, A M Lapshin, Yuriy I Sneshko and test pilot Yuriy A Garnayev participated in the development and trials of the *Toorbolyot*.

The initial research results obtained on the LL-MiG-17 were described in two reports prepared by LII in 1956. These research programmes provided valuable data for designing future VTOL aircraft – the Yak-36 *Freehand*, the Yak-38 *Forger* and ultimately the Yak-41 *Freestyle*.

153 Red, a MiG-17 fitted experimentally with a refuelling probe. Yefim Gordon archive

638 Blue (c/n 1406038), a MiG-17 used for aerodynamics research by LII. Note wingtip fairings, the frame with eight pitot heads on the port stabilizer and the cine camera faired into the canopy. Yefim Gordon archive

Two views of another LII aerodynamics research aircraft (813 Blue, c/n 54210813). The starboard wing is covered in wool tufts for airflow visualization, suggesting a modified airfoil; note cine camera installation.
Yefim Gordon archive

M-17 (MiG-17M), M-17MM (MiG-17MM), M-17MNM and M-17MNV target drones

In a similar way to the MiG-15M, a number of *Frescos* withdrawn from service were converted into remote-controlled target drones known at OKB-155 as MiG-17M and MiG-17MM. As with the MiG-15M (M-15), conversion took place at the Air Force's aircraft overhaul plant in L'vov. The designations M-17M and M-17MM have also been used, the M prefix denoting *mishen'* (target). Both versions featured guidance aerials in small cigar-shaped fairings mounted on short pylons under the wingtips and on the sides of the fin near the top, additional antenna fairings on the airbrake panels and a bulbous fairing under the centre fuselage over remote control equipment. The external differences between the two versions were obvious; the MiG-17M had small flattened teardrop fairings high on the aft fuselage sides housing additional aerials, while the MiG-17MM had a large dorsal teardrop fairing ahead of the fin and two smaller fairings under the wing roots. The MiG-17MM prototype was coded 01 Red.

Conversion took place in the late 1960s and throughout the 1970s. Depending on the original version, the drones were sometimes referred to at L'vov as M-17P (*Fresco-B*), M-17PF (*Fresco-D*), M-17F (*Fresco-C*) and M-17 (*Fresco-A*). Conversion proceeded in that order because, firstly, the PVO used up its own radar-equipped MiG-17s first and only then started obtaining retired *Frescos* from the VVS; secondly, the MiG-17F came before the *Fresco-A* because it was more numerous.

Two more target drone versions designated M-17MNM and M-17MNV have been reported. Details are not available but it seems logical that the last letter in the former designation stands for **mah**lovy**sot**naya [*mishen'*] – low-altitude target, while the V in the other designation stands for **vy**sot**naya** [*mishen'*] – high-altitude target. The drones' operational altitude has been quoted as 8,000 to 13,000m (26,246 to 42,651ft) and the time to maximum altitude as 17 minutes; endurance is 1 hour 10 minutes.

One MiG-17M coded 43 Red is preserved in the North Fleet Air Arm Museum in Severomorsk. This is a converted MiG-17AS fighter-bomber, as testified by the fairings for the detachable pylons outboard of the outer wing fences. The aircraft is unusual in having a small strake-like fairing ahead of the fin root and a cigar-shaped fairing on top of the fin instead of the customary lateral fin aerials.

Top: **This MiG-17 is a testbed of unknown purpose on which no information is available. The aircraft appears to be trailing a hose connecting the wingtips.** Yefim Gordon archive

Centre and bottom: **MiG-17M (M-17) target drones being readied for a mission. The characteristic equipment and antenna fairings under the centre fuselage, on the aft fuselage sides, airbrakes and fin and under the wingtips are clearly visible.** Yefim Gordon archive

MiG-17 target tug

The MiG-17 also found application as a target tug, working with various types of targets, including the PM-3Zh gliding target (*planee-rooyooschchaya mishen'*).

I-340 (*izdeliye* SM-1) development aircraft

In 1950 the design bureau led by Aleksandr Aleksandrovich Mikulin (OKB-500) produced the AM-3 axial-flow turbojet designed for heavy bombers; it powered the Myasishchev M-4 *Bison-A*, the Tu-16 – and the Tu-104 *Camel* airliner derived from the latter. The AM-3 had an unprecedented thrust in its day (8,750kgp/ 19,290lbst), but it was much too heavy and bulky to be installed in a fighter. Hence on 30th June 1950 Stalin summoned A I Mikoyan, Aleksandr Sergeyevich Yakovlev, A A Mikulin and Mikhail V Khroonichev (then Minister of Aircraft Industry) to the Kremlin for a meeting. The subject of the meeting was the project of a new Mikulin turbojet which would power the Mikoyan I-360 escort fighter[31] and the Yak-120 interceptor. This engine was duly designed as a scaled-down AM-3, receiving the designation AM-5.

In order to speed up development of the I-360 and the AM-5 engine A I Mikoyan proposed converting the first pre-production MiG-17 (SI-02) which had been withdrawn from use by then. (It would be more precise to say that some components of the SI-02 were used, since other airframe parts were utilised to build the MiG-17F prototype, 850 Red.) On 20th April 1951 the Council of Ministers issued directive No1282-648 tasking the Mikoyan OKB with developing the I-340 fighter, a MiG-17 derivative powered by two AM-5 turbojets, and submitting it for State acceptance trials in May 1952. The aircraft was to have a top speed of 1,160km/h (627kts) at 2,000m (6,561ft),

1,150km/h (621.6kts) at 5,000m (16,404ft) and 1,080km/h (583.78kts) at 10,000m (32,808ft). The time required to reach 5,000m and 10,000m was not to exceed 1.4 and 2.9 minutes respectively. The service ceiling was to be at least 16,500m (54,133ft). Range at 10,000m was set at 1,500km (810nm) on internal fuel only and 2,000km (1,081nm) with drop tanks, and the take-off run was not to exceed 400m (1,312ft).

Known in-house as *izdeliye* SM-1, the I-340 was an attempt to improve the MiG-17's performance but with only the expense of minimal redesign. (It has to be said here that even though Mikoyan OKB staff usually refer to the aircraft as 'nothing but a testbed for the AM-5',

the service-type designation *and* the very specific performance requirements set forth in the CofM directive suggest that the aircraft was viewed as a potential 'real' fighter.) The two AM-5s were located side by side in a new aft fuselage in the manner of the future MiG-19. Hence the aft fuselage had to be widened somewhat to accommodate the engines; it had almost constant width all the way and then tapered sharply aft of the engine nozzles.

The fuselage break point was much farther aft than on the MiG-15/MiG-17; hence changes were made to frame 13. The main (aft) engine attachment points were located on fuselage frame 18 and the forward attachment points on frame 14. Two small cooling air intakes in tandem were added on each side of the upper fuselage aft of frame 14. The engines were started electrically.

Changes were made to the forward fuselage. The inlet ducts were widened somewhat because of the increased mass airflow, and the air intake splitter was extended forward and sharpened – again *à la* MiG-19 (ie, it was level with the intake's leading edge and straight, not concave). The MiG-17's standard forward fuel cell holding 1,175 litres (258.5 Imperial gallons) was retained; it was augmented by a 350-litre (77 Imperial gallons) integral tank in the aft fuselage beneath the engine bay between frames 14 and 18.[32]

Top and below top: **A later M-17 with fin aerials and underwing equipment pods.**
Yefim Gordon archive

Above and left: **Two views of the MiG-17MM. It differed in having part of the guidance equipment located in a large dorsal fairing ahead of the fin.** Yefim Gordon archive

The SM-1's airbrakes of almost elliptical shape were mounted fairly low on the aft fuselage sides immediately ahead of the engine nozzles. A large actuator fairing ran the full length of each airbrake panel straight down the middle, starting some way ahead of it; unlike the MiG-17F, these fairings were of trapezoidal rather than semi-circular section. A 15m² (161.29ft²) brake parachute was housed in a ventral bay under the jetpipes.

The MiG-17's standard armament of one N-37D with 40 rounds and two NR-23s with 80rpg was retained. The aircraft was equipped with an ASP-4N optical sight integrated with an SRD-1 Radal' gun ranging radar. The avionics fit was identical to that of the production MiG-17 (OSP-48 ILS, SRO-1 IFF etc)

Preliminary design work on the I-340 (SM-1) began in May 1951 and the final manufacturing drawings were issued in September. However, prototype conversion had to be suspended at the end of the year because the AM-5 engines were still unavailable. The aircraft was finally completed and rolled out in March 1952, entering flight test soon afterwards; it was flown by Gheorgiy A Sedov and Konstantin K Kokkinaki, and A V Minayev was the engineer in charge of the test programme.

The SM-1 had its fair share of troubles, and these were associated not only with the new powerplant. Minayev later recalled that 'the

Top: **Two views of a late-production MiG-17P converted to a target drone. This version was called M-17P in L'vov.**
Yefim Gordon archive

Above and right: **Two views of the M-17PF, as the MiG-17PF target drone conversion was called. Note the strakes on the upper aft fuselage.**
Yefim Gordon

Above: **Three M-17s, including '12 Black outline', on the apron at the L'vov aircraft overhaul plant sometime in the 1980s. The Ural-375D truck is an APA-5D power cart.** Yefim Gordon archive

Left: **Conversion work in progress on a MiG-17MM in L'vov, with three more *Frescos* waiting their turn.** Yefim Gordon archive

Left and opposite page top: **Two views of an early-model M-17 with no aerials on the fin.** Yefim Gordon archive

Opposite page centre: **Another M-17 coded 57 Red with drop tanks.** Yefim Gordon archive

Opposite page bottom: **This 3/4 rear view of the SM-1 (I-340) clearly shows the wider rear end with the twin nozzles of the Mikulin AM-5 engines. The SM-1 was the first step towards the supersonic MiG-19.** Yefim Gordon archive

success of the MiG-19 was largely determined by the speedy flight tests and refinement of the engines [on the SM-1]. (The AM-5 was the precursor of the AM-9 (RD-9) powering the MiG-19 – *Auth*.) Of course, there were incidents like an engine tossing a turbine blade and lots of other things.' Sedov noted that 'the SM-1, dubbed 'Lucy', ...had poor cockpit pressurization; the system worked only when the engines were running. If they failed, which was a fairly common occurrence, you had to descend immediately because otherwise cockpit pressure fell rapidly and the pilot would start bleeding. (The blood vessels burst because of the pressure differential – *Auth*.)

The engines often surged or flamed out when the throttles were advanced sharply. We tried several ways of curing the problem in dozens of flights, but not until a fuel flow retarder was introduced did the axial-flow engines start operating normally.'

The original AM-5 was a non-afterburning turbojet rated at 2,000kgp (4,409 lbst). The aggregate thrust of two AM-5s was greater than that of a single VK-1F in full afterburner (3,380kgp/7,451 lbst) and the new powerplant weighed 88kg (194 lb) less. Still, the available thrust was not enough to achieve the specified performance target. In the course of the flight test programme the original engines were substituted with uprated AM-5As (also non-afterburning) delivering 2,150kgp (4,740 lbst) each; yet it soon became clear that even this was not good enough. Therefore, the Mikulin OKB developed the afterburning AM-5F rated at 2,150kgp dry and 2,700kgp (5,952 lbst) reheat. However, these engines took a long time to develop and were never fitted to the SM-1.

Still, even with the provisional AM-5As the aircraft had a noticeably higher thrust/weight

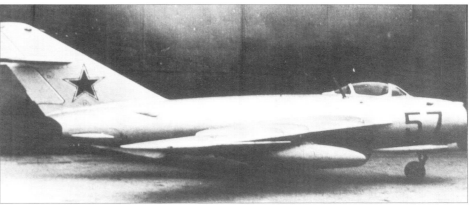

ratio than the standard MiG-17, and performance improved accordingly. Top speed at 5,000m (16,404ft) was 1,193km/h (644.86kts) or Mach 1.0, and the landing run was almost 30% shorter thanks to the brake parachute. Likewise, the more fuel-efficient engines and increased fuel capacity significantly improved the SM-1's combat radius.

Eventually the trials of the SM-1 and the I-360 (aka *izdeliye* SM-2) showed that the AM-5 was

not powerful enough to achieve truly supersonic performance. Mikulin engineers went back to the drawing board and developed the AM-5F into the even more powerful AM-9. As for the SM-1, the aircraft was later used to investigate the effect of gun blast gas ingestion on engine operation. This immediately opened a whole can of worms, since axial-flow engines are sensitive to gun blast gas ingestion, and caused the armament to be relocated on the MiG-19.

Chapter Three

Foreign Production

CHINESE-BUILT MiG-17s

Chinese licence production of the MiG-17 has been the subject of some controversy until recently. Contrary to claims by some Western sources, the original MiG-17 day fighter was never built in China; all Chinese *Fresco-As* were Soviet-supplied (built in Komsomol'sk-on-Amur, judging by the c/ns). However, as with the MiG-15*bis*, the aircraft nevertheless received the local designation Jianjiji-4 (often shortened to Jian-4 or J-4); some were resold to other nations as the F-4.

Shenyang J-5 (F-5) *Fresco-C* tactical fighter (type 56)

Manufacturing documents for the MiG-17F day fighter were handed over to the Shenyang aircraft factory in 1955, together with two pattern aircraft, 15 completely-knocked-down (CKD) kits and materials for a further ten aircraft. Licence production commenced in June 1956; serialled ⊕0101 (Chung 0101),[1] the first locally-manufactured aircraft made its first flight on 19th July 1956 at the hands of factory test pilot Wu Keming.[2] It was ultimately preserved at the People's Liberation Army Air Force Museum in Datangshan near Peking and listed as an 'Important Historical Monument' (!) by the Chinese government.

The licence-built version was originally known locally as 'type 56' but was redesignated Jianjiji-5 (Jian-5 or J-5) in 1964. The VK-1F turbojet manufactured in Harbin became the Wopen-5 (WP-5); the first engine passed acceptance trials on 19th June 1956. The J-5's performance was almost identical to that of the Soviet-built MiG-17F. Export aircraft were designated F-5.

Chengdu J-5A (F-5A) *Fresco-D* interceptor

Development of the first Chinese all-weather interceptor, the J-5A, began in 1961. This was virtually a straight copy of the early production MiG-17PF equipped with the RP-1 Izumrood-1 radar and armed with three NR-23 cannons.

Prototype production was assigned to the Chengdu aircraft factory (now the Chengdu Aircraft Corporation, CAC) in May 1961. The Shenyang factory sent a team of specialists to Chengdu to provide help, as well as a complete set of jigs and tooling. Manufacturing drawings were completed at the Chengdu factory in 1962 and component production began next March. The static test airframe (c/n 01) was completed in June 1964 and static tests continued until September. Finally, on 11th November 1964 the unserialled prototype (c/n 02) made its first flight at Yanliang airfield near Xian at the hands of Wu Youchang. Certification was obtained during 1964 and the J-5A entered production in Shenyang in 1965. The export version was designated F-5A.

Technical data stated for the J-5A differ slightly from those of the Soviet-built MiG-17PF. Wing span has been quoted as 9.6m (31ft 6in) versus 9.628m (31ft 7in); maximum TOW is 6,000kg (13,227 lb) versus 6,552kg (14,444 lb), top speed at 3,000m (9,842ft) is 1,145km/h (618.9kts) and range with drop tanks at an unspecified altitude is 1,560km (843nm).

A total of 767 single-seat J-5s (the proportion of 'pure' J-5s and J-5As is unknown) had been built when production ended in 1959; peak output was 25 aircraft per month. As well as being supplied to the Chinese Air Force, the aircraft was exported as the F-5A.

Shenyang J-5 *Fresco-C* torpedo bomber

A little-known fact is that the Shenyang factory developed a torpedo-bomber version (!) of the MiG-17F (J-5). The torpedo was carried under the fuselage; this required one of the cannons to be removed and the fuel load reduced to make up for the high weight of the torpedo. Trials showed that performance (except field performance) had deteriorated sharply as compared to the standard J-5 because of the high drag generated by the torpedo and the reduced fuel capacity. Thus the torpedo bomber did not progress beyond the prototype stage.

Serialled *Chung* 0101, the first J-5 (Chinese-built MiG-17F) took to the air on 19th July 1956.
Yefim Gordon archive

Chengdu/Shenyang JJ-5 (FT-5, F-5T, 'MiG-17UTI') advanced trainer (product 55?)

In 1964 the Chinese aircraft industry began development of an advanced trainer intended as a successor to the JJ-2 (a licence-built version of the UTI-MiG-15) which could not quite meet the requirement of training J-5 pilots. Designated Jianjiji Jiaolianji-5 (often shortened to Jianjiao-5 or JJ-5), it was a unique cross-breed between the UTI-MiG-15 and the MiG-17 – basically a UTI-MiG-15 cockpit section mated to a MiG-17 airframe. Interestingly, the shape of the nose resembled the MiG-17PF with its characteristic 'fat lip'. Yet the aircraft had no radar; the nose was all-metal and there was no intake centrebody.

The JJ-5 was powered by a Xian Wopen-5D (WP-5D or TJ-5D) non-afterburning turbojet – a licence-built VK-1A – rated at 2,700kgp (5,952 lbst), with a nozzle shape à la MiG-17. Nevertheless, it had 0.97m² (10.43ft²) airbrakes borrowed from the MiG-17F. In other words, it was the Fresco-A, Fresco-C, Fresco-D and Midget all rolled into one! At 11.5m (37ft 8¾in), the aircraft was 140mm (5½in) longer than the MiG-17PF (11.36m/37ft 3¼in); the other dimensions were identical.

Internal fuel capacity was 1,500 litres (330 Imperial gallons), and 400-litre (88 Imperial gallons) drop tanks could be carried. The Chinese engineers chose to eliminate the built-in weapons tray; the JJ-5 was armed with a single Type 23-1 (NR-23) cannon in a detachable belly pack on the starboard side. Additional pylons for air-to-ground weapons could be fitted outboard of the drop tank hardpoints. Finally, the aircraft was equipped with an SPU-2P intercom (samolyotnoye peregovornoye oostroystvo) and semi-automatic ejection seats; Jane's All the World's Aircraft described them as indigenous but they were probably just a locally-improved version of the original Soviet seat. The seats could not be used safely below 260m (853ft) at speeds up to 350km/h (188kts) or below 2,000m (6,561ft) at higher speeds.

Prototype construction began on 25th March 1965 and it first flew on 8th May 1966. After completing its flight test programme the trainer began production at Chengdu. (Some sources claim the JJ-5 was built by the Shenyang aircraft factory.) Deliveries to the PLAAF began on 30th November 1967; according to Jane's Aircraft Upgrades, a total of 1,061 examples had been built when production ended in late 1986.

A lineup of J-5s at a PLAAF airbase, including some of the first production aircraft (Chung 0101, Chung 0103, Chung 0201 and Chung 0202). The aircraft at the far end of the line have 'normal' serials without the Chung prefix.
Yefim Gordon archive

The first production aircraft earned the 'Important Historical Monument' title and is now on display at the PLAAF Museum in Datangshan.
Helmut Walther

The prototype J-5A interceptor (c/n 02) which took off on 11th November 1964.
Yefim Gordon archive

This J-5A preserved at the PLAAF Museum in Datangshan is unusual in having two additional wing pylons, possibly for heat-seeking AAMs.
Helmut Walther

63549 Red, a production JJ-5 of the PLAAF, taxies out for take-off. Note how the third and fifth digits of the serial (59) are repeated under the wing root, probably denoting this is the 59th aircraft in the unit. *AIR International*

Looking rather unhappy due to a collapsed nose gear and a damaged wing, 6717 Red is one of several JJ-5s preserved at the Datangshan museum. Helmut Walther

Surrounded by the fuselage and wing of a Tupolev Tu-124K VIP transport and the Solovyov D-20P turbofans from same, this unserialled JJ-5 painted in a stylish display colour scheme sits on the outskirts of the Datangshan museum. The damaged canopy has been replaced with sheet metal; note the lack of the gun camera.
Keith Dexter

CAC 0133 is owned by the Chengdu Aircraft Company which habitually allocated such 'registrations' to its demonstrator aircraft.
Yefim Gordon archive

The JJ-5 has two construction number systems, so the truth is possibly that the aircraft was actually built *both in Shenyang and in Chengdu*. One system (Chengdu production?) is straightforward – eg, 1609 (batch 16, ninth aircraft in batch). The other system (Shenyang production?) is a little more complicated – eg, 55-1206; the first two digits may be an in-house product code. However, it is just possible that this '55-' prefix was simply dropped after a certain number of batches had been built.

Chinese specialists claimed the JJ-5 outperformed the UTI-MiG-15, but that is a statement open to doubt. The JJ-5's specifications are indicated in the table below.

Overall length	11.5m (37' 9")
Wing span	9.6m (31' 6")
Height on ground	3.8m (12' 6")
Empty operating weight, kg (lb)	4,080 (8,995)
Normal TOW, kg (lb)	5,401 (11,907)
MTOW, kg (lb)	6,215 (13,700)*
Never-exceed speed, km/h (kts):	
at 5,000m (16,404ft)	1,048 (566.48)/
	Mach 0.932
at 9,750m (31,988ft)	902 (487.56)/
	Mach 0.92
Normal cruising speed, km/h (kts)	775 (418)
Rotation speed, km/h (kts)	250 (135)
Approach speed, km/h (kts)	280 (151)
Touchdown speed, km/h (kts)	240 (130)
Rate of climb at S/L, m/sec (ft/min)	27 (5,315)
Service ceiling, m (ft)	14,300 (46,916)
Take-off run, m (ft)	760 (2,493)
Landing run, m (ft)	780 to 830
	(2,559 to 2,723)
Range with max fuel	
at 12,000m (39,370ft), km (nm)	1,230 (664)*
Endurance at 13,700m (44,947ft) with	
400-litre (88 Imp gals) drop tanks	2 hrs 38 min

* Some sources state the MTOW as 6,087kg (13,419 lb) and maximum range as 1,160km (627nm).

The JJ-5 has been exported as the FT-5 (the designation F-5T has also been quoted). Known export customers are Albania (35), Pakistan (20), Sri Lanka (2) and Zimbabwe (2). Curiously, several publications call this aircraft 'MiG-17UTI'! Oh when are they going to stop inventing designations which don't exist...

POLISH-BUILT MiG-17s

Lim-5 *Fresco-C* tactical fighter (*produkt* CF)
In 1955 Poland obtained manufacturing rights for the MiG-17F and the VK-1F afterburning turbojet. Launching production would not be a problem, since the Polish aircraft industry association WSK PZL (*Wytwórnia sprzętu komunikacyjnego – Państwowe zakłady lotnicze*, Transport equipment manufacturer – State aircraft factories) had already built the *Fagot* under licence. The MiG-15 and MiG-15bis had been produced by the PZL plant in Mielec (pronounced '*Melets*') as the Lim-1 and Lim-2 respectively (Lim = *licencyjny myśliwiec* – licence-built fighter), while the RD-45F and VK-1 were produced by the Rzeszów (pronounced '*Zheh*-show') division as the Lis-1 and Lis-2 (*licencyjny silnik* – licence-built engine).[3]

The MiG-17F would be manufactured by WSK Mielec under the designation Lim-5 (for some obscure reason the designations Lim-3 and Lim-4 were left unused) and the VK-1F by WSK-Rzeszów as the Lis-5. Continuing the misconception which began with earlier licence-built MiGs, Polish documents referred to the aircraft as '*produkt* CF' (a corruption of the MiG-17F's OKB designation, '*izdeliye* SF').

WSK Mielec switched to *Fresco-C* production in a remarkably short time, but then, the first four aircraft (the pre-production batch) were assembled from Soviet-supplied CKD kits. The first Lim-5 (c/n 1C 00-01)[4] was manufactured on 28th November 1956 – only five days after the 500th and final Lim-2 had rolled off the production line.[5] Appropriately serialled 0001 Red, this aircraft became the personal hack of Polish Air Force C-in-C Gen Jan Frey-Bielecki after completing its factory tests. When it was finally retired in September 1994, 0001 Red went to OSL-4 (*Oficerska Szkoła Lotnicza* – Officers' Flying School) in Dęblin as a ground instructional airframe.

Three more aircraft serialled 002 Red through 004 Red (c/ns 1C 00-02 through 1C 00-04) were completed by the end of the year, and full-scale production began in 1957. The first production Lim-5 (c/n 1C 01-01) was actually a static test airframe. (Some sources claim that the three aircraft completed before the end of 1956 were c/ns 1C 01-02, 1C 02-01 and 1C 02-02!)

Between 8th February and 19th April 1957 the tenth Lim-5 built (ie, the sixth production aircraft, 201 Red, c/n 1C 02-01) underwent State acceptance trials at INB (*Instytut Naukowo-*

Badawczy – [Polish Air Force] Scientific Research Institute), the Polish equivalent of NII VVS, at Warsaw-Bemowo airfield.[6] The fighter was flown by test pilots Z Stręk, Z Korab and M Skowroński, with T Kuc as the engineer in charge of the flight tests programme.

Even though 201 Red was not yet fitted with the SRD-1M Radal'-M gun ranging radar (which, like the SRO-1 IFF transponder, had to be imported from the USSR), it was found to be 130kg (286 lb) heavier than a typical Soviet-built MiG-17F. However, some Polish sources disclaim this, stating that the weight of early-production Lim-5s matched the figures in the Soviet manufacturing documents. The INB trials report said that 'the tested aircraft has satisfactory handling and operational characteristics'; the Lim-5's performance was almost identical to that of the production Soviet-built MiG-17F.

The table below shows some performance figures of 201 Red (c/n 1C 02-01) which became the 'standard-setter' for production Lim-5s.

Top speed, km/h (kts)		Mach no.
at full military power		
at 1,000m (3,280ft)	1,045 (564.86)	n/a
at 3,000m (9,842ft)	1,055 (570.27)	0.864
at 5,000m (16,404ft)	1,060 (572.97)	0.977
at 10,000m (32,808ft)	1,027 (555.13)	0.999
at 11,000m (36,089ft)	1,015 (548.64)	1.0
in full afterburner		
at 1,000m (3,280ft)	n/a	n/a
at 3,000m (9,842ft)	1,154 (623.78)	0.864
at 5,000m (16,404ft)	1,138 (615.13)	0.977
at 10,000m (32,808ft)	1,076 (581.62)	0.999
at 11,000m (36,089ft)	1,061 (573.51)	1.0

Range on internal fuel was 659km (356nm) at 5,000m (16,404ft), 957km (517nm) at 10,000m (32,808ft) and 1,085km (586nm) at 12,000m (39,370ft).

Throughout its production run the Lim-5 received detail refinements. For example, an

unserialled Lim-5 (c/n 1C 07-07) which passed checkout trials at INB between 7th September and 19th October 1957[7] had an improved after-burner control system which allowed the after-burner to be selected even if the engine was at less than full military power. This feature enabled the pilot to adjust engine thrust in after-burner mode by advancing or retarding the throttle. The tables below indicated the perfor-mance of Lim-5 c/n 1C 07-07.

Normal TOW in 'clean' condition, kg (lb):	
with full fuel load	5,491 (12,105)
with 860kg (1,896 lb) of fuel	5,223 (11,514)
Landing weight, kg (lb):	
with 10% fuel reserves	4,364 (9,620)
without reserves	4,249 (9,363)
Service ceiling, m (ft):	
at full military power	14,850 (48,720)
in full afterburner	16,600 (54,542)

Rate of climb at full military power, m/sec (ft/min):	
at S/L	35.0 (6,890)
at 1,000m (3,280ft)	33.1 (6,515)
at 2,000m (6,561ft)	31.2 (6,141)
at 3,000m (9,842ft)	29.3 (5,767)
at 5,000m (16,404ft)	25.4 (5,000)
at 6,000m (19,685ft)	23.5 (4,626)
at 9,000m (29,527ft)	17.7 (3,484)
at 10,000m (32,808ft)	15.7 (3,090)
at 12,000m (39,370ft)	10.4 (2,047)
at 14,000m (45,931ft)	3.5 (689)
at 14,850m (48,720ft)	0.5 (98)

Rate of climb in full afterburner, m/sec (ft/min):	
at S/L	n/a
at 1,000m (3,280ft)	n/a
at 2,000m (6,561ft)	n/a
at 3,000m (9,842ft)	76.0 (14,960)
at 5,000m (16,404ft)	65.2 (12,834)
at 6,000m (19,685ft)	60.0 (11,811)
at 9,000m (29,527ft)	44.2 (8,700)
at 10,000m (32,808ft)	39.0 (7,677)
at 12,000m (39,370ft)	27.8 (5,472)
at 14,000m (45,931ft)	16.0 (3,150)
at 14,850m (48,720ft)	n/a

The aircraft's top speed was less than 1% lower than that of the 'standard-setter' Lim-5 (c/n 1C 02-01) and range was identical. The test report referred to 20 deviations from manufacturing technology, but only one of these complaints was serious, namely the short service life of the

Top and above: **1328 Red (c/n 1C 13-28) underwent checkout trials at INB in 1959.** Yefim Gordon archive

Below and bottom: **Lim-5 '1613 Red' (c/n 1C 16-13) was tested between 29th September 1959 and 25th March 1960.** Yefim Gordon archive

NR-23 cannons. Another Lim-5 which began tests at INB in September 1959 (1613 Red, c/n 1C 16-13) had a new SRO-2 Khrom (Chromium; NATO *Odd Rods*) IFF transponder instead of the SRO-1 Bariy-M fitted to earlier batches.

In little more than three and a half years a total of 477 (?) 'pure' Lim-5s – the original production version identical to the Soviet-built MiG-17F – was manufactured.[8] Production peaked in 1957 when WSK Mielec turned out 222 aircraft. Curiously, the last aircraft off the line (1914 Red, c/n 1C 19-14) completed on 30th June 1960 was the 14th aircraft of batch 19, just as had been the case with the last Lim-2 (1914 Red, c/n 1B 019-14). The last aircraft to be delivered, however, was 1910 Red (c/n 1C 19-10) which entered service on 29th July 1960.

Unlike the earlier licence-built MiGs, the Lim-5 was exported in substantial numbers, notably to East Germany. The East German Air Force received 120 aircraft from batches 6 (except c/n 1C 06-05), 7, 8, 9 and 10 (c/n 1C 10-01) between June 1957 and April 1958. A further 34 Lim-5s (c/ns 1C 11-05 through 1C 11-30 and 1C 12-01 through 1C 12-08) were built for unknown export customers in AprIL-July 1958, plus 29 more aircraft (c/ns 1C 18-01 through 1C 18-29) for unknown customers in April 1960. Other Lim-5s probably exported are c/ns 1C 14-21, 1C 15-03, 1C 15-04, 1C 15-07, 1C 15-10 and 1C 15-12 through 1C 15-26 (21 in all); these aircraft may have been supplied to Indonesia and Egypt.

Compared to the Soviet-built *Fresco-C*, the Lim-5 had a marginally higher all-up weight, even though internal fuel capacity was slightly reduced. Surprisingly enough, top speed at 3,000m (9,842ft) was quoted as 1,154km/h (623.78kts), which was better than the Lim-5's Soviet counterpart; this could be accounted for by a higher-quality surface finish (and hence less drag) or by an error in the test report – which was more likely.

The table above right illustrates the comparative performance of Lim-5s in different batches during checkout tests.

The table immediately to the right gives a performance comparison of the original MiG-17F and its Polish 'twin'.

The Lim-5 had its public debut (coincidentally with the Lim-2), appearing in the static park at the 1st Warsaw Air Show at Okęcie airport (26th August to 9th September 1956). The Lim-5 became a regular participant of various Polish airshows in the 1950s and 1960s. It remained the backbone of the Polish Air Force (PWL – *Polskie Wojsko Lotnicze*) fighter element until replaced in front-line service by the MiG-21 in the mid-60s, and even then the trusty *Fresco* soldiered on with training and research units until the early 1990s.

It has to be said that the PWL was not completely satisfied with the Lim-5's performance. The Air Force's opinion (shared by the engineers at WSK PZL) was that the fighter needed more effective high-lift devices. It was also deemed necessary to boost the aircraft's combat potential by adding provisions for a second pair of drop tanks and for unguided rockets, as well as to improve aerodynamics and uprate the engine. INB engineers even considered a complete redesign of the forward fuselage with lateral air intakes and the cockpit moved forward in order to improve cockpit visibility.

Many of the ideas, however, remained unrealised because the task was simply more than the four-man design team at WSK PZL could handle. (At its height the team tasked with improving the Lim-5 comprised 26 engineers, mostly fresh out of college.) The difficulties encountered by the team are illustrated by the instance when two young Polish engineers

Lim-5 performance comparison	Lim-5 c/n 1C 02-01	Lim-5 c/n 1C 07-07	Lim-5 c/n 1C 13-28	Lim-5 c/n 1C 16-13
Test date	8-2-57 to 19-4-57	7-9-57 to 19-10-57	1959	29-9-59 to 25-3-60
TOW in 'clean' condition, kg (lb):				
with full fuel load	5,500 (12,125)	5,491 (12,105)	5,500 (12,125)	5,500 (12,125)
with 1,050 litres (231 Imp gals)/ 860kg (1,896 lb) of fuel	5,235 (11,541)	5,223 (11,514)	5,235 (11,541)	5,229 (11,527)
Empty weight, kg (lb)	4,240 (9,347)	4,249 (9,367)	4,240 (9,347)	4,244 (9,356)
Landing weight, kg (lb)	4,368 (9,629)	4,364 (9,620)	4,368 (9,629)	4,372 (9,638)
Lis-5 engine c/n	556112	557148	557313	658290
Fuel capacity, litres (Imp gals):				
forward fuel cell	1,227 (269.94)	1,245 (273.9)	1,230 (270.6)	1,235 (271.7)
aft integral tank	150 (33.0)	145 (31.9)	150 (33.0)	155 (34.1)
drop tanks	2 x 390 (2 x 85.8)	2 x 397 (2 x 87.34)	2 x 395 (2 x 86.9)	2 x 395 (2 x 86.9)
Top speed, km/h (kts)*:				
at 1,000m (3.280ft)	1,045 (564.86)/ n/a	1,038 (561.08)/ n/a	1,036 (560.0)/ n/a	1,039.3 (561.78)/ n/a
at 3,000m (9.842ft)	1,055 (570.27)/ 1,154 (623.78)	1,048 (566.48)/ 1,149 (621.08)	1,049 (567.02)/ 1,147 (620.0)	1,050.7 (567.94)/ n/a
at 5,000m (16,404ft)	1,060 (572.97)/ 1,138 (615.13)	1,053 (569.2)/ 1,133.2 (612.54)	1,055 (570.27)/ 1,133 (612.43)	1,056.6 (571.13)/ n/a
at 11,000m (36,089ft)	1,015 (548.64)/ 1,061 (573.51)	1,005 (543.24)/ 1,057 (571.35)	1,010 (545.94)/ 1,055.5 (570.54)	1,010.8 (546.37)/ n/a
Rate of climb, m/sec (ft/min)*:				
at S/L	35.0 (6,890)/ n/a	35.0 (6,890)/ n/a	35.0 (6,890)/ n/a	35.0 (6,890)/ n/a
at 3,000m (9,842ft)	29.3 (5,767)/ 76.0 (14,960)	29.3 (5,767)/ 76.0 (14,960)	29.3 (5,767)/ 76.0 (14,960)	29.3 (5,767)/ 76.0 (14,960)
at 5,000m (16,404ft)	25.4 (5,000)/ 65.2 (12,834)	25.4 (5,000)/ 65.2 (12,834)	25.4 (5,000)/ 65.2 (12,834)	25.4 (5,000)/ 65.2 (12,834)
Climb time to 5,000m, min*	2.77/2.63	2.77/2.63	2.77/2.65	2.77/2.6
Service ceiling, m (ft)*	14,700 (48,228)/ 16,600 (54,542)	14,850 (48,720)/ 16,600 (54,542)	14,700 (48,228)/ 16,600 (54,542)	14,700 (48,228)/ 16,600 (54,542)

* At full military power/in full afterburner

MiG-17F & Lim-5 performance	MiG-17F c/n 0115302	Lim-5 c/n 1C 02-01
Powerplant	Klimov VK-1F	PZL-Rzeszów Lis-5
Overall length	11.09m (36' 4½")	11.09m (36' 4½")
Wing span	9.63m (31' 7")	9.63m (31' 7")
Height on ground	3.8m (12' 5½")	3.8m (12' 5½")
Wing area, m² (ft²)	22.6 (243.0)	22.6 (243.0)
Normal all-up weight, kg (lb)	5,324/5,340 (11,732/11,772)*	5,483 (12,087)
Maximum all-up weight, kg (lb)	6,048/6,064 (13,333/13,368)*	6,206 (13,681)
Top speed, km/h (kts)**:		
at 5,000m (16,404ft)	1,130 (610.8)	1,138 (615.13)
at 10,000m (32,808ft)	1,071 (578.9)	n/a
at 11,000m (36,089ft)	n/a	1,061 (573.51)
Rate of climb		
at 5,000m (16,404ft), m/sec (ft/min)**	65.0 (12,795)	65.2 (12,834)
Service ceiling in full afterburner, m (ft)	16,470 (54,035)	16,600 (54,542)
Time to height, min**:		
to 5,000m (16,404ft)	2.1	2.63
to 10,000m (32,808ft)	3.7	4.29

* Different documents give different data; ** In full afterburner in 'clean' condition

came to Moscow to tell their colleagues at OKB-155 about their attempts to develop all-flying (slab) stabilizers for the fighter. 'How many people do you have working on this?', the Mikoyan engineers asked. 'Forty!', the Poles replied, rightly believing that if they told the truth nobody would even listen to them. Yet even this inflated figure was not good enough for the OKB and the initiative did not win support. (Perhaps the *real* reason was that no mother has an ugly baby, and the Mikoyan engineers simply did not care for the idea of anyone messing around with their fighter!)

Lim-5P *Fresco-D* interceptor (*produkt* PF)

The 12 MiG-17PFs delivered in 1955 were not enough to suit the PWL's need for an all-weather-capable interceptor. Rather than buy additional *Fresco-Ds* in the Soviet Union, Poland obtained a licence to build this model as well. The licence-built MiG-17PF received the local designation Lim-5P ([*myśliwiec*] *przechwytujący* – interceptor fighter); it was also referred to in Polish documents as *produkt* PF.

The Poles wisely arranged to build the late-model MiG-17PF equipped with the RP-5 Izumrood-2 radar. In contrast, the Soviet-built aircraft supplied earlier had the original RP-1 Izumrood-1 radar; thus the locally-manufactured *Fresco-Ds* could be readily recognized by their larger centrebody radome. The Lim-5P was armed with three NR-23 cannons with up to 100rpg.

The first aircraft, 101 Red (c/n 1D 01-01), rolled off the line at WSK Mielec on 18th January 1959 and was delivered to the conversion training centre at Modlin AB on 12th February. The high priority attached to the interceptor – initially at least – is illustrated by the fact that the factory suspended production of the 'pure' Lim-5 for more than a year (from January 1959 to April 1960) in order to gear up for building the Lim-5P. In two years a total of 130 aircraft in six batches was built (129 plus a static test airframe, c/n 1D 01-05).[9] The final Lim-5P, 641 Red (c/n 1D 06-41), was completed on 29th December 1960.

The type served with the Polish Air Force until gradually phased out, starting in 1971; the last examples were retired in 1979. Many Lim-5Ps were converted to Lim-6M strike aircraft or Lim-6MR reconnaissance aircraft (these versions are described separately).

The Lim-5P was also exported, albeit on a much smaller scale. The East German Air Force took delivery of 40 aircraft in batches 1 (c/ns 1D 01-06 through 1D 01-10), 2 and 3; the

first five aircraft of batch 5 originally intended for the PWL were diverted to the Indonesian Air Force, and two Lim-5Ps (c/ns 1D 06-37 and 1D 06-38) were supplied to Bulgaria.

The Lim-5P's performance is shown in the table below.

Empty weight, kg (lb)	4,234 (9,334)
Normal AUW, kg (lb)	5,620 (12,389)
MAUW, kg (lb)	6,552 (14,444)
Internal fuel load, kg (lb)	1,160 (2,557)
Top speed in 'clean' condition, km/h (kts):	
at 11,000m (36,089ft)	1,123 (607.02)
at 3,000m (9,842ft)	1,060 (572.97)
Service ceiling, m (ft):	
with drop tanks	14,450 (47,408)
in 'clean' condition	16,300 (53,477)
Time to height*, min:	
to 5,000m (16,404ft)	2.5
to 10,000m (32,808ft)	4.5
Combat radius on internal fuel	
at 12,000m (39,370ft), km (nm)**	1,100 (594)
Combat radius with drop tanks	
in max efficiency cruise, km (nm)	1,730 (935)
Take-off run, m (ft)	730 to 930
	(2,395 to 3,051)
Landing run, m (ft)	885 (2,903)

* the afterburner was engaged at 3,000m (9,842ft).
** with 7% fuel reserves.

Lim-5P target tug conversion

Some Lim-5Ps – eg, 609 Red (c/n 1D 06-09) – were adapted for target towing duties, with a winch driven by a ram air turbine in a large fairing aft of the nose gear in a manner similar to the Czech MiG-15T and MiG-15*bis*T.[10] Unlike the latter types, the Lim-5P target tug retained its armament. The winch was removable, as a photo of 609 Red taken at a later date shows it in standard configuration.

Lim-5R tactical reconnaissance aircraft

The first locally-designed derivative of the MiG-17 was the Lim-5R (*rozpoznawczy*) tactical reconnaissance aircraft. It featured an AFA-39 camera mounted in similar fashion to the SBLim-2A – in a small ventral fairing immediately aft of the fuselage break point. Some aircraft, however, had a camera installation *à la* Lim-2R – in a large fairing offset to port immediately aft of the NR-23 cannons.

The Lim-5R prototype was converted from the sixth production aircraft (201 Red, c/n 1C 02-01) and tested at ITWL. Later, at least 35 other Lim-5s were converted to this standard.

Lim-5M tactical fighter project (CM-I – first use of designation)

The growing speeds and take-off weight of jet aircraft led several nations to investigate ways

and means of improving their field performance, starting in the late 1950s. This also implied the ability to operate from semi-prepared tactical airstrips. A typical solution to the problem was the use of jet-assisted take-off (JATO) bottles and brake parachutes.

Poland also conducted research in this direction. A team of engineers at WSK Mielec led by Feliks Borodzik developed the CM-I project (the first aircraft to use this designation), the M standing for *modyfikowany* – modified. The aircraft differed from the basic Lim-5 in having two SR (*startowa rakieta*) JATO bottles, each delivering 1,000kgp (2,204 lbst) for 12 seconds, on the aft fuselage sides. An SH-19 brake parachute (*spadochron hamujący*)[11] was stowed in a compartment under the jetpipe closed by double doors; this necessitated a redesign of the ventral fin which was now shorter and deeper. The CM-I's take-off weight was to be 5,697kg (12,559 lb) in counter-air configuration and 5,762kg (12,702 lb) in strike fighter configuration; the design maximum speed was 1,080km/h (583.78kts) and service ceiling was to be 14,100m (46,260ft).

Lim-5M tactical fighter (*produkt CM*)
(CM-II – first use of designation; later changed to CM-I – second use of designation)
In the late 1950s the Soviet Union and hence its Warsaw Pact allies began attaching considerable importance to fighter-bomber aircraft. This brought about an immediate problem: the basic Lim-5 was considered inadequate as a strike aircraft. If bombs were carried, the MTOW

limit imposed a limit on fuel quantity, thereby reducing combat range, and if drop tanks were used no bombs could be carried.

Hence, almost concurrently with the CM-I project, Feliks Borodzik's team developed the CM-II designed primarily for the close air support (CAS) role. The CM-II featured twin-wheel main gear units for operations from grass or dirt strips; quite simply, the standard units were modified to carry an extra brake wheel outboard of the shock strut on a straight-through axle. All four mainwheels had low-pressure tires.

The second major change was the aircraft's increased fuel capacity. 260-litre (57.2 Imperial gallons) conformal tanks were installed under the wing roots, increasing total usable fuel by 513 litres (112.86 Imperial gallons). From there, fuel was transferred to the aft fuselage integral tank via two prominent conduits which ran from the wing trailing edge to the airbrake actuator fairings. The tanks supplanted the usual drop tanks, leaving the standard wing hardpoints free for bombs or unguided rockets. They conveniently doubled as fairings for the redesigned main gear units; thus, appropriate changes were made to the gear doors.

The tanks protruded far beyond the wing leading edge, terminating about halfway between the air intake and the original wing root attachment point; the inboard boundary layer fences were extended considerably and wrapped around the leading edge to form the sidewalls. The curious shape of the tanks gave rise to such nicknames as *'szalik'* (scarf) or

'kołnierzyk' (little collar) when the aircraft finally entered service.

(Incidentally, these modifications necessitated a change in the aircraft's markings. The serial number was applied in much smaller digits and sometimes repeated on the conformal tank sidewalls, and the fuselage *szachownicy* (checkerboards, pronounced *shahovnitsy*) – the Polish national insignia – were located higher because of the conduits.)

The tail unit was reinforced, probably to absorb the increased structural loads during sharp manoeuvres at low altitude typical of CAS missions. Like the projected CM-I, the aircraft had an SH-19 brake parachute in a ventral compartment (and hence a new ventral fin) and provisions for JATO bottles, which also required some local reinforcement of the airframe.

Changes were made to the electric and pneumatic systems, as well as to the cockpit equipment. Finally, the dipole aerials of the RV-2 radio altimeter were moved from their usual underwing positions to the fuselage centreline.

The prototype CM-II was converted from a standard Lim-5 (1030 Red, c/n 1C 10-30). Unlike production aircraft, it had conformal tanks of all-metal construction. Bearing a slightly altered construction number (CM 10-30) and the service designation Lim-5M, the aircraft entered flight test on 2nd July 1959.

The main objective of the trials held at a semi-prepared airfield in the Pomorski Defence District was to verify the new landing gear and brake parachute and to determine the fighter's field performance. Stanisław Kruk was the engineer in charge of the trials programme. (Later, when production aircraft with construction numbers commencing 1F started coming off the line, the prototype's c/n was changed again to 1F 10-30.)

The test report said that 'the landing gear has passed the tests successfully and is cleared for operational use on CM fighters'. It also stated that 'the twin wheels make it possible to completely discontinue the operation of these aircraft from concrete or asphalt runways'. The report stressed that the twin mainwheels enhanced flight safety, making the aircraft less likely to veer off the runway in the event of a tyre explosion. On average the brake parachute reduced the landing run by 250m (820ft); however, there were cases when the parachute bay was damaged in a tail-down landing.

The Lim-5M entered production in 1960. Interestingly, the first Lim-5M to be completed at WSK Mielec was actually the *second* production aircraft (in terms of construction numbers) – 102 Red, c/n 1F 01-02, which passed checkout tests at ITWL between 19th August and 20th October. 102 Red had an empty weight of 4,473kg (9,861 lb), a normal AUW of 6,256kg (13,791 lb) and a maximum AUW of 6,954kg (15,330 lb). Top speed at 3,000m (9,842ft) was 1,108km/h (598.91kts). The aircraft had a service ceiling of 13,250m (43,471ft) at full military power and 15,200m (49,868ft) in full afterburner; it could reach 5,000m (16,404ft) and 10,000m (32,808ft) in 3.62 and 6.93 minutes respectively.

Concurrently, in late 1960 the prototype was used in a further trials programme to determine the durability of the nose gear unit during high gross weight take-offs and landings (6,890kg/ 15,189 lb and 5,800kg/12,786 lb respectively). After this, the nose gear was beefed up and this modified design was used on production aircraft. Meanwhile, work on refining the Lim-5M continued.

Full-scale production got under way on 30th November 1960 when the first production Lim-5M in terms of construction numbers (101 Red, c/n 1F 01-01) was completed. On production aircraft the conformal tanks had a 13mm (0.51in) laminated composite skin on a metal framework; their total capacity was slightly less than in the original all-metal version (475 litres/104.5 Imperial gallons). Minor changes were introduced along the way; eg, the radio altimeter aerials which were exposed on the first few Lim-5Ms were soon enclosed by dielectric fairings (possibly to prevent damage by stones or other objects thrown up by the nosewheel). With fairings, the aerials looked remarkably similar to the towing hook on a number of Lim-2s used for target towing.

According to the flight manual, the Lim-5M's take-off run in full afterburner was 710 to 770m (2,329 to 2,526ft), depending on runway class (paved or unpaved). With JATO bottles the fighter became airborne in 350 to 370m (1,148 to 1,214ft), which was an improvement of more than 50%. It should be noted that the take-off run was shorter than the standard Lim-5's, despite the higher gross weight, because the large conformal tanks created a ground effect, increasing lift.

Without brake parachute the landing run was 1,140m (3,740ft), but again, using the parachute halved this distance (670m /2,198ft). The armament consisted of the usual three cannons (one N-37D and two NR-23s); additionally, the Lim-5M could carry two FFAR pods of various models with 8, 15 or 25 S-5 rockets each.

Generally the Lim-5M was not particularly successful, and production ended on 10th May 1961 after only three batches (10, 20 and 30 aircraft respectively) had been built. The type served with both the PWL and the Polish naval air arm; it was not much of a 'pilot's airplane' and hence not very popular with its pilots. Of the 60 aircraft built, ten were lost in accidents, most of these being attributed to the type's difficult handling characteristics.[12] All surviving Lim-5Ms were eventually converted to Lim-6*bis* standard in 1964-65 (this version is described separately).

The following table shows the production Lim-5M's specifications as per manufacturer's documents.

Overall length	11.09m (36' 4½")
Wing span	9.628m (31' 7")
Height on ground	3.8m (12' 5½")
Wheel track	3.849m (12' 7½")
Fuel capacity, kg (lb)	1,555 (3,428)
Fuel capacity, litres (Imp gals)	1,890 (415.8)
Top speed in full afterburner, km/h (kts):	
at 3,000m (9,842ft)	1,108 (598.91)
at 5,000m (16,404ft)	1,097 (592.97)
at 10,000m (32,808ft)	1,035 (559.45)
Top speed at full military power, km/h (kts):	
at 3,000m (9,842ft)	932 (503.78)
at 5,000m (16,404ft)	934 (504.86)
at 10,000m (32,808ft)	925 (500.0)
Time to height in full afterburner*, min:	
to 5,000m (16,404ft)	3.62*
to 10,000m (32,808ft)	6.93*
Time to height at full military power, min:	
to 5,000m (16,404ft)	3.64
to 10,000m (32,808ft)	9.63
Rate of climb at S/L, m/sec (ft/min)	
in full afterburner	51 (10,039)
at full military power	27 (5,315)
Service ceiling, m (ft):	
in full afterburner	15,200
at full military power	13,250
Combat radius, km (nm):	
in full afterburner	225 (121)**
at full military power	n/a

* the afterburner was engaged at 3,000m (9,842ft).

** including 10 mins of air-to-air combat at 1,000m (3,280ft).

In standard configuration (with conformal tanks) the aircraft clocked a top speed of 1,046km/h (565.4kts), exhibiting a slight tendency to roll and some vibration at 800km/h (432.43kts). Without conformal tanks (with mainwheel fairings only), top speed rose to 1,091km/h (589.73kts); again, however, gradually decaying vibration and oscillations in all three control channels were discovered at 700km/h (378.37kts).

16 Red/01 Red, the prototype of the unsuccessful Lim-6 strike version. Yefim Gordon archive

Lim-5MR (*produkt* CMR)
tactical reconnaissance aircraft project

The Lim-5M generated a few spinoffs of its own. The first of these was the Lim-5MR (*mody-fikowany, rozpoznawczy*) tactical PHOTINT aircraft, aka *produkt* CMR. Unlike the production Lim-5R, it was to carry the cameras in wingtip pods increasing the wingspan to 10.58m (34ft 8½in); three combinations of AFA-39, AFA-BA-40R, AFA-BAF-21S and AFPN-21 cameras were envisaged. Yet the Lim-5MR remained a paper aircraft.

Lim-6 experimental tactical fighter
(*produkt* CM)
(CM-II – second use of designation)

Development of this version began even before the Lim-5M entered production, and the development process was long and tortuous. The most obvious new feature as compared to the Lim-5M was a relocated brake parachute housing. The 'chute was housed in a long 'stinger' fairing at the base of the rudder rather than under the jetpipe, and the standard long shallow ventral fin was reinstated.

There were two reasons for this change. Firstly, tests of the prototype Lim-5M (c/n CM 10-30) had shown that the ventrally attached brake parachute caused the aircraft to pitch down sharply; this meant it could only be deployed safely when the nosewheel was firmly on the ground. Conversely, a parachute located above the thrust line caused the fighter to pitch up, increasing drag; hence it could be deployed immediately after touchdown, reducing the landing run dramatically. Secondly, despite the tail bumper, there were cases when the ventral brake parachute housing was damaged in a tail-down landing.

The new arrangement was tested on the second prototype Lim-5M (ex-Lim-5 '1601 Red', c/n 1C 16-01) which, like the first prototype, had been retained by PZL as a 'dogship' for testing new equipment. As with the first prototype, the c/n was changed, becoming CM 16-01. Curiously, the aircraft had two serials (16 Red to port and 01 Red to starboard) making up the two halves of the original serial. The reason is not obvious, since there was still plenty of room on the nose for the complete serial.

Originally PZL installed a twin-canopy parachute system, hoping to get the most out of the new location. (This is part of the reason why the parachute housing was so long – ample room had to be provided for the two parachutes!) The two parachutes were attached on lines of unequal length (the starboard one was longer).

The test programme received the go-ahead in January 1960. However, tests quickly showed that the twin brake parachute system did not work – the port canopy (which was closer to the aircraft) influenced the starboard canopy in such a way as to prevent it from filling properly. Hence in October 1960 the prototype Lim-5M was modified to test a single brake parachute in the same location; this worked well and was later used on production aircraft.

Also in 1960, Lim-5M '16 Red/01 Red' was modified again, this time in an attempt to improve aerodynamics. A new, wider rear fuselage aft of the fuselage break point (frame 13) was fitted to make use of the area rule; this allowed the fuel pipelines from the conformal tanks to the aft integral tank to be housed internally. The single engine inspection panel on each side of the aft fuselage was replaced by two smaller panels. Yet tests showed once again that the conversion had no effect. Because of the conformal tanks/main gear fairings, the maximum fuselage cross-section was *ahead* of the new rear fuselage, which meant the area rule could not be used and the idea was abandoned.

Another way of improving the aircraft's field performance was the use of more efficient high-lift devices. In July 1960 PZL engineers completed the development of slotted blown flaps for the Lim-5M replacing the standard Fowler flaps. The flaps were blown by engine bleed air which exited via slots on the upper surface, delaying airflow departure and increasing lift; this required modifications to the engine compressor.

The blown flaps were tested in January 1961 on Lim-5M '16 Red/01 Red'. In this guise the aircraft was initially designated Lim-5M-II or *produkt* CM-II, the *original* CM-II (ie, the production Lim-5M) becoming *produkt* CM-I.[13] The modified engine, initially known as Lis-5M, was rated at 3,430kgp (7,561 lbst).

After Lim-5M production was completed in May 1961, WSK Mielec built an initial production batch of forty Lim-5M-IIs – even though the prototype (16 Red/01 Red) still had to be tested. (According to other sources, production began *after* the commencement of the prototype's trials but before they were completed.) As the Lim-5M-II entered production, the designations were changed again – the aircraft became the Lim-6 and the Lis-5M engine became the Lis-6. Interestingly, Lim-6 construction numbers continued the Lim-5M sequence, albeit with a different prefix, starting with batch 4 (1J 04-01 through 1J 04-40). At this stage, the prototype's c/n was changed again to 1J 16-01.

Apart from the relocated brake parachute, blown flaps and modified engine, the Lim-6 differed from the Lim-5M in a number of subtle ways. Flap uplocks were installed, which required the inboard and centre wing fences to be modified. The air intake lip was extended and the resulting change in aerodynamics increased top speed at low altitude. Spring-loaded blow-in doors were incorporated into the engine inspection panels on the upper rear fuselage to improve engine cooling.

Still, the Lim-6 never entered service; delivery had to be deferred because of several major problems. Firstly, the Lis-6 was prone to surging, and it took considerable time to find and eliminate the reason. The first case of engine surge on the Lim-6 prototype occurred on 7th January 1961 at 7,000m (22,965ft) and 350 to 400km/h (189 to 216kts). At first the

engineers believed that the extended intake lip was the cause of the problem and reverted to the original design. They were wrong – the surging persisted.

Next, the blow-in doors doors on the engine inspection covers were replaced by 'elephant's ear' intakes; then the covers were removed altogether to admit more air, but this did not help either. Eventually the cause of the problem was traced to the manifolds leading engine bleed air to the blown flaps. Only when WSK Rzeszów developed special unidirectional valves for these manifolds was the problem cured. From 6-8th July 1961 the Lim-6 prototype made five test flights in varying conditions and the engine showed no signs of surging.

The Lis-6 engine suffered from another serious problem – the exhaust gas temperature was too high. From 23rd to 27th December 1961 the prototype was test flown with the standard air intake lip refitted and the auxiliary intakes on the aft fuselage removed. When the afterburner was engaged and the flap blowing system switched on, exhaust gas temperature reached 718°C (1,324°F); by comparison, normal EGT for the standard Lis-5 engine was 670°C (1,238°F).

Testing continued in January 1962. At this stage the prototype was joined by the second and third production Lim-6s – 402 Red and 403 Red (c/ns 1J 04-02 and 1J 04-03). In order to compare the EGT two Lim-5s without the blown flaps were fitted experimentally with Lis-6 engines, but the results were inconclusive. Some modifications were made to the Lis-6 engine based on the test results, but later events led to this engine being abandoned.

Further research under the Lim-6 programme was halted when the prototype (16 Red/01 Red) commenced manufacturer's tests in definitive production configuration on 18th January 1962. Part of the manufacturer's test programme was performed on the fourth production aircraft (404 Red, c/n 1J 04-04). On 29th March however, the trials were terminated; so far the results were disappointing. The blown flaps reduced the take-off run only insignificantly and this improvement could not offset the handling and maintenance problems. In the trials report, test pilots Józef Menet and Zbigniew Słonowski noted that 'the aircraft's inadequate stability and insufficient elevator authority make operation extremely dangerous, especially when the CG is at its aft limit'. The conclusion was that 'in its current condition the aircraft is unsuitable for operation'; however, the report stating that 'the chief merit of this version is the twin-wheel [main] undercarriage'.

This opinion was shared by service pilots flying the Lim-5M. The significantly increased gross weight and the added drag generated by the conformal tanks impaired the aircraft's performance as compared to the standard Lim-5; this also increased fuel consumption to such an extent that the main goal of the redesign – an increase in combat radius – could not be reached. Also, as fuel from the conformal tanks was used up the CG shifted aft and the fibre-glass tank skins buckled at high speeds, disrupting the airflow; all of this affected handling in an unacceptable way.

Lim-6*bis* tactical fighter

Now since the conformal tanks were the main source of problems, the logical solution was to eliminate them. Hence on 6th April 1962, a few days after testing of the Lim-6 had been terminated, WSK PZL began tests of a further modified Lim-5 (1904 Red, c/n 1C 19-04), which had twin-wheel main gear units enclosed by small fairings but no conformal tanks. Two days later this aircraft was joined by the Lim-6 prototype which had been modified by removing the conformal tanks so that only the main gear fairings remained. These were quite large, terminating in line with the inboard wing fences; the latter thus ended at the wing leading edge as usual, but their forward edges were angular, not rounded.

The main purpose of the new test programme was to determine performance and handling with different types of fairings over the twin mainwheels and compare the aircraft's top speed as compared to the standard Lim-5 with single mainwheels. Stanisław Kuś, who had succeeded Feliks Borodzik as chief project engineer, was in charge of the test programme and Zbigniew Słonowski was project test pilot, though other pilots flew both test aircraft as well.

No fewer than ten different versions of mainwheel fairings were tested on 1904 Red in 33 flights, plus two versions on 16 Red/01 Red in 17 flights. As might be imagined, the test flights revealed vibration and oscillations, as well as a deterioration in performance as compared to the Lim-5. Besides, the port mainwheel fairing on 16 Red/01 Red failed during one of the test flights.

The test report said that 'additional trials are necessary to determine the character of vibration and oscillations and their effect on the aircraft's structural integrity and handling, especially during weapons aiming, before any decision on the suitability of aircraft with such fairings for service'. However, the report went on to say that 'no positive opinion can be made about the suitability of twin [main]wheels'.

The results of the mainwheel fairing tests performed on Lim-5 '1904 Red' are shown in the table at the top of the page.

The conclusion drawn after these tests was as follows. In the event Lim-6 production was resumed, the conformal tanks and blown flaps would have to be deleted to ensure normal operation, but the twin mainwheels, brake parachute at the base of the rudder and JATO boosters would be retained. A different way of enhancing the aircraft's potential as a fighter-bomber was proposed: two pylons would be fitted under the wings, leaving the standard 'wet' hardpoints free for 400-litre (88 Imperial gallons) drop tanks in order to achieve adequate range. This approach was nothing new: the

Type of fairing	Top speed km/h (kts)	Remarks
None (standard wings and main gear)	1,140 (616.21)	
Unfaired twin mainwheels	1,048 (566.48)	Vibration during take-off
Fairings ahead of mainwheels	1,070	Stick vibration at speeds above 950km/h (513.5kts)
Fairings aft of mainwheels	n/a	Gear won't lock in the up position
Fairings ahead and aft of mainwheels	1,050 (567.56)	Fuselage vibration and oscillations in all three control channels
Full teardrop fairings	1,080 (583.78)	Cockpit floor vibration at speeds above 700km/h (378.37kts)
Abbreviated teardrop fairings	1,082 (584.86)	Cockpit floor vibration at speeds above 700km/h (378.37kts)
'Type R' fairings starting at wing leading edge	1,070 (578.37)	Severe wing vibration at speeds above 500km/h (270.27kts)
'Type R' fairings with vortex generators and ventral strakes	1,011 (546.48)	Severe wing vibration at speeds above 620km/h (335.13kts)
'Type R' fairings with ventral strakes	1,047 (565.94)	Vibration and oscillations of entire aircraft at speeds above 800km/h (432.43kts)
'Type R' fairings with ventral and underwing strakes	1,070 (578.37)	Familiarization flights only

Configuration	Top speed km/h (kts)	Remarks
Twin mainwheels, inboard pylons, strakes on wing undersurface	1,053 (569.19)	Take-off performance as for standard Lim-5; acceleration marginally slower, handling satisfactory
As above, except strakes deleted	1,065 (575.67)	As above
Twin mainwheels, Mars-2 FFAR pods on inboard pylons	1,080 (583.78)	Configuration with single mainwheels (see next line) has better aerodynamics; handling identical to Lim-5
Standard single mainwheels fitted, fairings removed	1,080 (583.78)	
Twin mainwheels, camera pods on inboard pylons, drop tanks on outboard hardpoints, camera fairing under fuselage, TOW 6,500kg (14,329 lb)	981 (530.27)	Takeoff and landing behaviour identical to Lim-5 but poor stability and controllability
Single mainwheels, camera pods on inboard pylons, camera fairing under fuselage	n/a	Ventral camera fairing broke away at 1,000km/h (540.5kts); port PHOTINT pod and pylon broke away at 1,030km/h (556.75kts)
Single mainwheels, camera pod on one inboard pylon (2nd pylon removed), camera fairing under fuselage	n/a	Asymmetrical external stores severely impair lateral stability at 850km/h (459.45kts)

original Lim-5M project had envisaged *four* underwing pylons for unguided weapons but these were never fitted to the real thing.

Between 19th June and 6th August 1962 Lim-5 '1904 Red' made a total of 63 flights with dummy external stores on underwing pylons. The main objective of this new test programme was to determine the most aerodynamically efficient location for the pylons. The aircraft was flown by Z Słonowski, the design effort was led by engineer S Kuś and T Stepczyk was in charge of the test programme.

Six basic combinations of air-to-ground weapons and PHOTINT packs were tested. The best results were obtained with single-wheel main gear units and two Mars-2 FFAR pods – the Polish licence-built version of the UB-16-57U pod[14] accommodating sixteen 57mm S-5 rockets – on pylons located close to the fuselage.

The results of the external stores test programme on Lim-5 '1904 Red' are given in the table above.

No positive conclusion was reached as to the underwing camera pods. It should be noted that the camera pods were carefully streamlined in order to maximise combat radius; maximum combat radius was attained at 400 to 500km/h (216 to 270kts). However, test flights aimed at determining the top speed revealed that the pods were not strong enough, which meant a speed limit would have to be imposed in service. Since the PWL had no clearly defined operational requirement for fighter-bombers, it was not clear whether such a reduction in performance could be tolerated and the underwing camera pod issue remained unresolved.

It was easier with the fairing for the AFA-39 camera which had to be integrated with the aircraft's cannon armament. Originally the fairing was offset to port but it was quickly discovered that it was struck and damaged by spent cases from the portside NR-23 cannons. After that, the fairing was moved to starboard and the front portion protected with a steel armour plate. The result was much better – the fairing showed only a few scratches left by ammunition belt links.

When this series of tests with 1904 Red had been completed the State Commission ruled that 'utilising twin mainwheels significantly impairs the aircraft's aerodynamics, which manifests itself in vibration and oscillations at high speeds'. Note how the attitude towards the twin-wheel main gear changed from enthusiasm to doubt and then to open criticism.

These latest trials with external stores accelerated the development of the next Polish spin-off of the *Fresco*, the Lim-6*bis* (early project documents at WSK Mielec featured a slightly different presentation – Lim-6 '*bis*'). The original project still envisaged twin-wheel main gear units retracting into underwing fairings but the outer mainwheels could be removed in case of need (ie, the aircraft could be operated with both single and twin mainwheels). The Lim-6*bis* also featured a brake parachute at the base of the rudder, new SR 1055-00 JATO bottles rated at 1,200kgp (2,645 lbst) each and two pylons for carrying Mars-2 FFAR pods or 100-kg (220-lb) bombs. The sharply swept strut-braced (!) pylons were set at 1.147m (3ft 9in) from the fuselage centreline, just inboard of the inner wing fences.

In order to bring the already completed but undelivered 'pure' Lim-6s to the projected Lim-6*bis* performance standard, WSK Mielec issued a special bulletin concerning modifications to the aircraft. The Lis-6 engine and blown flaps were to be replaced by a standard Lis-5 and normal Fowler flaps; the conformal tanks were to be removed and the capacity of the aft fuselage integral tank reduced accordingly to maintain CG position. The bulletin was issued when the original Lim-6*bis* project described above was still on the drawing board. This project was to change before long; still, Lim-6 conversion work got under way, so that early *bises* actually retained the twin mainwheels for a while.

The single/twin mainwheel issue was finally resolved in late 1962 when the twin wheels were discarded. The Lim-5M prototype (1030 Red, c/n CM 10-30, later 1F 10-30) was converted again, becoming the Lim-6*bis* prototype. The manufacturer's flight test programme received the go-ahead on 7th November; originally it envisaged the use of JATO bottles but these were later deemed unnecessary and never fitted, since the Lim-6*bis*'s all-up weight was only marginally greater than the basic Lim-5's.

The Lim-6*bis* prototype with single mainwheels took to the air on 5th December 1962, completing its flight tests on 16th April 1963. The main objective of the tests was to determine the aircraft's performance and handling with various external stores. Each configuration had its own alphanumeric designator; the final configurations coded 1S-0-00 ('clean'), 1S-4-22 (with four Mars-2 FFAR pods) and 1S-2-42 (with two FFAR pods and two 400-litre drop

tanks) were studied with special care.[15] Still, the prototype did not allow the Lim-6*bis*'s performance to be recorded in full (eg, its take-off weight did not match the manufacturer's specifications for production *bises*). This was a result of the many conversions 1030 Red had undergone since it started life as a Lim-5 in 1957.

The test report said that 'regardless of external stores configuration, no phenomena unduly complicating flying or endangering flight safety have been discovered'. The conclusion was that 'the Lim-6*bis* tested in fighter-bomber configuration is suitable for operation by pilots trained to fly jet aircraft after taking a familiarization training course'. The main differences in piloting techniques as compared to the Lim-5 concerned take-off and landing techniques (the Lim-6*bis* had a higher rotation speed), marginally worse manoeuvrability with external stores, and a CG located further forward.

New-build Lim-6*bis* fighter-bombers began rolling off the assembly line at WSK Mielec in early 1963. Seventy aircraft in batches 5 and 6 (thirty and forty aircraft respectively) were built in this configuration; the last one, 640 Red (c/n 1J 06-40), was completed on 25th February 1964.

In September 1963 the prototype (1030 Red) was tested again to determine its combat radius. Between 15th April and 24th June 1964 a production-standard Lim-6*bis* (504 Red, c/n 1J 05-04) successfully passed its State acceptance trials at ITWL. The aircraft had an empty weight of 4,335kg (9,556 lb), a normal AUW of 5,550kg (12,235 lb) and an MAUW of 6,500kg (14,329 lb) with two Mars-2 FFAR pods and two 400-litre (88 Imperial gallons) drop tanks. Top speed at 3,000m (9,842ft) with external stores was 1,109km/h (550.8kts); the aircraft climbed to 5,000m (16,404ft) and 10,000m (32,808ft) in 4.0 and 8.3 minutes respectively. On 14th September 1964 the Lim-6*bis* officially joined the PWL inventory.

Meanwhile, all of the original 'pure' Lim-6s were converted to Lim-6*bis* standard at the Polish Air Force's overhaul plant No 4 near Warsaw (WZL-4, *Wojskowe zakłady lotnicze* – Military aircraft factories). The first aircraft to be converted, 407 Red (c/n 1J 04-07), left the plant on 23rd March 1963, followed two days later by the first production Lim-6 (401 Red, c/n 1J 04-01). The updated Lim-6s differed from the new-build *bises* in several ways – for instance, they retained the fittings for the JATO bottles on the aft fuselage sides which were later removed.

All surviving Lim-5Ms were also converted to Lim-6*bis* standard, starting on 7th April 1964. The last examples to be delivered to the PWL were the two long-suffering trials workhorses at WSK Mielec/ITWL – 1601 Red (c/n 1J 16-01) and 1030 Red (c/n 1F 10-30), which were handed over on 15th June 1965 and 30th September 1969 respectively. For some obscure reason the latter aircraft received a new con-

struction number, 1J 04-41, and was appropriately reserialled '441 Red'; this was unusual, since the c/ns of other Lim-5Ms did not change after conversion. Contrary to reports from some Western sources, the Lim-6*bis* was not exported.

The performance of the production Lim-6*bis* as per manufacturer's documents is indicated in the table below.

Weapons load, kg (lb)	780 (1,719)
Fuel capacity, litre (Imp gals)	1,415 (311.3)
Top speed, km/h (kts)	1,170 (632.43)
Service ceiling, m (ft)	16,000 (52,493)
Combat radius at low altitude, km (nm):	
on internal fuel only	120 (65)
with drop tanks	220 (119)
Combat radius at high altitude, km (nm):	
on internal fuel only	250 (135)
with drop tanks	430 (232)

The built-in armament was identical to that of the basic Lim-5 (MiG-17F), comprising one N-37D cannon with 40 rounds and two NR-23 cannons with 80rpg. There were four external stores options: two Mars-2 (UB-16-57U) FFAR pods on the inboard pylons plus two 400-litre drop tanks on the outer hardpoints; two Mars-2 FFAR pods inboard plus two 250-kg (551-lb) bombs outboard; two 100 to 140-kg (220 to 308-lb) bombs inboard plus two 250-kg (551-lb) bombs outboard; and two 100 to 140-kg bombs inboard plus two 400-litre drop tanks outboard.

At the opening stage of its service career the Lim-6*bis* lacked its characteristic underwing pylons, though the pylon attachment points were there from the start; the aircraft could be fitted with bomb shackles and launch rails for heavy unguided rockets. Later, when another series of armament trials was completed on the prototype (1030 Red) between 13th May and 6th August 1963 and the Mars-2 FFAR pod entered production at WSK Mielec, the pylons were fitted to late-production aircraft and the ones already delivered were returned to the factory to have the pylons retrofitted.

The abovementioned armament trials were intended to verify the Mars-2 FFAR pod, the pylons for same, the bomb shackles for 100-kg bombs, the electric trigger device and the ASP-4NM modified automatic gunsight. The armament could be serviced easily and safely, while live rocket launches and bomb drops demonstrated the high accuracy of the weapons and the possibility to use various tactical manoeuvres when attacking ground targets.

The Lim-6*bis* made its public debut (still minus pylons) on 22nd July 1964 when it participated in the grand military parade in Warsaw marking the 20th anniversary of the People's Republic of Poland. For many years it formed the backbone of the PWL's fighter-bomber aviation until gradually supplanted by the Su-7BMK. The last Lim-6*bis* was retired in February 1992.

Lim-6R (*produkt* CMR) tactical reconnaissance aircraft

Designated Lim-6R or *produkt* CMR, the PHOTINT version of the Lim-6*bis* was developed in parallel with the fighter-bomber, as illustrated by the tests of dummy camera pods on Lim-5 '1904 Red' in the summer of 1962. (Some WSK PZL documents called the aircraft 'Lim-6*bis*R', but this designation did not gain wide use.)

As originally designed in late 1962, the Lim-6R featured twin-wheel main gear units (though the outer mainwheels could be removed in case of need) and an AFA-39 camera in a ventral fairing *à la* Lim-5R. Additionally, two newly-developed CMR-9320-00 camera pods were to be carried on the outer wing hardpoints in lieu of drop tanks and the inner pylons would carry flare bombs for night sorties. The SRD-1M gun ranging radar was deleted to make up for the weight penalty incurred by the cameras and an oval metal plate was riveted over the slit in the forward avionics bay cover where the SRD-1M antenna used to be.

'Real-life' testing in order to determine the optimum reconnaissance configuration began when Lim-6*bis* production was under way. In the summer of 1964 a Lim-6*bis* – possibly the prototype (1030 Red) – was tested with an AFA-39 camera on a tilting mount under the fuselage and two oblique cameras.

Other cameras tested on the experimental CMR were the AFPN-21, the AFA-BAF-21S and the indigenous SzFP-02 wide-angle camera. However, when the Lim-6R finally entered service it was only equipped with a single AFA-39 in a small fairing immediately aft of the fuselage break point. Some aircraft had a camera fairing offset to port immediately aft of the NR-23 cannons.

Lim-6M fighter-bomber

By the early 1970s the Lim-5P interceptor had become obsolete. Hence, starting in 1971, the overhaul plant in Bydgoszcz (WZL-2) converted 40 Lim-5Ps to fighter-bombers designated Lim-6M. The conversion involved removing the radar (the radomes were left unchanged) and installing two pylons, as on the Lim-6*bis*, for carrying FFAR pods or bombs. (Later, when many Lim-6Ms received a tactical camouflage scheme, the dielectric parts were simply painted over in the basic camouflage colours.)

The DC battery was moved from the ventral fin area to the forward avionics bay to compensate, at least partly, for the CG shift caused by the removal of the radar. The avionics suite was upgraded – for example, the RV-2 radio altimeter was replaced by the more modern RV-UM. Unlike the Lim-6*bis*, the Lim-6M had no brake parachute.

The Lim-6M was operated both by the Air Force and the Navy until replaced by the Su-22M4 in 1987. Most aircraft were scrapped.

Lim-6MR tactical reconnaissance/ strike aircraft

Another 14 Lim-5Ps were similarly converted at the Bydgoszcz plant to Lim-6MR (*mody-fikowany, rozpoznawczy*) recce/strike aircraft. These were identical to the Lim-6M, except for the addition of an AFA-39 camera in a fairing under the centre fuselage, as on the Lim-6R. 602 Red (c/n 1D 06-02) was the first to be rebuilt on 31st March 1971; the conversion process ended with 641 Red (c/n 1D 06-41), the last Lim-5P built, which was rolled out as a Lim-6MR on 20th December 1974. The Lim-6MR remained in service with the PWL until 8th December 1988.

The forward fuselage of Lim-6R '505 Red' (c/n 1F 0505), showing the camera fairing. Yefim Gordon archive

Lim-6*bis* 206 Red wearing a rather unusual camouflage scheme. Wacław Holyś

Polish-built MiG-17 Specifications and Performance Comparison

	Lim-5 c/n 1C 02-01	Lim-5P	Lim-5M c/n CM 10-30	Lim-5M c/n 1F 01-02	Lim-6	Lim-6bis c/n 1J 05-04
Powerplant	Lis-5	Lis-5	Lis-5	Lis-5	Lis-6	Lis-5
Overall length	11.09m (36' 4½")	11.36m (37' 3¼")	11.09m (36' 4½")	11.09m (36' 4½")	11.09m (36' 4½")	11.09m (36' 4½")
Wing span	9.628m (31' 7")	9.628m (31' 77")	9.628m (31' 7")	9.628m (31' 7")	9.628m (31' 7")	9.628m (31' 7")
Height on ground	3.8m (12' 5½")	3.8m (12' 5½")	3.8m (12' 5½")	3.8m (12' 5½")	3.8m (12' 5½")	3.8m (12' 5½")
Wing area, m² (ft²)	22.6 (243.0)	22.6 (243.0)	22.6 (243.0)	22.6 (243.0)	22.6 (243.0)	22.6 (243.0)
Empty weight, kg (lb)	4,114 (9,069)	4,234 (9,334)	4,326 (9,338)	4,473 (9,861)	4,520 (9,964)	4,335 (9,556)
Normal AUW, kg (lb)	5,483 (12,087)	5,620 (12,389)	5,697 (12,559)	6,256 (13,791)	6,300 (13,888)	5,550 (12,235)
MAUW, kg (lb)	6,206 (13,681)	6,552 (14,444)	n/a	6,954 (15,330)	n/a	6,500* (14,329)
Internal fuel capacity, litre (Imp. gal)	1,377 (302.94)	1,395 (306.9)	1,377 (302.94)	1,890 (415.8)	1,890 (415.8)	1,415 (311.3)
Internal fuel load, kg (lb)	1,145 (2,524)	1,160 (2,557)	1,145 (2,524)	1,555 (3,428)	n/a	n/a
Fuel load in drop tanks, kg (lb)	721 (1,589)	732 (1,613)	n/a	n/a	n/a	n/a
Top speed, km/h (kts): *						
at 1,000m (3,280ft)	1,045 (564.86) / n/a	n/a	n/a	n/a	n/a	n/a
at 3,000m (9,842ft)	1,055 (570.27)/ 1,154 (623.78)	n/a/ 1,123 (607.02)	n/a	n/a/ 1,108 (598.91)	1,102 (595.67)	1,019 (550.8)†
at 5,000m (16,404ft)	1,060 (572.97)/ 1,138 (615.13)	n/a	n/a	n/a/ 1,097 (592.97)	n/a	n/a
at 11,000m (36,089ft)	1,015 (548.64)/ 1,061 (573.51)	n/a/ 1,060 (572.97)	n/a	n/a	n/a	n/a
at 12,000m (39,370ft)	n/a	n/a / 1,034 (558.91)	n/a	n/a	n/a	n/a
Rate of climb, m/sec (ft/min): *						
at S/L	35.0 (6,890) / n/a	33.8 (6,653) / n/a	n/a	n/a	n/a	n/a
at 1,000m (3,280ft)	n/a	31.8 (6,260) / n/a	n/a	n/a	n/a	n/a
at 3,000m (9,842ft)	29.3 (5,767)/ 76.0 (14,960)	n/a	n/a	n/a	n/a	n/a
at 5,000m (16,404ft)	25.4 (5,000)/ 65.2 (12,834)	n/a/ 55.0 (10,826)	n/a	n/a	n/a	n/a
at 10,000m (32,808ft)	n/a	n/a / 32.3 (6,358)	n/a	n/a	n/a	n/a
Service ceiling, m (ft) *	14,700 (48,228)/ 16,600 (54,542)	14,450 (47,408)/ 16,300 (53,477)	n/a n/a	13,250 (43,471)/ 15,200 (49,868)	13,050 (42,814)/ 15,000 (49,212)	n/a n/a
Climb time, min:						
to 5,000m	2.63	2.5	n/a	3.62 ‡	n/a	4.0 §
to 10,000m	4.29	4.5	n/a	6.93 ‡	n/a	8.3 §
Combat radius on internal fuel, km (nm): ¶						
at 5,000m (16,404ft)	659 (356)	n/a	n/a	n/a	n/a	n/a
at 10,000m (32,808ft)	657 (355)	n/a	n/a	n/a	n/a	n/a
at 12,000m (39,370ft)	1,085 (586)	1,110 (600)	n/a	n/a	n/a	n/a
Combat radius with drop tanks, km (nm)	n/a	1,730	n/a	n/a	n/a	n/a
Weight of JATO bottles, kg (lb)	–	–	–	260 (573)	–	–
Armament, built-in	1 x N-37D (40 rds) 2 x NR-23 (80rpg)	3 x NR-23 (100rpg)	1 x N-37D (40 rds) 2 x NR-23 (80rpg)	1 x N-37D (40 rds) 2 x NR-23 (80rpg)	1 x N-37D (40 rds) 2 x NR-23 (80rpg)	1 x N-37D (40 rds) 2 x NR-23 (80rpg)
Armament, external	2 bombs ? 100 to 250kg (220 to 551 lb)		2 FFAR pods or 2 bombs ? 100 to 250kg	2 FFAR pods or 2 bombs ? 100 to 250kg	2 FFAR pods + 2 bombs ? 100kg or 2 bombs ? 100kg + 2 x 250kg	2 FFAR pods + 2 bombs ? 100kg or 2 bombs ? 100 kg + 2 x 250kg

* in full afterburner/at full millitary power; † with two Mars-2 FFAR pods and two 400-litre (88 Imperial gallons) drop tanks; ‡ at full military power; § at full military power with external stores?
¶ with 7% fuel reserves.

Chapter Four

The MiG-17 in Action

Attaining IOC with the Soviet Air Force in the early 1950s, the MiG-17 quickly became an important part of the VVS inventory. It possessed such virtues as rugged reliability and ease of maintenance – valuable assets when operating from forward bases with limited ground support equipment. It was also fairly easy to fly, presenting no problems for the average pilot, and pilots who were familiar with the *Fagot* transitioned to the *Fresco* without any trouble. The UTI-MiG-15 was still used for conversion and proficiency training by MiG-17 units, since there was no dedicated trainer version of the *Fresco* in the USSR.

For the next six to eight years the *Fresco-A/C* was used in its main roles as a tactical and escort fighter. In so doing the MiG-17 even operated in a nuclear environment once. In September 1954 the 119th IAD comprising the 86th GvIAP, 157th IAP and 947th IAP,[1] all flying MiG-17s, relocated from Tiraspol' (Moldavia) to the Ural mountains to take part in a tactical nuclear exercise at the Totskoye training range. The exercise was commanded by Marshal Gheorgiy Konstantinovich Zhookov of Great Patriotic War fame.

On 14th September three regiments of IL-28 bombers (the entire 140th BAD)[2] took off and headed for the target in groups of nine; each bomber squadron was escorted by two flights of MiG-17s. The pilots were issued special goggles to protect their eyes from the flash of the nuclear explosion. When the nuke went off, creating the tell-tale mushroom cloud, the incoming armada started to take evasive action but suddenly a freak wind blew the cloud straight into its path. The jets were flying in close formation and there was not much room for manoeuvring because of the danger of collision; most aircraft managed to steer clear, but some went smack into the cloud. It is not known what the consequences were for the pilots or their jets.

All MiG-17 versions were stressed to 8 Gs when flown without external stores, ie, 'clean'. However, because of its aerodynamic peculiarities the aircraft could only pull 8 Gs at altitudes up to 5,000m (16,404ft). With full drop tanks the G limit was reduced to 4.5, rising to 6.5 when the drop tanks were empty.

As of 1st January 1955 the tactical arm of the Soviet Air Force (FA – *Fronto*va*ya aviah*tsiya,

Blue-coded MiG-17s, apparently operated by a PVO unit, share the ramp with three UTI-MiG-15 trainers. Yefim Gordon archive

Two red-coded late-production *Fresco-As* are being towed by GAZ-63 4 x 4 trucks. Yefim Gordon archive

lit. 'frontal aviation') had 2,150 MiG-17s on strength, not counting those operated by the PVO.

Since the MiG-17 was the Soviet Air Force's principal fighter type from the mid-50s onwards, its pilots shouldered the main workload of defending the Soviet Union's borders. And that workload was high, since in the Cold War years incursions by Western aircraft (chiefly reconnaissance aircraft) were quite common.

The first instance when Soviet MiG-17 fired their guns in anger was probably 29th July 1953. That day a USAF Boeing RB-50 entered Soviet airspace 130km (70nm) south of Gamov Cape near Vladivostok at 06:44 local time. (It has to be said that the Soviet Far East was a highly sensitive area with numerous military

installations.) At 07:01 it was intercepted by two 88th GvIAP MiG-17s (**not** MiG-15s, as sometimes reported!) flown by Capt Aleksandr D Rybakov and Lt (sg) Yuriy M Yablonovskiy. The intruder opened fire first, damaging Rybakov's aircraft, and was shot down into the Sea of Japan 15km (8nm) from Askol'd Island at 07:06.

The US Navy mounted a major search and rescue operation, first sending four SAR aircraft from Misawa AB in Japan and then a cruiser and four destroyers, but in vain. Of the 11 flight crew members and six 'crows' (reconnaissance equipment operators), only the co-pilot Lt John Roche was rescued and the bodies of three other crewmen recovered, the remaining 13 went missing in action. For this shootdown Rybakov received the Order of the Red Banner of Combat and Yablonovskiy was awarded the Order of the Red Star.

As noted earlier, the MiG-17P was the version which had the greatest difficulties entering service, mainly due to the lack of refined interception training techniques and the rather unwieldy GCI system. Distinguished Test Pilot Yuriy A Antipov (HSU) recalled: 'In the mid-50s the PVO units stationed around Baku were being regularly harassed by reconnaissance aircraft intruding from Iran. In theory, the solution was simple – send MiG-17Ps guided by ground control to intercept them, and that's it. In reality, however, all attempts to get at the intruders failed. The spyplane pilots knew well that the Caspian Sea area was divided equally between the air defence districts of Azerbaijan and Kazakhstan, and they put this knowledge to good use. It is no secret that the weakest point of any defence is the flanks. Following the border between the two districts and zigzagging from east to west, the spyplane would harass the air defences, complete its mission and calmly head for home.

As soon as the intruder got within range of the Azerbaijan district's AD radars, MiG-17P interceptors would be scrambled and directed towards it, but their pilots were unable to find the target. This gave rise to claims that the [aircraft's] targeting equipment was no good. Gheorgiy Timofeyevich Beregovoy (then a NII VVS test pilot – *Auth*.) and I immediately took an aircraft to Baku. It did not take long to find the reason; after making several demonstration interceptions of IL-28 target drones (IL-28M, *mishen'* – *Auth*.) we diagnosed the case – an excessively inert GCI system. While target information was passed along the chain of command and ultimately transmitted to the fighter pilot, the target would travel a sizeable distance and make confusing manoeuvres; as a result, the pilots ended up looking for the target in the wrong area.'

On 9th May 1954 Capt M Kitaïchik, the best sniper pilot of the North Fleet's air arm, attempted to intercept a Boeing RB-47 Stratojet near Arkhangel'sk in a brand-new MiG-17PF. After a brief exchange of fire the Stratojet, which was operating from one of the British bases, managed to get away.

The drifting reconnaissance balloons launched in large numbers from Western Europe were a major nuisance for the Soviet air defences in the 1950s. Capt L I Savichev was the first MiG-17 pilot who managed to shoot down such a balloon, destroying his quarry with just nine cannon shells at 10,000m (32,808ft) near the city of Chernovtsy in western Ukraine. A few days later Savichev took off again to intercept a reconnaissance balloon but could not destroy it, despite expending the entire ammunition supply – the balloon was flying too high.

In 1956 a MiG-17 pilot flying near Moscow spotted an unfamiliar aircraft cruising leisurely above him at around 20,000m (65,616ft). (The aircraft, as the reader may have guessed, was a Lockheed U-2 spyplane.) Of course, he attempted an attack but failed – the MiG's service ceiling was much lower. On landing the pilot reported the encounter but his commanders refused to believe him, as then the PVO was still unaware of the U-2's existence. To make matters worse, AD radar operators had not noticed a thing. On later occasions the radars briefly detected a high-flying target – no doubt a U-2 – but could not track it for an extended time.

Clarence 'Kelly' Johnson's elusive creation became the bane of the *Fresco* pilots' existence. In 1957 a pair of 17th IAP MiG-17Ps tried to catch up with a U-2 over the Soviet Far East but, of course, unsuccessfully. In the same year a 9th GvIAP pilot reached the MiG-17's ceiling

in pursuit of a U-2; still, that was all he could do – the target flew serenely on at around 20km, well out of range of the MiG's guns.

By the early 1960s the VVS and PVO were still short of interceptors, and the defence of the Soviet Union's airspace was a sore point. On 9th April 1960 a U-2 flown by none other than Francis Gary Powers took off from Peshawar airbase in Pakistan. Crossing the Soviet border, it made several passes at 20,000 to 21,000m (65,616 to 68,897ft) over the PVO test range near Lake Balkhash where the famous S-75 Tunguska (SA-2 *Guideline*) surface-to-air missile – the one that put a spectacular end to the U-2's incursions – was being tested. Only the fact that there were no live SAMs on site at the moment saved Powers. Then the U-2 over-flew the Baikonur space centre in Kazakhstan and escaped into Iran, crossing the border near the town of Maryy, Turkmenia (pronounced like the French name Marie) after spending 6 hours 48 minutes in Soviet airspace with impunity.

Naturally, the entire Soviet air defence system was in a turmoil. Neither PVO interceptors nor the Air Force's 73rd VA[3] fighters had been able to stop the intruder. Two 156th IAP MiG-17s from Maryy-2 AB tried to get at the U-2 over Turkmenia on the off-chance that it might descend on the way back; 73rd VA

Commander Gen Yuriy V Votintsev and 156th IAP CO Lt Col P Ye Koozin had authorised the pilots to cross the border in pursuit of the intruder. The pilots were quick to use this permission, flying 250 to 300km (135 to 162nm) into Iranian airspace, but to no avail – the target got away; running critically low on fuel, the pursuers had no choice but to head for home. Interestingly, the Teheran government made no comment whatever on the violation of Iranian airspace by Soviet fighters – probably knowing it was not in a position to raise a protest. To use a Russian slang expression, the cat knows whose meat it has eaten!

In the summer of 1963 a Rockwell Aero Commander 560 twin-engined light executive aircraft entered Soviet airspace from Iran. Two MiG-17Ps of the 12th Independent PVO Air Army/17th IAD commanded by Col A D Kotov scrambled to intercept it. Having located the intruder, the MiG pilots, Capt Stepanov and Lt (sg) Soodarikov, attempted to force it down on their home base; however, the Aero Commander pressed on towards the border in a determined attempt to escape. Stepanov had to open fire, damaging the intruder which crashed in flames in Iranian territory 1km (0.54nm) beyond the border. It was later established that an Iranian intelligence officer and a US Army

28 Blue, a late MiG-17, in flight.
Yefim Gordon archive

Naval MiG-17 '606 Red' (c/n 54210606) shows the early-standard slipper tanks.
Yefim Gordon archive

Left: **With a GAZ-69 jeep converted into a ground power cart in the foreground, a long line of VVS MiG-17Fs stands on the apron at a Soviet airbase.** Yefim Gordon archive

Below: **A pair of *Fresco-Cs* takes off on a sortie.** Yefim Gordon archive

Bottom: **On 25th May 1967 this MiG-17F fighter-bomber flown by a defecting VVS pilot made a belly landing near Dillingen. Note the pylons for air-to-ground weapons and the inscription 'Otlichnyy' (excellent), an excellent maintenance award. Here the aircraft is being lifted by a NATO recovery crew.** Sergey and Dmitriy Komissarov collection

colonel were among those killed in the crash. The incident occurred at a singularly inappropriate moment when a Soviet delegation headed by the Soviet leader Leonid I Brezhnev was making a friendly visit to Iran; makes one wonder if it had actually been *timed* to coincide with the visit!

At 07:00 on 8th May 1954 three 91st Strategic Reconnaissance Wing RB-47Es, including Lockheed-built 52-0268, took off from RAF Fairford on a seemingly routine mission over the Barents Sea skirting the Soviet border. Two of the Stratojets turned back to England off Murmansk, but the crew of 52-0268 had different orders. Flown by Capt Harold 'Hal' Austin (pilot), Capt Carl Holt (co-pilot) and Maj Vance Heavilin (navigator), the aircraft turned south and intruded into Soviet airspace over the Kola Peninsula. The mission was to photograph Soviet airbases in the area and find out how many of the new Myasischchev M-4 *Bison-A* bombers and MiG-17 fighters had been deployed.

As the crew recalled, shortly after passing Murmansk at noon at 40,000ft (12,192m) the RB-47E was intercepted by a flight of six MiG-15s, then a little later by six more *Fagots* over the White Sea, but strangely enough they made no attempt to attack. Only when the aircraft had turned west over Arkhangel'sk did the first attack come. Six 1619th IAP MiG-17s of the North Fleet air arm popped up and opened fire. Cannon shells hit the port wing and fuselage, knocking out the communications equipment; Holt returned fire but the cannon jammed.[4] It is possible that the MiGs were critically low on fuel, as they broke off the attack.

Shortly afterwards, when the Stratojet had passed Onega, photographing more airbases, six more MiG-17s, this time 614th IAP aircraft, repeated the attack but also unsuccessfully. The intruder got away – incidentally, only just managing to take on fuel from a standby Boeing KC-97 tanker from RAF Brize Norton on the way home. Reprisal for this failure came quickly: Lt Gen I I Borzov, Commander of the North Fleet air arm, was removed from office.

On 4th September 1954 a US Navy (VP-19) Lockheed P2V-5 Neptune was detected by AD radars near Nakhodka in the Far East. Two VVS Frescos scrambled from Tsentrahl'naya-Ooglovaya AB and shot the Neptune down 35km (18.9nm) south of Cape Ostrovnoy; the crew went MIA.

In the summer of 1964 another Iranian Rockwell Aero Commander 560 crossed the Soviet border near Serekhs. Once again a flight of 156th IAP MiG-17Ps led by Capt Pechonkin scrambled to intercept it. This time the intruder was forced to land on one of the reserve airfields near Maryy and the crew was captured. Later, it was handed over to the Iranian authorities; the fate of the aircraft is not known.

On 27th June 1958 two 34th VA MiG-17Ps piloted by Capt G F Svetlichnikov and Capt B F Zakharov intercepted a USAF Fairchild C-119 Flying Boxcar transport 30km (16.2nm) south of Yerevan. The intruder was ordered to land; however, the landing was unsuccessful and the C-119 crashed and burned 170km (92nm) from the border. The crew escaped unhurt and was handed over to US representatives on 7th July.

On 7th November 1958 two 30th VA MiG-17s attacked and damaged an RB-47 over the Baltic off Ventspils, Latvia. The spyplane managed to escape into international airspace but it may have ditched and sunk for all we know.

In the mid-50s the Soviet Air Force was reorganised: the ground attack arm (ShA – *Shtoormovaya aviahtsiya*) was disbanded and replaced by the fighter-bomber arm (IBA – *Istrebitel'no-bombardeerovochnaya aviahtsiya*) whose formation began in May 1957. By then the rapid development of new combat aircraft had rendered the MiG-17 family obsolescent; hence in 1960 several MiG-17 units were transferred to the IBA. In so doing the aircraft were updated to MiG-17AS standard, receiving the ability to carry 212mm S-21 HVARs and pods of 57mm ARS-57 (S-5) FFARs; 50-, 100- and 250-kg (110-, 220- and 551-lb) bombs were widely used.

Tactics used by MiG-17 fighter-bombers included bombing in level flight, dive bombing and toss bombing, firing cannons and rockets after making a yo-yo manoeuvre or a half loop, and ditto after making a loop over the target. In a nutshell, the tactics were similar to those employed by MiG-15 fighter-bombers, except that the attack was initiated at 870km/h (470kts) rather than 800km/h (432kts).

A peculiarity of the Soviet fighter-bomber aviation at the time (including MiG-17 units) was

the belief that using large groups of aircraft for strike duties was impossible or at any rate inadvisable. The official explanation was that the higher speeds and the allegedly much-reduced manoeuvrability as compared to yesterday's ground attack aircraft made flying in large formations too complicated and dangerous. Also, the military top brass were wont to exaggerate the MiG-17's potential as a fighter-bomber; in reality the *Fresco*, being designed as a pure fighter, could not meet the requirements applied to specialised strike aircraft.

In addition to its obvious uses as a mean fighting machine, the MiG-17 replaced the MiG-15*bis* in the display team at Kubinka AB (which, incidentally, could no longer be called the 'Red Five' since it now flew at least nine aircraft!). The 'Red Something-or-other' MiG-17s had a slightly different colour scheme (the upper fuselage, fin and wing upper surfaces were red/natural metal rather than solid red).[5] One aircraft is known to have been serialled 547 Red, but most photos of the team's MiG-17s show post-1955 two-digit tactical codes; known aircraft were coded 48 Red, 49 Red, 50 Red, 51 Red, 53 Red and 54 Red.

From 1954 onwards and well into the 1960s, the MiG-17 equipped Soviet fighter units stationed outside the USSR – for instance, in Poland (4th VA) and East Germany (16th VA), replacing the MiG-15*bis*. In Poland the *Fresco*

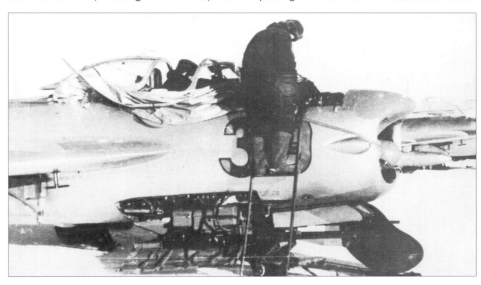

Early-production PVO MiG-17PFs with RP-1 radars undergoing routine maintenance on a wintry airfield. Yefim Gordon archive

Top left: **This shot of a rather weathered MiG-17PFU displays the RS-1-U missiles well.** Yefim Gordon archive

Top right: **The pilot of a MiG-17PFU poses for an official photo on the stepladder of his fully-armed aircraft. 'Let the dastardly imperialists beware...'** Yefim Gordon archive

Above: **Six MiG-17s from the Soviet Air Force's display team at Kubinka in the original colour scheme worn by these aircraft.** Yefim Gordon archive

Left: **This top view of one of the Kubinka aircraft illustrates clearly how the wings were painted.** Yefim Gordon archive

was operated, amongst others, by the 3rd IAP and 18th IAP (both 149th IAD) at Szprotawa AB, the 229th IAD/42nd *Tannenbergskiy* GvIAP[6] at Żagań AB and the 239th *Baranovichskaya* IAD/159th *Novorossiyskiy* GvIAP[7] at Kluczewo (Stargard) AB.

The 3rd IAP flew the MiG-17 from June 1955 to September 1961 when it re-equipped with the Sukhoi Su-7B *Fitter-A*, becoming the 3rd IBAP (*istrebitel'no-bombardeerovochnyy aviapolk* – fighter-bomber regiment) and moving to Krzywa AB. The 18th IAP flew the *Fresco* from 11th June 1955 to 1974, also re-equipping with the Su-7B (and becoming the 18th IBAP) in 1960. The 42nd GvIAP operated the MiG-17F and 'PF from May 1955 to 1972 when they were supplanted by MiG-21PF *Fishbed-Bs*; it also changed its identity to the 42nd GvIBAP in 1960. Finally, the 159th GvIAP received its first five *Fresco-As* in January 1954, followed by five MiG-17Ps and five MiG-17PFs two years later.

In East Germany the MiG-17F was used in the fighter-bomber role in 1956-1967 until replaced by the Su-7B *Fitter-A*; the MiG-17PFU was introduced in 1957. East German bases used by GSVG[8] MiG-17s included Allstedt, Altenburg (*Nöbitz*), Brand, Brandis, Cottbus, Damgarten (*Pütnitz*), Erfurt (1953), Falkenberg (*Alt Lönnewitz*), Finow (*Eberswalde*) (1954-1956), Finsterwalde, Groß-Dölln, Großenhain, Haßleben, Jüterbog-Altes Lager, Köthen, Lärz, Merseburg, Neuruppin, Parchim, Peenemünde, Stendal (*Borstel*), Templin (1955-69), Wittenberg, Wittstock (1954-58) and Zerbst.[9]

Allstedt was occupied by the 294th ORAP, Damgarten by the 16th IAD/773rd IAP (MiG-17PFU), Falkenberg by the 6th GvIAD/31st *Nikopol'skiy* GvIAP (MiG-17PFU), Jüterbog-Altes Lager by the 833rd IAP, Köthen by the 126th IAD/73rd GvIAP, Lärz by the 19th GvAPIB (MiG-17F/PF), Merseburg by the 6th GvIAD/85th GvIAP (MiG-17PFU), Peenemünde and Wittstock by the 16th GvIAD/33rd IAP, Templin by the 234th IAD/787th IAP (MiG-17F/PF), Zerbst by the 35th IAP (MiG-17F/PF) and 931st GvORAP. The 125th ADIB/20th GvAPIB was consecutively based at Neu-Welzow, Damgarten and Parchim, while the 105th ADIB/559th APIB moved from Falkenberg to Großenhain, Altenburg and finally Finsterwalde.

On one occasion when the East German authorities failed to warn the Soviet authorities of an impending test flight, 296th APIB MiG-17PFUs from Großenhain intercepted an IL-28R operating from nearby Dresden-Klotzsche airport. The aircraft, registered DM-ZZK (c/n 1207),

was a testbed for the 3,150-kgp (6,944 lbst) Pirna 014 turbojet developed for the Baade 152 medium-range airliner. The MiGs scrambled, expecting to find a Western spyplane – and for some obscure reason DM-ZZK had a West German flag on the fin (the coat of arms in the middle of the otherwise identical East German flag had been omitted), which certainly did not help! Luckily the situation was quickly clarified when the justifiably alarmed pilot called the tower, which promptly called the Soviet base and straightened things out. Still, it certainly must have been a nasty experience for the crew!

MiG-17 operations in Germany had their share of accidents. On 26th April 1964 a 559th APIB aircraft crashed near Finsterwalde (this is

unconfirmed, as some sources state the type as a Su-7). However, there are worse things than a crash. On 25th May 1967 a MiG-17F fighter-bomber coded 25 Blue and proudly wearing the inscription '*Otlichnyy*'[10] made a perfect belly landing on a grassy meadow near Dillingen, some 100km (54nm) from Stuttgart. It transpired that the pilot, a young lieutenant, had decided to 'go over the wall', and the event was widely publicised; some sources claim he requested political asylum in the USA. The aircraft (but not the pilot) was returned four days later via the East/West German border crossing at Herleshausen.

The MiG-17 had a long career in the Soviet Air Force. Besides (and after being phased out from) front-line service it was operated by the

With smoke generator pods under the wings, five *Fresco-As* from Kubinka make a spectacular formation loop during an airshow, probably in 1961. Yefim Gordon archive

14 Red, an early-production MiG-17PF, in the static display in Leningrad's Kirov Park during the 1968 Aviation Day. The display also featured a MiG-19 *Farmer-A* with the same tactical code.
Sergey Komissarov via Dmitriy Komissarov

DOSAAF, an organization that prepared Soviet youth for service with the armed forces.[11] As late as the early 1990s the MiG-17 was still in service with independent fighter squadrons based in Gor'kiy (possibly at Strighino airport which is also an air force base), Kostroma and at Bezrechnaya AB; the latter unit also operated Yak-28P *Firebar* interceptors.

Speaking of defections, on 14th August 1969 a Hungarian Air Force pilot, Maj Jozsef Biro, fled to Italy in his MiG-17F. In so doing his aircraft was fired upon and damaged by other *Fresco-Cs* scrambled to intercept the fugitive, crash-landing near Udine.

On 6th October 1969 a Cuban MiG-17 pilot defected to the USA, landing at Homestead AFB (Miami, Florida) at about 12:30 local time and sparking a fierce debate in the US Congress. The point of the debate was that the MiG was not detected until it was over the base and made a low pass over the parked Boeing VC-137C (Air Force One) which had brought President Richard Nixon to his residence on Key Biscayne. Had the Cuban pilot's intentions been anything other than defection, the consequences might have been very serious indeed. The message was clear: the US air defence system was no good. Senator Robert F Sykes (Rep.) promptly used the incident to urge the accelerated development of an early warning system which later became known as AWACS. As for the aircraft, it remained in the USA, of course.

Czech Air Force MiG-17PFs were used mainly to shoot down reconnaissance balloons and intercept aircraft intruding from beyond the Iron Curtain to probe the Czech air defences. However, on occasions they were also used to aid aircraft in distress. For example, in 1956 (the exact date is unknown) an 11. SLP (fighter regiment) *Fresco-D* flown by pilot Špinka took off to intercept an intruder. It turned out to be a Soviet Air Force Li-2 *Cab* coming from East Germany; the transport had strayed from the air route at night in a storm when the radio went down and was heading straight for a mountainous area near Děčín.

Having located the target by radar and identified it as a 'friendly', Špinka launched signal flares to catch the Li-2 crew's attention and guided the transport to a safe landing at Žatec AB. In a similar incident in 1957, Capt Emil Ptaček was guided by GCI to a Convair 240 which had been blown off course by strong winds, directing the airliner to České Budějovice AB.

The Czech Air Force also had its share of accidents. On 14th July 1966 MiG-17PF '0314' of the 7th Fighter Regiment (7. SLP) crashed near Piešťany during a low-level training interception, killing the pilot Maj Kadlíček.

Another fatal crash occurred on 30th November 1967 near Žatec AB when Lt Stopka (11. SLP) was killed in MiG-17PF '0203'.

The MiG-17 at war
Besides defending the Soviet borders during the Cold War, the MiG-17 had its fair share of

'hot' wars in various parts of the world. Though developed during the Korean War, it did not participate in that conflict (rumour has it that Stalin personally vetoed the sending of MiG-17s to North Korea), but there was to be enough action for it all the same. And, fighter technology development notwithstanding, it was not to be taken lightly. Possessing higher manoeuvrability than the faster and more modern jets that followed, the *Fresco* often emerged as the winner in dogfights with the Dassault Mystère – and even with the supersonic Dassault Mirage III and McDonnell F-4 Phantom II.

The MiG-17's first 'real' war was in 1956 – and, like its predecessor, the MiG-15, the type made its combat debut in China. In 1949 the differences between Mao Tse-tung's Communist Party and Chiang Kai-shek's nationalist Kuomintang Party escalated into an outright military conflict. Though the Nationalists were soon confined to Taiwan and the adjoining islands, they would not give it up. Hostilities between mainland China and Taiwan continued unabated after the Korean War as the Communist leaders strove to recapture the breakaway island.

By mid-1956 the Republic of China Air Force (ROCAF) had almost entirely re-equipped with Western jet aircraft, while the People's Liberation Army Air Force (PLAAF) started taking delivery of the licence-built MiG-17F (J-5). It was this aircraft which brought the Communist air arm its first-ever night 'kill' in June 1956; guided by GCI, pilot Liu Ming intercepted and destroyed a Taiwanese Boeing B-17 Flying Fortress. Liu Ming was a Korean War ace with eight 'kills' (including five Sabres) to his credit and was honoured with the Hero of the People's Republic of China title. Two months later pilot Chang Wang-yi shot down another ROCAF aircraft at night in poor weather.

The conflict between Peking and Taipei escalated sharply in 1958; this has come to be known as the Taiwan Crisis. Three years earlier Taiwan had signed a defensive pact with the USA. Supporting their Taiwanese allies, the Americans sent more than 700 aircraft to the island, including the latest supersonic fighters – North American F-100 Super Sabre, McDonnell F-101/RF-101 Voodoo and Lockheed F-104 Starfighter – and Martin Matador ground-launched cruise missiles able to carry nuclear warheads. Fortunately, the latter were never used; otherwise, the result could have been the Third World War.

Taiwan also hosted Martin RB-57D and Lockheed U-2 reconnaissance aircraft. While the former type was actually delivered to the Nationalists, the top-secret U-2s were flown by USAF pilots, wearing ROCAF markings just for appearance's sake. The higher to fly, the deeper to fall: the high-altitude spyplanes were not invulnerable, as it turned out. On 18th February 1958 a Taiwanese RB-57D was shot down into the sea by J-5s. The Chinese pilots got even luckier in mid-1958, shooting down a U-2; this Mission Impossible was achieved only because

the spyplane was suffering mechanical problems and flying lower than usual.

On 29th July 1958 a group of PLAAF MiG-17Fs (almost certainly J-5s) intercepted four ROCAF aircraft over Shantow (Swatow), Kwangtung Province, and shot down three of them. On 14th August, Chinese fighters engaged 12 Taiwanese F-86Fs over Pingtung Island; in the ensuing battle two Sabres were shot down and a third damaged. Pilot Chou Chung-fu scored both 'kills'; however, he was shot down immediately afterwards, losing his life. By 14th August, seven more ROCAF aircraft had been destroyed.

In September 1958 China began a blockade of the Kinmen (Quemoy) and Matsu islands held by Taiwan which the Nationalists viewed as a beachhead for possible strikes against the mainland. On 24th September there was a skirmish between some thirty MiG-17Fs (J-5s) and fourteen F-86Fs. For the first time the Nationalists used air-to-air missiles; according to Taiwanese reports, the Sabres destroyed four MiGs with AIM-9B Sidewinder heat-seeking AAMs and six more with machine-gun fire. The Chinese authorities claimed that only one *Fresco-C* had been shot down with AAMs and another came home *with an unexploded Sidewinder stuck in its fuselage*!

On 10th October 1958 a dogfight broke out between eight J-5s and six F-86Fs over Fukien Province. Pilot Tu Feng-chu shot down two Sabres but was also hit and had to eject. As he parachuted earthwards, the pilot of a third Sabre lined up on him and shot him dead. Yet Tu Feng-chu was avenged: immediately afterwards the murderous Sabre was destroyed by Chinese AA fire. One of the three F-86 pilots also ejected and was taken prisoner; the other two died in their aircraft.

There was relatively little action in 1959 as compared to the preceding year. In early 1959 a group of ROCAF Sabres intruded into Chinese airspace. A group of J-5s scrambled to intercept, shooting down one F-86 and damaging another; one of the J-5s was also damaged. On the night of 29th May 1959 Lt Hsiang Jie-lung destroyed an ROCAF B-17G in adverse weather conditions.

On 16th February 1960 four Sabres attacked a group of MiGs with Sidewinders over Fukien Province. The Nationalists claimed the destruction of at least one aircraft; in reality, however, the MiGs managed to evade the missiles and counter-attacked, damaging one F-86.

The first 'kill' scored by PLAAF J-5s in 1965 was reportedly another U-2 spyplane. However, this one and two more U-2s (ie, three out of four downed aircraft of this type exhibited at the People's Revolution Military Museum in Peking during 1965) were almost certainly shot down by SAMs.

PLAAF MiGs also had encounters with USAF and US Navy aircraft. For instance, on 12th May 1965, when the Vietnam War was already raging, five USAF F-4C Phantom IIs intruded into Chinese airspace over Yunnan Province and shot down a J-5 which was out on a training sortie. China filed a formal protest but the US government denied the charge, claiming that the MiG had been downed over North Vietnam.

MiG-17 operations in China also had an altogether peaceful and festive aspect. Like many air forces, the PLAAF had its own display team named 'August 1' and equipped with Shenyang JJ-5 advanced trainers. The aircraft wore a stylish red/natural metal colour scheme and non-standard three-digit serials; known aircraft were serialled consecutively 506 White through 513 White).

Here we have to go back in time a little. Say '1956' and one probably thinks of the Suez crisis; this was the second Arab-Israeli war and the second regional conflict in which the MiG-17 saw action. At the beginning of the conflict the Israelis were heavily outnumbered: the Israeli Defence Force/Air Force (*Heyl Ha'avir*) had 173 aircraft, including 114 combat aircraft (if you count the North American AT-6 Harvard trainers as light attack aircraft). They were opposed by 178 Egyptian combat aircraft; however, these included only twelve MiG-17Fs based at El Qabrit AB, which were still inoperative at the time.

During the Suez Crisis the MiG-17F was up against its French equivalent, the Dassault Mystère IVA which had its combat debut in that conflict. The first encounter between the two was on 30th October when a group of 12 MiGs, including several MiG-17s, jumped six *Heyl Ha'avir* Mystères of the 101st *Tayeset* (Squadron) based at Hatzor which were attacking El Qabrit AB. One Mystère flown by Lt Joseph Tzuk was seriously damaged but it is not known by what type. Later, the Israelis claimed two confirmed and two probable 'kills', while the Egyptians maintained that their MiG-17s attacked 'a large group of Mystères', shooting down three of them and putting the rest to flight! As with any war, 'kills' statistics are notoriously optimistic...

The air war peaked on 31st October; dogfights mostly took place over the roads along which Israeli troops moved and over Egyptian defensive positions. By noon the fighting was at its fiercest. At 12:10 two 101st Sqn Mystère IVAs piloted by Capt Yaakov 'Yak' Nevo and his wingman Lt Joseph Tzuk spotted and attacked three MiG-17Fs flying below them near El'Arîsh. Nevo recalled that two of the Egyptians panicked and fled, leaving their buddy to deal with the Israelis as best he could – one sought cover in the nearest cloud while the other hightailed it towards the Suez Canal.

Lt Tzuk dived straight at the third MiG, but he was not in a position to fire. Ordering him to break off the attack, Nevo applied the airbrakes to stay behind the MiG and pulled his Mystère into a climb in order to take aim. Only then did he realise that he was up against the newer and more dangerous MiG-17F, not a MiG-15*bis*; he could clearly see the redesigned wings of greater area with half a dozen boundary layer

fences. He had heard rumours that Nasser had received these fighters recently; now he knew it was true. Anyway, Nevo put his aiming pipper on the target and fired a short burst from the port cannon at about 180m (590ft) range; the starboard cannon had jammed. He could see his 30mm shells hitting the MiG – seemingly with no effect at first; then the enemy fighter abruptly rolled inverted and went down like a brick. At about 3,000m (10,000ft) after trying unsuccessfully to level out the Egyptian pilot ejected, but apparently his parachute did not open and he was killed. Seconds later the MiG burst into flames and hit the ground. This was the first MiG-17 to be lost in combat anywhere in the world.

At about 16:00 on 1st November a pair of Mystère IVAs patrolling over the Mitla Pass attacked a group of de Havilland Vampires escorted by MiG-17Fs which were attacking the positions of the Israeli 202nd Airborne Division. In the brief fight that followed one Egyptian aircraft was shot down, but it is not known whether it was a Vampire or a MiG.

After the Anglo-French utimatum concerning the Suez Canal, Egyptian President Gamal Abdul Nasser wisely moved many of his military aircraft (including some MiG-17Fs) to safe havens in Syria and Saudi Arabia to save them from being destroyed by Anglo-French air strikes on 1st November 1956. When the British and French troops left the Suez Canal area in January 1957, not only did these 'expatriates' come back but a major re-equipment programme was launched. In March 1957 three Romanian ships brought 15 MiG-17Fs and ten IL-28s to Alexandria; by late June the Egyptian Air Force had about 100 *Fresco-Cs* and about 40 *Beagles* on strength.

In his 25th July speech on occasion of Nasser's fifth anniversary as President, EAF Chief of Staff Air Vice-Marshal Mohammed Sidki stated that the Air Force's first-line assets had doubled as compared to the time immediately before the Suez Crisis. To add weight to his words, a formation of no fewer that 100 combat jets was to pass over Cairo that day. However, the show of force fizzled because the tech staff had managed to prepare only 42 aircraft for the display – eleven *Fagot-Bs*, eighteen MiG-17Fs and thirteen IL-28s. The watching crowd went wild all the same, but the message was clear: it would take years for the Egyptian Air Force to become fully combat-capable.

The Syrian Air Force, which did not take part in the Suez Crisis fighting, was in even worse shape, having lost nearly all its MiG-15s during that conflict when Royal Navy Westland Wyverns attacked Abu Sueir on 1st November 1956. However, in November Syria ordered sixty MiG-17Fs which were delivered between January and August 1957. When Egypt and Syria joined forces against Israel, creating the United Arab Republic on 1st February 1958, the Syrian Air Force had five day fighter squadrons equipped with *Fresco-Cs* plus one squadron of Gloster Meteor NF.13 night fighters which were

due for replacement with Soviet-built MiG-17PF interceptors.

Thus, Nasser's idea to create an air force outnumbering the *Heyl Ha'avir* four times seemed quite feasible. The Egyptian and Syrian components of the newly-created United Arab Republic Air Force (UARAF) were to comprise 30 and 10 squadrons respectively. The implementation of this grand plan, however, was hampered by aircrew training problems; in 1957 the USSR even reduced combat aircraft deliveries to Egypt because the UARAF did not have enough pilots to fly them! Technical staff training levels likewise remained low, and accident attrition was largely due to equipment failures caused by improper maintenance.

Also, UARAF top commanders were convinced that sheer strength in numbers was the key to success. It took the united efforts of Soviet, Polish, Czech and Indian military advisors and instructors, and then only in 1959, to make them change priorities and pay more attention to flight and ground crew training standards. By mid-1961 the Egyptian component of the UARAF was fully combat-capable. Yet the united air arm did not manage to benefit from this; in September 1961 the United Arab Republic ceased to exist, and Egypt and Syria (and their respective air forces) went their separate ways.

In the summer of 1961 Egypt began taking delivery of 80 Soviet-built MiG-19S *Farmer-C* supersonic day fighters;[12] in 1962 they were joined by 40 MiG-21F-13 *Fishbed-As* which could match the performance of Israeli Dassault Mirage IIICJs. Consequently the MiG-17Fs which no longer met current requirements were relegated to the strike role. Syria, which also received new Mikoyan fighters at the time, came to the same conclusion and Syrian *Frescos* were likewise converted to fighter-bombers.

Meanwhile, Egyptian and Syrian pilots were gaining experience in numerous clashes with the *Heyl Ha'avir* – chiefly negative experience. Until the Six-Day War of 1967 Israel continuously provoked its Arab neighbours. For instance, on 20th December 1958 two Mystère IVAs piloted by the 101st Sqn's new CO Maj Aharon Yoelli and the commander of Hatzor AB Mordechai 'Moti' Hod entered Egyptian airspace near El'Arîsh. Circling and gradually retreating towards the border, they drew the two MiG-17Fs sent to intercept the intruders into an ambush set by another pair of Mystères, the leader of which, Capt Yaakov Nevo, added another MiG 'kill' to his score.

Still, such provocative tactics did not always work out. On 14th February 1959 Syrian MiG-17Fs shot down a 'visiting' Mystère IVA near the Syrian border. On 4th November 1959 a Super Mystère B.2 flown by Maj David Ivri (who eventually became IDF/AF C-in-C) lost control and crashed during a dogfight with EAF MiG-17s.

In November 1959 a pair of Super Mystère B.2s (known as the *Sa'ar* in Israeli service) entered Egyptian airspace over the Gaza Strip and attacked two MiG-17Fs patrolling over the area, damaging one of them. Sometimes the Arabs answered in kind; for instance, on 25th May 1960 two Egyptian MiG-17Fs penetrated deep into Israeli airspace in the same area. They were intercepted by two IDF/AF fighters piloted by Capt Agaron and 1st Lt Yadin; Agaron managed to damage one of the intruders. Five days later a dogfight took place between four MiGs and two *Sa'ars*; according to Israeli press reports, one of the Egyptian fighters was damaged.

Skirmishes between Arab MiG-17s and Israeli fighters continued throughout the 1960s. On 28th April 1961 a pair of Super Mystère B.2s again met with a pair of UARAF MiG-17Fs near the Egyptian border. In the ensuing dogfight, pilot error caused one of the MiGs to go into a spin. After unsuccessful attempts at recovery the Egyptian pilot ejected; unfortunately for him, he did so over Israeli territory and was taken prisoner. Another battle occurred on 23rd July 1963 over the Negev Desert in Israel; the *Heyl Ha'avir* pilots claimed two MiGs shot down but, since both aircraft crashed in Egyptian territory, this could not be proved beyond reasonable doubt and the 'kills' were not credited.

There was quite a bit of action on the Israeli-Syrian border, too. In February 1960 four UARAF (Syrian) MiG-17Fs were attacked by *Heyl Ha'avir* 105th Sqn fighters but neither side suffered any losses. On 1st February 1962, as fighting raged over the Golan Heights, a pair of *Fresco-Cs* attacked and damaged a (101st Sqn?) *Sa'ar* which managed to reach Hatzor AB and land safely.[13]

Starting in 1962, during the eight year civil war Egyptian Air Force MiG-17Fs were in action in Yemen, supporting the Republicans who had overthrown the king. In March 1963 they had a few encounters with RAF Hawker Hunter FGA.9s; however, as in the case of the MiG-15*bis*, their main role was ground attack.

The most famous conflict in which the MiG-17 participated is, of course, the Vietnam War. Like Korea, Vietnam found itself divided into two countries – the Democratic Republic of Vietnam (DRV) in the north and the Republic of Vietnam (RVN) in the south. (It really is uncanny how this 'north and south' thing keeps recurring.) In 1964 American troops were pulled into South Vietnam. This elicited an allergic reaction from North Vietnam; on 2nd August 1964 North Vietnamese torpedo boats attacked the destroyers USS *Maddox* and USS *Turner Joy* in international waters in the Gulf of Tonkin.[14]

The US government was well aware that sending troops to North Vietnam in retaliation was out of the question; at best the Korean scenario with its 'one million of Chinese volunteers' would be repeated, and at worst the USA would end up starting a war with the Soviet Union. Therefore, the USA opted for massive bombardments in order to discourage North Vietnam from assisting South Vietnam's Front for National Liberation (FNL). If the North Viet-

namese persisted, the USAF would 'bomb them into stone age', as Gen Curtis LeMay put it. (Incidentally, the Americans could not resist the urge to take sweet revenge: the very first strike mission against North Vietnam on 5th August 1964 was directed at five torpedo boat bases on the coast.)

Gen LeMay believed that North Vietnam would be unable to resist the tremendous firepower of the USAF, and at first glance the task of bombing it into submission seemed easy. The North Vietnamese air defences were weak; at the start of the war the Vietnamese People's Air Force (VPAF) had only 40 to 60 obsolete aircraft, the most modern of which were 25 Chinese-built MiG-17Fs (F-5s).[15]

Strikes against North Vietnam in 1964 were conducted on a small scale because the USAF was short of funds. On the other hand, the Americans built and upgraded dozens of air-bases in Thailand and South Vietnam at this stage; also, two large tactical aviation groups were formed that year – Yankee Station (USAF) and Dixie Station (US Navy). The former group operated the North American F-100D Super Sabre, Republic F-105 Thunderchief, McDonnell F-101C/RF-101C Voodoo and F-4C/RF-4C Phantom II and even the Convair F-102 Delta Dagger. The naval group was equipped with the F-4B/RF-4B, Vought F8U-1 Crusader, Douglas A-1 Skyraider and A-4 Skyhawk.

On 7th February 1965 the USA launched Operation *Flaming Dart* involving systematic bombardment of North Vietnamese military installations and industrial centres; the Vietnam War had begun for real. At this stage the USAF and USN used large formations of up to 80 aircraft which dropped their bombs from 2,500 to 4,000m (8,202 to 13,123ft), often through cloud cover, staying safely out of range of the Vietnamese AAA. It was a different story with the fighters. The assorted MiGs were tasked mainly with point air defence of targets of importance.

The customary tactic used for this – ie, intercepting the incoming bombers at long range – did not work in Vietnam because the Americans enjoyed complete air superiority. Therefore, the Vietnamese pilots did the only possible thing, loitering at low altitude near the target they were defending and waiting for the enemy strike group to come up. The MiGs were camouflaged and could not be spotted so easily over the jungle. Having located the enemy, they popped up from their ambush and shot down the strike aircraft at point-blank range, taking advantage of the fact that the strike aircraft loaded with draggy and heavy external stores were sluggish and 200 to 300km/h (108 to 162kts) slower.

This tactic brought success for the first time on 4th April 1965 when four MiG-17Fs attacked eight F-105Ds near Thành Hoa. In this attack Capt Tranh Hanh and his wingman shot down two Thuds piloted by Capt James Magnusson and Maj Frank Bennet which became the first of 320 American aircraft lost in the Vietnam War.

To commemorate this victory 4th April has been declared Aviation Day in Vietnam.[16] Even if the MiGs failed to shoot down any fighter-bombers, the Americans would often drop their bombs hastily when under attack to improve manoeuvrability and speed – and that was just what the Vietnamese pilots had intended, for the strike mission would go down the drain.

Of course, surprise was the key to success, since the American aircraft were considerably more advanced. Tranh Hanh, by then promoted to Major, later said in an interview to the Soviet daily newspaper *Pravda* (Truth), *'They did not know yet that we had fighters, too. They just didn't believe that anyone would dare to approach them in the air. Of course, we had to use this... I opened fire at medium range and saw my tracer streams blowing holes in the port wing of one F-105, but it was not enough [to knock it down]. So I increased speed and came close enough to see the pilot's white helmet. The American pilot probably didn't realise what had happened to his aircraft. I could see him turn his head to inspect the wings and then lean forward towards the instrument panel. Then I squeezed off a long burst and the entire frame-work of one side of the aircraft became visible, frames and all that stuff; the F-105 went down like a brick.'*

After losing the first few aircraft the Americans grew more wary. Four days later, according to Western sources, they scored their first 'kill' in the war, and it was a US Navy crew that gained the distinction – but at a heavy price. At 08:40 on 9th April 1965 eight F-4Bs of VF-96 from USS *Ranger* out on a combat air patrol (MIGCAP) sortie spotted and attacked a flight of MiG-17Fs. One of the Phantoms (F-4B-16-MC BuNo 151403) destroyed a MiG with a Raytheon AIM-7 Sparrow AAM but was immediately shot down by one of the remaining MiGs. The aircraft fell into the Gulf of Tonkin, killing pilot Lt T Murphy and weapons systems operator (WSO) Flying Officer R Fagan.

However, there is a different account which sounds more credible – the loss of BuNo 151403 was a blue-on-blue incident. According to Chinese sources, the Phantoms intruded into Chinese, not Vietnamese, airspace over Hainan Island which lies near the Vietnamese coastline and were immediately pounced upon by PLAAF J-5s. It is possible that the American pilots were wilfully provoking the Chinese into attacking them; the idea was to shoot down a few Chinese fighters in purported self-defence and teach Red China a lesson for supplying arms to North Vietnam. However, the plan backfired. Murphy and Fagan damaged one J-5 with a Sparrow missile (the aircraft was *not* shot down and made it back to base), while another Phantom fired a missile at another J-5 but the missile locked onto BuNo 151403 instead and destroyed it.

Little by little the Vietnamese pilots gained combat experience which they initially lacked. On 3rd May 1965 Lt Phom Ngok Zanh shot down an A-4 in his MiG-17F. On 17th June four

MiG-17Fs sneaked up unnoticed on a group of Phantoms over Ninh Binh and gunned down two of them at point-blank range. The Americans did not manage to shoot down any of the attackers, but they were avenged all the same. In the heat of the battle the MiGs ran out of fuel and two of the pilots had to eject; a third MiG made a belly landing short of the base when the engine quit.

At 18:25 on 20th June a pair of *Fresco-Cs* attacked a flight of four AD-6 (A-1H) Skyraiders of VA-25/CVW-2 (USS *Midway*) over the sea. One of the MiGs overshot and was destroyed by the powerful 20mm cannons of a Skyraider flown by Lt Clint Johnson (BuNo 139768/ 'NE-577'). According to American sources, between February and July 1965 the US Navy destroyed four MiG-17Fs; three of them were shot down by F-4Bs. The USAF opened its list of aerial victories in Vietnam on 10th July 1965 when two 2nd AD/45th TFS F-4C-22-MCs (64-0679, pilot Capt Thomas S Roberts/WSO Capt Ronald C Anderson and 64-0693, pilot Capt Kenneth E Holcombe/WSO Capt Arthur C Clark) shot down one MiG-17F each. American losses in the same period were four or five F-105Ds, two naval attack aircraft and one F-4B.

In July 1965 the S-75 (SA-2 *Guideline*) surface-to-air missile was introduced on the Vietnamese theatre of operations. The consequent sharp increase in combat losses over North Vietnam – and not least the psychological effect of the SAMs – led the US command to change tactics. Since the S-75 was optimised for destroying targets at high and medium altitudes, USAF and USN aircraft switched to low-level and ultra-low-level nap-of-the-earth flying in order to evade SAMs and AD radars which guided the Vietnamese fighters. Speaking of which, initially the Vietnamese were the only ones to use radar for guiding fighters. It was not until 1967 that the Americans started using radar control – mostly in an early-warning capacity. There was a cruiser in the Gulf of Tonkin (code-named Red Crown) and Lockheed EC-121M Warning Star AEW aircraft patrolling over nearby Laos (code-named Disco).

This change of tactics complicated things a lot for the MiG pilots which now received accurate GCI information much less often. The effect of MiG-17 ambushes was drastically reduced. Yet this did not make things easier for the Americans, as at low level they were fired upon by all kinds of AAA (sometimes even from above, from mountain ridges!) and even Vietnamese soldiers with Kalashnikov AKM assault rifles.

Another change of tactics concerned fighter escort of strike groups. Until then, Vietnamese fighters popping up from below engaged the low-flying strike aircraft, and when the American fighters flying top cover descended on them it was often too late for the escortees. Hence the escort fighters started flying on the same level or lower than the MiGs. Having located them visually or by radar, the F-4s

caught up with the MiGs and destroyed them with AAMs.

That is, if they were lucky enough. Firstly, the Americans had a lot of trouble with the AIM-7 Sparrow which was the Phantom's main weapon. The guidance system of the early versions was based on vacuum tubes and frequently failed; it was not until the advent of the AIM-7F with solid-state avionics that reliability was improved. Secondly, while being nowhere near as fast as the F-4, the MiG-17F had excellent manoeuvrability and often managed to dodge the missiles if the pilot was skilful enough. Thirdly, the Vietnamese pilots tried to force a WW II-style dogfight on the enemy and the MiG-17F could get into the Phantom's six o'clock fairly easily (to say nothing of the F-105 which was the MiGs' favourite prey and had an appallingly high loss ratio). This was because the *Fresco* had a much lower wing loading and weighed only about as much as the Phantom's internal fuel load. Finally, the Americans were not allowed to fire unless the target had been positively identified – and this gave the MiG pilots an advantage, since the larger F-4 was easier to identify as the enemy from a good long way off.

Then the Americans invented a new stratagem: if MiGs and Phantoms started chasing each other in circles, one or two F-4s would break out of the circle and make a 'high-speed yo-yo' in order to dive down on the enemy's tail or make a flank attack. After losing six *Frescos* this way the Vietnamese resorted to a hit-and-run tactic, making a single firing pass at top speed and heading for home.

By early 1966 the VPAF already had the supersonic MiG-19S, and deliveries of the all-weather MiG-21PF-V *Fishbed-D*[17] began in April that year. Still, the MiG-17F remained a trusted workhorse even after the still more advanced MiG-21PFM was added to the VPAF inventory, as every little bit helped in 'the struggle against the US imperialist aggression'. The Vietnamese operated the *Frescos* in flexible interaction with the more modern *Fishbeds*, quickly reacting to changing enemy tactics. One ploy favoured by the Vietnamese was to send a natural metal MiG-17F or MiG-19S out as bait; American fighters would go for the lone fighter which was plainly visible against the jungle – and be counterattacked by a camouflaged MiG-17F or MiG-21PF-V waiting in ambush. Another co-operative tactic was this: the MiG-17Fs, which fought well at low altitude, forced the Phantoms to climb in order to gain an advantage and hopefully attack from above; up there they would be engaged by high-altitude MiG-21s.

Also in 1966, new versions of the MiG-17 made their appearance in Vietnam, albeit on a small scale. The first of these was the J-5A (the Chinese copy of the radar-equipped MiG-17PF) armed with three NR-23 cannons. About 1968 the VPAF started using MiG-17Fs armed with two R-3S (AA-2 *Atoll*) IR-homing AAMs in addition to the standard cannons.

The arrival of the MiG-21 changed things dramatically. In the first four months of 1966 the USAF and USN had lost eleven aircraft and the VPAF nine, which meant the 'kill' ratio was 1.2:1; in comparison, between May and December 1966 (ie, after the introduction of the *Fishbed*) the USA and North Vietnam lost 47 and 12 aircraft respectively, which meant the 'kill' ratio was 4:1! According to American sources, the USAF and USN scored 20 'kills' that year, including five MiG-21s and two Antonov An-2 *Colt* utility biplanes used for *Tha Vo* (Free Fall) resupply missions; the rest were MiG-17Fs.

Some Vietnamese *Fresco-Cs* – eg, 2047 Red – were reportedly fitted with a brake parachute for operation from *ad hoc* tactical airstrips. On 19th April 1972 ace Nguyen Van Bai took off in this aircraft from a secret airbase in Quang Binh Province and, together with his wingman Le Xuan Di, made a surprise attack on two US Navy destroyers (USS *Higbee* and USS *Oklahoma* City) which were shelling Dong Hoi, damaging both ships. Nguyen Van Bai delivered a 250-kg (551-lb) bomb squarely on the superstructure of the USS *Higbee*, causing extensive damage. This action was claimed by the Vietnamese as the first aerial attack on the US Seventh Fleet since WW II and earned the aircraft a place in the VPAF Museum in Hanoi. Four commando junks were also sunk by similarly equipped MiG-17s.

One peculiarity of the opening stage of the Vietnam War was the use of tactical aircraft (notably F-4s) in the strategic bomber role. A formation of Phantoms led by a Douglas EB-66D Destroyer communications jammer aircraft would typically drop their bombs from high altitude, often through cloud. Later, when the VPAF built up its MiG-17 and MiG-21 fleet and the Vietnamese air defences got SAMs and radars, the Phantoms reverted to their original escort fighter role. In encounters with MiGs, a hit-and-run tactic with missile launch at long range usually brought success, but if a close-in dogfight began, the Phantom crews were in for a tough time.

The F-4's main advantage over the MiG-17F was its missile armament – AIM-7 Sparrow medium-range AAMs and AIM-9 Sidewinder short-range AAMs. Hence the MiG pilots tried to stay close to the Phantoms, knowing that the F-4 had no built-in cannon and that the Americans would not fire missiles if they were within minimum range or if there was a chance of hitting one of their own; besides, unlike the Sidewinder, early-model AIM-7s were notoriously unreliable. Soon, however, the MiGs were stripped of this cover when the Phantom got the General Electric M61A1 Vulcan six-barrel 20mm Gatling cannon – originally in podded form (SUU-16/A and SUU-32/A) and later, on the F-4E, in the fuselage nose.

USAF and US Navy pilots admitted that the MiG-17F was a difficult opponent to get to grips with. Col Robin Olds,[18] the popular CO of the 8th Tactical Fighter Wing 'Wolfpack' operating from Ubon RTAFB,[19] scored four of the unit's 24 'kills' in the Vietnam War. Here are some of his observations on the MiG-17: *'Our combat aircraft were usually designed as multi-purpose ones. An aircraft originally developed for one role could fill others in the specific conditions of a war; eg, the F-4 was conceived as a shipboard strike aircraft but it soon became clear that it could perform a variety of tasks.*

...In the case of the Vietnam War we had to fly very long distances and be capable of fighting the enemy over his own airfield. You have to remember this when comparing our aircraft to theirs. The MiG-17 and MiG-21 were designed for point air defence of targets located near their bases.

...The chief difference between our aircraft and theirs was size and weight. The MiGs' low wing loading and high thrust/weight ratio was a great advantage in combat near their own airfield. Our big and heavy jets would be hard pressed because we had to fight the Vietnamese while trying to conserve fuel in order to make it back home.

Our press wrote little about the MiG-17 and sometimes underestimated North Vietnam's air power. But you can take my word for it that the MiG-17 could give you a hard time! ...Of course, you can say that the F-4 can go faster than Mach 2, but when the aircraft is carrying a full load of bombs, drop tanks and other stuff – remember, we flew strike missions, – you will never get Mach 2 out of it! Sure, you're still going fast, but your speed is the speed at which the MiG-17 is at its best, however old it may be. And if it catches up with you, look out! It is a light and amazingly agile aircraft; there's no way the F-4 can outturn it. No matter how good the F-4 is in air-to-air combat, it is no match for the MiGs if you fight the way they do – and that's WW II-style dogfighting.

...The often-quoted fact that we had numerical superiority doesn't really mean that much. Say, you're flying in a group of 36 or 48 aircraft to hit a ground target. You have to get there, you've got everything timed right down to the second and there's no time to tangle with enemy fighters. And when you get there, the air defences will be shooting all they got at you. The enemy is free to choose if he wants to attack, and then to attack straight away or make a deceptive manoeuvre. He may have only a dozen aircraft up against your 48, but he may concentrate on one or two flights, and then it's him who has numerical superiority! A classic example is 20th May 1967. We were escorting a group of F-105s which were raiding a Vietnamese airfield near Kep, and our eight Phantoms were attacked by sixteen MiGs. Talk about numerical superiority!

For the MiGs a strike group was a tough nut to crack. But frequently they did crack it, and even though they were often outnumbered four times, the fight often ended in a draw. So don't ever think that fighting in Vietnam was easy!'

The big problem facing American fighter pilots was that they never studied classic dogfight tactics and thus were unable to use the capabilities of their aircraft to the full. Hence after summing up the results of the first series of air strikes against North Vietnam which ended in 1968 the US Navy established the Navy Fighter Weapons School at NAS Miramar (San Diego, California) under the aegis of Capt Frank W Ault. Popularly known as 'Top Gun', this outfit used the A-4E Skyhawk (aka Mongoose) to simulate the performance of the MiG-17 and the Northrop T-38A Talon to simulate the MiG-21. Naval pilots were trained in air combat manoeuvring (ACM) and gunnery, and the results soon became patently clear. According to American sources, the US Navy's 'kill' ratio improved from 3.7:1 to 8:1 (some sources even state a whopping 13:1!); in contrast, the USAF's 'kill' ratio dropped from 2.5:1 to 1.8:1.

Other figures have been quoted, too. North Vietnamese reports stated that in 1967 the VPAF destroyed 124 American aircraft, losing 60 of its own (which makes for a 2:1 'kill' ratio). According to Western press reports referring to US sources, the VPAF lost 67 aircraft in this period. These included 59 aircraft destroyed by the USAF (17 MiG-21s and 19 MiG-17s shot down by Phantoms plus 23 MiG-17s shot down by Thunderchiefs); the Navy was responsible for 17 'kills' (three MiG-21s and three MiG-17s shot down by F-4s, ten *Fresco-C*s, including at least one J-5, destroyed by F-8s and one MiG-17 by an A-4C).

Other publications (again referring to US sources) state that the USAF alone shot down 60 MiG-17s and 25 MiG-19s in 1965-68; the Navy destroyed 25 *Fresco-C*s, nine *Fishbed-D*s and two An-2s. In 1972-73 the USAF claimed the destruction of 43 MiG-21s and eight MiG-19s, while naval pilots shot down 15 *Fresco-C*s, eight *Fishbed-D*s and one 'unidentified aircraft'.[20] Still, these figures have to be taken with a grain of salt; the *real* 'kill' statistics of both sides will probably be established sometime in the future when all archive data are accessible.

Speaking of 'kills', the MiG-17's fuselage designed in two sections for engine access sometimes produced interesting results. On several occasions a missile flew right up the MiG's jetpipe and the resulting explosion spectacularly took off the entire tail section which tumbled end over end. This happened, eg, on 6th March 1972 in the 'kill' scored by pilot Lt Garry Weigand and WSO Lt (JG) Bill Freckleton in F-4B BuNo 153019/'NL-201'[21] (CVW-15/VF-111, USS *Coral Sea*). Another example was the 'kill' scored by pilot LCDR Jerry 'Devil' Houston and WSO Lt K I Moore in F-4B-14-MC BuNo 150456/'NL-100' (CVW-15/VF-51, USS *Coral Sea*) exactly two months later.

Until the Vietnam War, enemy aircraft shot down were credited to the pilot while the aircraft on which he scored the 'kills' did not come into the picture. In Vietnam, however, a new trend originated. Since assorted MiGs made up the vast majority of the enemy aircraft downed in Vietnam, the aircraft that destroyed them were known as 'MiG killers' and proudly bore their 'kill' markings even when the pilot moved on to another aircraft – in fact, long after the war in many cases.

In another flashback of the Korean War, MiGs really seem to have a way of generating geographical names! The area between Phuc Yen and Kep in the northern part of North Vietnam – both major MiG bases – was soon christened 'MiG Ridge'. (In comparison, the nearby Tam Dao ridge which large formations of Thunderchiefs habitually followed on their way to the target was known as 'Thud Ridge'.)

In the spring of 1972 the USA launched Operation Linebacker II, resuming massive bombardments of North Vietnam after a four-year respite. Now the USAF employed Boeing B-52G Stratofortress strategic bombers which, among other things, were much used for night raids against Hanoi. The Vietnamese soon discovered that the 'Buffs' invariably used the same routes and altitudes for target approach, and they put this knowledge to good use. A MiG-17F would patrol the Hanoi area, keeping a lookout for the B-52s. Having located the bomber stream, the pilot would alert the missile control centre and indicate target range, whereupon the missile crews would simply set the detonators of the S-75 SAMs for the bombers' flight level and blast away at them. Unlike the fighters, the huge B-52s could not take violent evasive action, and 17 bombers were shot down.[22] American POWs watching these battles from the 'Hanoi Hilton' prison recalled that it was a terrifying sight when the stricken B-52 plunged earthwards, blazing and breaking up as it fell.

One of the best VPAF pilots, ace Col Thomb, became a legend among the US pilots in Vietnam. He alternately flew a MiG-17F and a MiG-21PF-V, knocking down American aircraft with considerable success. During the war North Vietnam never officially acknowledged his existence, so he was something of an avenging spirit. The Americans never really believed these disclaimers, and when a camouflaged MiG-17F serialled 3020 Red and a natural metal MiG-21PF-V serialled 4326 Red were publicly displayed in Hanoi, bearing seven and thirteen 'kill' stars respectively, the Americans immediately 'identified' them as Col Thomb's mounts.

On 10th May 1972 an F-4J-35-MC of CVW-9/VF-96 (BuNo 155800/'NG-100') flown by pilot Lt Randy Cunningham and WSO Lt (jg) Willie Driscoll catapulted from USS *Constellation*. They were exceptionally lucky that day, adding two MiG-17Fs to their previous two 'kills' – one MiG-21PF-V and one MiG-17F – scored on another aircraft. This gave them a chance to become the Navy's first aces, and that chance came soon enough. Shortly afterwards they met a lone MiG-17F coming towards them. Cunningham tried a head-on attack at first, intending 'to scare the s**t out of this gomer' – and almost got killed because the MiG opened fire without the slightest hesitation ('his whole nose lit up like a Christmas tree!').

A running fight ensued; Cunningham and Driscoll tried vainly to get into position to launch their two remaining Sidewinders – the MiG kept so close that they could clearly see the pilot, leather helmet, goggles, scarf and all.[23] The Vietnamese pilot 'was flying damn good airplane', as Cunningham put it; not only did he follow the Phantom's vertical manoeuvres, which very few MiG-17 pilots did, but he opened fire whenever the F-4 got out in front of him. Only when the MiG got low on fuel and ran for home did Cunningham manage to get a shot at him. The last-but-one Sidewinder did not appear to do any damage at first but a few seconds later the MiG burst into flames and dived into the ground; the pilot did not attempt to eject and was killed.[24]

Cunningham and Driscoll later claimed they had shot down Col Thomb himself, saying that nobody else could fight so well in so good an aircraft. Whoever the Vietnamese pilot was, he was avenged. On the way back to the ship the Phantom was hit by a SAM near Nam Dinh and all hydraulic systems failed one by one, rendering the aircraft uncontrollable. Fortunately, Cunningham and Driscoll managed to reach the coast before the last system died and ejected safely, joining the Gulf of Tonkin Yacht Club; they were rescued by US Marines helicopters from the USS Okinawa.

Despite all its activity, the VPAF fighter aviation played only a secondary part in fending off US air raids. The mainstay of the North Vietnamese air defences was constituted by SAMs and AAA, including S-60 57mm (2.24in) AA guns aimed by radar.

Having looked at Vietnam, we have to travel back in time again. The longest conflict on the African continent in which the MiG-17 took part was the bitter two-year civil war in Nigeria. In April 1967 a coup d'état occurred in this populous country and the corrupt government was toppled by Gen Irons, C-in-C of the Nigerian Armed Forces. During May, however, Irons was killed in a new coup organised by Col Ojukwu, governor of the Eastern province and one of the leaders of the Ibo tribe. The rebels declared their intention to secede, forming the State of Biafra named after a bight in the Gulf of Guinea. This immediately sparked an all-out war between the separatists and the federal government.

The Biafran separatists had a North American B-25 Mitchell bomber and a couple of Douglas B-26 Invaders; an ex-Nigeria Airways Fokker F.27 Friendship was adapted for use as a bomber and two North American AT-6 Texan trainers for light attack. The B-25 and B-26s were soon destroyed on the ground by Federal Nigerian Air Force (FNAF) raids on Enugu and Port Harcourt. After that, the Biafrans largely relied on Malmö MFI-9B light aircraft converted into makeshift attack aircraft. Flown by mercenary pilots led by the Swedish Count Carl Gustav von Rosen, these aircraft were known locally as Minicons – probably a corruption of 'mini-COIN' (counter-insurgency aircraft).

The FNAF originally used six impressed Nigeria Airways Douglas DC-3s (ex-5N-AAN, 5N-AAP etc) and 12 Czech-supplied Aero L-29 Delfin advanced trainers in the bomber and strike roles respectively. Soon, however, it obtained real combat aircraft from Arab nations supporting the Islamic government in Lagos in its struggle against the Christian Ibo separatists. Egypt was the first to extend help, supplying 41 MiG-17Fs (misidentified as MiG-15s by some sources) and, together with Algeria, six IL-28 bombers throughout the war. Unlike the Beagles, which were flown by Egyptian crews, the MiGs were flown by British and South African mercenary pilots, operating from Benin City.

The war presented no great danger for FNAF fighter pilots and bomber crews, since the Biafran Air Force had no aircraft capable of air-to-air combat. The Minicons could only attack ground targets – which they did with some success, destroying a MiG-17F at Benin City, a Pan African Airways DC-4 at Port Harcourt[25] and a B-26 at Enugu. They also damaged an IL-28 at the latter location, plus a DC-3 at Benin City and a MiG-17F at Port Harcourt (all three aircraft were later repaired). Only one combat loss of an FNAF MiG-17F has been recorded; the aircraft was damaged beyond repair by flak while attacking a rebel gunboat on the Orashi River around July 1969. It was subsequently stripped for spares, thus saving the one damaged at Port Harcourt.

Still, the FNAF lost more than 20 aircraft in the first year of the war, mostly in accidents (only one L-29 was actually shot down by Biafran air defences). Most of these accidents were caused by poor pilot training. For example, FNAF C-in-C Col Shittu Alao was killed in an unsuccessful emergency landing in an L-29 on 15th October 1969 when he lost his way in poor weather and ran out of fuel 72km (45 miles) north of Benin City.

The Nigerian MiG-17Fs performed the usual fighter missions. For example, in February 1969 they escorted ex-Nigeria Airways DC-3s paradropping supplies to a brigade of the 3rd Federal Army Division surrounded by rebel forces at Owerri. The MiG drivers managed to score a few 'kills'. On 9th November 1969 they shot down a Biafran Air Force AT-6 over Binui Province; 20 days later they destroyed two Minicons, tailing them back to their jungle airstrip after a raid and shooting them up on the ground. The Frescos also operated in the fighter-bomber role; to this end some aircraft were fitted with launch rails for eight 76mm rockets.

(Incidentally, when attempts to unblock the surrounded brigade failed and all the DC-3s were grounded for repairs after being hit by flak over Owerri, the Nigerians commandeered a Pan African Airways DC-4 which had landed at Port Harcourt, loaded it with ammunition and ordered the captain to fly to Owerri with an IL-28 providing escort (!). However, the captain cunningly simulated an engine failure and persuaded his captors to turn back, thus probably saving both his life and the aircraft.)

There was also a tragic episode involving the shootdown of a civil airliner. The war had caused famine in Biafra, and the International Committee of the Red Cross (ICRC) organised the delivery of food and medicine to Uli, the sole Biafran airfield which remained intact, using chartered civil aircraft (for example, ex-USAF Boeing C-97s leased from the Swiss airline Balair). With typically bizarre wartime humour, the aircraft carrying humanitarian cargo to Uli were dubbed 'powdermilk bombers' (possibly a play on the 'Berlin candy bombers' taking part in the 1948 Berlin airlift).

However, the Lagos government accused the ICRC of smuggling war materials to the separatists and the FNAF was ordered to shoot down any aircraft heading for Uli. In mid-1969 a pair of MiG-17Fs out on a routine patrol mission intercepted a Swedish Red Cross DC-7B (SE-ERP, c/n 45401) near Port Harcourt at dusk. Ignoring orders to change course and land at Port Harcourt, the airliner attempted to dive into the clouds and get away. Warning shots were also ignored; next thing, one of the MiGs set one of the airliner's engines on fire and the DC-7 blew up in mid-air, crashing near Eket and killing the crew – an American captain and three Swedish crewmen.

In 1967 there was trouble in the Middle East again. MiG-17Fs and Super Mystère B.2s clashed again in the third Arab-Israeli war, commonly referred to as the Six-Day War. The Israelis had been planning this war long and carefully – right down to building five mock Egyptian airbases in the Negev Desert where they constantly practiced raids against the real thing. Within a year all IDF/AF combat squadrons had passed a training course at these facilities.

Building on the results of this training, the Israeli high command developed a 'preemptive attack' plan known as the Moked Plan. The combined air forces of the Arab nations outnumbered the IDF/AF almost three times, so it was decided to destroy them on the ground rather than tangle with them in the air. The first wave of strike aircraft was to attack 19 airfields deep in Egyptian territory, knocking out the aircraft based there, but it was decided to spare the runways at the four bases located on the Sinai Peninsula so that Israeli aircraft could use them once the peninsula had been occupied. The first strike was scheduled between 08:35 and 09:10 when the Egyptian fighters were not expected to be out on combat air patrol and the base commanders usually were not on site. This would be followed by three more waves of strike aircraft which were to destroy the greater part of the Egyptian Air Force on the ground by 14:00. After that, the strike force would be redirected at airbases in Syria, Jordan and Iraq.

By the spring of 1967 it became clear that war was imminent; skirmishes on the Israeli-Syrian border in which both sides used heavy weapons and aircraft were becoming increasingly more frequent. On 17th May Egypt started concentrating troops on the Israeli border; four

By 15:00 *Heyl Ha'avir* aircraft attacked Syrian and Iraqi airbases. In Iraq they annihilated nine MiG-21F-13s, five Hunters and two IL-14s. The fighting in Syria was more intense and the Syrian losses were accordingly higher – 32 MiG-21s, 23 MiG-15*bises* and MiG-17Fs, two IL-28s and three Mil' Mi-4 *Hound* helicopters. Some of the MiG-17Fs were downed while attacking Israeli army positions. The Israelis also lost a few aircraft, including two Mystères shot down over Damascus.

After noon the Egyptians managed to get their AD radars working so that the GCI system could be brought into play. By then the Israeli land offensive had started, and during the next day the remnants of the EAF were put into action against enemy troops. The MiG-17Fs bore the brunt of the air war at this stage, their pilots managing to score a few 'kills'.

In the afternoon of 6th June, Egyptian MiG-17Fs strafed an Israeli tank column advancing towards Ismailia. Super Mystères were summoned to the rescue and the MiG pilots downed one of them. On 9th June two groups of Syrian MiGs attacked another tank column and the airfield at Bir Gafgafa on the Golan Heights, effortlessly shooting down one of the counterattacking Mystères. It was a different story near Ismailia where Israeli Mirage IIICJs shot down three of several MiG-17Fs still hammering away at the advancing troops.

After that, Egyptian MiGs attacked the enemy with a do-or-die resolve that even the Israelis acknowledged. In the final hours of the battle all available aircraft were flung into the fray to cover the Egyptian troops retreating from the Suez Canal. At the cost of 13 fighters shot down the Egyptians managed to check the Israeli onslaught for a few hours.

Meanwhile, up north the Syrians shelled Israeli territory, including IDF/AF bases. Since the Syrian Air Force had taken a less serious mauling compared to the EAF, the Syrian MiGs made a few post-attack reconnaissance sorties over Israel. Those were their last sorties in the war; after that, they stayed on the ground until the ceasefire on 11th June.

In the following years until the next war there were many unconfirmed reports of battles between Egyptian and Israeli aircraft over the Suez Canal; however, the MiG-17Fs did not participate in them. Only in mid-May 1970, when the IDF/AF started bombing targets some 30km (18.6 miles) west of the Suez Canal, did Egypt launch a series of retaliatory strikes against Israeli targets east of the canal; seven *Fresco-Cs* were lost during these sorties.

The Arab nations continued operating the MiG-17F well into the 1970s. By then, however, the Israelis were well familiar with the type and its strengths and weaknesses, especially since two intact MiG-17Fs had fallen into their hands. This mishap occurred when their Syrian pilots

days later Egypt and Israel called a mobilization of the army reserve, and on 22nd May President Nasser declared the Suez Canal closed for Israeli ships.

The Arab nations (Egypt, Syria, Jordan, Lebanon and Iraq) had a total of some 800 combat aircraft at the start of the conflict. Of this total, the EAF had about 100 MiG-21F-13s and MiG-21PFs, 40 MiG-19Ss, 150 MiG-15*bis* and MiG-17F fighters (the proportion is unknown), 35 IL-28s and 30 Tu-16s (including Tu-16KS-1 missile strike aircraft). The fifteen Su-7BMK *Fitter-A* fighter-bombers and Su-7U *Moujik* trainers delivered in April were not yet operational. The Iraqi Air Force had some 30 first-line aircraft in ten squadrons. The MiG-21 made up the backbone of the fighter force, serving alongside the MiG-17F/PF, MiG-19 and Hawker Hunter; there were also a few BAC Strikemaster light attack aircraft and 16 IL-28 and Tu-16 bombers. Syria had about 40 MiG-21PFs and 60 MiG-17Fs. The Royal Jordanian Air Force had 24 Hunter F.6s and sixteen Vampire FB.9 fighter-bombers, which could be augmented by the few Lebanese military aircraft.

The EAF allocated five fighter-bomber squadrons equipped with *Fagot-Bs* and *Fresco-Cs* for close air support of the land forces; these units reported directly to the Army command. Three more squadrons equipped with MiG-17Fs and MiG-19Ss were temporarily relocated to Dumayr AB in Syria, from where they operated until 1975. The remaining MiG-15s, MiG-17s and MiG-19s were to fill the air defence or escort fighter roles.

All Syrian *Fishbeds* were formed into two fighter squadrons, while the MiG-17Fs equipped three attack squadrons. The Jordanian Hunters equipped two fighter squadrons and the Vampires were operated as a separate unit. The Iraqi Air Force would mainly be tasked with bombing raids in the coming war; Iraqi fighters were unlikely to participate, since Iraq was not on very good terms with Syria and Jordan.

The Israelis were quick in taking their decision to wipe out the Arab air forces, and the reason is known. The Egyptian Chief of the General Staff Marshal Amir, EAF C-in-C General Sidik and several other top-ranking officers were arriving at Tamada (Bir Tamada) airbase on the Sinai Peninsula; the opportunity to eliminate all of them at once was too good to be

missed. And even though the Egyptians had been expecting an Israeli attack, they were taken completely by surprise. True, they did patrol the area along the Israeli border with a squadron of MiG-21s and a squadron of MiG-17Fs, but only between 05:00 and 08:00; no one could even suppose that the Israelis would have the nerve to attack in broad daylight.

On the morning of 5th June 1967 a massive assault was launched against Arab airbases. For instance, four Israeli fighters raided Jebel Libni AB, destroying 13 MiG-17Fs and MiG-19Ss; two of the attackers also shot down the pair of MiG-17Fs on quick-reaction alert (QRA) just as it became airborne. It was the same story at El'Arîsh where six *Fresco-Cs* were destroyed on the ground; another MiG-17F was lost in a dogfight with *Heyl Ha'avir* 105th Sqn fighters. On the credit side, several MiG-21s managed to scramble from Hurgada and shot down two Super Mystère B.2s bombing Abu Sueir.

During the day another flight of four Super Mystère B.2s led by the now famous Capt Yaakov Nevo attacked El Qabrit AB. Leaving several MiG-15s and MiG-17Fs and two IL-14T *Crate* transports burning on the ground, they made for home at low altitude. A pair of MiG-17Fs scrambled and gave chase; attempting to get away, two of the Israeli fighters lost control and collided with the ground.

The Israelis met almost no resistance. Only at Luxor, where the memory of the French air strikes of 1956 was still fresh, the Egyptians met the attackers with a hail of AA fire. The gunners managed to shoot down one Sud-Ouest SO 4050 Vautour, but little good did it do because the bomber fell squarely on the flight line, destroying four MiG-17Fs.

At 10:20 came the first retaliatory action on the part of the Arabs: Jordanian aircraft attacked the Israeli section of Jerusalem and Kefar Sirkin AB where four fighters were present. By 14:00, however, all but three of the 24 Jordanian Hunters had been destroyed; some were shot down while others crashed while attempting to land on runways cratered by Israeli bombardments. This effectively ended the air war on this front. After this, the action shifted north where a lone EAF Tu-16 bombed the coastal town of Netanya in central Israel and was shot down by the air defences.

landed on the Israeli auxiliary airfield at Bezel near the Lebanese border because of a navigation error (possibly in 1970).

It should be noted that the Syrian Air Force had stepped up its activities in that area, especially after Israel invaded Lebanon on 12th May 1970. That day a group of *Heyl Ha'avir* A-4Es headed into Lebanon was attacked by six MiG-17Fs. The MiGs had two of the Skyhawks pinned down to the ground and ready for killing, and these would almost certainly have been shot down, had not the Mirage IIICJs flying top cover descended on the attackers, destroying three of them. In the afternoon the Syrian MiG-17Fs twice strafed Israeli troops, suffering no losses this time. These attacks caused the Israelis to concentrate on hunting Syrian aircraft, which left fewer aircraft available for close air support.

While Prince Norordom Sihanouk was still in power, Cambodian MiG-17Fs were used to protect Cambodia's neutrality in the Vietnam War. After the March 1970 uprising, however, the National Khmer Aviation (NKA) began using them against South Vietnamese FNL partisans making raids into Kampuchean territory. For instance, on 7th April 1970 they attacked FNL positions in the captured village of Thai Phu, some 160km (99 miles) southeast of Phnom Penh and 16km (9.9 miles) from the Vientamese border.

The MiGs frequently operated from USAF bases in South Vietnam alongside USAF Phantoms. The two types made an interesting comparison when parked together – the massive F-4 was nearly twice as big! According to some reports, NKA MiG-17Fs were even used in combat against VPAF aircraft over North Vietnam ('MiG eat MiG'?). Most of them, however, were destroyed on the ground by FNL partisans on 21st January 1971.

Uganda used its MiG-17Fs in a border conflict with Tanzania in 1972. Unfortunately, little is recorded about this war.

1973 saw the outbreak of yet another Arab-Israeli war known as the Holy Day War, or Yom Kippur War (6-24th October). The Arabs were the first to attack. The day was chosen carefully: firstly, 6th October was a Jewish religious holiday, Yom Kippur (Atonement Day), and the Arabs knew well that the Israelis do not expect to fight on holidays. Secondly, 6th October was the tenth day of the holy month of Ramadan. Legend has it that on this day the prophet Mohammed began preparations for the battle of Badr, which he won and entered Mecca in triumph ten days later. Hence the Arab offensive was code-named Operation *Badr*.

After a massive shelling the Egyptians broke through the supposedly impregnable Bar Lev line along the Suez Canal and secured beachheads on its eastern bank. At the same time, the Syrians attacked Israeli positions on the Golan Heights. In both cases the land offensive was supported by strike aircraft (mainly Su-7BMKs and the perennial MiG-17Fs). The

Syrian Air Force was most active in using its surviving *Fresco-Cs*, mainly against ground targets on the Golan Heights and IDF/AF bases in Galilee; by then, only about a third of the original 60 aircraft remained. The EAF used its MiG-17Fs against the Bar Lev line. Its age notwithstanding, the small and agile *Fresco* was a bigger challenge for the Israeli air defences than the larger and faster *Fitter*.

The Israelis tried to use the tactic which had worked well during the Six-Day War – ie, destroy the enemy's air forces on the ground. This time, however, they were in for a disappointment. The Egyptians and Syrians now kept their aircraft in hardened aircraft shelters (HASs) capable of taking a hit of a medium-calibre bomb and the air defences around their bases were reinforced considerably.

Then the Israelis tried bombing the runways at Egyptian and Syrian bases and mining them with the help of submunitions pods. For example, on 11th October eight *Heyl Ha'avir* F-4Es attacked Mezze AB near Damascus, cratering the runway in six places; it took the Syrians six hours to repair it. The air defences were taken by surprise and the Phantoms suffered no losses; however, when they tried a second raid later in the day they were met by a hail of AA fire and had to turn back.

Next morning six F-4Es made another attack on Mezze, dropping two bombs on the runway which took three hours to repair. Within the next four days the Israelis raided the base three or four times a day. They succeeded in destroying one UTI-MiG-15, one MiG-17F, one Mi-8T *Hip-C* helicopter and one Antonov An-24B *Coke* airliner (YK-ANB; c/n 87304204?)[26] parked in the open, and two more *Frescos* were damaged by unguided rockets which flew into open HAS doors. However, this cost them six Phantoms shot down by AA fire, and bombing accuracy was greatly reduced because of the need to take evasive action.

The Syrians quickly discovered that the Phantoms invariably used the same tactic, approaching the bases at ultra-low level and following canyons to escape detection by radar, and they took appropriate countermeasures. They posted observers equipped with telephones on the directions from which the Phantoms were most likely to appear, and when the Phantoms reached their target the AA gunners were ready and eager.

During the 18-day war the Syrian Air Force brigade equipped with Su-7BMKs, Su-20 *Fitter-Cs* and MiG-17Fs lost a total of 31 aircraft. These included 12 MiGs, three of which were shot down by HAWK anti-aircraft missiles, four by AAA and shoulder-launched SAMs, three more by IDF/AF Mirage IIICJs and the other two by 'friendly fire'. On the credit side, MiG-17F pilots shot down two Mirages; Lt Khaled who scored the first 'kill' became the first Hero of the Syrian Arab Republic.[27]

Some combat and non-combat losses were caused by the (still) poor training level of Arab pilots. For example, some sources claim that

four EAF MiG-17Fs collided with the ground while attacking Israeli HAWK batteries.

The success of the MiG-17F in the Yom Kippur War was one of the major events in the type's combat career, allowing it to remain in service for another ten years or so. Interestingly, in May 1976 the British magazine *Air International* questioned the advisability of designing specialised attack aircraft, given that the obsolete MiG-17F could still attack targets on the battlefield without the benefit of an automatic weapons control system, and without sustaining excessive losses at that.

In June 1976 Sudan extended aid to the rebel Eritrea province which was seeking independence from Ethiopia. Thus, two different kinds of F-5 met in combat over Eritrea – Ethiopian Air Force Northrop F-5A/E Tigers were up against Sudanese Shenyang F-5s (MiG-17Fs). Several F-5s (the Chinese kind) were shot down or damaged by the Ethiopian fighters.[28] A ceasefire between Ethiopia and Eritrea was agreed in March 1978.

In July 1977, while still at war with the Eritrean Liberation Front, Ethiopia clashed with Somalia in a territorial dispute over the Ogaden area. Both sides had Soviet-supplied MiG-17s, so again it was a case of 'MiG eat MiG'. According to Ethiopian sources, more than 23 Somalian MiGs were destroyed in the first six moths of the war. The Soviet Union supported Ethiopia in this conflict – and, of course, promptly 'fell out' with Somalia as a result.

In 1988-90, Somalian Aeronautical Corps MiG-17s were used by dictator Siad Barre in his attempts to stomp out rebellion in the northern regions of Somalia. The aircraft operated out of Hargeisa along with Shenyang F-6Cs (MiG-19Ss) against Somali National Movement insurgents. However, when things got too hot for comfort, Barre fled the country in 1991 and in the ensuing anarchy the Somalian Aeronautical Corps effectively ceased to exist.

MiG-17s and MiG-17Fs were used by the Afghan Republican Air Force against Mujahideen rebels during the civil war in Afghanistan. However, the morale of Najibullah's pilots was low and defections not uncommon. On 25th March 1983 a MiG-17 pilot defected to Pakistan, crash-landing at Mushlab airfield.

The last conflict in which the MiG-17 took part with absolute certainty[29] is the civil war in Mozambique, where Mozambique People's Air Force (FPA) *Fresco-A/Cs* were in action against the so-called Mozambique Resistance Movement backed by the South African Republic. No combat losses have been reported. However, on 14th June 1989 a MiG-17F crashed while attempting to land in a storm, killing the pilot; the exact location of the crash is unknown. On 8th July 1981 the pilot of an FPA MiG-17 coded 23 Black defected to South Africa; surprisingly enough, the aircraft was later returned.

In all nations operating the MiG-17 it was rated highly by its pilots. Its chances in a dogfight with other fighter types depended chiefly on pilot skill and tactics.

MiG-17 Operators Worldwide

The MiG-17 served with the air forces of more than 40 nations, including all of the socialist states, whether members of the Warsaw Pact or not. MiG-17s – often second-hand aircraft – were also operated by many third-world nations. According to *Interavia*, more than 4,000 *Frescos* were still operational around the world in late 1978.

style insignia used during the Afghan War (a red star on a white roundel edged in green, red and black), indicating that the type remained in service at least until 1982. Indeed, a survey of the world's air forces published in *Flight International* says the Afghan Air Force still had 30-plus *Frescos* in late 1991!

AFGHANISTAN

The Afghan Republican Air Force (*Afghan Hanai Qurah*) took delivery of its first MiG-17s in 1957. The aircraft were based at Mazar-i-Sharif, equipping Afghanistan's first air defence fighter unit, and initially flown by Soviet instructors. By 1967 the Afghan Republican Air Force had 32 MiG-17Fs equipping four squadrons; by 1979 this number reportedly increased to 50 aircraft.

Only five aircraft, MiG-17Fs '102 Black' and '107 Black' (the latter aircraft belonged to the 335th SAP' at Kandahar) and late-production MiG-17s serialled 104 Red (335th SAP), 109 Blue and 111 Blue, have been identified to date; MiG-17Fs serialled 32, 61, 97,112, 127 and 136 through 138 have also been reported. The latter aircraft was preserved in some museum, possibly the Armed Forces Museum in Kabul.

The *Fresco* was the main combat aircraft of the Kabul government in the civil war which followed the April Revolution of 1978 (and ultimately led to the Afghan War) until superseded by more modern Mikoyan types. Col Valeriy I Ablazov (retd.), a former Soviet military advisor in Afghanistan, recalled, '*When we arrived in Afghanistan and saw MiG-17s and IL-28s taking off at the local bases, it was like travelling several decades back in a time machine. Here, these types turned out to be the best choice for operations both in the mountains and in the desert. The pilots and tech staff for them were trained by the local flying school. ...The MiG-17s were used as interceptors for the air defence system and practiced live firing, while the IL-28s were flown in visual meteorological conditions, once per month at the most, and used to put on a show of force at military parades. When the intensity of air force operations began increasing, the Afghan leaders requested that our factories build an additional batch of these aircraft and send more instructors for pilot training. However, it was quickly established that all the tooling had ben long since thrown away and the MiG-17 was not even operated by the DOSAAF any longer, and the idea was dropped.*

*...In order to speed up the transition to the MiG-21 our instructors, referring to operational experience at the Chernigov flying school, recommended that pilots be trained directly on this type without using the MiG-17 as a stepping stone. But the Afghan commanders' reply was a firm no. Once we were standing with Afghan Air Force C-in-C Mir Ghausuddin somewhere in the mountains, watching a group of Pushtu nomads passing by. The Commander said, 'Your kids are born to the babbling of a TV set, they can turn on the lights and the tape recorder and play with the steering wheel of a car before they're old enough to talk. When they grow up, they are not scared to let go of one control stick and grab hold of another. **Our** kids are just letting go of a donkey's tail or mother's skirt, and you want to put them into a modern aircraft? Get real. Don't push us and don't hurry'.*'

Afghan Air Force *Frescos* mostly flew in natural metal finish, though MiG-17 '104 Red' had a two-tone green camouflage. MiG-17F '102 Black' and MiG-17 '104 Red' had the early-style solid red roundels introduced immediately after the revolution, while the others had the later-

ALBANIA

According to press reports, the Albanian People's Republic Air Force (*Forcat Ushtarake Ajore Shquipëtare*, later renamed *Aviacione Ushtarak Shquipëtare*) took delivery of an initial ten Soviet-built MiG-17s in the mid-50s. When Albania severed diplomatic relations with the USSR in 1962, China began extending help; starting in 1965, an estimated ten Shenyang F-5 (MiG-17F) day fighters and an unspecified number of F-5A (MiG-17PF) all-weather interceptors was delivered. (In some sources the Albanian name has been rendered *Aviatika Militar e Republika Popullóre e Shqipërise*.)

In 1971 the Albanian Air Force had about four ground attack squadrons flying the F-5, although the type was being augmented and supplanted by the Shenyang F-6 (licence-built MiG-19S). The latter was being transferred from fighter units re-equipping with the Guizhou F-7A (licence-built MiG-21F-13).

According to the *Euromil – Military Air Arms in Europe* handbook, by 1995 Albania had 23 Soviet-built MiG-17Fs and 12 F-5s in service, plus at least twelve F-5A interceptors operated by the 1875th Regiment/1st Sqn at Kucovë AB near Berat (!?). *Air International* provides a much more realistic figure – eleven F-5s flown by the 1875th Regt (since redesignated the 4030th Regt) and no mention of radar-equipped F-5As! Incidentally, the type has worked up an absolutely fantastic safety record with the Albanian Air Force: in 30 years of service, only one aircraft had been lost in an accident.

According to the same handbook, 35 Shenyang FT-5 advanced trainers were purchased to bridge the gap between the UTI-MiG-15 and the MiG-19. However, *Air International* says that only eight FT-5s (obstinately referred to by both sources as 'MiG-17UTI'!) were delivered in 1961 and six were still in service by December 1992. Of these, two aircraft were operated by the 2nd and 3rd Sqns of the 1875th (now 4030th) Regt and the remaining four aircraft by the 5646th (now 4010th) Regt/1st Sqn of the Zadrima AB near Lezha.

Registration	C/n	Version	Remarks
211	?	MiG-17F (F-5?)	
212	?	MiG-17F (F-5?)	
215	?	MiG-17F (F-5?)	
221	?	MiG-17F (F-5?)	
230	?	MiG-17F (F-5?)	
234	?	MiG-17F (F-5?)	
241	?	MiG-17F (F-5?)	
4-01	?	MiG-17F (F-5?)	1875th Regt.
4-10	1707?	MiG-17F (F-5?)	1875th Regt; c/n read off poor-quality photo.
4-14	?	MiG-17F (F-5?)	1875th Regt.
4-16	?	MiG-17F (F-5?)	1875th Regt.
4-21	?	MiG-17F (F-5?)	1875th Regt.
4-25	?	F-5A	1875th Regt/1st Sqn.
4-37	?	F-5A	1875th Regt/1st Sqn.

4-39	?	F-5A	1875th Regt/1st Sqn.
4-40	?	F-5A	1875th Regt/1st Sqn.
4-65	?	FT-5	1875th Regt/1st Sqn.
8-08	?	FT-5	5646th Reg/1st Sqn.
8-09	?	FT-5	5646th Regt.
8-12	?	FT-5	5646th Regt.
8-31	?	FT-5	5646th Regt/1st Sqn.

A survey of the world's air forces in *Flight International* shows that 35-plus F-4s (MiG-17s) were in service in late 1991; however, Albania has never been known to operate the *Fresco-A*.

ALGERIA

The Algerian Air Force (*Al Quwwat al Jawwiya al Jaza'eriya/Force Aérienne Algerienne*) took delivery of 60 MiG-17Fs (enough to equip three squadrons) in the 1960s. By 1979 they were relegated to the ground attack role and reportedly replaced by MiG-23s. According to *Interavia*, the Algerian Air Force had a handful of MiG-17Fs in use as advanced trainers alongside MiG-21U *Mongols* in early 1987; the total number of both types was stated as 20 but the proportion is unknown. However, *Flight International* claims that more than 50 MiG-17Fs were operated as trainers in late 1991.

ANGOLA

There have been conflicting reports of MiG-17 operations in this African country. Some reports say the Soviet Union supplied ten *Frescos* – almost certainly MiG-17Fs – to the Angolan Air Force (FAA – *Força Aérea Angolana*) by 1976 and the fighters were initially flown by Cuban pilots.

Other sources give a different account. Soon after Angola gained independence from Portugal it was torn apart by civil war as three political factions scrambled for power. These were the UNITA (*União Nacional por Independencia Total de Angola*) led by Dr. Jonas Savimbi (and backed by the South African Republic), the pro-Zaïrean FNLA (*Frente Nacional de Liberacão de Angola*) and the ruling MPLA (*Movimento Popular de Liberacão de Angola*). Finding itself in an embattled position, the MPLA turned to Cuba for help. Among other things, Cuba assisted in establishing the Angolan Air Force, donating three UTI-MiG-15s, eight MiG-17Fs and an unspecified number of MiG-21F-13s. The two latter types formed the backbone of the FAA until the early 1980s when they were succeeded by more modern types such as the MiG-23MF; however, at least eight were reportedly still operational in late 1991.

The MiG-17Fs were based near the Angolan capital of Luanda. Four aircraft serialled C21 through C24 have been identified to date. C-23 (*sic* – the serials were applied differently) flew in natural metal finish with a black serial, while C24 had a two-tone camouflage and a red serial. The C prefix to the serials means *caça* (fighter); by comparison, Angolan Air Force trainer serials are prefixed I for *instrução*, helicopter serials are prefixed H etc

AUSTRALIA

At least three Polish Air Force MiG-17s were sold to warbird collectors down under in the early 1990s. Unfortunately, little is known of the civil identities of these aircraft.

Registration	C/n	Version	Remarks
VH-ALG	1J 04-34	Lim-6*bis*	Ex-PWL 434, acquired 1989. Owned by Randal W MacFarlane (Brisbane, Qld, d/d 3-89), later Hockey Treloar (Bankstown, NSW).
VH-...	1C 16-19	Lim-5	Ex-PWL 1619, acquired 1992. Owned by Ian Kenny, stored pending restoration.

VH-...	1F 01-02	Lim-6*bis*	Ex-PWL 102, acquired 1989. Owned by Randal W MacFarlane, later Jack McDonald (Caboolture, Qld).

BANGLADESH

The Bangladesh Air Wing (*Biman Bahini*) reportedly operated a few Shenyang F-5s and FT-5s supplied by China. While the information concerning F-5s is extremely doubtful, one FT-5 serialled 1724 (c/n 1724) has been identified; the aircraft was operated by the unit based at Tezgaon AB near Dacca (Dhaka).

BULGARIA

The Bulgarian Air Force (BVVS – *Bolgarski Voyenno Vozdooshni Seeli*; also reported as BVVS – *Bolgarski Vozdooshni Voyski*) operated both MiG-17Fs and MiG-17PFs which began replacing the *Fagot-A/B* in the air defence units in 1955-56 (some sources state the first *Frescos* arrived in 1953). Two of the *Fresco-Ds* were Polish-built Lim-5Ps (c/ns 1D 06-37 and 1D 06-38). In 1963 the 26th ORAP (*Otdelen Razuznavatelen Aviopolk* – independent reconnaissance regiment) took delivery of a small number of MiG-17R reconnaissance aircraft equipped with AFA-39 cameras.

Six squadrons of MiG-17s were reportedly on strength. In the early 1960s the *Frescos* were replaced by MiG-19S *Farmer-Cs* and MiG-19P *Farmer-Bs* and transferred to ground attack units. However, the *Farmer's* low reliability and high attrition rate caused the 21st IAP (*Iztrebitelen Aviopolk* – fighter regiment) at Uzundzhovo AB to reconvert to the proven MiG-17F/PF.

According to *Euromil*, sixty-odd MiG-17Fs and MiG-17PFs were still operational in 1995. Known examples are listed below.

Serial	C/n	Version	Remarks
12	?	MiG-17PF	Camouflaged.
14	?	MiG-17F	
16	4616?	MiG-17F	
21 Red	7137	MiG-17PF	Camouflaged. Preserved Bulgarian AF Museum (Graf Ignatiev AB, Plovdiv).
22	?	MiG-17PF	Preserved Bulgarian AF Museum.
30 Red	?	MiG-17PF	Preserved Bulgarian AF Museum.
31	?	MiG-17F	
32	?	MiG-17F	
33	?	MiG-17F	
34	?	MiG-17F	
35	?	MiG-17F	
38	?	MiG-17F	
71 Red	7207	MiG-17F?	Preserved Bulgarian AF Museum; reported as MiG-17PF but c/n too high for this!
72	?	MiG-17F	Preserved Dobroslavtsi AB museum.
100	?	MiG-17F	Preserved Bulgarian AF Academy Museum (Dolna Metropoliya AB, Pleven).
101	?	MiG-17F	
126 Red	?	MiG-17 (late)	Camouflaged; wfu Dolna Metropoliya AB.
136	?	MiG-17F	Preserved Dobroslavtsi AB museum.
147	?	MiG-17F	Preserved Bulgarian AF Academy Museum.
150	7138	MiG-17F?	Preserved Bulgarian AF Museum; reported as MiG-17PF but c/n too high for this!
152	?	MiG-17F	
181	?	MiG-17F	
261	?	MiG-17F	
299	?	MiG-17F	
323	?	MiG-17F	
374	?	MiG-17F	
379	?	MiG-17F	

A line-up of Afghan Air Force/335th SAP MiG-17Fs at Kandahar. *World Air Power*

An 1875th Regiment aircraft, FT-5 4-65. Judging by the Chinese characters on the forward fuselage, the aircraft may have been acquired secondhand from the PLAAF. *Key Publishing Group*

Camouflaged Bulgarian AF MiG-17F '150 Red', also preserved at Graf Ignatiev AB. *Keith Dexter*

CAMBODIA (KAMPUCHEA)

During the reign of Prince Norodom Sihanouk who was on good terms with the Soviet Union, Cambodia received Soviet weapons as a gift from Nikita S Khruschchov. Among other things, the Royal Khmer Aviation (RKhA) operated a number of MiG-17Fs, the first three of which were delivered on 8th February 1964. Seventeen were reportedly in service in 1967; known examples were serialled 0612, 0742, 0760, 0767, 1024, 1721 and 7205 (the serials probably matched the c/ns). The aircraft formed the backbone of the RKhA together with a small number of MiG-19S *Farmer-Cs*.

After the March 1970 pro-American uprising which forced Prince Sihanouk to leave the country the air arm was renamed National Khmer Aviation (NKA). The original blue-outlined red roundels with an image of the Angkor Wat temple gave way to insignia strongly reminiscent of the USAF 'stars and bars'; the blue disc in the centre had a red upper left quadrant bearing the Angkor Wat image with three small white stars immediately to the right of it. MiG-17F '1024' thus marked was briefly evaluated by the USAF and the South Vietnam Air Force at Pleiku (Play Cu) AB in South Vietnam before being destroyed on the ground by a North Vietnamese mortar attack on 24th April 1970.

Together with MiG-15*bises* and Fouga CM.170-1 Magisters, the MiG-17Fs equipped a single fighter-bomber squadron. Most of them were destroyed on 22nd January 1971 when South Vietnamese FNL partisans raided two airbases near Phnom Penh, including Pochentong (which is now Phnom Penh's international airport). The surviving aircraft equipped a fighter-bomber unit in June 1971 but were eventually rendered unserviceable by spares shortages and hastily replaced by American fighters.

CHINA (PEOPLE'S REPUBLIC OF CHINA)

According to some reports, the People's Liberation Army Air Force (PLAAF, or *Chung-kuo Shen Min Taie-Fang-Tsun Pu-tai*) took delivery of its first Soviet-built *Fresco-As* (known locally as the J-4) and *Fresco-Cs* in the mid-50s. Licence production of the MiG-17F (J-5) started in 1956 and the type served with the PLAAF and the People's Liberation Army Naval Air Force (PLANAF) in large numbers, equipping at least 20 fighter regiments. Known aircraft are listed below.

Serial	C/n	Version	Remarks
✚0101 Red*	0101?	J-5	First production J-5. Preserved Datangshan museum.
✚0102 Red?	0102?	J-5	
✚0103 Red	0103?	J-5	
✚0201 Red	0201?	J-5	
✚0202 Red	0202?	J-5	
016 Red	?	J-5A	
063 Red	2705?	J-5	C/n also reported as 2507. Sold to the USA/private owner as N1VC.
506 White	?	JJ-5	'August 1' display team, red/natural metal colour scheme.
507 White	?	JJ-5	'August 1' display team, red/natural metal colour scheme, non-standard wraparound windscreen *sans* bulletproof windshield. Preserved Datangshan museum.
509 White	?	JJ-5	'August 1' display team, red/natural metal colour scheme; unconfirmed (drawing only).
510 White	?	JJ-5	'August 1' display team, red/natural metal colour scheme.
511 White	?	JJ-5	'August 1' display team, red/natural metal colour scheme.
512 White	?	JJ-5	'August 1' display team, red/natural metal colour scheme.
513 White	?	JJ-5	'August 1' display team, red/natural metal colour scheme.
518 White	?	JJ-5	'August 1' display team, red/natural metal colour scheme.
0110 Red	?	J-5	
0268 Red	?	J-5	
0327 Red	?	J-5	
0362 Red	?	J-5	
0363 Red	?	J-5	
0364 Red	?	J-5	
0365 Red	?	J-5	
0537 Red	?	J-5	
0539 Red	?	J-5	
1030 Red	?	J-5	Red upper fin section.
1033 Red	?	J-5	Red upper fin section.
1049 Red	?	MiG-17 (J-4)	
1059 Red	?	J-5	
1063 Red	?	J-5	
1228 Red	?	J-5	
1229 Red	?	J-5	
1232 Red	?	J-5	
1248 Red	?	MiG-17 (J-4)	
1340 Red	?	MiG-17 (J-4)	
1441 Red	?	MiG-17 (J-4)	
1599 Red	?	J-5	
1623 Red	?	J-5A	
1849 Red	?	J-5A	
2074 Red	?	J-5A	Preserved Datangshan museum, with 2 AAM pylons.
2218 Red	?	JJ-5	Preserved Datangshan museum.
4332 Red	?	JJ-5	
4333 Red	?	JJ-5	
4334 Red	?	JJ-5	
4336 Red	?	JJ-5	
6537 Red	?	J-5	
6539 Red	?	J-5	
6717 Red	?	JJ-5	Preserved Datangshan museum, damaged nose gear and port wing.
7523 Red	?	J-5	
7526 Red	?	J-5	
7530 Red	?	J-5	
8079 Red	?	J-5	Preserved Datangshan museum.
11606 Red	?	J-5A	
11607 Red	?	J-5A	
11608 Red	?	J-5A	
11609 Red	?	J-5A	
12461 Red	?	MiG-17 (J-4)	Preserved in Taiwanese (?) museum.
13288 Red	?	J-5	Preserved Datangshan museum in anti-corrosion compound.
30474 Red	?	MiG-17 (J-4)	Preserved Datangshan museum.
31482 Red	5735	MiG-17 (J-4)	Preserved Datangshan museum.
31580 Red	5821	J-5	Preserved Datangshan museum.
31581 Red	5738	MiG-17 (J-4)	Preserved Datangshan museum.
31583 Red	5846	J-5	Preserved Datangshan museum.
31584 Red	5753	J-5	
31585 Red	5830	J-5	
31586 Red	?	J-5?	Exact version unknown. Preserved Datangshan museum.
31681 Red	5835	J-5	Preserved Datangshan museum.
31682 Red	5734	J-5	
31685 Red	5713	MiG-17 (J-4)	Preserved Datangshan museum.
51230 Red	?	J-5	Preserved Datangshan museum.
51623 Red	?	J-5A	
51694 Red	?	J-5	
63041 Red†	?	J-5	01†
63043 Red	?	J-5	03?
63243 Red	?	J-5	23
63540 Red	?	JJ-5	50?
63543 Red	?	JJ-5	53?

63546 Red	?	JJ-5	56?
63549 Red	?	JJ-5	59
63640 Red	?	JJ-5	60
63642 Red	?	JJ-5	62?
63646 Red	?	JJ-5	66?
63649 Red	?	JJ-5	69?
63740 Red	?	JJ-5	70?
63748 Red	?	JJ-5	78?
86501 Red	?	J-5	Unconfirmed (drawing only).
CAC 0133	?	JJ-5	Chengdu Aircraft Corporation demonstrator.
none	?	JJ-5	Preserved Datangshan museum, blue/white display colour scheme, damaged forward canopy section.
none	02	J-5A	Prototype.
not known	54211566	MiG-17 (J-4)	Sold to the USA/private owner as N6180M.
not known	54211214	MiG-17 (J-4)	Sold to the USA/private owner as N6351J.
not known	0704	MiG-17 (J-4)	Sold to the USA/private owner as N306DM.
not known	1327	JJ-5	Sold to the USA/private owner as N69PP.

* ⊕ is the hieroglyph 'Chung' making up the first part of the country's name in Chinese.
† As noted earlier, the first two digits may be a code denoting one of the eleven defence districts, the fourth digit a unit code, while the third and fifth digits make up the individual number of the aircraft in the unit. Adding weight to this theory, on some PLAAF Mikoyan fighters the third and fifth digits are repeated in small characters under the starboard wing root (eg, 63243 Red = 23, 63549 Red = 59 etc).

Top left: **J-5 '30474 Red' preserved at the Chinese Army museum in Peking.** Helmut Walther

Top right: **Apparently the entire personnel of a PLAAF unit rallying before their J-5s (bedecked in Chinese characters for the occasion), with all the drums and whistles and pictures of Mao Tse-tung. The aircraft have non-standard two-digit serials on the fins.** Yefim Gordon archive

Centre: **Nay, folks, it ain't rusty. Coated in anti-corrosion compound (some of it already removed), J-5 '13288 Red' is one of the less lucky aircraft preserved at the PLAAF museum in Datangshan.** Helmut Walther

Bottom: **Busy scene at a PLAAF airbase choked with J-5s. Some of the aircraft are apparently brand-new and have no serials applied yet.** Yefim Gordon archive

Below: **A PLAAF J-5A returns from a night training sortie; more *Fresco-Ds* are coming up behind.** China Aircraft

An estimated 3,500 to 4,500 aircraft, including some 1,700 J-5s/J-5As/JJ-5s, were in service with the PLAAF in the 1960s and 1970s. Of these, about 100 MiG-17 derivatives were still active in 1997.

When the MiG-17 was replaced by the licence-built MiG-19S (J-6) and its locally-developed versions, Chinese *Frescos* were put into storage. Unlike the more affluent Western nations which were extremely efficient when it came to scrapping obsolete military hardware (with the result that many warbirds are now nowhere to be found), China was reluctant to throw away its old fighters. Huge stockpiles of vintage MiGs were built up in the belief they might come in handy one day – and they did. Starting in 1986, ex-Chinese MiG-17s found their way to private operators in the West (notably in the USA).

CONGO-BRAZZAVILLE

In late 1991 the Congo Air Force (*Force Aérienne Congolaise*) reportedly had a single squadron of *Frescos* (eight aircraft). Often reported in error as MiG-17Fs, they were in fact late-production *Fresco-As*. By 1991 all of them had been withdrawn from use at Pointe-Noire (Agostinho Neto airport). Known aircraft are serialled 106 Black, 112 Black, 118 Black and 120 Black.

CUBA

After the 1st March 1959 revolution which toppled the Batista regime the newly-established Cuban Air Force (FAR – *Fuerza Aérea Revolucionaria*) had only a handful of WW II-vintage aircraft of US and British origin with which to fight the anti-Communists opposition based in the USA. It was these aircraft which helped foil the notorious Bay of Pigs invasion in March 1961. Soon, however, they were replaced by Soviet-supplied combat jets; at the same time, FAR pilots received jet training in the USSR.

In keeping with a Soviet-American accord aimed at resolving the Cuban missile crisis the Soviet Union withdrew the 33 (42?) IL-28N nuclear-capable tactical bombers briefly deployed to Cuba in 1962.[2] This left the FAR with thirty-odd MiG-17s, plus similar numbers of MiG-15*bis* fighter-bombers and MiG-19 interceptors, as its main strike element. Apparently, however, fighter deliveries continued as a sort of compensation, since 75 MiG-17s were reportedly in service by 1971.

In the 1970s the *Fresco* was likewise transferred to the fighter-bomber role when MiG-21s and MiG-23s displaced it from front-line service; up

Left: **A line of Congolese MiG-17 *Fresco-A*s in rather dilapidated condition; the old-style *Force Aérienne Congolaise* roundels have all but disappeared.** *Air Forces Monthly*

Above left: **0201, an early-production MiG-17PF with RP-1 radar, at the Czech military museum at Prague-Kbely (VM VHÚ). The radome colour varied widely on Czech AF *Fresco-D*s.** *Létectvi + Kosmonautika*

Above right: **Another CzAF MiG-17PF with white radomes, possibly a 3. SLP machine.** Yefim Gordon archive

Left: **Lim-5P (MiG-17PF) '430 Red' (c/n 1D 02-01) sitting in front of a floodlit hangar.** Yefim Gordon archive

Left: **Lim-5P '460 Red' (c/n 1D 01-07) taxies out for a sortie.** Yefim Gordon archive

to 80 MiG-17Fs were in service with four squadrons. In 1969-71 the FAR reportedly took delivery of an additional 18 *Frescos* (probably MiG-17Fs) which were used as fighter-bombers. According to *Flight International*, the FAR still operated more than 18 MiG-17s in the ground attack role in late 1991.

Only one Cuban MiG-17, a late-production *Fresco-A* serialled 232 Blue, has been identified to date. In 1969 this aircraft, reportedly armed with anti-tank guided missiles on underwing launchers, was used for maritime patrol duties against boats inserting anti-Castro sabotage groups. (In reality 232 Blue was almost certainly armed with ordinary unguided rockets, since it is extremely improbable that it could be fitted with missile guidance equipment.)

CZECHOSLOVAKIA

Czechoslovakia was one of the first foreign nations to receive the MiG-17. Yet the Czechoslovak Air Force (CzAF or ČVL *Československé Vojenské Létectvo*) was not a major operator of the type. First, two MiG-17Fs[3] were delivered in November 1955 as pattern aircraft with a view to starting licence production at Aero-Vodochody (pronounced '*Vodokhod*y') 20km (12.4 miles) north of Prague. However, the plan did not materialise and the two aircraft became the personal hacks of Maj Gen Jozef Kúkel and Deputy Defence Minister (Air Force and Air Defence Force) Lt Gen Josef Vosáhlo.

The first aircraft (c/n 0872) had been manufactured in March 1952 and placed in storage after a few checkout flights. It was not until mid-October that the crated fighter arrived at Prague-Kbely AB and was unpacked and reassembled at the Kbely overhaul plant (LOK – Letecké Opravny Kbely). This was no small task, as someone had neglected to include the assembly manuals etc and assembling the fighter was pretty much a 'seat of the pants' thing. Nevertheless, the MiG-17F was duly assembled by 25th October and reflown a few days later. The ARK-5 ADF promptly went unserviceable on 29th October and a substitute unit had to be hastily assembled and fitted so that the aircraft could be delivered to VÚ 5957 (*vyzkumný útvar* – test unit) and Lt Gen Vosáhlo on 1st November as planned.

Nor was the MiG-17PF (known locally as the S-104)[4] built in Czechoslovakia, since the Czech authorities decided it was more advisable to build the supersonic MiG-19S and MiG-19P. The former type eventually entered production at Aero-Vodochody as the S-105 and formed the backbone of the fighter element until the CzAF re-equipped with the Mach 2 MiG-21F-13 (also built locally as the S-107) and later versions of the *Fishbed*.

Only a handful of MiG-17PF interceptors was on strength between 1955 and the mid-60s. All Czech MiG-17PFs were apparently Tbilisi-built. Aircraft from batches 1 to 4 and 7 had the original RP-1 Izumrood-1 radar, while the final aircraft from batches 10 and 11 were equipped with the more capable RP-5 Izumrood-2.

The 11. SLP (*stíhací létecký pluk* – fighter regiment) at Žatec AB was the first to re-equip with the MiG-17PF. Later operators of the type were the 1. *Zvolenský* SLP at České Budějovice AB, the 3. SLP at *Brno-Tuřany* AB, the 7. SLP at Košice AB (from 1957 onwards; later relocated to Piešťany AB) and the 8. SLP at Prague-Kbely AB. The latter unit later moved to Bratislava and was subsequently disbanded, turning its aircraft over to the 7. SLP. The 3. SLP was also disbanded in the mid-70s as surface-to-air missile units were formed in the Czech air defence system.

Regular checks and maintenance took place at Zvolen, Brno and České Budějovice. For major overhaul, however, the aircraft were ferried to the Polish Air Force's repair plant in Bydgoszcz (WZL-2) which handled the Lim-5P, the Polish-built version of the MiG-17PF. This was a rather lengthy affair and could take up to six months.

In order to increase the number of the CzAF's interceptor units a two-month conversion training course was established at Žatec AB. This was the first programme of its kind in Czechoslovakia; previously the pilots had to go to the USSR. Conversion to the MiG-17PF was slow, as training was hampered by lack of aircraft. For instance, the 7. and 8. SLPs

had only four aircraft each, and these were flown mostly by pilots with higher-than-average skill levels. Some units (eg, the 3. SLP) had aircraft equipped strictly with the old RP-1 radar, while others operated a mix of 'old' and 'new' aircraft (with the RP-5 radar).

Initially CzAF aircraft had serials consisting of one or two letters and two digits separated by a dash. The letters were a code denoting the squadron; the serial was painted on the forward fuselage in huge characters. A different system was introduced in mid-1957, with four-digit serials matching the last four of the aircraft's c/n; the serial was painted on the rear fuselage.

The MiG-17 soldiered on with the CzAF for 14 years until superseded by the MiG-21F-13. According to some reports, 40 were still in service as late as 1971, but this figure is obviously incorrect as only 30 MiG-17PFs were delivered, not to mention the fact that the type was retired in 1969!

Serial	C/n	Version	Remarks
EP-01	0952?	MiG-17F	Reserialled 0952 in 1957?
HF-13	1...	MiG-17PF	RP-5 radar, 11. SLP/1. *letka*.
HF-18	1...	MiG-17PF	RP-5 radar, 11. SLP/1. *letka*.
HF-20	1...	MiG-17PF	RP-5 radar, 11. SLP/1. *letka*.
IW-11	0311	MiG-17PF	RP-1 radar, 1. *Zvolenský* SLP/1. *letka*. Reserialled 0311 in 1957.
0101	0101	MiG-17PF	RP-1 radar. D/D 17-5-55, retired 8-9-69; preserved Czech aerospace museum (VM VHÚ)*, Prague-Kbely.
0201	0201	MiG-17PF	RP-1 radar. D/D 1-8-55. Last flown by the 3. SLP; preserved VM VHÚ.
0202	0202	MiG-17PF	RP-1 radar.
0203	0203	MiG-17PF	RP-1 radar, 11. SLP. Crashed near Žatec 30-11-67.
0302	0302	MiG-17PF	RP-1 radar.
0310	0310	MiG-17PF	RP-1 radar.
0311	0311	MiG-17PF	Ex-IW-11, 1. *Zvolenský* SLP/1. *letka*.
0313	0313	MiG-17PF	RP-1 radar.
0314	0314	MiG-17PF	RP-1 radar, 7. SLP. Crashed near Piešťany 14-7-66.
0406	0406	MiG-17PF	RP-1 radar.
0407	0407	MiG-17PF	RP-1 radar.
0409	0409	MiG-17PF	RP-1 radar, 7. SLP.
0410	0410	MiG-17PF	RP-1 radar.
0701	0701	MiG-17PF	RP-1 radar.
0871	0871?	MiG-17F	Existence unconfirmed! Possible confusion with, see below.
0872	0872	MiG-17F	Damaged 1-3-56 in a forced landing and repaired. To 8. SLP, later to 3. SLP. Damaged again 2-2-60 in major accident and reflown after repairs 28-9-60. Preserved VM VHÚ.
0952	0952?	MiG-17F	Ex-EP-01?
1003	1003	MiG-17PF	RP-5 radar.
1005	1005	MiG-17PF	RP-5 radar.
1006	1006	MiG-17PF	RP-5 radar.
1007	1007	MiG-17PF	RP-5 radar.
1008	1008	MiG-17PF	RP-5 radar.
1009	1009	MiG-17PF	RP-5 radar.
1010	1010	MiG-17PF	RP-5 radar.
1011	1011	MiG-17PF	RP-5 radar.
1012	1012	MiG-17PF	RP-5 radar.
1013	1013	MiG-17PF	RP-5 radar, 11. SLP.
1014	1014	MiG-17PF	RP-5 radar.
1015	1015	MiG-17PF	RP-5 radar. Preserved VM VHÚ.
1018	1018	MiG-17PF	RP-5 radar.
1101	1101	MiG-17PF	RP-5 radar.
1106	1106	MiG-17PF	RP-5 radar.
1107	1107	MiG-17PF	RP-5 radar.

* VM VHÚ = *Vojenské muzeum Vojenského historického ústavu* – Military Museum of the Military Historical Society.

CzAF MiG-17Fs serialled 3213, 3232 and 3233 were also reported erroneously in some Western sources; however, these were actually S-103s (licence-built MiG-15bis Fagot-Bs).

The Czech MiG-17Fs made their public debut on 2nd September 1956 during the Aviation Day display at Prague-Ruzyne airport. Maj Gen Jozef Kúkel made a low pass in EP-01; the ear-splitting roar of the engine at full reheat and the long sheet of flame from the nozzle certainly left the spectators impressed! After landing, Kúkel demonstrated the new G suit which had been unheard of in the CzAF until the MiG-17PF came along. The static display at Prague-Ruzyne included an unserialled MiG-17F (c/n 0872) which had been flown there for the occasion from Prague-Kbely by Lt Gen Josef Vosáhlo the day before.

Equally impressive was the type's appearance at the military parade in Prague in April 1957 when a trio of 11. SLP MiG-17PFs piloted by Špinka, Novák and Tobola made a formation flypast in full afterburner. The ground troops unlucky enough to be parading below at the moment must have been extremely impressed (not being at liberty to plug the ears)! In June 1969 České Budějovice AB hosted an air fête, during which the static display included MiG-17PF '1013' of the resident 1. SLP.

The colour of the radomes on Czech MiG-17PFs varied widely;for instance, it was red on HF-13, HF-18 and HF-20, blue outlined in red on 0311 and 0409, white outlined in red on 0201 and dark green on 1015. As for serials, initially CzAF aircraft had serials consisting of one or two letters and two digits separated by a dash; the letters were a code denoting the squadron. The 11. SLP/1 Sqn had serials with the squadron code HF; this gained its pilots the sobriquet 'Žatečti hafani', which can be loosely translated as 'the barking dogs of Žatec' – both for purely alliterative reasons and referring to the unit's 'watchdog of the sky' role, since this was the quick-reaction alert squadron. Fresco-Ds of the second and third squadrons of the same unit were serialled in the HX and LE blocks respectively.

1. SLP aircraft had serials commencing IW (1 Sqn), JW (2 Sqn) and KU (3 Sqn); on photos intended for the popular press the IW prefix was sometimes altered to TW by military censors. (Speaking of which, such photos were rare; Czech MiG-17PFs were generally veiled in secrecy due to their important air defence role.)

EAST GERMANY

Starting in the summer of 1957, the MiG-17F became the first standard multi-role jet fighter of the LSK/LV (Luftstreitkräfte und Luftverteidigung der Deutschen Demokratischen Republik – Air Force and Air Defence Force of the German Democratic Republic). Most of the East German Fresco-Cs were Polish-built Lim-5s; nevertheless, in East Germany they were invariably referred to by their Soviet designation. The powerful armament comprising three heavy cannons, bombs and unguided rockets allowed the MiG-17F to be used as a fighter-bomber.

A German book states that approximately 100 Fresco-Cs were flown by all six LSK/LV fighter wings in the day fighter role between 1957 and 1968. However, this figure seems understated, since 120 Lim-5s (the entire batches 6, 7, 8 and 9, less one aircraft, plus one aircraft from batch 10) were delivered to the East German Air Force by Poland alone during June 1957 and April 1958, ferried by pilots of the Polish Air Force's 39. PLM (fighter regiment). And then there were aircraft of Soviet origin as well! (The first batch of ex-Soviet Air Force MiG-17Fs, all built in Komsomol'sk-on-Amur, was likewise delivered in 1958.)

JFG 1 (Jagdfliegergeschwader – fighter wing) at Cottbus (later renamed JG 1 'Fritz Schmenkel') had 19 MiG-17Fs on strength in January 1961; in 1962 this number increased to 32. FG 2 (Fliegergeschwader – air wing) at Trollenhagen, Mecklenburg/Vorpommern (later JFG 2, still later JG 2 'Yuriy Gagarin'), flew the F in 1957-68. The 3rd Staffel (squadron) of FG 3 (later 3/JFG 3 and 3/JG 3 'Vladimir Komarov') at Preschen, Brandenburg, took delivery of sixteen Fresco-Cs in October 1957 and operated the type until 1962.

FG 7 (later JFG 7 and JG 7 'Wilhelm Pieck') at Drewitz, Brandenburg, operated the MiG-17F in 1960-66. 3/FG 8 (later 3/JFG 8 and 3/JG 8 'Her-

mann Matern') at Marxwalde, Brandenburg,[5] had 21 MiG-17Fs delivered on 10th October 1957 which remained in service until 1968. FG 9 (later JFG 9 and JG 9 'Heinrich Rau'), also at Drewitz (the unit moved to Peenemünde in 1961), flew the first MiG-17F sortie on 13th July 1957.[6]

Curiously, the 'pure' MiG-17 was delivered later than the MiG-17F; these were likewise ex-VVS aircraft from various factories. A total of 122 Fresco-As was operated by JG 1/JG 2/JG 7 and the training units (see below) in 1960-66. In the former units they were allocated to young pilots fresh from flying schools, while the latter units used them for proficiency training. Most of the MiG-17s were the late model with 0.88m² airbrakes and an irreversible hydraulic actuator in the elevator control circuit; such aircraft received the unofficial East German designation MiG-17H (for [nicht umkehrbarer] Hydraulikbooster). In LSK/LV slang the Fresco-A was known as the 'MiG-17 glatt', i.e. with no suffix letters to the designation. However, the nickname also had an altogether literal meaning ('smooth' MiG-17) and may have been derived from the smooth rear end lacking the afterburner nozzle and, in the case of early aircraft, airbrake actuator fairings.

More second-hand MiG-17Fs – again built in Komsomol'sk-on-Amur – arrived at about the same time. These aircraft and the Fresco-As were distributed in a very unconventional way. The fighters were ferried to Cottbus by Soviet pilots. Each LSK/LV fighter squadron sent technicians to the base; these were to line up in front of the aircraft and, after receiving the 'Go!' command, race across the flight line to secure an aircraft for themselves! The reason for this innovative approach was that the condition of the fighters varied widely; some aircraft were real junk usable only for spares or as ground instructional airframes. The world is up for grabs, and may the best man win!

From 1959 onwards the radar-equipped MiG-17PF gave the LSK/LV day/night all-weather intercept capability. Once again, the aircraft were Polish-built Lim-5Ps but were invariably referred to as MiG-17PFs. 40 aircraft (c/ns 1D 01-06 through 1D 01-10, 1D 02-01 through 1D 02-15 and 1D 03-01 through 1D 03-20) were delivered – according to Polish sources, between January and 6th May 1959. However, the abovementioned German book says that JFG 1, the first LSK/LV unit to operate the type, did not take delivery of the first six Fresco-Ds until April 1959! These were allegedly followed by seven more later that month, and during May the complement increased to 20 aircraft (1 squadron).

LSK/LV technicians were sent to Czechoslovakia for training in radar maintenance. One Lim-5P crashed on 19th July 1959; the remaining 19 aircraft were transferred to JG 2 which flew them in 1966-68. The type was also operated by JG 7 and JG 9 (the latter flew its first sortie on 22nd May 1959).

Because of East Germany's extremely limited territory, the numerous GSVG units, the three international air corridors to Berlin (which, together with the Berlin ATC zone, made up 1/7th of the country's area) and the domestic civil air traffic, operations from most LSK/LV bases, except Peenemünde, were restricted to three days a week. The Soviet units likewise had three days a week, so that Soviet and East German military aircraft flew intermittently to avoid 'getting in each other's way'. Moreover, most of the bases were located so close to the Polish border that the aircraft had to enter Polish airspace, which meant that appropriate clearances had to be obtained. To coordinate LSK/LV operations the VHZ-14 (Vereinigte Hauptzentrale – united main control centre) staffed by Russian-speaking East German officers was established in 1975 at the Soviet 16th Air Army HQ in Wünsdorf, Zossen.

In the late 1960s the High Command of the Warsaw Pact demanded closer co-operation between ground forces and the Air Force as a result of the Soviet military analysts' perception of the recent hostilities in the Middle East. Pressured by Big Brother, the WarPac nations (including East Germany) began building up the ground attack component of their air forces. However, the aircraft then in service with the LSK/LV were not particularly suitable for this role.

Faced by economic constraints, the East German leadership had to find the most cost-effective solution. The breakthrough came when the LSK/LV fighter units re-equipped with the state-of-the-art MiG-21 during 1962-68, relegating the MiG-17F to secondary roles. At the time the Soviet

Union, Poland and Czechoslovakia were all investigating the possibility of turning the *Fresco* into a viable fighter-bomber. Thus in 1973-75 all East German MiG-17Fs and Lim-5s remaining in good condition were retrofitted with two strut-braced pylons just inboard of the inner wing fences *à la* Polish Lim-6*bis* and Lim-6M fighter-bombers; the brake parachute installation of the Lim-6*bis* was not fitted as this was considered too labour-intensive. (Reports by some sources of Lim-6*bis* fighter-bombers being delivered to the LSK/LV are completely erroneous.)

The modification was performed by the Dresden Aircraft Repair Plant (FWD – *Flugzeugwerft Dresden*),[7] using conversion kits supplied by WSK PZL, and enabled the aircraft to carry Mars-2 pods – the Polish version of the UB-16-57 – with sixteen 57mm S-5 FFARs each. The converted *Frescos* were operated by JBG 31 'Klement Gottwald' (*Jagdbombenfliegergeschwader* – fighter-bomber wing) at Drewitz[8] which had up to 43 MiG-17Fs on strength since its formation in October 1971, until the type was finally retired in 1983 after 28 years of service. (The rest, including all *Fresco-As* and Lim-5Ps, had been withdrawn from use in 1968 and mostly scrapped.)

Originally the aircraft retained their natural metal factory finish, but a dark green/dark earth camouflage was later applied to the upper surfaces. Between 1980 and 1985 the MiG-17F was progressively phased out and replaced by the MiG-23BN *Flogger-F* fighter-bomber. Most aircraft were scrapped. However, twelve MiG-17Fs (plus a single UTI-MiG-15) officially listed as scrapped were refurbished by FWD, reserialled and clandestinely delivered to Mozambique (referred to as *Land 58* in documents for security reasons) in August 1981. (In fact, there may have been more than twelve, but very little paperwork has survived on aircraft retired by the LSK/LV before 1972 and the fate of these aircraft remains unknown.)

The *Fresco* was also in service with the LSK/LV's support units, including two training units. FAG 15 'Heinz Kapelle' (*Fliegerausbildungsgeschwader* – flight training wing) in Rothenburg operated the MiG-17 from 1960 and the MiG-17F from 1959 (both versions were phased out on 28th July 1966), and FAG 25 'Leander Ratz' in Bautzen, Sachsen, had five aircraft of an unspecified version in 1963-65. Also, ZDK 33 (*Zieldarstellungskette* – target towing flight) in Peenemünde operated several MiG-17s transferred from JG 1.

East German pilots were extremely pleased with the *Fresco*; the aircraft was sturdy and reliable. The only major shortcoming of the MiG-17F/PF was the strictly limited afterburner operation time due to overheating problems; it was all too easy to exceed the limit and as the afterburner's service life drew to an end the unit had to be permanently disengaged. Known LSK/LV MiG-17s are listed in the table below (all serials are red).

Serial	C/n	Version	D/Date	Remarks
'4'	?	MiG-17F		Photo exists ('retouched' serial?); possibly Lim-5.
07	2054	MiG-17		Late-model ('MiG-17H'). Reportedly **not** operated by the LSK/LV, origin unknown! Preserved Hoyerswerda, later to *Technik- und Verkehrsmuseum Stade*.
'08'	0630	MiG-17F		Ex-Soviet AF. SOC 19-8-81, GIA at MTS Bad Düben, fake serial? Preserved *Luftwaffenmuseum Appen*, Uetersen; later Bautzen Museum.
22	?	MiG-17		Ex-Soviet AF. Preserved in See bei Niesky.
001	?	MiG-17		Ex-Soviet AF. JG 2. Preserved Trollenhagen, fake serial?
'091'	1D 0...-...	Lim-5P	1959	Preserved *Luftwaffenmuseum Berlin-Gatow* with fake serial, identity unknown.
'093'	1D 0...-...	Lim-5P	1959	Preserved with fake serial, identity and location unknown.
172	54211280	MiG-17	1961	Ex-Soviet AF, late-model ('MiG-17H'); crashed 1963.
194	54212067	MiG-17	1961	Ex-Soviet AF, late-model ('MiG-17H').
195	?	MiG-17		Ex-Soviet AF.
201	1C 06-01	Lim-5	6-57	JG-1.
202	1C 06-02	Lim-5	6-57	JBG 31. SOC 31-12-84, scrapped.
203	1C 06-03	Lim-5	6-57	
206	0527	MiG-17F	1961	Ex-Soviet AF.
207	1C 08-21	Lim-5	1957	JG 1.
209	1C 07-03	Lim-5	8-57	JG 1. To JBG 31; SOC 23-10-85, scrapped.
210	1C 08-22	Lim-5	11-57	JBG 31. SOC 30-12-80; reserialled 128 Red, sold to Mozambique 8-81.
211	0619	MiG-17F	12-61	Ex-Soviet AF. JBG 31. SOC 14-4-80; reserialled 129 Red, sold to Mozambique 8-81.
212	?	MiG-17		Ex-Soviet AF, late-model ('MiG-17H').
214	1C 07-05	Lim-5		
219	?	MiG-17		Ex-Soviet AF.
222	1415337	MiG-17	1961	Ex-Soviet AF, late-model ('MiG-17H'). Preserved in pioneer camp near Karlshagen.
223	1C 07-09	Lim-5	8-57	JBG 31. SOC 23-10-85, scrapped.
263	?	MiG-17		Ex-Soviet AF. JBG 31. SOC 4-80.
264	?	MiG-17		Ex-Soviet AF.
274	?	MiG-17F		Unconfirmed (drawing only).
300	1C 06-30	Lim-5	8-57	JBG 31. SOC 30-11-85, pres. *Militärhistorisches Museum Dresden*, later to *Luftfahrthistorische Sammlung Finow*.
301	1C 07-01	Lim-5		JG 2. SOC 4-68.
303	1C 06-13	Lim-5	7-57	
304	0338	MiG-17F		Ex-Soviet AF.
305	7349	MiG-17F		Ex-Soviet AF. JG 2. SOC 10-68, transferred to FWD.*
306	0505	MiG-17F		Ex-Soviet AF.
307	1C 06-17	Lim-5	7-57	
308	0228	MiG-17F		Ex-Soviet AF. JG 2. SOC 4-68, transferred to FWD.
309	7122	MiG-17F		Ex-Soviet AF.
312	1D 02-03	Lim-5P	1959	
314	1C 06-14	Lim-5	6-57	JG 1. To JG 7, later to JBG 31. SOC 30-12-80; reserialled 130 Red, sold to Mozambique 8-81.
318	1C 06-18	Lim-5	6-57	
320	1D 03-02	Lim-5P	1959	
322	1C 06-22	Lim-5	8-57	JG 1; D/D also quoted as 6-57. To JG 7, later to JBG 31. SOC 30-12-80; reserialled 131 Red, s/t Mozambique 8-81.
325	1D 02-04	Lim-5P	1959	
328	1D 03-04	Lim-5P	1959	
333	1C 06-23	Lim-5	8-57	JG 8. To JBG 31; crashed 28-5-77.
334	1C 06-24	Lim-5	8-57	JBG 31. SOC 10-8-84, scrapped.
344	?	MiG-17F		Unconfirmed (drawing only).
345	1C 06-25	Lim-5	8-57	Ultimately transferred to FWD.
346	1C 07-23	Lim-5	10-57	JBG 31. SOC 30-11-85, std Drewitz; to *Deutsches Museum München*, later to *Luftwaffenmuseum Berlin-Gatow*.
352	1D 03-16	Lim-5P	1959	
383	7473	MiG-17F		Ex-Soviet AF.
387	7503	MiG-17F		Ex-Soviet AF.
388	7424	MiG-17F		Ex-Soviet AF.
392	7432	MiG-17F		Ex-Soviet AF.
393	0479	MiG-17F	1-58	Ex-Soviet AF. JG 7, to JBG 31. SOC 30-12-80; reserialled 132 Red, s/t Mozambique 8-81.
402	54211959	MiG-17	1961	Ex-Soviet AF, late-model ('MiG-17H'). Pres. *Historisch-Technisches Info-Zentrum Peenemünde* as '009 Red'.
413	1C 07-02	Lim-5	8-57	
418	1D 03-17	Lim-5P	5-59	
420	1D 01-10	Lim-5P	1-59	JG 7; crashed 12-1-69.
425	1C 07-04	Lim-5	8-57	
427	1D 02-11	Lim-5P	4-59	
428	1D 0...-...	Lim-5P	1959	C/n is either 1D 01-09 or 1D 03-18.

Serial	C/n	Type	Date	Notes
430	1D 02-01	Lim-5P	3-59	
435	1C 06-04	Lim-5	6-57	JBG 31. SOC 31-12-84, scrapped.
437	1D 02-12	Lim-5P	4-59?	Preserved *Armeemuseum Potsdam* as '2001 Red', later '2009 Red', still later '850 Red' (see this serial); now preserved in *Flugplatzmuseum Cottbus* (as '1171 Red'?).
438	1D 03-19	Lim-5P	5-59	
439	1C 07-06	Lim-5	8-57	JBG 31. SOC 23-10-85, scrapped.
440	1D 02-02	Lim-5P	3-59	
442	1C 07-08	Lim-5	8-57	JG 7, to JBG 31. SOC 23-10-85, scrapped.
444	1C 06-08	Lim-5	7-57	JBG 31. SOC 25-6-80, sold to Guinea-Bissau.
447	1D 02-13	Lim-5P	4-59	
448	1D 03-20	Lim-5P	5-59	
450	1D 01-06	Lim-5P	1-59	
456	1C 06-10	Lim-5	7-57	JG 1.
457	1D 03-09	Lim-5P	1959	
458	1D 03-06	Lim-5P	1959	
460	1D 01-07	Lim-5P	1-59	
467	1D 03-10	Lim-5P	1959	
468	1D 03-07	Lim-5P	5-59	JG 1; crashed 27-8-66.
470	1D 01-08	Lim-5P	1-59	JG 2. SOC 11-68.
471	1C 06-11	Lim-5	7-57	
475	1C 06-06	Lim-5	6-57	
477	1D 03-11	Lim-5P	1959	
478	1D 03-08	Lim-5P	5-59	
480	1C 06-07	Lim-5	7-57	JBG 31. SOC 23-10-85, scrapped.
483	1C 07-11	Lim-5		
'491'	1D 0...-...	Lim-5P	1959	JG 9; really 591 Red ('retouched' serial for publicity photo)?
494	1C 06-12	Lim-5	8-57	
496	1C 07-13	Lim-5		
500	1C 06-20	Lim-5	7-57	
501 (a)	1C 06-21	Lim-5	7-57	
501 (b)	7126?†	MiG-17F	1962	Ex-Soviet AF.
502	1C 09-02	Lim-5		Donated to Dresden Pioneers' Palace, now preserved in *Flugplatzmuseum Cottbus*.
505	1C 06-15	Lim-5		
506	1C 09-16	Lim-5		
513	1C 09-13	Lim-5	2-58	JBG 31. SOC 31-12-84, scrapped.
516	1C 07-20	Lim-5		
519	1C 06-19	Lim-5	7-57	JG 9. To JG 8, later to JBG 31. SOC 31-12-80; reserialled 133 Red, sold to Mozambique 8-81.
523	1C 09-03	Lim-5		JG 7. Crashed 10-8-67.
527	1C 06-27	Lim-5		JG 7. To JG 2; SOC 4-68, transferred to FWD.
528	1C 06-28	Lim-5	8-57	JG 9. To JG 8, later to JBG 31. SOC 14-4-80; reserialled 134 Red, sold to Mozambique 8-81.
537	1C 09-17	Lim-5	2-58	JBG 31. SOC 31-12-84, preserved on a plinth at Drewitz AB in front of HQ building, later to *Flugplatzmuseum Cottbus*.
539	1C 07-25	Lim-5		
542	1D 03-05	Lim-5P	1959	JG 2. SOC 11-68.
564	1D 03-12	Lim-5P	1959	
568	1D 03-15	Lim-5P	1959	
569	1C 09-19	Lim-5	2-58	JG 9. To JG 7, later to JBG 31. SOC 14-4-80; reserialled 135 Red, sold to Mozambique 8-81.
573	1D 02-05	Lim-5P	3-59	JG 2. SOC 11-68.
580	7124	MiG-17F		Ex-Soviet AF.
585	0937	MiG-17F		Ex-Soviet AF.
589	?	MiG-17		Ex-Soviet AF.
591	1D 02-06	Lim-5P	3-59	JG 2. SOC 11-68.
592	?	MiG-17F		Possibly Lim-5.
600	1C 07-27	Lim-5	10-57	JBG 31. SOC 25-6-80, sold to Guinea-Bissau.
601	1C 10-01	Lim-5	4-58	
610	1C 07-29	Lim-5		Crashed 3-66.
611	0947	MiG-17F		Ex-Soviet AF.
615	1D 02-08	Lim-5P	1959	
621	1707	MiG-17		Ex-Soviet AF, late-model ('MiG-17H'). JG 7. SOC 31-12-63, preserved *Armeemuseum Potsdam* in pre-1956 markings, ultimate fate unknown.
630	1C 09-30	Lim-5	1957	JG 2. SOC 10-68, transferred to FWD.
634	?	MiG-17F		Possibly Lim-5.
643	1D 02-09	Lim-5P	1959	
648	0326	MiG-17F		Ex-Soviet AF.
650 (a)	1C 08-05	Lim-5		
650 (b)	0401	MiG-17F		Ex-Soviet AF.
651	0654	MiG-17F		Ex-Soviet AF.
653	0432	MiG-17F		Ex-Soviet AF.
656	0851	MiG-17F	11-57	Ex-Soviet AF. JBG 31. Crashed 23-5-78.
658	1C 08-06	Lim-5		JG 2. SOC 4-68, transferred to FWD.
660	0993	MiG-17F		Ex-Soviet AF.
667	0659	MiG-17F		Ex-Soviet AF.
668	1C 08-07	Lim-5	10-57	JBG 31. SOC 31-12-84, scrapped.
670	1C 08-11	Lim-5		
685	1D 02-07	Lim-5P	1959	
695	1C 08-09	Lim-5	1957	JG 2. SOC 4-68, transferred to FWD.
700	1C 07-17	Lim-5	10-57	JBG 31. SOC 25-6-80, sold to Guinea-Bissau.
707	1C 07-18	Lim-5		JG 2.
715	1C 07-19	Lim-5		JG 2.
727	1C 07-10	Lim-5		
731	1C 07-21	Lim-5		SOC 4-68, transferred to FWD.
735	1C 07-22	Lim-5		
739	1C 07-24	Lim-5		
743	1C 07-26	Lim-5		
747	1C 07-28	Lim-5		
752	1C 06-09	Lim-5		JG 2. SOC 4-68, transferred to FWD.
757	1C 08-24	Lim-5	11-57	JG 3. To FAG 15, to JG 2, to JBG 31. SOC 30-12-80; reserialled 136 Red, sold to Mozambique 8-81.
761	1D 0...-...	Lim-5P	1959	C/n is either 1D 01-09 or 1D 03-18.
769	1C 07-14	Lim-5	10-57	JBG 31. SOC 23-10-85, scrapped.
773	1C 07-12	Lim-5		JG 2. SOC 4-68, transferred to FWD.
774	0337	MiG-17F		Ex-Soviet AF.
775	54211431	MiG-17		Ex-Soviet AF, late-model ('MiG-17H').
777	1C 08-25	Lim-5	11-57	JBG 31. SOC 20-1-84, scrapped.
781	1C 07-15	Lim-5		
784	0467	MiG-17F		Ex-Soviet AF. JG 2. SOC 4-68, transferred to FWD.
785	0436	MiG-17F	7-57	Ex-Soviet AF. JBG 31. SOC 31-12-84, scrapped.
799	1C 07-16	Lim-5		
800	1C 08-08	Lim-5		JG 2. SOC 4-68, transferred to FWD.
802	1D 03-01	Lim-5P	1959	JG 1; crashed 5-7-68.
806	1C 08-15	Lim-5	11-57	JBG 31. SOC 20-1-84, scrapped.
808	?	MiG-17F		Possibly Lim-5.
810	1C 08-12	Lim-5		
815	1C 08-10	Lim-5		JG 2. SOC 4-68, transferred to FWD.
820	1C 09-20	Lim-5		Crashed 11-5-67.
823	1C 09-23	Lim-5	2-58	
824	1C 08-13	Lim-5		
827	1D 02-14	Lim-5P	4-59	JG 2. SOC 11-68.
831	1C 09-21	Lim-5		
834	1D 03-14	Lim-5P	1959	
839	1C 06-29	Lim-5	3-58	
842	1C 09-22	Lim-5	2-58	JBG 31. SOC 23-10-85, scrapped.
845	1C 08-14	Lim-5	1957	JG 2. SOC 4-68, transferred to FWD.
850	1C 07-30	Lim-5		
853	1D 03-03	Lim-5P	1959	
855	1C 09-25	Lim-5	1957	JG 2. SOC 4-68, transferred to FWD.
856	1D 02-10	Lim-5P	1959	
859	1C 08-01	Lim-5		

Above: **A much-publicised shot of Lim-5P '450 Red' (c/n 1D 01-06).** Yefim Gordon archive

Right: **An LSK/LV pilot climbs into the cockpit of his Lim-5P '312 Red' (c/n 1D 02-03).**
Sergey and Dmitriy Komissarov collection

Above: **Hungarian Air Force MiG-17PF '315 Red' (c/n 58210315) operated by the 50th Fighter Regiment.** Yefim Gordon archive

Right: **Two-digit serials were rare on Hungarian MiGs.** Yefim Gordon archive

Right: **405 Red, a Hungarian Air Force MiG-17PF preserved in Szolnok.** Peter Davison

863	1C 08-02	Lim-5		
866	1C 09-26	Lim-5	2-58	JBG 31. Crashed 11-4-78.
867	1C 09-27	Lim-5	2-58	JBG 31. SOC 23-10-85, scrapped.
873	1D 03-13	Lim-5P	1959	
875	1C 08-04	Lim-5	1957	JG 2. SOC 10-68, transferred to FWD.
879	1C 08-29	Lim-5	1957	
886	1C 06-16	Lim-5	7-57	JG 8, to JBG 31. SOC 14-4-80; reserialled 137 Red, sold to Mozambique 8-81.
888	1C 09-28	Lim-5	3-58	
892	1C 08-03	Lim-5		
895	1D 02-15	Lim-5P	1959	
900	1C 08-18	Lim-5	1957	JG 1.
902	1C 08-19	Lim-5	1957	JG 1.
903	?	MiG-17		Ex-Soviet AF.
904	0443	MiG-17F		Ex-Soviet AF. JG 2. SOC 10-68, transferred to FWD.
905	1C 08-20	Lim-5	7-57	JG 1, to JBG 31; last MiG-17F overhauled by FWD. SOC 23-10-85, pr. *Luftwaffenmuseum Appen*, later *Luftwaffenmuseum Berlin-Gatow*.
906	7126?†	MiG-17F		Ex-Soviet AF.
910	7134	MiG-17F	7-57	Ex-Soviet AF. JG 8, to JBG 31. SOC 30-12-80; reserialled 138 Red, s/t Mozambique 8-81.
911	1C 08-16	Lim-5	11-57	JG 1, to JBG 31. SOC 30-12-80; reserialled 139 Red, sold to Mozambique 8-81.
912	1C 09-01	Lim-5		
914	1C 08-04	Lim-5	2-58	JBG 31; D/D also stated as 1-58. SOC 31-12-84, scrapped.
915	0426	MiG-17F	1958	Ex-Soviet AF. JBG 31. SOC 31-12-84, scrapped.
916	1C 09-05	Lim-5		
917	1C 09-06	Lim-5		JBG 31; crashed 26-6-75.
921	1C 09-07	Lim-5		
923	1C 09-08	Lim-5	1957	JG 2. SOC 10-68, transferred to FWD.
925	1C 07-07	Lim-5		
926	7129			JG 2. SOC 4-68, transferred to FWD.
941	1C 08-17	Lim-5	1957	JG 2. SOC 4-68, transferred to FWD.
945	1C 09-09	Lim-5	1-58	JBG 31. SOC 31-12-84, scrapped.
946	1C 09-10	Lim-5	1957	JG 2. SOC 4-68, transferred to FWD.
951	1C 09-11	Lim-5		
954	1C 09-12	Lim-5		
955	1C 09-14	Lim-5	1-58	JBG 31. SOC 31-12-84, scrapped.
960	1C 09-15	Lim-5		
971	1C 08-23	Lim-5	11-57	
973	1C 09-24	Lim-5	3-58	
974	1C 08-26	Lim-5	1957	JG 2. SOC 4-68, transferred to FWD.
976	54212017	MiG-17		Ex-Soviet AF, late-model ('MiG-17H').
977	1C 08-27	Lim-5		
978	1C 08-28	Lim-5		Crashed 10-65.
985	1C 08-29	Lim-5	1-58	
991	1C 08-30	Lim-5	1-58	JBG 31. SOC 23-10-85, GIA at OHS TI‡, later scrapped.
993	0448	MiG-17F		Ex-Soviet AF.

* The fate of the 22 aircraft transferred to FWD after being phased out is unknown; they may have been used for spares, or overhauled and sold to third-world countries.

† German sources quote the same c/n (7126) for MiG-17Fs '501 Red' No 2 and '906 Red'. Since there are no remarks about serial changes in either case, one of the c/ns has to be a misquote; it is not clear which one is correct.

‡ OHS TI = *Offizierhochschule für Truppeninstandsetzung* – Officers' High School of In-Service Repairs. The aircraft was obviously used for training in battle damage control techniques.

Lim-5s '346 Red', '537 Red' and '905 Red' are sometimes erroneously reported as scrapped. 346 Red was the *Traditionsmaschine* (traditional aircraft) of JBG 31, ie, an aircraft retained for memories' sake when the unit re-equips with a later type. Another MiG-17 survivor in Germany was a Soviet Air Force *Fresco-C* coded 47 Red which was mounted on a plinth at Großenhain at least until 1993.

EGYPT (UNITED ARAB REPUBLIC; ARAB REPUBLIC OF EGYPT)

The first 12 Soviet-built MiG-17Fs were delivered to the Egyptian Air Force (*al Quwwat al-Jawwiya IL-Misriya*) in the autumn of 1956 to bolster the EAF's fighter arm in view of the growing political tension in the Suez Canal area. None of them were operational when the Suez Crisis fighting broke out; eventually, however, they did take part in the conflict, operating from El Qabrit AB. At least one of them was shot down during the conflict (on 31st October 1956).

More *Fresco-Cs* were delivered after the withdrawal of British and French troops from the Suez Canal area, starting in March 1957; by late June the EAF had nearly 100 MiG-17Fs based, for example, at Almaza AB near Cairo. In the 1960s, many UARAF/EAF *Fresco-Cs* were transferred to ground attack units and retrofitted with two or four double launch rails for four or eight 76mm (3in) unguided rockets outboard of the drop tank hardpoints. Some aircraft also had bomb racks on the forward fuselage just aft of the guns for carrying two bombs. The upgrade was performed at the maintenance facility in Helwan.

Originally Egyptian MiG-17Fs flew in natural metal finish and wore no serials, making individual aircraft identification impossible. Four-digit serials had been introduced by May 1967 but the aircraft were still unpainted. This changed fast after the Six-Day War of June 1967 – a three-tone desert camouflage was hastily introduced.

According to *Interavia*, 60 MiG-17F fighter-bombers were still in service with the EAF in early 1987 but were being withdrawn. One aircraft crashed on 21st April 1970. Aircraft sighted to date are listed below.

Serial	Remarks
2034 Black	Camouflaged, post-UAR markings.
2115 Black	Camouflaged, post-UAR markings.
2271 Black*	Natural metal, UARAF markings, red/white checkered rudder, red ID bands on aft fuselage and wingtips; fighter-bomber with four rocket launch rails.
2782 Black	Camouflaged, post-UAR markings.
2961 White	Camouflaged, post-UAR markings; fighter-bomber with four rocket launch rails and bomb racks under fuselage. Preserved Cairo.
2975 Black	Camouflaged, post-UAR markings; fighter-bomber with four rocket launch rails and bomb racks under fuselage.
3147 Black	Camouflaged, post-UAR markings.
4021 Black	Camouflaged, post-UAR markings.

* 2271 has been reported as Egyptian but may be Syrian.

ETHIOPIA

The Ethiopian Air Force received at least 40 MiG-17Fs from Soviet stocks; this is the figure quoted by *Air International* in July 1978. However, only 20 were reportedly in service by 1979, which may reflect the losses sustained in the wars with enemies within (the Eritrean Liberation Front) and outside (Somalia). 15 were still used as fighter-bombers in late 1991.

GUINEA (GUINEA REPUBLIC)

The Guinea Air Force (*Force Aérienne de Guinée*) had eight MiG-17Fs based at Conakry. The fighters were supplied by the Soviet Union in return for letting Soviet Navy (Northern Fleet/392nd ODRAP)[9] Tupolev Tu-95RTs *Bear-D* maritime reconnaissance/over-the-horizon targeting aircraft use Guinean bases. Six MiG-17Fs were in service at least until late 1991.

Pilots from neighbouring Guinea-Bissau reportedly took training in these aircraft after initial conversion training in UTI-MiG-15s. The intention was to borrow the fighters for use against Portuguese forces in Guinea-Bissau's armed struggle for independence. However, the 'Carnation Revolution' in the former metropoly, one of the goals of which was to grant independence to Portuguese colonies, rendered this unnecessary.

GUINEA-BISSAU

The Guinea-Bissau Air Force (*Force Aérienne de Guinée-Bissau*) reportedly included a squadron of MiG-17Fs based at Bissalanca. At least three of these were Lim-5s purchased from East Germany in the early 1980s (ex-LSK/LV 444 Red, c/n 1C 06-08; ex-600 Red, c/n 1C 07-27; and ex-700 Red, c/n 1C 07-17); the rest may have been loaned from the Guinea Air Force (see above). According to *Flight International*, however, only five were ever delivered. At least two of these fighters were lost in crashes; the remaining three were still in service in late 1991.

HUNGARY

MiG-17 deliveries to the Hungarian Air Force (MHRC – *Magyar Honvedseg Repülö Csapatai*) began in 1956. Both MiG-17Fs and MiG-17PFs were operated – the latter model, eg, by the 50th *Honi Vadaszrepülö Ezred* (fighter regiment) at Taszár AB. Known aircraft are listed below.

Serial	C/n	Version	Remarks
12 Red	?	MiG-17PF	
17 Red	0404	MiG-17F	Ex-'1975 Red'. Preserved *Ozigetvar Muzeum*, Vécses.
071 Red	...071	MiG-17F	Gate guard at Borgond AB.
315 Red	58211315?	MiG-17PF	50th HVre Ezred; preserved *Haditechnikai Park*, Budapest.
402 Red	...402	MiG-17F	
405 Red	58211405?	MiG-17PF	Preserved *Magyar Repülestorteneti Muzeum*, Szolnok.
409 Red	...409	MiG-17F	
434 Red	...434	MiG-17F	
461 Red	...461	MiG-17F	
472 Red	...472	MiG-17F	
522 Red	...522	MiG-17F	Gate guard at Pécs AB.
805 Red	58210805?	MiG-17PF	
838 Red	58210838?	MiG-17PF	
847 Red	58210847?	MiG-17PF	50th HVre Ezred; preserved in museum in Taszár?
862 Red	...862	MiG-17F	
891 Red	...891	MiG-17F	
898 Red	...898	MiG-17F	
'1974 Red'	?	MiG-17PF	Phoney serial, preserved *Hadtorteneti Muzeum*, Budapest.
'1975 Red' (1)	?	MiG-17PF	Phoney serial, dumped Vécses storage depot, later to *Ozigetvar Muzeum*.
'1975 Red' (2)	?	MiG-17PF	Phoney serial, dumped Vécses storage depot, later to *Ozigetvar Muzeum*.
'1976 Red'	?	MiG-17F	Phoney serial, preserved *Csapatai Muzeum* (Aeronautical Museum), Kécskemet.

INDONESIA

The Indonesian Air Force (AURI – *Angkatan Udara Republik Indonesia*) had 60 MiG-17s supplied via Czech sources but probably built in Poland; these included five Lim-5P (MiG-17PF) interceptors delivered in June 1959 (c/ns 1D 05-01 through 1D 05-05). The *Frescos* were operated by the No11 Sqn; like all AURI fighters, they had serials prefixed F. Ironically, these aircraft were actively used in the anti-Communist coup d'état which sealed their fate.

Known aircraft are listed below, but it is highly probable that the intervening serials were used as well (ie, the MiG-17Fs were serialled consecutively F 1101 through F 1155 and the Lim-5Ps were serialled F 1181 through F 1185).

Serial	C/n	Version	Remarks
F 1108	1C 1...-...?	MiG-17F (Lim-5?)	Preserved Bandjarmasin airport, Borneo.
F 1116	1C 1...-...?	MiG-17F (Lim-5?)	
F 1119	1C 1...-...?	MiG-17F (Lim-5?)	
F 1122	1C 1...-...?	MiG-17F (Lim-5?)	
F 1123	1C 1...-...?	MiG-17F (Lim-5?)	
F 1129	?	MiG-17 *Fresco-A*?	Version unconfirmed (drawing only); probably MiG-17F.
F 1151	1C 1...-...?	MiG-17F (Lim-5?)	
F 1152	1C 1...-...?	MiG-17F (Lim-5?)	
F 1182	1D 05-0...	Lim-5P (MiG-17PF)	

In October 1972 Air Marshal Sukendar stated that the AURI was 'in a difficult situation' since spares for the MiG-17s had to be acquired for a down payment in hard currency (rather than the proverbial 10,000 goatskins – *Auth*.), but Indonesia was 'not currently considering replacing the MiG'. However, at the time the AURI *was* already preparing to re-equip with Australian-built (Commonwealth Aircraft Company) F-86 Sabres. It is extremely doubtful that these fighters could be acquired for anything except hard currency. Thus, what Sukendar was really saying was probably 'We cannot obtain spares for the MiGs, currency or no currency, because of political differences with the Soviet Union; still, why throw the fighters away while they are still flyable?' The MiGs were finally replaced by Western fighters in the mid-70s.

IRAQ

The Iraqi Air Force (*al Quwwat al-Jawwiya al-Iraqiya*) received about 15 MiG-17Fs and 20 MiG-17PFs in the mid-60s. 30 *Frescos* were reportedly still in service According to *Interavia*, 100 Shenyang F-6 fighter-bombers were in service with the EAF in early 1987; in fact, according to some reports, the aircraft survived long enough to take part in the opening stages of the Gulf War (the Iraqi invasion of Kuwait) in 1988. Only two MiG-17Fs serialled 452 and 482 have been identified so far.

ISRAEL

The Israelis captured two Syrian Air Force MiG-17Fs (1033 and 1041) sometime before 1973 – probably in 1970 – when the fighters landed at the Israeli airbase at Bezel because of a navigation error. Some sources, however, maintain that this was a planned defection. The aircraft were carefully examined and probably flown by the Israeli Defence Force/Air Force (IDF/AF or *Heyl Ha'avir*).

MADAGASCAR (MALAGASY REPUBLIC)

Eight MiG-17Fs were delivered to the *Armée de l'Air Malgache* (reportedly from North Korea) after Madagascar attained independence, but only half of them were reportedly operational by late 1991. The aircraft were based at Ivato; no serials are known.

MALI

Five MiG-17Fs were delivered to the Mali Air Force (*Force Aérienne de la Republique du Mali*) in the mid-60s when Mali still enjoyed 'friendly nation' status with the USSR. The aircraft equipped an *Escadrille de Chasse* (fighter squadron) probably based at Bamako and were reportedly still operational in late 1991.

1119, one of the Indonesian Air Force's 60 MiG-17Fs. Yefim Gordon archive

This Mozambique Air Force MiG-17 was briefly evaluated by the South African Air Force when its pilot defected. *World Air Power Journal*

NAF 612, one of the Federal Nigerian Air Force's 41 MiG-17Fs, about to take off on another sortie against the Ibo separatists; note the crudely hand-painted serial. Yefim Gordon archive

MONGOLIA

The Mongolian People's Army Air Force operated a number of ex-Soviet Air Force MiG-17s, including *Fresco-A* '003 Red', in 1969-79. The latter aircraft was natural metal overall with the national *zoyombo* markings on the fin. In the early 1980s the MiG-17s were supplanted by more modern (but still well-used) MiG-21s, but at least 12 MiG-17Fs were reportedly still operational in late 1991.

MOROCCO

After attaining independence from France Morocco sought help wherever possible to build up its nascent armed forces, purchasing military equipment from East and West alike. On 10th February 1961 the Soviet freighter S/S *Karaganda* brought 12 (some sources say 20) MiG-17s and two UTI-MiG-15 trainers for the Royal Moroccan Air Force (*al Quwwat al-Jawwiya al-Malakiya Marakishiya*, also called *Aviation Royale Chérifienne*). Nearly 100 Soviet instructors and support personnel came to Morocco to help the RMAF master both types. The *Frescos* had a brief career with the RMAF, being mothballed in 1966 and remaining in storage until the early 1980s; later, Morocco operated only Western types.

Only one Moroccan MiG-17 has been identified, a late-production *Fresco-A* serialled 10-1FJ. The c/n has been quoted in a Czech book as 140616, but this is obviously in error and the correct c/n should be 1406016.

MOZAMBIQUE

The Mozambique People's Air Force (FPA – *Força Popular Aérea de Moçambique*) had at least 30 MiG-17 and MiG-17F (Lim-5) fighter-bombers, some acquired from the East German AF in the early 1980s. The type stayed in service at least until 1991; 14 aircraft have been identified.

Serial	C/n	Version	Remarks
21 Black	?	MiG-17	Ex-EGAF?
23 Black	5238	MiG-17	Built in Komsomol'sk-on-Amur?
			Defected to South Africa 8-7-81.
?	0479	MiG-17F	Ex-EGAF 132 Red, ex-393 Red.
?	0619	MiG-17F	Ex-EGAF 129 Red, ex-211 Red.
?	7134	MiG-17F	Ex-EGAF 138 Red, ex-910 Red.
?	1C 06-14	Lim-5	Ex-EGAF 130 Red, ex-314 Red.
?	1C 06-16	Lim-5	Ex-EGAF 137 Red, ex-886 Red.
?	1C 06-19	Lim-5	Ex-EGAF 133 Red, ex-519 Red.
?	1C 06-22	Lim-5	Ex-EGAF 131 Red, ex-322 Red.
?	1C 06-28	Lim-5	Ex-EGAF 134 Red, ex-528 Red.
?	1C 08-16	Lim-5	Ex-EGAF 139 Red, ex-911 Red.
?	1C 08-22	Lim-5	Ex-EGAF 128 Red, ex-210 Red.
?	1C 08-24	Lim-5	Ex-EGAF 136 Red, ex-757 Red.
?	1C 09-19	Lim-5	Ex-EGAF 135 Red, ex-569 Red.

THE NETHERLANDS

Several Polish-built MiG-17s were sold to the Netherlands in the early 1990s. At least one of them (003 Red) received a civil registration, but most went on to languish at various sites around the country.

Registration	C/n	Version	Remarks
PH-...	1C 00-03	Lim-5	Ex-PWL 003, acquired 8-10-91.
PH-...?	1C 04-18	Lim-5	Ex-PWL 418, acquired 1-91.
PH-...?	1C 12-20	Lim-5	Ex-PWL 1220, acquired 12-91.
PH-...?	1J 04-17	Lim-6*bis*	Ex-PWL 417, acquired 1-91.
PH-...?	1J 04-18	Lim-6R	Ex-PWL 418, acquired by 1991.

Additionally, one more Lim-5 (1213 Red, c/n 1C 12-13) is preserved as an exhibit in Rotterdam.

NIGERIA

Eight MiG-17s and 28 MiG-17Fs were supplied to the Federal Nigerian Air Force in August 1967 for use against the Ibo separatists in the eastern province (the so-called State of Biafra). The *Fresco-Cs* mostly came from Egyptian Air Force stocks (according to some sources, via the USSR); some of the aircraft may have been Lim-5P *Fresco-D* interceptors. The *Fresco-As*, on the other hand, were ex-East German Air Force aircraft. The aircraft were delivered to Kano in northern Nigeria by Soviet Air Force Antonov An-12 *Cub-A* transports.

Serial	C/n	Version	Remarks
NAF 603	?	MiG-17F	
NAF 604	?	MiG-17F	
NAF 605	?	MiG-17F	
NAF 606	?	MiG-17F	
NAF 607	?	MiG-17F	
NAF 608	?	MiG-17F	
NAF 609	0515317?	MiG-17F	
NAF 610	?	MiG-17F	
NAF 611	?	MiG-17F	
NAF 612	?	MiG-17F	
NAF 613	?	MiG-17F	
NAF 614	?	MiG-17F	
NAF 615	?	MiG-17F	Destroyed on the ground at Port Harcourt 10-11-69 by a Biafran AF T-6G Harvard.
NAF 616	?	MiG-17F	Crashed near Osobe 25-6-69.
NAF 617	?	MiG-17F	
NAF 618	?	MiG-17F	
NAF 619	?	MiG-17F	
NAF 620	?	MiG-17F	Damaged beyond repair at Port Harcourt 22-5-69 by Biafran AF Malmö MFI-9B Minicons.
NAF 621	?	MiG-17F	
NAF 622	?	MiG-17F	
NAF 623	?	MiG-17F	Crashed near Port Harcourt 19-7-69.
NAF 624	?	MiG-17F	
NAF 625	?	MiG-17F	
NAF 626	?	MiG-17F	
NAF 627	?	MiG-17F	
NAF 628	?	MiG-17F	
NAF 629	?	MiG-17F	
NAF 630	?	MiG-17F	
NAF 631	?	MiG-17	D/D 13-10-69. W/O in crash landing at Makurdi 19-12-69.
NAF 632	?	MiG-17	D/D 13-10-69.
NAF 633	?	MiG-17	D/D 13-10-69.
NAF 634	?	MiG-17	D/D 13-10-69.
NAF 635	?	MiG-17	D/D 13-10-69.
NAF 636	?	MiG-17	D/D 18-10-69.
NAF 637	?	MiG-17	D/D 18-10-69.
NAF 638	?	MiG-17	D/D 18-10-69.

The fighters were flown by British and South African mercenary pilots and based at Benin City. Some aircraft were delivered as fighter-bombers with underwing launch rails for eight 76mm rockets of the same type as used by the Egyptian Air Force. About 12 to 16 *Frescos* were operational at any one time, the rest remaining in storage. The MiG-17F remained the FNAF's only jet fighter until 1975 when it was gradually supplanted by the MiG-21.

The MiGs flew in natural metal finish, being supplied, as it were, before the Six-Day War and the introduction of camouflage in Egypt. There was no clear standard of national insignia and the aircraft show three different styles. NAF 612 had late-style markings with a green/white/green roundel on the fin but a crudely hand-painted serial; NAF 618, NAF 624 and NAF 625 had a stencilled serial and a Nigerian flag fin flash, while NAF 615 also had a roundel on the fuselage separating the two parts of the serial.

No1 FCU FT-5 55-1201 'up close and personal'. Key Publishing Group

Lim-5 '1414 Red' of the WSP (*Wyższa Szkoła Pilotażu* – Higher Flying School). This aircraft later became a Lim-5R reconnaissance aircraft with the 21. SPLR. *Skrzydlata Polska*

NORTH KOREA

After the end of the Korean War the North Korean Air Force (aka Korean People's Army Air Force) began a massive re-equipment effort, taking delivery of the latest Soviet combat aircraft. The first Soviet-built MiG-17Fs were reportedly delivered in 1956, followed by MiG-17PFs in 1958.

According to press reports, 150 *Frescos*, including Shenyang F-5s, had been supplied by 1956. Deliveries obviously continued after this date because more than 150 MiG-17F/PFs were still operational in the early 1990s. Only two aircraft – MiG-17F '409 Red' (c/n ...415309?) and MiG-17PF '919 White' (c/n 58210919?) – have been identified to date.

NORWAY

A MiG-17 (*sic*) owned by Bjørn Bostad was placed on the Norwegian civil register on 17th February 1992 as LN-MIG. The c/n has been quoted as 1321 and it has been said that the aircraft is an ex-Polish Air Force machine; however, this is not Lim-5 '1321 Red' (c/n 1C 13-21), since that aircraft was sold to the USA as N69RB, and the origin of LN-MIG is a mystery.

PAKISTAN

The Shenyang FT-5 was the sole MiG-17 version, or rather derivative, operated by the Pakistan Air Force (PAF, or *Pakistan Fiza'ya*) since 1975. At least 20 FT-5s were delivered to the No1 Fighter Conversion Unit (FCU) at Mianwali AB. Aircraft serialled 55-1136, 55-1201, 55-1202, 55-1206, 55-1208, 55-1210, 55-1216, 1524, 1525, 1609, 2211, 2213, 2214, 2215, 2216, 2218 and 2219 have been identified to date (the serials match the construction numbers); it is quite probable that some of the intervening aircraft have also been delivered to the PAF. They wore three colour schemes: natural metal, white overall, and medium grey overall.

The training course on the FT-5 lasted five months and included approximately 85 sorties. This was broken down into several phases as follows: transition (24 sorties), IFR training (16 sorties), close formation flying (14 sorties), battle formation flying (six sorties), high-level navigation (three sorties), low-level navigation (two sorties), advanced handling (including aerobatics; 20 sorties) and finally five or six sorties as a lead-in to the next stage of training.

Generally the PAF was satisfied with the FT-5, the only major complaint being the type's limited endurance (training sorties rarely lasted longer than 40 minutes). The FT-5's WP-5A engines are overhauled at the PAF's Faisal Shaheed maintenance base near Karachi. However, the aircraft is getting long in the tooth and looks set to be replaced by the Sino-Pakistani NAMC K-8 Karakoram basic trainer which will be produced at Kamra.

POLAND

The first MiG-17s to be operated by the Polish Air Force (PWL – *Polskie Wojsko Lotnicze*) were twelve Tbilisi-built MiG-17PFs equipped with the RP-1 Izumrood-1 radar. The interceptors came in two batches (in May and August 1955), equipping the newly-formed 21. SELM (*samodzielna eskadra lotnictwa myśliwskiego* – independent fighter squadron) at Bemowo AB, whose primary task was to defend the city of Warsaw. In August 1956 four of them were transferred to the 28. PLM (*pułk lotnictwa myśliwskiego* – fighter regiment) at Rędzikowo AB near Słupsk to provide air defence for the Baltic coast, serving with the unit until replaced by MiG-19Ps in the mid-60s. These aircraft and the seven survivors from the 21. SELM were later divided between four fighter regiments – the 4. PLM at Goleniow (later transformed into the 2. PLM), the 29. PLM at Orneta, the 40. PLM at Świdwin and the 41. PLM at Malbork. The MiG-17PFs formed interceptor flight within the four regiments and were eventually replaced by Polish-built Lim-5s in the mid-70s.

By then only eight of the original MiG-17PFs remained airworthy. They were considered obsolete for the interceptor role and transferred to the fighter-bomber regiment at Świdwin (40. PLM-Sz, *pułk lotnictwa myśliwsko-szturmowego* – fighter/ground attack regiment, ex-40. PLM) and the Polish Navy's 7. PLM-B (*pułk lotnictwa myśliwsko-bombowego* – fighter-bomber regiment) at Siemirowice which later became the 7. PLS (*pułk lotnictwa specjalnego* – special air regiment). The type was finally retired in the mid-80s.

The Lim-5 *Fresco-C* was by far the most numerous version operated by the PWL. The first four pre-production Lim-5s were delivered to the 5. DLM (*dywizja lotnictwa myśliwskiego* – fighter division) at Bemowo AB in November 1956. As noted earlier, the first of them (0001 Red, c/n 1C 00-01) was used as the personal mount of the Polish Air Force C-in-C Gen Jan Frey-Bielecki.

The first units to completely re-equip with the Lim-5 between February and March 1957 were the 25. PLM at Pruszcz Gdański and the 39. PLM at Mierzęcice, since they were based close to Poland's northern and southern borders and would be among the first to deal with intruders. Other fighter units flying the type were the 1. PLM 'Warszawa' at Minsk-Mazowiecki AB, the 2. PLM at Kraków-Balice AB (later renamed the 10. PLM and moved to Łask), the 3. PLM at Wrocław, the 4. PLM, the 11. PLM at Dębrzno, the 13. PLM at Leczyca (since disbanded), the 26. PLM at Zegrze Pomorskie (later renamed the 9. PLM), the 28. PLM at Słupsk, the 31. PLM at Łask, the 41. PLM and the 62. PLM at Poznań-Krzesiny AB.

The 12 MiG-17PFs delivered in 1955 were not enough to provide an effective all-weather air defence system. Hence they were soon supplemented by the licence-built version, the Lim-5P. The first such aircraft was delivered to the CSL on 12th February 1959; service introduction with the 29. PLM at Orneta followed on 4th May 1959. The Lim-5P was also operated by the 3., 4., 13. and 26. PLM. The latter unit was the last to operate the Lim-5P in the interceptor role, as the aircraft was rapidly becoming obsolete; the last dozen or so Lim-5Ps were retired at Zegrze Pomorskie in 1979.

Lim-5M fighter-bombers had their service debut with the 5. DLM in December 1960. It was also operated by the 5., 6., 30. and 48. PLM-Sz and the 17. EL DLO (eskadra lotnicza dowództwa lotnictwa operacyjnego – operational command and control, ie, HQ squadron). The improved Lim-6bis came in 1963; the 53. PLM-Sz at Miroslawiec (renumbered 8. PLM-Sz in 1967) was the first unit to take delivery of this version on 25th March. All surviving Lim-5Ms were converted to Lim-6bis standard in 1964-65. Naval bises serving with the 7. PLM-B at Siemirowice were withdrawn in 1988, while the last Air Force examples were retired by the 45. PLM-B at Babimost in February 1992. (In some sources this unit has been referred to as the 45. LPSz-B, lotniczy pułk szkolno-bojowy – advanced training air regiment.)

Additionally, in 1971-74 forty obsolescent Lim-5Ps were converted into Lim-6M fighter-bombers, while another 14 were rebuilt as Lim-6MR strike/reconnaissance aircraft. They entered service with the 40. PLM-B at Świdwin and the Navy's 7. PLM-B. The latter unit transferred 14 of its Lim-6M/Lim-6MRs to the 8. PLM-B at Miroslawiec in February 1982. These versions had a shorter career, being largely phased out by 1987; the last few examples were retired by the 45. PLM-B on 8th December 1988.

In the reconnaissance role, the first 36 Lim-5s converted to Lim-5R standard Lim-5R were operated by the 21. SPLR (samodzielny pułk lotnictwa rozpoznawczego – independent aerial reconnaissance regiment) at Sochaczew, entering service on 7th July 1960. Subsequent Lim-5R conversions (eg, 513 Red, 516 Red and 518 Red) were delivered to various ground attack regiments, forming reconnaissance cells within these units. In 1963 the 21. SPLR started taking delivery of the improved Lim-6R.

In the early 1970s the 'pure' Lim-5s were gradually replaced in first-line service by MiG-21s and transferred to training units. The 58. LPSz (lotniczy pułk szkolny – training air regiment) at Dęblin was the first to receive the displaced Lim-5s, followed by the 38. LPSz-B at Modlin which operated the type in 1979-88. The 61. LPSz-B at Biała Podlaska was the longest user of the Lim-5 in the training role, the last examples being replaced in 1991 by indigenous PZL TS-11 Iskra trainers. Various Lims were also operated by the WOSL (Wyższa Oficerska Szkoła Lotnicza – Officers' Higher Flying School) – popularly known as Szkoła Orląt (Eaglets' School) – at Dęblin and the conversion training centre (CSL, Centrum Szkolenia Lotniczego – Air Training Centre) at Modlin

The Fresco also served with various support units – for example, the 19.EH (eskadra holownicza – target towing squadron) at Słupsk and the 45. LED (lotnicza eskadra doświadczalna – experimental aviation squadron) at Modlin each had a couple of Lim-5s.

As with the Lim-1/-2, originally all Lim-5/-6s flew in their natural metal factory finish. In the late 1960s, two- or three-tone tactical camouflage was introduced. Camouflage colours and patterns varied widely from aircraft to aircraft (slate grey/olive drab or dark green/tan with light grey

undersurfaces, light grey/olive drab/tan or foliage green/olive drab/tan with light grey undersurfaces, or three shades of green with blue undersurfaces). The serials usually remained red, though at least one Lim-6R (612) had a low-visibility white outline serial. Some Lim-5Ps received a light grey air superiority colour scheme. In the Lims' latter days many aircraft were extremely weathered, with large areas of natural metal showing; such patches were often painted up with whatever colour was available, giving the aircraft a rather untidy appearance.

On 20th February 1992 the MiG-17 made its last flight on active duty with the PWL; the honour belonged to Lim-6bis '522 Red' (c/n 1J 05-22) and 2nd Lt Hubert Jaroszynski. The real last flight, however, was performed by Lim-5 '1717 Red' (c/n 1C 17-17) operated by the 45. LED at Modlin on 12th July 1993, thus marking the end of the Fresco's nearly 40-year-long career with the Polish Air Force.

Retired Lims were stored at the PWL overhaul plant No 2 (WZL-2) at Bydgoszcz and the Katowice storage depot; most aircraft were ultimately scrapped. Amongst those arriving at Katowice was the longest-serving Lim-5 (003 Red, c/n 1C 00-03); it arrived on 12th June 1990 after nearly 34 years in service. (And even that was not the end of its flying career, for the aircraft was sold to a private owner in the Netherlands!)

Some aircraft, including a surprisingly large number of Lim-5Ps, became ground instructional airframes at the TSWL (Techniczna Szkoła Wojsk Lotniczych – Air Force Technical School) at Zamość, while others served the same purpose at the CSSTWL (Centrum Szkolenia Specjalistów Technicznych Wojsk Lotniczych – Air Force Technical Specialists' Instruction and Training Centre) at Oleśnica. Such aircraft were marked with a big yellow C (for ćwiczenia – training) on the upper fin section.

Polish Air Force MiG-17s are listed in the table below. Since the serials of Polish-built versions often coincide, the aircraft have been sorted by version (as built) for the sake of convenience, with subsequent conversions detailed as appropriate. All serials are red.

Serial	C/n	Version	D/Date	First Unit	Remarks
305	0305	MiG-17PF	24-8-55	21. SELM	Preserved Ekspozicja Muzealna Łódź.
306	0306	MiG-17PF	24-8-55	21. SELM	WFU.
307	0307	MiG-17PF	24-8-55	21. SELM	WFU 15-9-80, preserved Muzeum Braterstwa Broni, Drzonów, 14-5-81; c/n also quoted as 58310307. Now painted in camouflage c/s as '507 Red'? (see note at end of table)
308	0308	MiG-17PF	24-8-55	21. SELM	WFU 29-8-80.
309	0309	MiG-17PF	24-8-55	21. SELM	Derelict Dęblin.
310	0310	MiG-17PF	24-8-55	21. SELM	WFU.
921	0921	MiG-17PF	13-5-55	21. SELM	Crashed 27-4-57.
926	0926	MiG-17PF	13-5-55	21. SELM	WFU 13-9-80, preserved Muzeum Marynarki Wojennej (Navy Museum), Gdynia, 29-6-82.
938	0938	MiG-17PF	13-5-55	21. SELM	WFU 11-4-79.
948	0948	MiG-17PF	13-5-55	21. SELM	Preserved Dęblin.
949	0949	MiG-17PF	13-5-55	21. SELM	WFU.
1001	1001	MiG-17PF	13-5-55	21. SELM	Preserved Muzeum imieni Orla Białego (White Eagle Museum), Skarzysko Kamienna.
0001	1C 00-01	Lim-5	28-11-56	5. DLM	GIA WOSL, Dęblin 9-94.
002	1C 00-02	Lim-5	28-11-56	5. DLM	WFU 7-2-72.
003	1C 00-03	Lim-5	28-11-56	5. DLM	WFU 12-6-90, sold to the Netherlands 8-10-91.
004	1C 00-04	Lim-5	18-1-57	WOSL	GIA Dęblin 9-94.
102	1C 01-02	Lim-5	27-3-57	25. PLM	WFU 22-6-90.
103	1C 01-03	Lim-5	13-2-57	39. PLM	Crashed 21-10-66.
104	1C 01-04	Lim-5	13-2-57	39. PLM	WFU.
105	1C 01-05	Lim-5	13-2-57	39. PLM	WFU 7-2-72.
201	1C 02-01	Lim-5	19.11.57	INB	Converted to, see below.
		Lim-5R		21. SPLR	WFU 2-10-90.
202	1C 02-02	Lim-5	13-2-57	39. PLM	WFU.
203	1C 02-03	Lim-5	27-3-57	25. PLM	Crashed 23-9-59.

204	1C 02-04	Lim-5	13-2-57	39. PLM	WFU 9-2-72.
205	1C 02-05	Lim-5	13-2-57	39. PLM	WFU.
206	1C 02-06	Lim-5	13-2-57	39. PLM	Crashed 18-10-79.
207	1C 02-07	Lim-5	13-2-57	39. PLM	WFU 13-6-88, stored Bydgoszcz 1991.
208	1C 02-08	Lim-5	27-3-57	25. PLM	WFU.
209	1C 02-09	Lim-5	27-3-57	25. PLM	WFU, stored Katowice 6-91.
210	1C 02-10	Lim-5	13-2-57	39. PLM	WFU.
301	1C 03-01	Lim-5	13-2-57	39. PLM	WFU.
302	1C 03-02	Lim-5	27-3-57	25. PLM	WFU.
303	1C 03-03	Lim-5	27-3-57	25. PLM	WFU 7-2-72.
304	1C 03-04	Lim-5	27-3-57	25. PLM	WFU 2-10-90.
305	1C 03-05	Lim-5	27-3-57	25. PLM	WFU, stored Katowice 9-94.
306	1C 03-06	Lim-5	27-3-57	25. PLM	WFU 1990, stored Katowice; sold to the USA/pvt owner after 5-93 as N217JG.
307	1C 03-07	Lim-5	27-3-57	25. PLM	Crashed 21-12-78, mid-air collision with Lim-5 '1716 Red'.
308	1C 03-08	Lim-5	12-4-57	31. PLM	WFU.
309	1C 03-09	Lim-5	27-3-57	10. DLM	WFU. Sold to the USA/private owner as N1060M?
310	1C 03-10	Lim-5	8-4-57	WOSL	WFU.
311	1C 03-11	Lim-5	8-4-57	WOSL	WFU 12-6-90, stored Katowice 6-91.
312	1C 03-12	Lim-5	12-4-57	31. PLM	WFU.
313	1C 03-13	Lim-5	8-4-57	WOSL	WFU.
314	1C 03-14	Lim-5	12-4-57	31. PLM	WFU 7-6-86.
315	1C 03-15	Lim-5	12-4-57	31. PLM	Converted to, see below.
		Lim-5R		21. SPLR	WFU 2-10-90.
401	1C 04-01	Lim-5	13-5-57	39. PLM	WFU 12-6-90.
402	1C 04-02	Lim-5	13-5-57	39. PLM	Crashed 31-5-58.
403	1C 04-03	Lim-5	8-4-57	WOSL	WFU.
404	1C 04-04	Lim-5	8-4-57	WOSL	WFU 22-6-90, stored Katowice 6-91.
405	1C 04-05	Lim-5	12-4-57	31. PLM	WFU.
406	1C 04-06	Lim-5	12-4-57	31. PLM	Sold to USAF/DTESA 1988.
407	1C 04-07	Lim-5	13-5-57	39. PLM	WFU.
408	1C 04-08	Lim-5	13-5-57	39. PLM	Preserved *Ekspozicja Muzealna Łódź*.
409	1C 04-09	Lim-5	15-5-57	28. PLM	WFU.
410	1C 04-10	Lim-5	15-5-57	28. PLM	WFU.
411	1C 04-11	Lim-5	13-5-57	39. PLM	WFU.
412	1C 04-12	Lim-5	15-5-57	28. PLM	Crashed 13-6-72.
413	1C 04-13	Lim-5	13-5-57	39. PLM	WFU 7-11-78, GIA CSSTWL.
414	1C 04-14	Lim-5	13-5-57	39. PLM	WFU 13-6-88, stored Bydgoszcz 1991.
415	1C 04-15	Lim-5	15-5-57	28. PLM	Preserved *Muzeum Lotnictwa i Astronautyki* (MLiA), Kraków.
416	1C 04-16	Lim-5	13-5-57	39. PLM	WFU.
417	1C 04-17	Lim-5	13-5-57	39. PLM	WFU.
418	1C 04-18	Lim-5	15-5-57	28. PLM	WFU 20-6-88, sold to the Netherlands 1-91.
419	1C 04-19	Lim-5	13-5-57	39. PLM	WFU, GIA CSSTWL.
420	1C 04-20	Lim-5	15-5-57	28. PLM	WFU.
501	1C 05-01	Lim-5	15-5-57	28. PLM	WFU.
502	1C 05-02	Lim-5	13-5-57	39. PLM	WFU.
503	1C 05-03	Lim-5	15-5-57	28. PLM	WFU.
504	1C 05-04	Lim-5	15-5-57	28. PLM	WFU.
505	1C 05-05	Lim-5	13-5-57	39. PLM	WFU.
506	1C 05-06	Lim-5	14-6-57	31. PLM	Converted to, see below.
		Lim-5R		21. SPLR	WFU 1990; preserved MLiA, Kraków.
507	1C 05-07	Lim-5	14-6-57	31. PLM	Converted to, see below.
		Lim-5R		21. SPLR	WFU 2-10-90.
508	1C 05-08	Lim-5	14-6-57	3.KLM	WFU; sold to the UK 3-88.
509	1C 05-09	Lim-5	14-6-57	31. PLM	Converted to, see below.
		Lim-5R		21. SPLR	WFU 22-11-90, stored Katowice 6-91.
510	1C 05-10	Lim-5	14-6-57	31. PLM	Crashed 19-3-58.
511	1C 05-11	Lim-5	14-6-57	31. PLM	Converted to, see below.
		Lim-5R		21. SPLR	WFU 2-10-90.
512	1C 05-12	Lim-5	14-6-57	31. PLM	Crashed 11-4-58.
513	1C 05-13	Lim-5	14-6-57	1. PLM	Converted to, see below.
		Lim-5R			WFU 27-5-88.

514	1C 05-14	Lim-5	14-6-57	1. PLM	WFU.
515	1C 05-15	Lim-5	14-6-57	1. PLM	WFU.
516	1C 05-16	Lim-5	14-6-57	1. PLM	Converted to, see below.
		Lim-5R			WFU 11-7-78, GIA CSSTWL.
517	1C 05-17	Lim-5	14-6-57	1. PLM	WFU.
518	1C 05-18	Lim-5	14-6-57	1. PLM	Converted to, see below.
		Lim-5R			WFU.
519	1C 05-19	Lim-5	14-6-57	1. PLM	WFU.
520	1C 05-20	Lim-5	14-6-57	1. PLM	WFU 22-6-90, stored Katowice 6-91.
605	1C 06-05	Lim-5	26-4-58	3. PLM	WFU 27-6-88, stored Bydgoszcz 1991.
none	1C 07-07	Lim-5		INB	Temporarily with PWL, trials aircraft; delivered to E German AF as 925 Red.
'948'	?	Lim-5M			Preserved WOSL. C/n quoted as 1C 09-48 which does not make sense.
1002	1C 10-02	Lim-5	26-4-58	3.KOPL	WFU.
1003	1C 10-03	Lim-5	26-4-58	3.KOPL	WFU.
1004	1C 10-04	Lim-5	26-4-58	3. PLM	WFU.
1005	1C 10-05	Lim-5	26-4-58	3. PLM	WFU.
1006	1C 10-06	Lim-5	11-4-58	39. PLM	WFU.
1007	1C 10-07	Lim-5	15-4-58	28. PLM	WFU.
1008	1C 10-08	Lim-5	15-4-58	26. PLM	WFU 23-5-90, stored Bydgoszcz 1991.
1009	1C 10-09	Lim-5	15-4-58	26. PLM	WFU 2-10-90.
1010	1C 10-10	Lim-5	15-4-58	26. PLM	Sold to USAF/DTESA 1988, to 010 Red.
1011	1C 10-11	Lim-5	26-4-58	62. PLM	WFU 1990, stored Katowice 9-94.
1012	1C 10-12	Lim-5	26-4-58	62. PLM	W/O in landing accident 25-1-61.
1013	1C 10-13	Lim-5	26-4-58	62. PLM	WFU.
1014	1C 10-14	Lim-5	26-4-58	62. PLM	Crashed 26-6-58, mid-air collision with Lim-2 '0929 Red'.
1015	1C 10-15	Lim-5	26-4-58	62. PLM	Crashed 24-6-58.
1016	1C 10-16	Lim-5	26-4-58	62. PLM	WFU 27-8-90.
1017	1C 10-17	Lim-5	26-4-58	62. PLM	WFU.
1018	1C 10-18	Lim-5	26-4-58	3. PLM	WFU 2-10-90.
1019	1C 10-19	Lim-5	15-4-58	26. PLM	WFU.
1020	1C 10-20	Lim-5	1-2-58	ITWL	WFU 1990, std Katowice 6-91 to 5-93. Sold to USA/pvt owner 3-94 as N117MG.
1021	1C 10-21	Lim-5	15-4-58	26. PLM	WFU 27-8-90.
1022	1C 10-22	Lim-5	15-4-58	26. PLM	WFU.
1023	1C 10-23	Lim-5	15-4-58	25. PLM	Preserved MLiA, Kraków.
1024	1C 10-24	Lim-5	15-4-58	28. PLM	WFU.
1025	1C 10-25	Lim-5	15-4-58	28. PLM	WFU.
1026	1C 10-26	Lim-5	15-4-58	28. PLM	WFU.
1027	1C 10-27	Lim-5	15-4-58	25. PLM	Crashed 24-6-58.
1028	1C 10-28	Lim-5	15-4-58	25. PLM	WFU.
1030	1C 10-30	Lim-5	15-4-58	25. PLM	Converted to, see below.
	CM 10-30;				
	1F 10-30	Lim-5M	20-9-61	ITWL	Lim-5M prototype/trials aircraft. Converted to Lim-6R '441 Red', which see, in 1969 (c/n changed to 1J 04-41).
1101	1C 11-01	Lim-5	26-4-58	3. PLM	Converted to, see below.
		Lim-5R			WFU 27-8-90, stored Katowice 6-91.
1102	1C 11-02	Lim-5	26-4-58	3. PLM	WFU.
1103	1C 11-03	Lim-5	26-4-58	3. PLM	WFU 8-2-61, GIA CSSTWL.
1104	1C 11-04	Lim-5	15-4-58	26. PLM	WFU.
1209	1C 12-09	Lim-5	24-7-58	11. PLM	WFU.
1210	1C 12-10	Lim-5	24-7-58	11. PLM	WFU 1990, std Katowice 6-91 to 9-94.
1211	1C 12-11	Lim-5	24-7-58	11. PLM	WFU 1990, stored Katowice 6-91 to 9-94; sold to Classic Aviation (UK) as G-BWUF.
1212	1C 12-12	Lim-5	24-7-58	11. PLM	WFU 1975.
1213	1C 12-13	Lim-5	24-7-58	11. PLM	WFU 7-6-88; sold to the Netherlands 1-91, preserved Rotterdam.
1214	1C 12-14	Lim-5	24-7-58	11. PLM	WFU.
1215	1C 12-15	Lim-5	24-7-58	11. PLM	WFU.
1216	1C 12-16	Lim-5	31-7-58	13. PLM	WFU.
1217	1C 12-17	Lim-5	24-7-58	11. PLM	WFU 1990, stored Katowice 6-91. Pres. *Muzeum Wojska Polskiego*, Warsaw.

Serial	c/n	Type	Date	Unit	Remarks
'1217'	?	Lim-5			Preserved *Muzeum Katynskie*, Warsaw, fake serial.
1218	1C 12-18	Lim-5	24-7-58	11. PLM	WFU.
1219	1C 12-19	Lim-5	24-7-58	11. PLM	WFU.
1220	1C 12-20	Lim-5	24-7-58	11. PLM	WFU 12-6-90, stored Katowice 1991. Sold to the Netherlands 12-91.
1221	1C 12-21	Lim-5	24-7-58	26. PLM	WFU.
1222	1C 12-22	Lim-5	24-7-58	26. PLM	WFU.
1223	1C 12-23	Lim-5	24-7-58	26. PLM	WFU.
1224	1C 12-24	Lim-5	24-7-58	26. PLM	WFU.
1225	1C 12-25	Lim-5	24-7-58	26. PLM	WFU.
1226	1C 12-26	Lim-5	24-7-58	26. PLM	WFU.
1227	1C 12-27	Lim-5	24-7-58	26. PLM	WFU.
1228	1C 12-28	Lim-5	30-7-58	2. PLM	WFU 1987; sold to the UK 3-88.
1229	1C 12-29	Lim-5	6-8-58	WSP	WFU 6-8-68.
1230	1C 12-30	Lim-5	30-7-58	2. PLM	WFU 7-6-88, stored Bydgoszcz 1991.
1231	1C 12-31	Lim-5	30-7-58	2. PLM	WFU.
1301	1C 13-01	Lim-5	24-7-58	11. PLM	WFU 1990, stored Katowice 5-93. Sold to the USA 3-94.
1302	1C 13-02	Lim-5	11-8-58	WSP	WFU.
1303	1C 13-03	Lim-5	31-7-58	ITWL	Sold to USAF/DTESA 1988, to 303 Red?
1304	1C 13-04	Lim-5	31-7-58	13. PLM	WFU 1990: Katowice 6-91.
1305	1C 13-05	Lim-5	30-7-58	2. PLM	WFU 7-6-86.
1306	1C 13-06	Lim-5	30-7-58	2. PLM	WFU.
1307	1C 13-07	Lim-5	31-7-58	13. PLM	WFU.
1308	1C 13-08	Lim-5	31-7-58	13. PLM	WFU 1990, std Katowice 6-91 to 9-94.
1309	1C 13-09	Lim-5	30-7-58	2. PLM	WFU 27-5-88.
1310	1C 13-10	Lim-5	30-7-58	2. PLM	WFU 7-6-88.
1311	1C 13-11	Lim-5	31-7-58	13. PLM	WFU 22-6-90.
1312	1C 13-12	Lim-5	31-7-58	13. PLM	Converted to, see below.
		Lim-5R		21. SPLR	WFU 1990, stored Katowice 6-91. Sold to the USA by 1994.
1313	1C 13-13	Lim-5	31-7-58	13. PLM	WFU 7-6-88.
1314	1C 13-14	Lim-5	31-7-58	13. PLM	WFU 2-10-90, stored Katowice 6-91.
1315	1C 13-15	Lim-5	2-8-58	45. PLM	WFU.
1316	1C 13-16	Lim-5	2-8-58	45. PLM	Crashed 3-3-59.
1317	1C 13-17	Lim-5	2-8-58	45. PLM	WFU 12-6-90.
1318	1C 13-18	Lim-5	2-8-58	45. PLM	WFU.
1319	1C 13-19	Lim-5	2-8-58	45. PLM	WFU 1990, stored Katowice 1991. Sold to the USA 3-94.
1320	1C 13-20	Lim-5	30-7-58	2. PLM	WFU.
1321	1C 13-21	Lim-5	2-8-58	45. PLM	WFU, sold to the USA/private owner 22-11-93, registered N69RB by 1-94.
1322	1C 13-22	Lim-5	31-7-58	13. PLM	WFU 27-5-88.
1323	1C 13-23	Lim-5	2-8-58	45. PLM	WFU 27-5-88.
1324	1C 13-24	Lim-5	2-8-58	45. PLM	WFU.
1325	1C 13-25	Lim-5	2-8-58	3. PLM	WFU.
1326	1C 13-26	Lim-5	2-8-58	3. PLM	WFU 7-6-86, GIA TSWL; later preserved Linz, Austria?
1327	1C 13-27	Lim-5	2-8-58	3. PLM	WFU.
1328	1C 13-28	Lim-5R?	7-7-59	ITWL	Undernose fairing offset to port. WFU.
1329	1C 13-29	Lim-5	2-8-58	3. PLM	WFU.
1330	1C 13-30	Lim-5	2-8-58	3. PLM	WFU 2-10-90, stored Katowice 6-91. Preserved Waganiec nad Toruń.
1401	1C 14-01	Lim-5	2-8-58	62. PLM	WFU.
1402	1C 14-02	Lim-5	2-8-58	62. PLM	WFU.
1403	1C 14-03	Lim-5	2-8-58	62. PLM	Crashed 26-6-63.
1404	1C 14-04	Lim-5	2-8-58	62. PLM	Converted to, see below.
		Lim-5R		21. SPLR	WFU 27-8-90.
1405	1C 14-05	Lim-5	2-8-58	62. PLM	WFU.
1406	1C 14-06	Lim-5	2-8-58	62. PLM	WFU.
1407	1C 14-07	Lim-5	2-8-58	62. PLM	WFU.
1408	1C 14-08	Lim-5	6-8-58	WSP	WFU.
1409	1C 14-09	Lim-5	11-8-58	WSP	WFU 24-8-90, stored Katowice 6-91 - 9-94.
1410	1C 14-10	Lim-5	18-10-58	41. PLM	WFU.
1411	1C 14-11	Lim-5	18-10-58	41. PLM	To the 45. LED, development aircraft? WFU 1990, stored Katowice 1991.
1412	1C 14-12	Lim-5	22-1-59	34. PLM	Crashed 19-8-66.
1413	1C 14-13	Lim-5	22-1-59	34. PLM	Converted to, see below.
		Lim-5R		21. SPLR	WFU 1990, stored Katowice 1991. Sold to the USA by 11-94.
1414	1C 14-14	Lim-5	15-9-58	WSP	Converted to, see below.
		Lim-5R		21. SPLR	WFU 24-8-90, stored Katowice 6-91. Preserved MLiA, Kraków.
1415	1C 14-15	Lim-5	15-9-58	WSP	WFU 13-06-88.
1416	1C 14-16	Lim-5	19-11-58	ITWL	WFU.
1417	1C 14-17	Lim-5	15-9-58	WSP	WFU 1990, std Katowice 1991 to 9-94.
1418	1C 14-18	Lim-5	18-10-58	41. PLM	Converted to, see below.
		Lim-5R		21. SPLR	WFU 27-6-88, std Bydgoszcz 1991 (also reported derelict Modlin – 45. LED?)
1419	1C 14-19	Lim-5	15-9-58	WSP	WFU 11-90, std Katowice 1991 to 9-94. Preserved *Muzeum Wyzwolenia Miasta Poznania* (Poznań Liberation Museum).
1420	1C 14-20	Lim-5	18-10-58	41. PLM	WFU.
1422	1C 14-22	Lim-5	18-10-58	41. PLM	Crashed 17-3-59.
1423	1C 14-23	Lim-5	22-1-59	34. PLM	WFU; sold to the USA/private owner by 11-93, to N17QS.
1424	1C 14-24	Lim-5	19-11-58	41. PLM	Converted to, see below.
		Lim-5R		21. SPLR	WFU 12-6-90, stored Katowice 1991.
1425	1C 14-25	Lim-5	19-11-58	41. PLM	Converted to, see below.
		Lim-5R		21. SPLR	WFU 2-10-90, stored Katowice 6-91.
1426	1C 14-26	Lim-5	19-11-58	41. PLM	WFU 1990, std Katowice 6-91 to 9-94.
1427	1C 14-27	Lim-5	19-11-58	41. PLM	Converted to, see below.
		Lim-5R			WFU 27-6-88, stored Bydgoszcz 1991.
1428	1C 14-28	Lim-5	19-11-58	41. PLM	WFU.
1429	1C 14-29	Lim-5	19-11-58	41. PLM	WFU.
1430	1C 14-30	Lim-5	22-1-59	34. PLM	WFU.
1501	1C 15-01	Lim-5	22-1-59	34. PLM	WFU Minsk-Mazowiecki 1991.
1502	1C 15-02	Lim-5	22-1-59	34. PLM	WFU, stored Katowice 06.91-09.94.
1505	1C 15-05	Lim-5	19-11-58	41. PLM	WFU 23-3-89; sold to Finland 1989, preserved Paimio.
1506	1C 15-06	Lim-5	19-11-58	41. PLM	WFU.
1508	1C 15-08	Lim-5	22-1-59	34. PLM	WFU; stored Kraków, later to MLiA.
1509	1C 15-09	Lim-5	22-1-59	34. PLM	WFU 1990, stored Katowice 1991.
1511	1C 15-11	Lim-5			Crashed on test flight at WSK Mielec 25-10-58.
1513	1C 15-13	Lim-5			Photo exists, no other info available (probably never delivered to the PWL and diverted to export).
1527	1C 15-27	Lim-5	22-1-59	34. PLM	WFU.
1528	1C 15-28	Lim-5	22-1-59	34. PLM	Crashed 25-6-63, mid-air collision with Lim-2 '1322 Red'.
1529	1C 15-29	Lim-5	22-1-59	34. PLM	Converted to, see below.
		Lim-5R		21. SPLR	WFU 1990, std Katowice 1991. Sold to the USA/pvt owner by 4-94, to N117BR.
1530	1C 15-30	Lim-5	22-1-59	34. PLM	Converted to, see below.
		Lim-5R		21. SPLR	WFU.
1601	1C 16-01	Lim-5	26-7-60	11. DLM	Converted to, see below.
16 (stbd)/ 01 (port)	CM 16-01	Lim-5M		ITWL	Trials aircraft, converted by 12-65. Converted to, see below
	1J 16-01	Lim-6		ITWL	Trials aircraft. Converted to, see below.
1601		Lim-6*bis*	15-6-65	53. PLM-Sz	WFU 20-5-88.
1602	1C 16-02	Lim-5	8-4-60	28. PLM	WFU.
1603	1C 16-03	Lim-5	8-4-60	28. PLM	WFU 1990, stored Katowice 1991-93. Sold to the USA by 1994.
1604	1C 16-04	Lim-5	21-4-60	26. PLM	WFU 1990, stored Katowice 6-91. Preserved *Muzeum Katyńskie*, Warsaw.
1605	1C 16-05	Lim-5	19-7-60	41. PLM	WFU 23-5-90, stored Katowice 1991-94. Sold to the USA 3-94.
1606	1C 16-06	Lim-5	4-5-60	29. PLM	WFU.
1607	1C 16-07	Lim-5	14-4-60	13. PLM	WFU 1990, std Katowice 1991-94. Sold to the USA/pvt owner 4-94 as N606BM.

No.	c/n	Type	Date	Unit	Notes
1608	1C 16-08	Lim-5	14-5-60	4. PLM	Crashed 9-3-65.
1609	1C 16-09	Lim-5	14-4-60	13. PLM	WFU 27-5-88.
1610	1C 16-10	Lim-5	16-4-60	39. PLM	WFU.
1611	1C 16-11	Lim-5	16-4-60	39. PLM	WFU 1990, stored Katowice 1991. Sold to the USA by 11-94.
1612	1C 16-12	Lim-5	14-5-60	4. PLM	Crashed 10-04-61.
1613	1C 16-13	Lim-5	23-6-60	26. PLM	Ex-INB trials aircraft. Converted to, see below.
	Lim-5R			21. SPLR	WFU 1990, stored Katowice 1991-94.
1614	1C 16-14	Lim-5	19-7-60	41. PLM	WFU.
1615	1C 16-15	Lim-5	21-4-60	26. PLM	WFU 1990, std Katowice 6-91 to 9-94.
1616	1C 16-16	Lim-5	4-5-60	29. PLM	Converted to, see below.
	Lim-5R			21. SPLR	Crashed 4-4-79.
1617	1C 16-17	Lim-5	4-5-60	29. PLM	WFU; sold to the USA 1988.
1618	1C 16-18	Lim-5	4-5-60	29. PLM	WFU.
1619	1C 16-19	Lim-5	14-5-60	3. PLM	WFU; sold to Australia 1992.
1620	1C 16-20	Lim-5	29-7-60	4. PLM	Converted to, see below.
	Lim-5R			21. SPLR	WFU 1990, stored Katowice 6-91.
1621	1C 16-21	Lim-5	19-4-60	3. PLM	WFU.
1622	1C 16-22	Lim-5	19-4-60	3. PLM	WFU.
1623	1C 16-23	Lim-5	29-7-60	4. PLM	Converted to, see below.
	Lim-5R			21. SPLR	WFU 13-6-88, std Bydgoszcz 1990-91.
1624	1C 16-24	Lim-5	29-7-60	4. PLM	Converted to, see below.
	Lim-5R			21. SPLR	WFU 18-1-91, stored Katowice 6-91.
1625	1C 16-25	Lim-5	20-4-60	45. PLM	Crashed 30-6-66.
1626	1C 16-26	Lim-5	26-6-60	CSL	WFU 27-6-88, std Bydgoszcz 1990-91.
1627	1C 16-27	Lim-5	7-6-60	45. PLM	WFU.
1628	1C 16-28	Lim-5	4-5-60	29. PLM	Converted to, see below.
	Lim-5R			21. SPLR	Crashed 21-6-79.
1629	1C 16-29	Lim-5	26-6-60	CSL	WFU 26-11-90, stored Katowice 1991? (possibly sold to USAF/DTESA).
1630	1C 16-30	Lim-5	23-6-60	29. PLM	WFU.
1701	1C 17-01	Lim-5	21-4-60	26. PLM	WFU.
1702	1C 17-02	Lim-5	11-5-60	45. PLM	WFU.
1703	1C 17-03	Lim-5	10-5-60	1.KOPL	Converted to, see below.
	Lim-5R			21. SPLR	WFU 23-5-90, stored Katowice 1991. Sold to the USA 3-94.
1704	1C 17-04	Lim-5	11-5-60	45. PLM	To the 45. LED 9-94, trials acft; WFU.
1705	1C 17-05	Lim-5	26-6-60	CSL	WFU 1990, std Katowice 6-91. Sold to the USA/private owner 1993 as N1705.
1706	1C 17-06	Lim-5	26-6-60	CSL	WFU 1990, std Katowice 1991 to 9-94.
1707	1C 17-07	Lim-5	11-5-60	45. PLM	WFU 1990, std Katowice 6-91 to 9-94; sold to the USA/pvt owner as N9143Z.
1708	1C 17-08	Lim-5	11-5-60	13. PLM	WFU.
1709	1C 17-09	Lim-5	11-5-60	13. PLM	WFU 23-3-89.
1710	1C 17-10	Lim-5	4-5-60	29. PLM	WFU 1990, stored Katowice 6-91.
1711	1C 17-11	Lim-5	22-6-60	40. PLM	WFU, stored Katowice 9-94.
1712	1C 17-12	Lim-5	7-7-60	21. SPLR	Converted to, see below.
	Lim-5R				WFU 27-6-88, std Bydgoszcz 1990-91.
1713	1C 17-13	Lim-5	9-5-60	2. PLM	WFU 1990, stored Katowice 1991-94. Sold to the USA 3-94.
1714	1C 17-14	Lim-5	2-5-60	4. PLM	WFU 27-6-88, std Bydgoszcz 1990-91.
1715	1C 17-15	Lim-5	9-5-60	2. PLM	WFU.
1716	1C 17-16	Lim-5	2-5-60	4. PLM	Converted to, see below.
	Lim-5R				Crashed 21-12-78, mid-air collision with Lim-5 '307'.
1717	1C 17-17	Lim-5	9-5-60	2. PLM	To the 45 LED, development aircraft; WFU Modlin; sold to the USA/private owner after 9-94, later to N1717M.
1718	1C 17-18	Lim-5	2-5-60	4. PLM	Converted to, see below.
	Lim-5R			21. SPLR	WFU 13-6-88, std Bydgoszcz 1988-91.
1719	1C 17-19	Lim-5	26-6-60	CSL	Converted to, see below.
	Lim-5R			21. SPLR	WFU 1990, stored Katowice 1991; sold to the USA by 11-94 as N1719.
1720	1C 17-20	Lim-5	4-5-60	29. PLM	WFU.
1721	1C 17-21	Lim-5	4-5-60	29. PLM	Converted to, see below.
	Lim-5R			21. SPLR	WFU 1990, std Katowice 1991 to 9-94.
					Preserved *Muzeum Braterstwa Broni* (Brotherhood-in-arms Museum), Drzonów.
1722	1C 17-22	Lim-5	11-6-60	3. PLM	Crashed 3-9-68.
1723	1C 17-23	Lim-5	4-5-60	29. PLM	WFU 7-6-88, stored Bydgoszcz 1991.
1724	1C 17-24	Lim-5	2-5-60	4. PLM	WFU.
1725	1C 17-25	Lim-5	2-5-60	4. PLM	WFU 1990, stored Katowice 6-91.
1726	1C 17-26	Lim-5	7-6-60	45. PLM	WFU 1990, stored Katowice 1991; sold to the USA by 11-94.
1727	1C 17-27	Lim-5	2-5-60	4. PLM	WFU.
1728	1C 17-28	Lim-5	15-6-60	2.KOPL	Converted to, see below.
	Lim-5R			21. SPLR	WFU 1990, std Katowice 1991 to 9-94.
1729	1C 17-29	Lim-5	15-6-60	2.KOPL	WFU.
1730	1C 17-30	Lim-5	7-7-60	21 SPLR	Converted to, see below.
	Lim-5R			21. SPLR	WFU; preserved Łódź Museum.
1809	1C 18-09	Lim-5			Pr. *Muzeum Braterstwa Broni*, Drzonów.
1830	1C 18-30	Lim-5	19-7-60	41. PLM	WFU.
1901	1C 19-01	Lim-5	19-7-60	41. PLM	WFU 27-5-88.
1902	1C 19-02	Lim-5	19-7-60	41. PLM	Converted to, see below.
	Lim-5R			21. SPLR	WFU 2-10-90.
1903	1C 19-03	Lim-5	23-6-60	29. PLM	Converted to, see below.
	Lim-5R			21. SPLR	WFU 1990, stored Katowice 1991.
1904	1C 19-04	Lim-5	23-6-60	29. PLM	WFU.
1905	1C 19-05	Lim-5	26-6-60	CSL	Converted to, see below.
	Lim-5R			21. SPLR	Sold to USAF/DTESA 1988, to 904 Red.
1906	1C 19-06	Lim-5	22-6-60	40. PLM	Converted to, see below.
	Lim-5R			21. SPLR	WFU 1990, std Katowice 1991 to 9-94.
1907	1C 19-07	Lim-5	26-7-60	11. DLM	WFU.
1908	1C 19-08	Lim-5	22-6-60	40. PLM	WFU 1990, stored Katowice 6-91.
1909	1C 19-09	Lim-5	26-6-60	CSL	WFU, stored MLiA, Kraków, 1991-93.
1910	1C 19-10	Lim-5	29-7-60	4. PLM	Converted to, see below.
	Lim-5R			21. SPLR	WFU 1990, stored Katowice 6-91. Preserved MLiA, Kraków.
1911	1C 19-11	Lim-5	22-6-60	40. PLM	WFU 12-6-90.
1912	1C 19-12	Lim-5	22-6-60	40. PLM	WFU 7-6-86; GIA TSWL.
1913	1C 19-13	Lim-5	26-6-60	CSL	Converted to, see below.
	Lim-5R			21. SPLR	Preserved Łódź Museum.
1914	1C 19-14	Lim-5	7-7-60	17. EL DLO	WFU.
101	1D 01-01	Lim-5P	12-2-59	CSL	Converted to, see below.
	Lim-6MR				WFU 30-8-85, preserved Siemirowice.
102	1D 01-02	Lim-5P	12-2-59	CSL	Converted to, see below.
	Lim-6M				Preserved Czaplinek.
103	1D 01-03	Lim-5P	5-2-59	39. PLM	Crashed 9-5-61.
104	1D 01-04	Lim-5P	5-2-59	39. PLM	WFU 4-8-70.
401	1D 04-01	Lim-5P	14-5-59	13. PLM	Converted to, see below.
	Lim-6M				Crashed 12-8-75.
402	1D 04-02	Lim-5P	14-5-59	13. PLM	Converted to, see below.
	Lim-6M				Preserved Miroslawiec as '1988 Red'.
403	1D 04-03	Lim-5P	4-5-59	29. PLM	Converted to, see below.
	Lim-6M				WFU.
404	1D 04-04	Lim-5P	6-5-59	3. PLM	WFU 21-1-79, GIA TSWL.
405	1D 04-05	Lim-5P	14-5-59	13. PLM	WFU 11-1-79, GIA TSWL.
406	1D 04-06	Lim-5P	6-5-59	3. PLM	GIA WAT, Warsaw.
407	1D 04-07	Lim-5P	6-5-59	3. PLM	WFU 11-1-79, GIA TSWL.
408	1D 04-08	Lim-5P	4-5-59	29. PLM	Derelict Oleśnica 1992.
409	1D 04-09	Lim-5P	25-6-60	26. PLM	Converted to, see below.
	Lim-6M				WFU.
410	1D 04-10	Lim-5P	21-4-60	26. PLM	Converted to, see below.
	Lim-6M				WFU.
411	1D 04-11	Lim-5P	16-7-60	13. PLM	WFU 11-1-79, GIA TSWL.
412	1D 04-12	Lim-5P	24-5-60	26. PLM	WFU 11-1-79.
413	1D 04-13	Lim-5P	14-4-60	13. PLM	Converted to, see below.
	Lim-6M				WFU.
414	1D 04-14	Lim-5P	2-4-60	1. PLM	Converted to, see below.
	Lim-6M				WFU.
415	1D 04-15	Lim-5P	2-4-60	1. PLM	Converted to, see below.
	Lim-6M				Crashed 17-6-78.

No.	c/n	Type	Date	Unit	Notes
416	1D 04-16	Lim-5P / Lim-6MR	27-6-60	11. PLM	Converted to, see below. / WFU.
417	1D 04-17	Lim-5P	2-4-60	1. PLM	Crashed 23-3-61.
418	1D 04-18	Lim-5P / Lim-6M	16-7-60	2. PLM	Converted to, see below. / WFU.
419	1D 04-19	Lim-5P	3-7-60	11. PLM	WFU 11-1-79, GIA TSWL.
420	1D 04-20	Lim-5P	15-7-60	11. PLM	Crashed 15-8-63.
506	1D 05-06	Lim-5P / Lim-6M	2-4-60	2. PLM	Converted to, see below. / WFU.
507*	1D 05-07	Lim-5P / Lim-6M	2-4-60	2. PLM	Converted to, see below. / WFU; *see note at end of table*
508	1D 05-08	Lim-5P	4-7-60	25. PLM	Crashed 30-4-64.
509	1D 05-09	Lim-5P	2-4-60	2. PLM	WFU 11-1-79, GIA TSWL.
510	1D 05-10	Lim-5P	2-4-60	2. PLM	WFU 1972 (stored Mierzęcice AB?)
511	1D 05-11	Lim-5P / Lim-6M	24-5-60	26. PLM	Converted to, see below. / Sold to USAF/DTESA 1988.
512	1D 05-12	Lim-5P / Lim-6M	8-4-60	25. PLM	Converted to, see below. / WFU.
513	1D 05-13	Lim-5P / Lim-6M	8-4-60	25. PLM	Converted to, see below. / WFU.
514	1D 05-14	Lim-5P / Lim-6M	8-4-60	25. PLM	Converted to, see below. / WFU.
515	1D 05-15	Lim-5P	8-4-60	25. PLM	WFU 11-1-79.
516	1D 05-16	Lim-5P / Lim-6M	20-4-60	45. PLM	Converted to, see below. / WFU.
517	1D 05-17	Lim-5P / Lim-6M	20-4-60	45. PLM	Converted to, see below. / WFU.
518	1D 05-18	Lim-5P	20-4-60	45. PLM	WFU 11-1-79, GIA TSWL.
519	1D 05-19	Lim-5P	2-4-60	1. PLM	Crashed 26-11-65.
520	1D 05-20	Lim-5P / Lim-6M	20-4-60	45. PLM	Converted to, see below. / WFU.
521	1D 05-21	Lim-5P	4-4-60	3. PLM	WFU 11-1-79, GIA TSWL.
522	1D 05-22	Lim-5P	28-5-60	11. PLM	Crashed 26-1-66.
523	1D 05-23	Lim-5P / Lim-6MR	4-5-60	40. PLM	Converted to, see below. / WFU 30-8-85, preserved Siemirowice.
524	1D 05-24	Lim-5P / Lim-6M	8-6-60	ITWL	Converted to, see below. / WFU.
601	1D 06-01	Lim-5P / Lim-6M	26-11-60	3. PLM	Converted to, see below. / Crashed; SOC 12-8-75.
602	1D 06-02	Lim-5P / Lim-6MR	22-11-60	1. PLM	Converted to, see below. / WFU.
603	1D 06-03	Lim-5P / Lim-6M	26-11-60	3. PLM	Converted to, see below. / WFU 29-12-83.
604	1D 06-04	Lim-5P / Lim-6M	26-11-60	3. PLM	Converted to, see below. / WFU.
605	1D 06-05	Lim-5P / Lim-6M	2-12-60	45. PLM	Converted to, see below. / WFU.
606	1D 06-06	Lim-5P / Lim-6M	26-11-60	45. PLM	Converted to, see below. / Preserved MLiA, Kraków.
607	1D 06-07	Lim-5P	19-12-60	45. PLM	Crashed 25-10-68.
608	1D 06-08	Lim-5P / Lim-6MR	22-11-60	1. PLM	Converted to, see below. / WFU.
609	1D 06-09	Lim-5P	29-11-60	2. PLM	WFU 11-1-79, GIA CSSTWL.
610	1D 06-10	Lim-5P	22-11-60	1. PLM	WFU 11-1-79, GIA TSWL.
611	1D 06-11	Lim-5P / Lim-6M	29-11-60	11. PLM	Converted to, see below. / WFU.
612	1D 06-12	Lim-5P	22-11-60	1. PLM	Crashed 28-7-61.
613	1D 06-13	Lim-5P / Lim-6M	22-11-60	1. PLM	Converted to, see below. / WFU.
614	1D 06-14	Lim-5P / Lim-6M	2-12-60	41. PLM	Converted to, see below. / WFU.
615	1D 06-15	Lim-5P / Lim-6M	29-11-60	11. PLM	Converted to, see below. / WFU.
616	1D 06-16	Lim-5P / Lim-6M	29-11-60	25. PLM	Converted to, see below. / WFU 28-9-81.
617	1D 06-17	Lim-5P / Lim-6MR	29-11-60	25. PLM	Converted to, see below. / Crashed; SOC 31.12.75
618	1D 06-18	Lim-5P / Lim-6MR	2-12-60	41. PLM	Converted to, see below. / Preserved MLiA, Kraków.
619	1D 06-19	Lim-5P / Lim-6M	2-12-60	26. PLM	Converted to, see below. / WFU 26-11-81.
620	1D 06-20	Lim-5P	2-12-60	26. PLM	WFU 11-1-79. / Sold to the USA 1-96 as N620PF.
621	1D 06-21	Lim-5P	1-12-60	2. PLM	WFU 11-1-79.
622	1D 06-22	Lim-5P / Lim-6M	1-12-60	34. PLM	Converted to, see below. / WFU.
623	1D 06-23	Lim-5P / Lim-6M	1-12-60	34. PLM	Converted to, see below. / WFU.
624	1D 06-24	Lim-5P / Lim-6M	1-12-60	34. PLM	Converted to, see below. / WFU.
625	1D 06-25	Lim-5P / Lim-6M	1-12-60	34. PLM	Converted to, see below. / WFU 8-12-88.
626	1D 06-26	Lim-5P / Lim-6M	1-12-60	34. PLM	Converted to, see below. / WFU.
627	1D 06-27	Lim-5P / Lim-6M	1-12-60	34. PLM	Converted to, see below. / WFU.
628	1D 06-28	Lim-5P / Lim-6M	11-1-61	40. PLM	Converted to, see below. / WFU.
629	1D 06-29	Lim-5P	11-1-61	40. PLM	WFU.
630	1D 06-30	Lim-5P / Lim-6M	10-1-61	29. PLM	Converted to, see below. / WFU.
631	1D 06-31	Lim-5P	11-1-61	40. PLM	Crashed 24-9-63.
632	1D 06-32	Lim-5P / Lim-6M	10-1-61	41. PLM	Converted to, see below. / WFU.
633	1D 06-33	Lim-5P / Lim-6MR	10-1-61	41. PLM	Converted to, see below. / WFU.
634	1D 06-34	Lim-5P / Lim-6MR	10-1-61	29. PLM	Converted to, see below. / Sold to USAF/DTESA 1988.
635	1D 06-35	Lim-5P / Lim-6MR	10-1-61	29. PLM	Converted to, see below. / Preserved Skarzysko Kamienna museum.
636	1D 06-36	Lim-5P / Lim-6MR	11-1-61	4. PLM	Converted to, see below. / WFU.
639	1D 06-39	Lim-5P / Lim-6MR	11-1-61	4. PLM	Converted to, see below. / WFU.
640	1D 06-40	Lim-5P / Lim-6MR	11-1-61	4. PLM	Converted to, see below. / WFU.
641	1D 06-41	Lim-5P / Lim-6MR	11-1-61	4. PLM	Converted to, see below. / WFU.
101	1F 01-01	Lim-5M / Lim-6*bis*	2-12-60	6. PLM-Sz	Converted to, see below. / To 45. LPSz-B 6-91. / Preserved *Muzeum Katyńskie.*
102	1F 01-02	Lim-5M / Lim-6*bis*	26-1-61	ITWL	Converted to, see below. / WFU 19-5-88; sold to Australia 1989.
103	1F 01-03	Lim-5M / Lim-6*bis*	2-12-60	5. DLM	Converted to, see below. / WFU 19-11-86.
104	1F 01-04	Lim-5M	2-12-60	6. PLM-Sz	Fate unknown (crashed ?)
105	1F 01-05	Lim-5M / Lim-6*bis*	1-12-60	5. DLM	Converted to, see below. / Preserved MLiA, Kraków.
106	1F 01-06	Lim-5M / Lim-6*bis*	10-5-61	6. PLM-Sz	Converted to, see below. / WFU.
107	1F 01-07	Lim-5M	14-4-61	5. PLM-Sz	Crashed 23-5-64.
108	1F 01-08	Lim-5M / Lim-6*bis*	1-12-60	5. DLM	Converted to, see below. / Crashed 5-9-77.
109	1F 01-09	Lim-5M / Lim-6*bis*	2-12-60	6. PLM-Sz	Converted to, see below. / Crashed 4-8-76, mid-air collision with a Soviet Air Force Mi-8.
110	1F 01-10	Lim-5M / Lim-6*bis*	13-3-61	30. PLM-Sz	Converted to, see below. / WFU 25-1-88.
201	1F 02-01	Lim-5M / Lim-6*bis*	13-3-61	30. PLM-Sz	Converted to, see below. / Crashed 27-3-85.
202	1F 02-02	Lim-5M	21-3-61	48. PLM-Sz	Crashed 21-8-64.
203	1F 02-03	Lim-5M / Lim-6*bis*	12-4-61	48. PLM-Sz	Converted to, see below. / WFU.

No.	Code	Type	Date	Unit	Notes
204	1F 02-04	Lim-5M / Lim-6bis	12-4-61	48. PLM-Sz	Converted to, see below. WFU.
205	1F 02-05	Lim-5M	12-4-61	48. PLM-Sz	Fate unknown (crashed ?)
206	1F 02-06	Lim-5M / Lim-6bis	12-4-61	48. PLM-Sz	Converted to, see below. WFU 21-5-88, stored Katowice 6-91.
207	1F 02-07	Lim-5M	5-5-61	30. PLM-Sz	Crashed 28-7-64.
208	1F 02-08	Lim-5M / Lim-6bis	12-4-61	48. PLM-Sz	Converted to, see below. WFU.
209	1F 02-09	Lim-5M / Lim-6bis	12-4-61	48. PLM-Sz	Converted to, see below. WFU
210	1F 02-10	Lim-5M / Lim-6bis	12-4-61	48. PLM-Sz	Converted to, see below. WFU.
211	1F 02-11	Lim-5M / Lim-6bis	5-5-61	30. PLM-Sz	Converted to, see below. WFU 25-1-88.
212	1F 02-12	Lim-5M / Lim-6bis	10-5-61	6. PLM-Sz	Converted to, see below. WFU 25-1-88; preserved Cersola, Italy?
213	1F 02-13	Lim-5M / Lim-6bis	5-5-61	30. PLM-Sz	Converted to, see below. WFU.
214	1F 02-14	Lim-5M	2-5-61	30. PLM-Sz	Fate unknown (crashed?)
215	1F 02-15	Lim-5M / Lim-6bis	2-5-61	30. PLM-Sz	Converted to, see below. WFU 25-1-88, dismantled at Bydgoszcz 1991.
216	1F 02-16	Lim-5M / Lim-6bis	5-5-61	30. PLM-Sz	Converted to, see below. WFU 20-5-88.
217	1F 02-17	Lim-5M / Lim-6bis	10-5-61	6. PLM-Sz	Converted to, see below. Crashed 30-5-87.
218	1F 02-18	Lim-5M / Lim-6bis	13-3-61	30. PLM-Sz	Converted to, see below. WFU 25-1-88.
219	1F 02-19	Lim-5M / Lim-6bis	1-12-60	5. DLM	Converted to, see below. WFU.
220	1F 02-20	Lim-5M / Lim-6bis	2-12-60	6. PLM-Sz	Converted to, see below. WFU.
301	1F 03-01	Lim-5M / Lim-6bis	19-1-61	48. PLM-Sz	Converted to, see below. WFU Katowice 6-91.
302	1F 03-02	Lim-5M	17-3-61	6. PLM-Sz	Fate unknown (crashed?)
303	1F 03-03	Lim-5M / Lim-6bis	12-4-61	48. PLM-Sz	Converted to, see below. WFU.
304	1F 03-04	Lim-5M / Lim-6bis	19-1-61	48. PLM-Sz	Converted to, see below. WFU.
305	1F 03-05	Lim-5M	20-1-61	5. PLM-Sz	Crashed 1961.
306	1F 03-06	Lim-5M / Lim-6bis	20-1-61	5. PLM-Sz	Converted to, see below. WFU; sold to France 19-10-89, preserved Savigny.
307	1F 03-07	Lim-5M / Lim-6bis	20-1-61	5. PLM-Sz	Converted to, see below. Pr. *Muzeum Braterstwa Broni*, Drzonów.
308	1F 03-08	Lim-5M	18-3-61	5. PLM-Sz	Crashed 7-2-64.
309	1F 03-09	Lim-5M	19-1-61	48. PLM-Sz	Crashed 26-4-61.
310	1F 03-10	Lim-5M / Lim-6bis	17-3-61	6. PLM-Sz	Converted to, see below. WFU.
311	1F 03-11	Lim-5M / Lim-6bis	20-1-61	5. PLM-Sz	Converted to, see below. WFU 18-5-88, stored Katowice 6-91.
312	1F 03-12	Lim-5M / Lim-6bis	17-3-61	6. PLM-Sz	Converted to, see below. WFU.
313	1F 03-13	Lim-5M / Lim-6bis	18-3-61	5. PLM-Sz	Converted to, see below. WFU 18-5-88.
314	1F 03-14	Lim-5M / Lim-6bis	17-3-61	6. PLM-Sz	Converted to, see below. WFU 25-1-88.
315	1F 03-15	Lim-5M / Lim-6bis	20-1-61	5. PLM-Sz	Converted to, see below. WFU.
316	1F 03-16	Lim-5M / Lim-6bis	18-3-61	5. PLM-Sz	Converted to, see below. WFU 19-11-86, preserved Polish Navy Museum, Gdynia.
317	1F 03-17	Lim-5M / Lim-6bis	17-3-61	6. PLM-Sz	Converted to, see below. WFU 18-5-88.
318	1F 03-18	Lim-5M / Lim-6bis	17-3-61	6. PLM-Sz	Converted to, see below. WFU.
319	1F 03-19	Lim-5M / Lim-6bis	18-3-61	5. PLM-Sz	Converted to, see below. To the 45. LPSz-B 6-91. WFU 2-92, std Katowice 5-93; sold to the USA by 3-94.
320	1F 03-20	Lim-5M / Lim-6bis	12-4-61	48. PLM-Sz	Converted to, see below. WFU.
321	1F 03-21	Lim-5M / Lim-6bis	18-3-61	5. PLM-Sz	Converted to, see below. Photo exists as Lim-6R with camera fairing aft of nose gear. To the 45. LPSz-B 6-91. WFU 2-92, stored Katowice 1991-93.
322	1F 03-22	Lim-5M / Lim-6bis	14-4-61	5. PLM-Sz	Converted to, see below. WFU.
323	1F 03-23	Lim-5M / Lim-6bis	10-5-61	6. PLM-Sz	Converted to, see below. WFU.
324	1F 03-24	Lim-5M / Lim-6bis	12-4-61	48. PLM-Sz	Converted to, see below. WFU 19-11-86.
325	1F 03-25	Lim-5M / Lim-6bis	12-4-61	48. PLM-Sz	Converted to, see below. WFU 25-1-88, stored Bydgoszcz 1991. Sold to the USA/private owner.
326	1F 03-26	Lim-5M / Lim-6bis	12-4-61	48. PLM-Sz	Converted to, see below. Crashed 31-1-79.
327	1F 03-27	Lim-5M / Lim-6bis	13-4-61	17. EL DLO	Converted to, see below. WFU 19-11-86.
328	1F 03-28	Lim-5M / Lim-6bis	18-3-61	5. PLM-Sz	Converted to, see below. Crashed 1972.
329	1F 03-29	Lim-5M / Lim-6bis	2-5-61	30. PLM-Sz	Converted to, see below. WFU 19-5-88.
330	1F 03-30	Lim-5M / Lim-6bis	10-5-61	6. PLM-Sz	Converted to, see below. Crashed 2-4-80.
401	1J 04-01	Lim-6 / Lim-6R	8-6-65	21. SPLR	Converted to, see below. WFU.
402	1J 04-02	Lim-6 / Lim-6bis / Lim-6R	8-4-63	51. PLM-Sz	Converted to, see below. Converted to, see below. WFU.
403	1J 04-03	Lim-6 / Lim-6bis / Lim-6R	8-4-63	51. PLM-Sz	Converted to, see below. Converted to, see below. WFU 28-4-71.
404	1J 04-04	Lim-6 / Lim-6bis / Lim-6R	8-4-63	51. PLM-Sz	Converted to, see below. Converted to, see below. WFU 24-3-80, GIA TSWL.
405	1J 04-05	Lim-6 / Lim-6bis / Lim-6R	28-3-63	53. PLM-Sz	Converted to, see below. Converted to, see below. WFU.
406	1J 04-06	Lim-6 / Lim-6bis	25.05.63	5. PLM-Sz	Converted to, see below. WFU 15-6-88, stored Katowice 1991.
407	1J 04-07	Lim-6 / Lim-6bis / Lim-6R	28-3-63	53. PLM-Sz	Converted to, see below. Converted to, see below. WFU.
408	1J 04-08	Lim-6 / Lim-6R	28-3-63	53. PLM-Sz	Converted to, see below. WFU.
409	1J 04-09	Lim-6 / Lim-6bis / Lim-6R	28-3-63	53. PLM-Sz	Converted to, see below. Converted to, see below. WFU.
410	1J 04-10	Lim-6 / Lim-6bis	8-4-63	51. PLM-Sz	Converted to, see below. To the 45. LPSz-B 6-91. WFU 2-92, stored Katowice 1993.
411	1J 04-11	Lim-6 / Lim-6bis / Lim-6R	28-3-63	53. PLM-Sz	Converted to, see below. Converted to, see below. WFU.
412	1J 04-12	Lim-6 / Lim-6bis / Lim-6R	28-3-63	53. PLM-Sz	Converted to, see below. Converted to, see below. Crashed 1972.
413	1J 04-13	Lim-6 / Lim-6bis / Lim-6R	28-3-63	53. PLM-Sz	Converted to, see below. Converted to, see below. WFU 13-6-88, stored Bydgoszcz 1991.

No.	Code	Type	Date	Unit	Notes
414	1J 04-14	Lim-6			Converted to, see below.
		Lim-6bis	28-3-63	53. PLM-Sz	To the 45. LPSz-B 6-91. WFU 2-92, stored Katowice 1993.
415	1J 04-15	Lim-6			Converted to, see below.
		Lim-6bis	28-3-63	53. PLM-Sz	Converted to, see below.
		Lim-6R			WFU.
416	1J 04-16	Lim-6			Converted to, see below.
		Lim-6bis	8-4-63	51. PLM-Sz	Converted to, see below.
		Lim-6R			Crashed 17-7-63.
417	1J 04-17	Lim-6			Converted to, see below.
		Lim-6bis	28-3-63	53. PLM-Sz	WFU 13-6-88; sold to the Netherlands 1-91.
418	1J 04-18	Lim-6			Converted to, see below.
		Lim-6bis	8-4-63	51. PLM-Sz	Reported in Polish source as Lim-6R but photo shows aircraft as 'pure' Lim-6bis. WFU, stored Katowice 5-91; sold to the Netherlands 1991.
419	1J 04-19	Lim-6			Converted to, see below.
		Lim-6bis	8-4-63	51. PLM-Sz	Converted to, see below.
		Lim-6R			WFU 22-6-88, stored Bydgoszcz 1991.
420	1J 04-20	Lim-6			Converted to, see below.
		Lim-6bis	8-4-63	51. PLM-Sz	Converted to, see below.
		Lim-6R			WFU.
421	1J 04-21	Lim-6			Converted to, see below.
		Lim-6bis	8-4-63	51. PLM-Sz	Converted to, see below.
		Lim-6R			WFU.
422	1J 04-22	Lim-6			Converted to, see below.
		Lim-6bis	8-4-63	51. PLM-Sz	Converted to, see below.
		Lim-6R			WFU 15-6-88, stored Katowice 6-91.
423	1J 04-23	Lim-6			Converted to, see below.
		Lim-6bis	29-4-63	51. PLM-Sz	Converted to, see below.
		Lim-6R			WFU.
424	1J 04-24	Lim-6			Converted to, see below.
		Lim-6bis	29-4-63	53. PLM-Sz	WFU.
425	1J 04-25	Lim-6			Converted to, see below.
		Lim-6bis	29-4-63	53. PLM-Sz	Crashed 11-9-63.
426	1J 04-26	Lim-6			Converted to, see below.
		Lim-6bis	29-4-63	51. PLM-Sz	WFU 21-5-88, stored Katowice 6-91.
427	1J 04-27	Lim-6			Converted to, see below.
		Lim-6bis	29-4-63	53. PLM-Sz	Preserved Łódź Museum.
428	1J 04-28	Lim-6			Converted to, see below.
		Lim-6bis	29-4-63	51. PLM-Sz	Converted to, see below.
		Lim-6R			WFU.
429	1J 04-29	Lim-6			Converted to, see below.
		Lim-6bis	25-3-63	53. PLM-Sz	WFU.
430	1J 04-30	Lim-6			Converted to, see below.
		Lim-6bis	25-3-63	53. PLM-Sz	WFU.
431	1J 04-31	Lim-6			Converted to, see below.
		Lim-6bis	25-3-63	53. PLM-Sz	To the 45. LPSz-B 6-91. WFU 2-92, stored Katowice 1993.
432	1J 04-32	Lim-6			Converted to, see below.
		Lim-6bis	29-4-63	51. PLM-Sz	To the 45. LPSz-B 6-91. WFU 2-92, stored Katowice 1993.
433	1J 04-33	Lim-6			Converted to, see below.
		Lim-6bis	25-5-63	5. PLM-Sz	WFU.
434	1J 04-34	Lim-6			Converted to, see below.
		Lim-6bis	25-5-63	5. PLM-Sz	WFU 20-5-88; sold to Australia/private owner 1989 as VH-ALG.
435	1J 04-35	Lim-6			Converted to, see below.
		Lim-6bis	25-5-63	53. PLM-Sz	WFU.
436	1J 04-36	Lim-6			Converted to, see below.
		Lim-6bis	29-4-63	53. PLM-Sz	WFU.
437	1J 04-37	Lim-6			Converted to, see below.
		Lim-6bis	29-4-63	51. PLM-Sz	Converted to, see below.
		Lim-6R			WFU.
438	1J 04-38	Lim-6			Converted to, see below.
		Lim-6bis	29-4-63	53. PLM-Sz	To the 45. LPSz-B 6-91. WFU 2-92; sold to the USA/private owner 16-2-94 as N2153V.
439	1J 04-39	Lim-6			Converted to, see below.
		Lim-6bis	25-5-63	5. PLM-Sz	Crashed 6-4-64.
440	1J 04-40	Lim-6			Converted to, see below.
		Lim-6bis	25-5-63	53. PLM-Sz	To the 45. LPSz-B 6-91. WFU 2-92, stored Katowice 1993.
441	1J 04-41	Lim-6bis	30-9-69	6. PLM-Sz	Cvtd Lim-5M '1030' (c/n 1F 10-30). Converted to, see below.
		Lim-6R			Crashed 19-11-71.
501	1J 05-01	Lim-6R	16-8-63	53. PLM-Sz	WFU.
502	1J 05-02	Lim-6R	16-8-63	53. PLM-Sz	Crashed, SOC 10-6-70.
503	1J 05-03	Lim-6R	16-8-63	53. PLM-Sz	Crashed, SOC 26-6-72.
504	1J 05-04	Lim-6R	13-1-65	ITWL	WFU 21-5-88, stored Katowice 6-91.
505	1J 05-05	Lim-6R	16-8-63	53. PLM-Sz	WFU 2-92, stored Katowice 1993. Sold to the USA/private owner 15-2-94 as N2153K.
506	1J 05-06	Lim-6R	12-11-63	53. PLM-Sz	To the 45. LPSz-B 6-91. WFU 2-92; sold to the USA by 10-93.
507	1J 05-07	Lim-6R	12-11-63	53. PLM-Sz	WFU.
508	1J 05-08	Lim-6R	12-11-63	53. PLM-Sz	WFU 2-92, stored Katowice 5-93. Sold to the USA 3-94.
509	1J 05-09	Lim-6R	12-11-63	53. PLM-Sz	WFU.
510	1J 05-10	Lim-6R	12-11-63	53. PLM-Sz	To the 45. LPSz-B 6-91. WFU 2-92, stored Katowice 1994. Sold to the USA as N17JL.
511	1J 05-11	Lim-6R	12-11-63	51. PLM-Sz	To the 45. LPSz-B 6-91. WFU 2-92, std Katowice 5-93. Sold to the USA 3-94.
512	1J 05-12	Lim-6R	12-11-63	51. PLM-Sz	To the 45. LPSz-B 6-91. WFU 2-92, stored Katowice 1993.
513	1J 05-13	Lim-6R	12-11-63	51. PLM-Sz	WFU.
514	1J 05-14	Lim-6R	14-11-63	51. PLM-Sz	To the 45. LPSz-B 6-91. WFU 2-92, std Katowice 05.93. Sold to the USA 3-94.
515	1J 05-15	Lim-6R	14-11-63	51. PLM-Sz	WFU.
516	1J 05-16	Lim-6R	14-11-63	51. PLM-Sz	To the 45. LED, development aircraft? WFU.
517	1J 05-17	Lim-6R	14-11-63	51. PLM-Sz	WFU.
518	1J 05-18	Lim-6R	15-11-63	6. PLM-Sz	WFU.
519	1J 05-19	Lim-6R	14-11-63	51. PLM-Sz	WFU.
520	1J 05-20	Lim-6R	14-11-63	51. PLM-Sz	WFU 16-2-88.
521	1J 05-21	Lim-6R	15-11-63	6. PLM-Sz	Crashed, SOC 16-9-68.
522	1J 05-22	Lim-6R	15-11-63	6. PLM-Sz	To the 45. LPSz-B 6-91. WFU 20-2-92, std Katowice 5-93. Sold to the USA 3-94.
523	1J 05-23	Lim-6R	15-11-63	6. PLM-Sz	To the 45. LPSz-B 6-91. WFU 2-92, std Katowice 5-93; sold to the USA 3-94.
524	1J 05-24	Lim-6R	15-11-63	6. PLM-Sz	WFU.
525	1J 05-25	Lim-6R	15-11-63	6. PLM-Sz	WFU 31-12-87.
526	1J 05-26	Lim-6R	14-11-63	5. PLM-Sz	WFU 14-1-91, preserved Zawiercie.
527	1J 05-27	Lim-6R	15-2-64	6. PLM-Sz	To the 45. LPSz-B 6-91. WFU 2-92, preserved Warsaw-Żoliborz.
528	1J 05-28	Lim-6R	14-11-63	5. PLM-Sz	To the 45. LPSz-B 6-91. WFU 2-92, std Katowice 5-93. Sold to the USA 3-94 as H17HQ.
529	1J 05-29	Lim-6R	14-11-63	5. PLM-Sz	WFU, stored Katowice 1991.
530	1J 05-30	Lim-6R	14-11-63	5. PLM-Sz	WFU.
601	1J 06-01	Lim-6R	5-1-64	21. SPLR	WFU 20-5-88.
602	1J 06-02	Lim-6R	5-1-64	21. SPLR	WFU.
603	1J 06-03	Lim-6bis	25-1-64	30. PLM-Sz	WFU.
604	1J 06-04	Lim-6R	5-1-64	21. SPLR	WFU 24-3-80, GIA TSWL; later sold to the USA/private owner as N604LS.
605	1J 06-05	Lim-6R	16-1-64	21. SPLR	To the 45. PLM-B; preserved Babimost barracks as '1982'.
606	1J 06-06	Lim-6R	16-1-64	21. SPLR	WFU.
607	1J 06-07	Lim-6R	16-1-64	21. SPLR	WFU.
608	1J 06-08	Lim-6R	16-1-64	21. SPLR	Preserved Łódź Museum.
609	1J 06-09	Lim-6R	27-7-64	21. SPLR	To the 45. LPSz-B 6-91. WFU 2-92, stored Katowice 9-94.

610	1J 06-10	Lim-6R	16-1-64	53. PLM-Sz	WFU.
611	1J 06-11	Lim-6R	16-1-64	21. SPLR	WFU 13-6-88, stored Bydgoszcz 1991.
612	1J 06-12	Lim-6R	15-2-64	16. DLM-Sz	WFU.
613	1J 06-13	Lim-6R	16-1-64	53. PLM-Sz	WFU (stored Mieręzcice AB?)
614	1J 06-14	Lim-6R	16-1-64	21. SPLR	WFU.
615	1J 06-15	Lim-6bis	25-1-64	30. PLM-Sz	WFU 14-1-91, stored Katowice 1991.
616	1J 06-16	Lim-6bis	25-1-64	30. PLM-Sz	WFU 19-5-88.
617	1J 06-17	Lim-6bis	25-1-64	30. PLM-Sz	WFU.
618	1J 06-18	Lim-6bis	25-1-64	30. PLM-Sz	WFU.
619	1J 06-19	Lim-6R	16-1-64	53. PLM-Sz	WFU 2-92; sold to the USA/private owner as N619M.
620	1J 06-20	Lim-6R	25-1-64	30. PLM-Sz	WFU 21-5-88.
621	1J 06-21	Lim-6bis	25-1-64	30. PLM-Sz	WFU.
622	1J 06-22	Lim-6bis	25-1-64	30. PLM-Sz	WFU 16-2-88.
623	1J 06-23	Lim-6bis	25-1-64	30. PLM-Sz	WFU.
624	1J 06-24	Lim-6R	25-1-64	30. PLM-Sz	WFU.
625	1J 06-25	Lim-6R	25-1-64	30. PLM-Sz	WFU 18-5-88.
626	1J 06-26	Lim-6R	25-1-64	30. PLM-Sz	WFU.
627	1J 06-27	Lim-6R	25-1-64	30. PLM-Sz	WFU.
628	1J 06-28	Lim-6R	25-1-64	30. PLM-Sz	WFU 14-1-91, stored Katowice 6-91.
629	1J 06-29	Lim-6R	25-1-64	30. PLM-Sz	Converted Lim-6bis? (photos show no camera fairings). WFU 14-1-91, stored Katowice 6-91.
630	1J 06-30	Lim-6R	25-1-64	30. PLM-Sz	WFU.
631	1J 06-31	Lim-6R	2-3-64	30. PLM-Sz	To the 45. LPSz-B 6-91. WFU 2-92, stored Katowice 9-94. Sold to the USA/private owner as N73568.
632	1J 06-32	Lim-6R	2-3-64	30. PLM-Sz	WFU 18-5-88.
633	1J 06-33	Lim-6R	2-3-64	30. PLM-Sz	WFU 14-1-91, stored Katowice 6-91.
634	1J 06-34	Lim-6R	2-3-64	30. PLM-Sz	WFU 20-5-88.
635	1J 06-35	Lim-6R	13-3-64	21. SPLR	Pr. Muzeum Braterstwa Broni, Drzonów.
636	1J 06-36	Lim-6R	13-3-64	21. SPLR	WFU.
637	1J 06-37	Lim-6R	6-3-64	21. SPLR	Preserved Łódź Museum.
638	1J 06-38	Lim-6R	6-3-64	21. SPLR	WFU.
639	1J 06-39	Lim-6bis	2-3-64	30. PLM-Sz	WFU.
640	1J 06-40	Lim-6R	2-3-64	30. PLM-Sz	Reported in Polish source as 'pure' Lim-6bis but photo clearly shows aft camera pod. WFU.

KLM = korpus lotnictwa myśliwskiego – fighter corps; KOPL = korpus obrony przeciwlotniczej – air defence corps; WSP – Wyższa Szkoła Pilotażu – Higher Flying School (location unknown); DLM-Sz = dywizja lotnictwa myśliwsko-szturmowego – fighter/ground-attack division; WAT = Wojskowa Akademia Techniczna – Military Technical Academy in Warsaw.

* 507 Red is something of a mystery aircraft. An unidentified Polish museum contains a camouflaged Fresco-D serialled 507 Red; however, this aircraft is of obviously Soviet origin (with RP-1 radar and no pylons) and thus cannot be Lim-6M c/n 1D 05-07. On the other hand, Polish sources give no indication of a MiG-17PF with this serial (c/n 58210507 or 0507) being operated by the PWL. Thus, the aircraft is very probably ex-307 Red at Drzonów. Some Polish museums have a habit of regularly repainting aircraft displayed in the open as their finish deteriorates – and, worse, painting them in phoney markings in so doing.

Another mystery aircraft whose identity is unknown is a Lim-5 with the phony serial 1952 Red preserved at Słupsk AB. Also, an unserialled Lim-5P with the tail painted in rainbow colours and the System rolet okiennych 'Perfecta' logo on the fuselage advertising for a brand of Venetian blinds is preserved near a petrol station in Wrocław; its identity is likewise unknown.

As a point of interest, the Euromil handbook seems to have created some confusion by the entries contained in its Polish MiG-17 section. For example, it lists a Lim-5 serialled 101 Red (c/n 1C 10-01) preserved at Bemowo AB; however, 1C 10-01 is in fact an export aircraft, whereas the serial '101 Red' belonged to 1C 01-01. Likewise, it includes a lot of aircraft which never existed – Lim-5s (c/ns 1C 00-05, 1C 00-07, 1C 00-10, 1C 02-12, 1C 02-15, 1C 02-18 through 1C 02-20, 1C 02-24, 1C 02-30 and 1C 19-28), Lim-5Ps (c/ns 1D 07-01, 1D 07-02, 1D 07-05 through 1D 07-07, 1D 07-11, 1D 07-14, 1D 07-20, 1D 07-21, 1D 07-25 through 1D 07-27 and 1D 09-05), Lim-5Ms (c/ns 1F 05-14, 1F 05-23, 1F 08-03, 1F 08-10, 1F 08-14, 1F 08-18 and 1F 15-13) and Lim-6bises (c/ns 1J 06-51, 1J 09-05, 1J 09-06, 1J 09-08, 1J 09-11, 1J 09-15, 1J 09-16, 1J 09-21, 1J 09-26 and 1J 09-48). Lim-5 '307 Red', which was destroyed in a crash, is listed as preserved at Muzeum Braterstwa Broni in Drzonów; conversely, 1021 Red and 1028 Red, which allegedly crashed, were actually simply retired after running out of service life. Another Western handbook, Militair'82, has Lim-5 '1119 Red' (actually an export aircraft), Lim-5Ps '137 Red' and '814 Red'.

ROMANIA

The Romanian Air Force (Fortele Aeriene ale Republicii Socialişte Române) received the MiG-17F day fighter and the MiG-17PF interceptor in 1956. The Fresco served alongside the Fagot-A/B, equipping two mixed fighter regiments in the 1950s and 1960s. All known Romanian MiG-17PFs had the early-model RP-1 Izumrood-1 radar.

In the early 1970s the MiG-17s were transferred to ground attack units (two regiments and several independent squadrons) which could still perform general fighter tasks if required. According to Western sources, more than 70 MiG-17s were still operational in the 1970s; however, no more than ten remained in use as tactical trainers by late 1991.

Serial	C/n	Version	Remarks
26	?	?	
41	?	?	
58	?	?	
66	?	?	
76	?	?	
79	?	?	
84	?	?	
91	?	?	
93	?	?	
95	?	?	
96	?	?	
97	?	?	
104	...104?	?	
112	...112?	?	
413	...413	MiG-17PF	C/n is 58210413 or 0413.
418	...418	MiG-17PF	C/n is 58210418 or 0418.
442	...442	MiG-17F	Preserved Museul Aviaţiei, Bucharest-Otopeni airport.
443	...443	MiG-17F	
502	0502?	MiG-17PF	Tbilisi-built? Preserved Balta Verde AB, Craiova.
0904	0904?	MiG-17PF	Tbilisi-built? Preserved Museul Aviaţiei.

Photographs on the opposite page:

Top: **442 Red, an overall light grey MiG-17F preserved at the Museul Militar Naţional in Bucharest.** Peter Davison

Centre: **444 Red, another Romanian Air Force Fresco-C on display at the Museul Militar Naţional in immaculate condition.** Peter Davison

Bottom left: **This rather battered MiG-17PF (418 Red) is preserved at an unspecified Romanian museum.** Peter Davison

Bottom right: **Early MiG-17PF '0904 Red', another Museul Militar Naţional exhibit. Unlike the Fresco-Cs, the Romanian Fresco-Ds retained their natural metal finish throughout.** Peter Davison

SOMALIA

From 1963 onwards the Somalian Aeronautical Corps (*Dayuuradaha Xoogga Dalka Somaliyeed*) operated at least 12 late-production MiG-17 *Fresco-As* (some sources claim that 54 had been delivered by 1967). Most of them were based in Mogadishu, but a MiG detachment was also established at Hargeisa in the former British Somaliland. The MiG-17s wore two-tone green or green/brown camouflage and had serials in the 100 block, though some of these were allocated to MiG-15s.

Many of the *Fresco-As* were lost during Somalia's war with Ethiopia in the summer of 1977. The survivors quickly became unserviceable in the 1980s after Somalia terminated its friendship treaty with the USSR in November 1977. Only four MiG-17s have been identified; these were derelict by the early 1990s.

Serial	C/n	Remarks
CC 125	1025?	Derelict Mogadishu.
CC 129	1029?	Derelict Kismayu.
CC 134	1034?	Derelict Mogadishu.
CC 136	1036	Built in Komsomol'sk-on-Amur; derelict Mogadishu.

Another unserialled MiG-17 was abandoned at Hargeisa in relatively good condition.

Some sources claim the Somalian Aeronautical Corps received some 40 MiG-17Fs (?), only ten of which were flyable. However, there is no tangible evidence of *Fresco-Cs* ever being delivered to Somalia.

SOVIET UNION

As noted earlier, Soviet Air Force MiG-17s originally had three- or four-digit serials based on the c/n and allowing more or less positive identification. After 1955 these were later replaced by two-digit tactical codes rendering identification impossible unless the c/n is known. More or less positively identified aircraft are listed below; post-1955 tactical codes are indicated in bold type.

Serial/code	C/n	Version	Remarks
01 Red (a)	54210101	MiG-17 (SI-01)	First pre-production aircraft.
01 Red (b)	?	MiG-17*	Preserved Russian Air Force Museum, Monino.
01 Red (c)	54211827	MiG-17†	Ex-827 Red. GSVG; scrapped Rangsdorf AB 1992.
01 Red (d)	?	MiG-17MM	Prototype, NII VVS trials aircraft.
'01 Red' (e)	?	MiG-17AS	Large airbrakes aft of wings. Preserved in pioneer camp near Moscow, phoney tactical code.
02 White outline	1407100	MiG-17†	Ex-71. Preserved Kiev (Army Museum), non-authentic tan/olive drab/light green/dark green camouflage. Tactical code later changed to 02 Red.
02 Black outline	7444	MiG-17F	GSVG; scrapped Rangsdorf AB 1992.
02 Blue	1409010	MiG-17†	Ex-910 Red. GSVG; scrapped Rangsdorf AB 1992.
05 Red	54210461	MiG-17	Ex-461 Red. GSVG; scrapped Rangsdorf AB 1992.
06 Red	54211006?	MiG-17 (SDK-5)	Avionics testbed, Mikoyan OKB.
09 Red	1408003	MiG-17	Ex-803 Red. GSVG; scrapped Rangsdorf AB 1992.
15 Blue	54210565	MiG-17	Ex-565 Red, fighter-bomber conversion prototype, Mikoyan OKB.
16 Red	7421?	MiG-17F?	Built in Komsomol'sk-on-Amur? C/n read off poor-quality photograph.
17 Red (a)	54210349	MiG-17	Ex-349 Red. GSVG; scrapped Rangsdorf AB 1992.
17 Red (b)	1215391	MiG-17†	Ex-1291 Red. Preserved Central Aviation and Spaceflight Museum, Moscow; later to open-air museum at Moscow-Khodynka.
17 Yellow	?	MiG-17†	Kubinka display team, solid red top version.
17 Blue	0988 (?)	MiG-17F	Ex-988 Red? C/n off air intake cover (full c/n may be 54210988 or 0915388!).
19 Yellow	?	MiG-17†	Kubinka display team, solid red top version.
20 Red (a)	1409011	MiG-17†	Ex-911 Red. GSVG; scrapped Rangsdorf 1992.
20 Red (b)	?	MiG-17†	Preserved Central Armed Forces Museum, Moscow.
21 Yellow	?	MiG-17†	Kubinka display team, solid red top version.
24 Blue	1032 (?)	MiG-17F	Ex-1032 Red? C/n off air intake cover (full c/n may be 54211032 or 1015332!).
25 Red (a)	54211076	MiG-17†	GSVG; scrapped Rangsdorf AB 1992.
25 Red (b)	0515347?	MiG-17†	Preserved Soviet Army Museum, Moscow; c/n read off poor-quality photo. Tactical code later changed to 25 Red outline.
25 Blue	?	MiG-17F	Fighter-bomber. Defected to West Germany 25-5-67.
27 Red	0822	MiG-17	Built in Komsomol'sk-on-Amur? Ex-822 Red. GSVG; scrapped Rangsdorf AB 1992.
27 Yellow	?	MiG-17†	Kubinka display team, solid red top version.
28 Red	1115328	MiG-17†	
28 Yellow	?	MiG-17†	Kubinka display team, solid red top version.
31 Blue	7238	MiG-17F	
32 Red	?	MiG-17†	Avionics testbed.
33 Red	2194	MiG-17	Built in Komsomol'sk-on-Amur
35 Yellow	?	MiG-17†	Kubinka display team, solid red top version.
37 Red	1515399	MiG-17†	Ex-1599 Red. GSVG; scrapped Rangsdorf 1992.
43 Red	?	MiG-17M	Converted MiG-17AS, preserved North Fleet Air Arm Museum, Severomorsk.
48 Red	?	MiG-17†	Kubinka display team, red/natural metal top version.
49 Red	?	MiG-17†	Kubinka display team, red/natural metal top version.
50 Red	?	MiG-17†	Kubinka display team, red/natural metal top version.
51 Red	?	MiG-17†	Kubinka display team, red/natural metal top version.
53 Red (a)	?	MiG-17†	Kubinka display team, red/natural metal top version.
53 Red (b)	54210958	MiG-17†	Ex-958 Red. GSVG; scrapped Rangsdorf AB 1992.
54 Red (a)	?	MiG-17†	Kubinka display team, red/natural metal top version.
54 Red (b)	6231	MiG-17†	Built in Komsomol'sk-on-Amur? Ex-231 Red. GSVG; scrapped Rangsdorf AB 1992.
54 Red (c)	0815312	MiG-17 (†?)	Ex-0812 Red? GSVG; scrapped Rangsdorf AB 1992.
55 Red (a)	54211761	MiG-17†	Ex-761 Red. GSVG; scrapped Rangsdorf AB 1992.
55 Red (b)	?	MiG-17F	Preserved Kubinka AB museum; fake tactical code.
57 Red	54210525	MiG-17	Ex-525 Red. GSVG; scrapped Rangsdorf AB 1992.
61 Red	54211860	MiG-17†	Ex-860 Red. DOSAAF, preserved Moscow-Khodynka.
69 Red	?	MiG-17M	
71 Red (a)	54211513	MiG-17†	Ex-513 Red. GSVG; scrapped Rangsdorf AB 1992.
71 Red (b)	?	MiG-17†	Preserved in museum, location unknown.
75 Red	1407009	MiG-17	Ex-709 Red. GSVG; scrapped Rangsdorf AB 1992.
81 Red	0815366	MiG-17 (†?)	Ex-0866 Red? GSVG; scrapped Rangsdorf AB 1992.
88 Red	1801	MiG-17	Built in Komsomol'sk-on-Amur? Ex-801 Red. GSVG; scrapped Rangsdorf AB 1992.

Code	C/n	Type	Notes
91 Red	0915369	MiG-17 (†?)	Ex-0969 Red? GSVG; scrapped Rangsdorf AB 1992.
95 Red	54211076	MiG-17†	GSVG; scrapped Rangsdorf AB 1992.
005 Red	54211005	MiG-17† (SI-16)	Development aircraft, Mikoyan OKB.
007 Red	54211007	MiG-17† (SDK-5)	Avionics testbed, Mikoyan OKB.
008 Red	58211008?	MiG-17PF	
017 Red	54212017	MiG-17†	
028 Red	54211028	MiG-17†	
054 Red	2054	MiG-17†	Built in Komsomol'sk-on-Amur?
067 Red	54212067	MiG-17†	
100 Red	?	MiG-17AS	Preserved at a DOSAAF airfield near Vilnius, pylons removed.
102 Red (a)	1401002	MiG-17* (SI-??)	Development aircraft, Mikoyan OKB.
102 Red (b)	0115302	MiG-17F	NII VVS, trials aircraft.
103 Red	1401003	MiG-17*	Converted to, see below.
none		MiG-17P (SP-7)	Prototype, Mikoyan OKB; engine and airbrakes to MiG-17PF standard.
104 Red	1401004	MiG-17* (SI-19)	Development aircraft, Mikoyan OKB.
105 Red	54211745	MiG-17†	Ex-745 Red. GSVG; scrapped Rangsdorf AB 1992.
111 Red	54211768	MiG-17†	Ex-768 Red. DOSAAF, preserved Moscow-Khodynka.
114 Red	54210114	MiG-17 (SG-5)	Development aircraft, Mikoyan OKB.
116 Red	1116	MiG-17	Built in Komsomol'sk-on-Amur?
121 Red	1409029	MiG-17†	Ex-929 Red. GSVG; scrapped Rangsdorf AB 1992.
133 Red	54211133	MiG-17†	
139 Red	54211399	MiG-17†	DOSAAF. Preserved Great Patriotic War Museum, Poklonnaya Gora, Moscow as '39 Red'.
153 Red	?	MiG-17†	Hose and drogue refuelling system testbed, Mikoyan OKB.
167 Red	54211167	MiG-17†	
175 Red	54211175?	MiG-17†	
208 Red	...2...08	MiG-17†	C/n is 1402008, 31...208 or ...208.
209 Red	58210209	MiG-17PF	Development aircraft, Mikoyan OKB?
214 Red	54210214	MiG-17* (SI-10)	Development aircraft, Mikoyan OKB.
225 Red	54210225?	MiG-17†	
231 Red	6231	MiG-17	Coded 54 Red in 1955.
251 Red (?)	54211873	MiG-17†	Tactical code as reported in German book; ex-873 Red. GSVG; scrapped Rangsdorf AB 1992.
280 Red	54211280	MiG-17†	
349 Red	54210349	MiG-17	Coded 17 Red in 1955.
404 Red	54210404	MiG-17 (SR-2)	Prototype, Mikoyan OKB.
416 Red	3416	MiG-17†	Built in Komsomol'sk-on-Amur?
421 Red	54210421	MiG-17 (SI-21)	Development aircraft, Mikoyan OKB.
431 Red	54211431	MiG-17†	
443 Red	54210443	MiG-17 (SI-21)	Development aircraft, Mikoyan OKB.
461 Red	54210461	MiG-17	Coded 05 Red in 1955.
513 Red	54211513	MiG-17†	Coded 71 Red in 1955.
525 Red	54210525	MiG-17	Coded 57 Red in 1955.
565 Red	54210565	MiG-17	To Mikoyan OKB, coded 15 Blue in 1955.
568 Red	54211568	MiG-17†	
606 Red	54210606	MiG-17†	
607 Red	54210607	MiG-17† (SI-O)	Development aircraft, Mikoyan OKB.
611 Blue	54210611?	MiG-17†	LII testbed.
625 Red	58210625	MiG-17PF	First MiG-17PF with RP-5 Izumrood-2 radar.
627 Red	58210627	MiG-17PF (SP-9)	Development acft, Mikoyan OKB; cvtd to, see below.
		MiG-17PF (SP-10)	Development aircraft, Mikoyan OKB.
628 Red	54210628	MiG-17†	
629 Red	54210629	MiG-17†	
630 Red	54210630	MiG-17†	
631 Red	..6...31	MiG-17†	C/n 1406031 or ...631? Apparently not Gor'kiy-built.
632 Red	54210632	MiG-17†	AV-MF/Baltic Fleet.
638 Blue	1406038	MiG-17†	LII, aerodynamics research aircraft.
670 Black	54210670?	MiG-17	Airbrakes immediately aft of wings.
671 Red	54210102	MiG-17 (SI-02)	Second pre-production aircraft. Built from parts of MiG-15bis c/n 53210671, hence serial 671 Red.
707 Red	1707	MiG-17†	Built in Komsomol'sk-on-Amur?
709 Red	1407009	MiG-17†	Coded 75 Red in 1955.
723 Red	1407023	MiG-17†	
745 Red	54211745	MiG-17†	Coded 105 Red in 1955.
761 Red	54211761	MiG-17†	Coded 55 Red in 1955.
768 Red	54211768	MiG-17†	To DOSAAF, eventually coded 111 Red.
801 Red	1801	MiG-17	Built in Komsomol'sk-on-Amur? Coded 88 Red in 1955.
803 Red	1408003	MiG-17†	Coded 09 Red in 1955.
813 Blue	54210813	MiG-17†	LII, aerodynamics research aircraft.
822 Red	0822	MiG-17	Built in Komsomol'sk-on-Amur? Coded 27 Red in 1955.
827 Red	54211827	MiG-17	Coded 01 Red in 1955.
850 Red	53210850	MiG-17F (SF)	Prototype, Mikoyan OKB; converted MiG-15bis (hence c/n commencing 53...)
860 Red	54211860	MiG-17†	To DOSAAF, eventually coded 61 Red.
873 Red	54211873	MiG-17†	Coded 253 Red (?) in 1955.
909 Red	...9...09	MiG-17†	C/n is 1409009, 31...909 or ...909.
910 Red	1409010	MiG-17†	Coded 09 Blue in 1955.
911 Red	1409011	MiG-17†	Coded 20 Red in 1955.
929 Red	1409029	MiG-17†	Coded 121 Red in 1955.
932 Red	1409039?	MiG-17†	
941 Red	58210941?	MiG-17PF	Unconfirmed (drawing only).
948 Red	54210948	MiG-17† (SI-P)	Development aircraft, Mikoyan OKB.
958 Red	54210958	MiG-17†	Coded 53 Red in 1955.
959 Red	54210959	MiG-17†	
0124 Red	0115324	MiG-17F	
0451 Red	0415351	MiG-17F	First aircraft with SRD-1 gun ranging radar.
0476 Red	0415376	MiG-17F (SF-3)	Development aircraft, Mikoyan OKB.
0477 Red	0415377	MiG-17F	
0478 Red	0415378	MiG-17F	
0812 Red?	0815312	MiG-17	Serial could be 812 Red. Coded 54 Red in 1955.
0839 Red?	0815339	MiG-17 (†?)	Serial could be 839 Red
0866 Red?	0815366	MiG-17	Serial could be 866 Red. Coded 81 Red in 1955.
0969 Red?	0915369	MiG-17	Serial could be 969 Red. Coded 91 Red in 1955.
1185 Red	1115385	MiG-17†	
1291 Red	1215391	MiG-17†	Coded 17 Red in 1955.
1437 Red	1415337	MiG-17†	
1599 Red	1515399	MiG-17†	Coded 37 Red in 1955.
1628 Red	1615328	MiG-17†	AV-MF/Baltic Fleet? B-374 weapons system testbed.
1642 Red	1615342	MiG-17†	AV-MF/Baltic Fleet.
not known	54210565	MiG-17	Ex-565 Red. Fighter-bomber conversion prototype, Mikoyan OKB.
not known	54211959	MiG-17†	Ex-959 Red. Sold to EGAF 1961 as 402 Red.
not known	54211133	MiG-17†	Ex-133 Red. GSVG; scrapped Rangsdorf AB 1992.
not known	54211280	MiG-17†	Ex-280 Red. Sold to EGAF 1961 as 172 Red.
not known	54211431	MiG-17†	Ex-431 Red. Sold to EGAF as 775 Red.
not known	54211568	MiG-17†	Ex-568 Red. GSVG; scrapped Rangsdorf AB 1992.
not known	54212017	MiG-17†	Ex-017 Red. Sold to EGAF as 976 Red.
not known	54212067	MiG-17†	Ex-067 Red. Sold to EGAF as 194 Red.
not known	1407023	MiG-17†	Ex-723 Red. GSVG; scrapped Rangsdorf AB 1992.
not known	0715364	MiG-17F	Ex-0764 Red? GSVG, scrapped (Rangsdorf AB?)
not known	0815339	MiG-17 (†?)	Ex-0839 Red? GSVG; scrapped Rangsdorf 1992.

not known	1115385	MiG-17†	Ex-1185 Red. GSVG; scrapped Altenburg AB.
not known	1415337	MiG-17†	Ex-1437 Red. Sold to EGAF 1961 as 222 Red.
not known	0228	MiG-17F	Sold to East German Air Force as 308 Red.
not known	0326	MiG-17F	Sold to East German Air Force as 648 Red.
not known	0337	MiG-17F	Sold to East German Air Force as 774 Red.
not known	0338	MiG-17F	Sold to East German Air Force as 304 Red.
not known	0401	MiG-17F	Sold to East German Air Force as 650 Red.
not known	0426	MiG-17F	Sold to E German Air Force 1958 as 915 Red.
not known	0432	MiG-17F	Sold to East German Air Force as 653 Red.
not known	0436	MiG-17F	Sold to E German Air Force 7-57 as 785 Red.
not known	0443	MiG-17F	Sold to East German Air Force as 904 Red.
not known	0448	MiG-17F	Sold to East German Air Force as 993 Red.
not known	0467	MiG-17F	Sold to East German Air Force as 784 Red.
not known	0479	MiG-17F	Sold to E German Air Force 1-58 as 393 Red.
not known	0505	MiG-17F	Sold to East German Air Force as 306 Red.
not known	0527	MiG-17F	Sold to E German Air Force 1961 as 206 Red.
not known	0619	MiG-17F	Sold to E German Air Force 12-61 as 211 Red.
not known	0630	MiG-17F	Sold to E German Air Force, serial not known.
not known	0654	MiG-17F	Sold to East German Air Force as 651 Red.
not known	0659	MiG-17F	Sold to East German Air Force as 667 Red.
not known	0851	MiG-17F	Sold to E German Air Force 11-57 as 656 Red.
not known	0937	MiG-17F	Sold to East German Air Force as 585 Red.
not known	0947	MiG-17F	Sold to East German Air Force as 611 Red.
not known	0993	MiG-17F	Sold to East German Air Force as 660 Red.
not known	1116	MiG-17	Built in Komsomol'sk-on-Amur? Ex-116 Red. GSVG; scrapped Rangsdorf AB 1992.
not known	1707	MiG-17†	Ex-707 Red. Sold to EGAF as 621 Red.
not known	2054	MiG-17†	Ex-054 Red. Sold to EGAF as 07 Red.
not known	3416	MiG-17†	Ex-416 Red. GSVG; scrapped Rangsdorf AB 1992.
not known	5004	MiG-17F?	Built in Komsomol'sk-on-Amur? Photo exists.
not known	7122	MiG-17F	Sold to East German Air Force as 309 Red.
not known	7124	MiG-17F	Sold to East German Air Force as 580 Red.
not known	7126	MiG-17F	Sold to EGAF 1962 as 501 Red or 906 Red.
not known	7134	MiG-17F	Sold to E German Air Force 7-57 as 910 Red.
not known	7349	MiG-17F	Sold to East German Air Force as 305 Red.
not known	7424	MiG-17F	Sold to East German Air Force as 388 Red.
not known	7432	MiG-17F	Sold to East German Air Force as 392 Red.
not known	7473	MiG-17F	Sold to East German Air Force as 383 Red.
not known	7503	MiG-17F	Sold to East German Air Force as 387 Red.

Airbrake type is indicated where known for *Fresco-As*.
* denotes early-production aircraft with 0.522m² airbrakes;
† denotes late-production aircraft with 0.88m² airbrakes.

Sri Lanka Air Force *Fresco-As* in a hangar. RART

2433, a very weathered and canopy-less Syrian Air Force MiG-17F. *World Air Power Journal*

SPAIN

Spain was never an *operator* of the type. Still, it is worth noting that the aviation museum at Madrid-Cuatro Vientos airport contains a late-production *Fresco-A* with 0.88m² airbrakes. The ex-Bulgarian Air Force aircraft was acquired in May 1998 and wears an absolutely unbelievable colour scheme – bright red overall with huge yellow stars on the aft fuselage and upper fin half and a yellow hammer and sickle on the nose and lower fin half. Cold War-era Hollywood could hardly have done a worse job! What were those Spanish guys thinking (or drinking)?

SRI LANKA (CEYLON)

Sri Lanka became the last Asian nation to receive the type when it requested military aid to quell an uprising in March 1971.[10] On 22nd April that year the Sri Lankan Air Force (SLAF), formerly the Royal Ceylon Air Force (RCyAF), took delivery of five late-production MiG-17 *Fresco-As*. The aircraft were serialled CF 902 through CF 906 (CF 901 was the SLAF's sole UTI-MiG-15).

In January 1972 the fighters were grounded because of economic constraints but operations resumed a year later. The MiG-17s were operational with the 6th Sqn at Katunayake (China Bay) until 1979.

In 1991 Sri Lanka established links with China which was the only country willing to give any tangible support in the struggle against the LTTE rebels. In July 1991 the SLAF acquired two Shenyang FT-5 trainers serialled CTF 701 and CTF 702. Unlike the Soviet-supplied aircraft which were flown in natural metal finish, the FT-5s were painted light grey overall and operated by the 5th Jet Sqn at Katunayake.

SUDAN

After the 1969 revolution and until the early 1970s Sudan was on good terms with the Soviet Union and China. Hence the Sudanese Air Force (*al Quwwat al-Jawwiya as-Sudaniya*; also reported as *Silakh al-Jawwiya as-Sudaniya*) received 20 Shenyang F-5/FT-5s (the exact proportion is unknown). (Some sources state the single-seaters were F-4s, ie, Soviet-built ex-PLAAF MiG-17s.) The aircraft were probably based in Khartoum. 17 were reportedly in service in June 1976; by late 1991 this number had decreased to ten. 18 single-seat F-5s serialled 158, 160,161,163,164,170 and 710 through 712 have been identified, along with twelve FT-5 trainers serialled 168, 180 through 184, 186 through 188, 190, 713 and 714.

SYRIA
(UNITED ARAB REPUBLIC; SYRIAN ARAB REPUBLIC)

In November 1956 Syria signed an agreement with the Soviet Union for the delivery of 60 MiG-17Fs. Twenty Syrian Air Force (*al Quwwat al Jawwiya al-Arabiya as-Suriya*) pilots were sent to the USSR to take their training; another 18 went to Poland and still others were trained *in situ*. *Fresco-C* deliveries began in January 1957 and were completed in August. AN unspecified number of *Fresco-Ds* was also delivered.

The MiG-17s formed the Syrian component of the UARAF in 1958-61. Like the Egyptian MiGs, they were hastily camouflaged as a result of lessons learned in the Six-Day War. Later the type was replaced by various versions of the MiG-21 and the MiG-23MS; however, more than 30 were reportedly still in service as tactical trainers in late 1991. Only four Syrian MiG-17s are known.

Serial	Version	Remarks
39	MiG-17F	Natural metal, pre-UAR markings.
452	MiG-17PF	In service 1973.
1033	MiG-17F	Camouflaged, captured by Israel.
1041	MiG-17F	Camouflaged, captured by Israel.

TANZANIA

Among other military equipment of Chinese origin, the Air Wing of the Tanzanian People's Defence Force planned to purchase 48 F-5s (MiG-17Fs). The first 12 aircraft arrived in 1973, equipping a fighter unit based at Mikumi AB 130km (80 miles) north of Dar es Salaam. The other 12 were never delivered, as Tanzania ordered the more capable F-6C (MiG-19S) and F-7M Airguard (MiG-21F-13) instead.

According to other reports, the Air Wing of the Tanzanian People's Defence Force had only eight or ten F-4s (ex-PLAAF MiG-17s); eight aircraft survived until late 1991.

UGANDA

According to press reports, the Uganda Army Air Force (UAAF) received seven MiG-17Fs from the USSR in 1966; this number later increased to 12. The *Militair'82* handbook, however, says 12 ex-Czech Air Force aircraft and six ex-East German examples were supplied; known serials are U-601 through U-604. These aircraft equipped Uganda's first combat squadron and contributed a lot to making the UAAF one of the most potent air arms on the African continent over a ten-year period. By 1976 the MiG-17F had been supplanted by the MiG-21PF as Uganda's main fighter and relegated to the ground attack role.

Four UAAF MiG-17Fs, among other things, were blown up by Israeli Commandos at Entebbe Airport in 1976 during the widely publicised hijack drama. The Commandos had been sent to liberate the passengers of an airliner hijacked to Entebbe by Palestine Liberation Organization (PLO) terrorists. Many of the passengers were Israelis and the terrorists were holding them hostages with the connivance of the Ugandan dictator Idi Amin. However, the destroyed fighters were reportedly replaced later by new deliveries from the USSR.

UNITED KINGDOM

Three former Polish Air Force Lim-5s serialled 508 Red (c/n 1C 05-08), 1211 Red (c/n 1C 12-11) and 1228 Red (c/n 1C 12-28) were sold to the UK in March 1988. 508 Red and 1228 Red were resold to the Cavanaugh Flight Museum (USA) in April 1995 as N1917M and N1817M respectively. 1211 Red is owned by Classic Aviation Ltd; it resides in airworthy condition at the Imperial War Museum in Duxford and is registered G-BWUF.

UNITED STATES OF AMERICA

A small quantity of MiG-17s obtained officially (from Poland in the late 1980s) and unofficially ('lost, or stolen, or strayed') was operated by the US Air Force's Defense Test and Evaluation Support Agency (DTESA) at Kirtland AFB, New Mexico and reportedly at the classified Groom Lake facility in Nevada ('The Ranch'). The aircraft were used alongside other Soviet types for evaluation purposes and threat simulation during exercises such as Red Flag. Known aircraft are listed below.

Serial	C/n	Version	Remarks
010 Red	1C 10-10	Lim-5	Ex-PWL 1010, acquired 1988; To USAF Aircraft Maintenance and Regeneration Center (AMARC) at Davis-Monthan AFB (Tucson, AZ) by 10-90.
303 Red?	1C 13-03	Lim-5	Ex-PWL 1303, acquired 1988; to AMARC by 10-90.
406 Red?	1C 04-06	Lim-5	Ex-PWL 406 Red, acquired 1988; to AMARC by 10-93.
511 Red?	1D 05-11	Lim-6M	Ex-PWL 511, acquired 1988. To AMARC by 10-92; preserved.

634 Red	1D 06-34	Lim-6M?	Reported in Polish sources as Lim-6MR but has no recce camera fairing. To AMARC; to Pima Air Museum as 'Soviet Air Force 634 Blue' by 4-93.
905 Red	1C 19-05	Lim-5R	Ex-PWL 1905 Red, acquired 1988. To AMARC 1991; to Pima Air Museum by 4-93 as VPAF 1903 Red.
1629 Red	1C 16-29?	Lim-5	Ex-PWL 1629 Red?
'15751'	?	MiG-17F	ie, 61-5751? Origin unknown (may be Lim-5 or J-5).

MiG-17F '15751' flew in natural metal finish with full USAF markings. Conversely, the ex-Polish aircraft were all repainted with white upper-surfaces, deep blue undersurfaces, no national insignia and the DTESA horse's head and lightning logo in black on the fin, except 1629 Red which retained its natural metal finish. The Lims were all retrofitted with Western communications and navigation equipment, as demonstrated by the non-standard blade aerials on port side aft of canopy and ILS aerials on both sides of the upper fin section.

Apart from that, several surplus MiG-17s were acquired and restored to flying condition by warbird collectors. Known civil *Frescos* operated in the USA are listed below.

Registration	C/n	Version	Remarks
N1VC	2705?	J-5	C/n also reported as 2507! Ex-PLAAF. Owned by Morgan Merrill (Alexandria, VA, d/d 88), later Steven M Rosenberg (Novato, CA, d/d 90), then Terence G Klingele (Belleville, IL), registration date 13-12-94. Painted in Chinese markings as '063 Red'.
N17HQ	1J 05-28	Lim-6R	Ex-PWL 528. Owned by Brunetto Flying Services (d/d 3-94), then H J Quamme, then Phoenix Warbirds (Phoenix, AZ), then Josephs Four, Inc. (Fayetteville, GA)
N17QS	1C 14-23	Lim-5	Ex-PWL 1423. Owned by Ferrante Aviation, Inc. (Vandergrift, PA), regn date 7-11-93.
N17JL	1J 05-10	Lim-6R	Ex-PWL 510.
N69PP	1327	JJ-5	Ex-PLAAF. Owned by Poly Technologies, Inc. (d/d 13-2-90), then Peter Franks (Angel Fire, NM, d/d 3-90).
N69RB	1C 13-21	Lim-5	Ex-PWL 1321. Owned by Roy H Bischoff (Fairview Heights, IL), d/d 22-11-93, registered by 1-94.
N117BR	1C 15-29	Lim-5R	Ex-PWL 1529. Owned by MiG Magic, Inc. (Tualatin, OR), registration date 29-4-94.
N117MG	1C 10-20	Lim-5	Ex-PWL 1020, imported 3-94. Owned by James B Rossi (Ocala, FL), regn date 6-5-95.
N217JG	1C 03-06	Lim-5	Ex-PWL 306, imported 3-94. Owned by Jerry H Gallup (Byron, CA), regn date 13-1-98.
N306DM	0704	MiG-17	Ex-PLAAF. Owned by Consolidated Aviation Enterprises (Burlington, VT, d/d 1-88), then Dean Martin/Warplanes, Inc. (Burlington, VT, d/d 1990). Red overall. W/O after in-flight fire at Aurora, OR, 1-3-94.
N406DM	0613	MiG-17	Owned by Consolidated Aviation Enterprises (d/d 1-88), then Dean Martin/Warplanes, Inc. (d/d 1990), then Douglas C Schultz (Kissimmee, FL), registration date 17-6-91.
N2153K	1J 05-05	Lim-6R	Ex-PWL 505. Owned by Amjet Corp. (St. Paul, MN), d/d 15-2-94. *Reregistered 22-6-94 as N505MG.*
N2153V	1J 04-38	Lim-6*bis*	Ex-PWL 438. Owned by Amjet Corp., d/d 16-2-94. *Reregistered 7-94 as N438MG.*
N604LS	1J 06-04	Lim-6R	Ex-PWL 604. Owned by Larry E Steever (Puyallup, WA), registration date 20-1-2000.
N606BM	1C 16-07	Lim-5	Ex-PWL 1607, acquired 4-94.
N619M	1J 06-19	Lim-6*bis*	Ex-PWL 619. Owned by George Lazik (Van Nuys, CA, d/d 21-7-93) as 'PWL 619'
N620PF	1D 06-20	Lim-5P	Ex-PWL 620.
N905DM*	?	MiG-17?	Owned by Consolidated Aviation Enterprises (d/d 1-88), then Dean Martin/Warplanes, Inc. (d/d 10-89), then Brunstad Enterprises (Ridgefield, CT), registration date 3-2-96.
N968	1C 17-05	Lim-5?	Ex-PWL 1705. Owned by Terence G Klingele, d/d 3-93. *Sold/rereg 12-5-94 as, see below.*
N1060M?	1C 03-09?	Lim-5	Ex-PWL 309? Registration read off poor-quality photo. Black overall and with pre-1955 Soviet AF markings as '309 Red'. Owned by Mario Feola (Gretna, LA).
N1705			
N1717M	1C 17-17	Lim-5	Ex-PWL 1705, imported after 9-94. Owned by North American Aviation Group LLC (Rockford, IL), registration date 9-2-99.
N1719	1C 17-19	Lim-5R	Ex-PWL 1719, imported by 11-94. Crashed at Dallas, TX, 6-9-96.
N1817M	1C 12-28	Lim-5	Ex-PWL 1228, imported from the UK. Owned by Cavanaugh Flight Museum, Inc. (Addison, TX), registration date 11-4-95.
N1917M	1C 05-08	Lim-5	Ex-PWL 508, imported from the UK. Owned by Cavanaugh Flight Museum, Inc. (Addison, TX), registration date 11-4-95.
N6180M	54211566	MiG-17	Ex-PLAAF. Owned by James A McKean (Mabank, TX), registration date 10-10-97.
N6351J	54211214	MiG-17	Ex-PLAAF. Owned by James A McKean (Mabank, TX), registration date 10-10-97.
N7105	?	Lim-5?	Reported in *Euromil* as ex-PWL 705 (c/n 1D 07-05), ie, Lim-5P, but no Lim-5P with this c/n existed (only 6 batches built).
N9143Z	1C 17-07	Lim-5	Ex-PWL 1707, imported after 9-94. Owned by MA, Inc. (Oshkosh, WI), regn date 26-3-96.
N73568	1J 06-31	Lim-6R	Ex-PWL 631. Owned by Michael F Bauman (Olney, IL), registration date 3-95.
not known	1C 13-01	Lim-5	Ex-PWL 1301. Owned by Brunetto Flying Services (Coolidge, AZ), d/d 3-94.
not known	1C 13-12	Lim-5R	Ex-PWL 1312, acquired by 1994, delivered to Mesa field, AZ.
not known	1C 13-19	Lim-5	Ex-PWL 1319. Owned by Brunetto Flying Services, d/d 3-94.
not known	1C 14-13	Lim-5R	Ex-PWL 1413, acquired by 11-94.
not known	1C 16-03	Lim-5	Ex-PWL 1603, acquired by 1994.
not known	1C 16-05	Lim-5	Ex-PWL 1605. Owned by Brunetto Flying Services, d/d 3-94.
not known	1C 16-11	Lim-5	Ex-PWL 1611, acquired by 11-94.
not known	1C 16-17	Lim-5	Ex-PWL 1617, acquired 1988. Preserved Planes Of Fame Museum as 'PWL 1617', later Cal-Aero Field as 'Vietnamese People's Air Force 1617 Red'.
not known	1C 17-03	Lim-5R	Ex-PWL 1703. Owned by Brunetto Flying Services, d/d 3-94.
not known	1C 17-13	Lim-5	Ex-PWL 1713. Owned by Brunetto Flying Services, d/d 3-94.
not known	1C 17-19	Lim-5R	Ex-PWL 1719, acquired by 11-94.
not known	1C 17-26	Lim-5	Ex-PWL 1726, acquired by 11-94.
not known	1F 03-19	Lim-6*bis*	Ex-PWL 319. Owned by Brunetto Flying Services, d/d 3-94.
not known	1F 03-25	Lim-6*bis*	Ex-PWL 325. Loaned to Quonset Air Museum (North Kingston, RI)
not known	1J 05-06	Lim-6R	Ex-PWL 506, acquired by 10-93.
not known	1J 05-08	Lim-6R	Ex-PWL 508. Owned by Brunetto Flying Services, d/d 3-94.
not known	1J 05-11	Lim-6R	Ex-PWL 511. Owned by Brunetto Flying Services, d/d 3-94.
not known	1J 05-14	Lim-6R	Ex-PWL 514. Owned by Brunetto Flying Services, d/d 3-94.

Top and right: **A fake Vietnamese. Lim-5 G-BWUF at the Imperial War Museum was painted in VPAF colours as 1211 Red which is its original Polish serial. It is seen here at Duxford 'unbuttoned' for maintenance.** Helmut Walther

Below: **The same aircraft, 1211 Red seen in one piece outside at the Imperial War Museum, Duxford. It is an ex-PWL Lim-5 (c/n 1C 12-11).** Yefim Gordon

Bottom: **MiG-17F '15751' (ie, 61-5751?) on test with the USAF.** Sergey and Dmitriy Komissarov collection

Above and left: **These are fake Yankees! Several MiG-17Ps were painted in USAF colours for the early 1970s Soviet movie *Night Without Mercy*.** Sergey and Dmitriy Komissarov collection

Left: **This privately owned MiG-17F is eloquently registered N1VC (for 'Viet Cong') but is actually an ex-Chinese J-5.** Yefim Gordon archive

Below: **This supposedly North Vietnamese J-5 displayed at Pima Air Museum (Tucson, Arizona) is actually an ex-Polish Air Force Lim-5R (c/n 1C 19-05). Earlier, this aircraft was flown by the USAF's Defense Test and Evaluation Support Agency (DTESA) as 905 Red.** Helmut Walther

| not known | 1J 05-22 | Lim-6R | Ex-PWL 522. Owned by Brunetto Flying Services, d/d 3-94. |
| not known | 1J 05-23 | Lim-6R | Ex-PWL 523. Owned by Brunetto Flying Services, d/d 3-94. |

* The c/n of N905DM has been reported as 551604 but this doesn't make sense, unless this is a Shenyang J-5. However, it is equally possible that this is a misprint for 54(21)1604 – or that the c/n is actually 55211604 (but then this is not a MiG-17 at all, but a MiG-15*bis*R!).

As a point of interest, it can be noted that at least three late-production Soviet Air Force MiG-17Ps starred in the early 1970s movie *Night Without Mercy*, impersonating USAF fighters. The aircraft wore spurious markings, with huge U.S.AIR FORCE titles on the fuselage, huge one-digit numbers on the noses (!?) and large USAF serials on the fins – for example, '26222' (ie, 62-6222?). The correct paint job would have been large buzz numbers on the aft fuselage and small U.S.AIR FORCE titles on the fins above the serial.

Conversely, the Pima Air Museum (Pima County, Arizona) has a MiG-17PF painted in pre-1955 Soviet Air Force markings as 634 Blue to suggest c/n 58210634. However, the two pylons for FFAR pods identify it as a Lim-6M (ex-Polish Air Force 634 Red, c/n 1D 06-34)! In addition, the aircraft has the tracking antenna radome painted blue and the guidance antenna (centrebody) radome painted bright yellow, which is absolutely non-authentic.

The USAF Museum at Wright-Patterson AFB (Dayton, Ohio) has a MiG-17F – probably a J-5 – painted as Vientamese People's Air Force 3026 Red. The museum at Cal-Aero Field, California, contains another MiG-17F painted in Vietnamese markings as 1617 Red; this aircraft wears a natural metal finish with a red upper fin section. Yet again this aircraft is an impostor, being actually a Lim-5 (ex-Polish Air Force 1617 Red, c/n 1C 16-17). A third MiG-17F in Vietnamese markings, painted light grey overall (!) and serialled 1211 Red, is preserved at an unidentified American museum. Once again, this aircraft could be a Lim-5 (ex-Polish Air Force 1211 Red, c/n 1C 12-11). On this and the previous aircraft the serial number style does not match the one used in Vietnam.

Finally, grey-painted MiG-17F, this time in North Korean markings and serialled 547 Red, is a gate guard at Nellis AFB (Las Vegas, Nevada) outside the Threat Training Facility. While the origin of this aircraft remains a secret, this is *not* an ex-PWL Lim-5; in fact, the serial is almost certainly derived from the fact that the fighter was operated by the 547th Intelligence Sqn. Curiously, despite the North Korean markings, the aircraft carries the name of its pilot, Lt Gen David J McCloud (mis-spelled as 'McLoud'). 'Our man in Pyongyang'?

Decode for US States

Occasional reference is also made in the text to State and Territory abbreviations. They follow the official government standards and may be de-coded as follows:

AL = Alabama	IL = Illinois	NC = North Carolina	SD = South Dakota
AK = Alaska	IN = Indiana	ND = North Dakota	TN = Tennessee
AR = Arkansas	KS = Kansas	NH = New Hampshire	TX = Texas
AZ = Arizona	KY = Kentucky	NJ = New Jersey	UT = Utah
CA = California	LA = Louisiana	NM = New Mexico	VA = Virginia
CO = Colorado	MA = Massachusetts	NV = Nevada	VI = Virgin Islands
CT = Connecticut	MD = Maryland	NY = New York	VT = Vermont
DC = Dist of Columbia	ME = Maine	OH = Ohio	WA = Washington
DE = Delaware	MI = Michigan	OK = Oklahoma	WI = Wisconsin
FL = Florida	MN = Minnesota	OR = Oregon	WV = West Virginia
GA = Georgia	MO = Missouri	PA = Pennsylvania	WY = Wyoming
HI = Hawaii	MS = Mississippi	PR = Puerto Rico	
IA = Iowa	MT = Montana	RI = Rhode Island	
ID = Idaho	NB = Nebraska	SC = South Carolina	

VIETNAM

The Vietnamese People's Air Force (VPAF, or *Không Quan Nham Dan Viêt Nam*) operated MiG-17Fs of both Soviet and Chinese provenance; the first of these were delivered in the late 1950s. (According to some sources, F-5 deliveries began in 1964, followed by Soviet-built MiG-17Fs in 1965.) About 70 were estimated to be in service during the Vietnam War (1969-72).

After the war the surviving *Frescos* were replaced by more modern fighter types and used as strike aircraft; more than 70 were reportedly still operated in this role in late 1991 but this is extremely doubtful. Known examples are listed below; the serials may match the c/ns.

Serial	Version	Remarks
2011	MiG-17F (F-5?)	923rd Sqn, natural metal, 9 'kills'. Preserved VPAF Museum, Bac Mai airfield, Hanoi.
2015	MiG-17F (F-5?)	Mottled green camouflage.
2047	MiG-17F (F-5?)	Natural metal, 7 'kills'. Preserved VPAF Museum.
2072	MiG-17F (F-5?)	Mottled green camouflage; unconfirmed (drawing only).
2531	F-5	Natural metal; unconfirmed (drawing only).
2533	MiG-17F (F-5?)	Natural metal, red upper fin section *à la* some Chinese J-5s.
2535	MiG-17F (F-5?)	Natural metal, red upper fin section; unconfirmed (drawing only).
2754	F-5	Mottled green camouflage; unconfirmed (drawing only).
3020	MiG-17F (F-5?)	Mottled green camouflage, 7 'kills'. Possibly shot down by F-4J-35-MC BuNo 155800/'NG-100' (CVW-9/VF-96, USS *Constellation*) 10-5-72.
3026?	MiG-17F (F-5?)	Mottled green camouflage; identically painted J-5 preserved in US museum.

The nine 'kills' scored by MiG-17F '2011 Red' include F-4C-20-MC 63-7614 (366th TFW/390th TFS) which was shot down on 12th May 1967 by Lt Ngo Duc Mai. The pilot of the Phantom, Col Norman Gaddis, ejected and was taken prisoner; the WSO, 1st Lt James Milton Jefferson, went missing in action.

The other *Fresco-C* on display at the VPAF Museum (2047 Red) is reportedly fitted with a brake parachute, which enabled it to operate from short runways. On 19th April 1972 this aircraft made a successful bomb attack on the USS *Higbee*. Finally, another MiG-17F (unmarked) is preserved at the Lenin Park (*Công Viên Lê Nin*) in Hanoi.

NORTH YEMEN (YEMEN ARAB REPUBLIC)

The Yemen Arab Republic Air Force (YARAF) received about 30 MiG-17Fs after the 1972 civil war. Nine were still in service in 1979 (some sources say twelve aircraft remained but were probably non-operational). Of these, according to *Interavia*, six were used in the advanced trainer role by early 1987 and were being withdrawn. One YARAF MiG-17F crashed on 25th February 1979.

SOUTH YEMEN (PEOPLE'S DEMOCRATIC REPUBLIC OF YEMEN)

Reports on the number of MiG-17Fs operated by the South Yemen Air Force (PDRYAF) vary. 37 and 12 were reported by different sources to be in service in 1979; the former figure seems more likely, as *Interavia* reported 30 *Fresco-Cs* still operational in the ground attack role by early 1987. The aircraft were probably based at Khormaksar.

ZIMBABWE

The Zimbabwe Air Force reportedly received an unspecified number of Shenyang F-5s and two FT-5 trainers in 1986. The latter were still operational in late 1991 while the single-seaters had been withdrawn and replaced by Guizhou F-7M Airguards.

The MiG-17 was also reportedly operated by the air forces of the Congo Republic (*l'Armee de l'Air du Congo*), Laos (AFPLA – Air Force of the People's Liberation Army) and Yugoslavia (JRV – *Jugoslovensko Ratno Vazduhoplovstvo*), but no details are known.

Chapter Six

The MiG-17 in Detail

Type

Single-engined tactical fighter with limited strike capability/interceptor designed for day and night operation in visual meteorological conditions (VMC) and instrumental meteorological conditions (IMC).

Fuselage

Semi-monocoque all-metal stressed-skin structure with frames, longerons and stringers. The riveted fuselage structure is made mainly of V95 aluminium alloy. Fuselage length is 8.08m (26ft 6in), fuselage diameter 1.45m (4ft 9in), and air intake diameter 0.747m (2ft 5⅛in). Maximum cross-section area (less cockpit canopy) is 1.65m² (17.74ft²) and aspect ratio is 6.7.

Structurally the fuselage consists of two sections: forward (up to frame 13, which is the fuselage break point) and rear. The latter is detachable for engine maintenance and removal.

The *forward fuselage* incorporates the forward avionics/equipment bay (frames 1 to 4), the nosewheel well, the pressurized cockpit (frames 4 to 9), the armament bay (except on the MiG-17PFU interceptor) and aft avionics/equipment bay located under it, and the No1 fuel tank (frames 9 to 13). The circular air intake located at frame No1 has a vertical splitter which divides it into two elliptical-section air ducts passing along the fuselage sides, flanking the cockpit, nosewheel well, No1 fuel tank and avionics bays.

The forward fuselage has 13 frames (including four mainframes absorbing the main structural loads, Nos 4, 5A, 9 and 13) and three auxiliary frames. Mainframes Nos 4 and 5A serve as attachment points for the nose gear unit and gun tray respectively; wing spar attachment fittings are installed at frames Nos 9, 11 and 13. The latter also carries the engine bearer with ten attachment points for the engine. Frame 1 has a flanged cutout on top for the S-13 gun camera; the nose fairing with the intake splitter is attached to this frame. The forward fuselage skin is 1.2mm (0.047in) thick and the skin of the inlet ducts 0.8mm (0.031in) thick.

The cockpit is contained by pressure bulkheads at mainframes 4 and 9; it is enclosed by a bubble canopy and protected by armour from the front and from below. The fixed windshield has two curved triangular Perspex sidelights 8mm (0.31in) thick and an elliptical optically-flat bulletproof glass 64mm (2.5in) thick. The stamped duralumin windshield frame is hermetically riveted to the forward fuselage structure. The aft-sliding canopy incorporates a TS-27 periscope for rearward vision and can be jettisoned manually or pyrotechnically in an emergency. The blown Perspex glazing is likewise 8mm thick. The cockpit features an ejection seat (with guide rails attached to the rear pressure bulkhead), an instrument panel and side control consoles.

On the MiG-17P/PF/PFG/PFU interceptors the forward fuselage is longer, with structural changes up to frame 9 to accommodate the radar; it incorporates a dielectric radome in the intake upper lip and an intake centrebody with a second radome, and the gun camera is relocated to the starboard side of the intake. The canopy windshield is lengthened, with trapezoidal sidelights and an additional upper glazing panel.

The *rear fuselage* (frames 14 to 31) houses the engine with its accessories and jetpipe, the two-section rear fuel tank and control linkages. The engine jetpipe is attached to frame 28 by a special flexible fitting. The rear fuselage structure consists of 18 frames, ten longerons and a number of stringers supporting the skin. Skin thickness varies from 1.0 to 1.5mm (0.039 to 0.059in). The rear fuselage incorporates two lateral airbrakes, each with an area of 0.522m² (5.61ft²) on early-production MiG-17s and MiG-17Ps, 0.88m² (9.46ft²) on late-production MiG-17s and MiG-17Ps, 0.64m² (6.88ft²) on initial-production MiG-17Fs and 0.97m² (10.43ft²) on late-production MiG-17Fs and 'PFs. The airbrakes are electrohydraulically-actuated and deflected 55°.

Wings

Cantilever mid-wing monoplane. Leading-edge sweep 49° inboard and 45° 30' outboard, with kink at half-span; sweepback at quarter-chord 45° inboard and 42° outboard, anhedral 3°, incidence 1°, aspect ratio 4.08, taper 1.23. The wings utilise TsAGI S-12A (SR-12S) laminar airfoil at the root and TsAGI SR-11 airfoil at the tip; mean aerodynamic chord (MAC) is 2.19m (7ft 2¼in), and mean thickness/chord ratio 12% at the root and 8% airfoil at the tip. Wingspan is 9.6m (31ft 6in) and wing area 22.6m² (243.0ft²).

The wings are of all-metal, three-spar stressed-skin structure, with forward spar, main spar and auxiliary rear spar; they are one-piece structures joined to the fuselage at the root rib. Each wing has 25 ribs and two beams which, together with the main spar, form the main wheel well. Each wing incorporates a 5.1-kg (11.24-lb) anti-flutter weight and has three boundary layer fences on the upper surface. The detachable tip fairings are attached by screws and anchor nuts. The wing/fuselage joint is covered by a fillet attached to fuselage and wing in similar fashion. The wings have hydraulically-actuated, one-piece TsAGI flaps (modified Fowler flaps) located between ribs 1 and 18, with an area of 2.86m² (30.75ft²). Flap settings were 20° for take-off and 60° for approach.

Tail unit

Cantilever cruciform tail surfaces of all-metal stressed-skin construction. Fin leading-edge sweep 55° 41', sweepback at quarter-chord 45°. Both fin and stabilizers utilise a symmetrical NACA-M airfoil. Stabilizer leading-edge sweep 45°; stabilizer incidence ground-adjustable. Total vertical tail area 4.26m² (45.8ft²) and total horizontal tail area 3.1m² (33.3ft²). A small ventral fin is installed under the aft fuselage to improve directional stability of the aircraft.

Landing gear

Hydraulically-retractable tricycle type, with pneumatic extension in emergency; wheel track 3.849m (12ft 7½in), wheelbase 3.368m (11ft ½in). Nose unit retracts forward, main units inward into wings so that the wheels lie in the wing roots ahead of the main spar. In the retracted position the landing gear is secured by uplocks, in the extended position by shutoff valves trapping hydraulic fluid in the retraction jacks which double as downlocks.

All three landing gear struts have oleo-pneumatic shock absorbers. The main units have single 600 x 160mm (23.6 x 6.3in) wheels with expander-tube brakes. The nose unit has a single 480 x 200mm (18.9 x 7.87in) non-braking wheel and is equipped with a shimmy damper. The castoring nosewheel can turn ±50° for taxying; steering on the ground is by differential braking.

The nosewheel well is closed by twin lateral doors, the mainwheel wells by triple doors (one segment is hinged to the front spar, one to the root rib and a third segment attached to the oleo leg). All doors remain open when the gear is down. Landing gear position is indicated by warning lamps on the instrument panel and by mechanical indicators. A sprung tail bumper built into the ventral fin protects the rear fuselage and jetpipe in a tail-down landing.

Powerplant

The MiG-17 and MiG-17P are powered by one Klimov VK-1 or VK-1A non-afterburning turbojet rated at 2,700kg (5,952 lbst) or 2,740kg (6,040 lbst) respectively; the MiG-17F/PF/PFU have a VK-1F afterburning turbojet rated at 2,600kgp (5,732 lbst) dry and 3,380kgp (7,451 lbst) reheat. The VK-1F's maximum thrust is attained at 11,560rpm in full afterburner.

The engine has a single-stage centrifugal compressor (with dual inlet ducts), nine straight-flow combustion chambers, a single-stage axial turbine, a subsonic fixed-area nozzle (VK-1/VK-1A) or an afterburner with a two-position axisymmetrical convergent-divergent nozzle (VK-1F), and an extension jetpipe. The latter is attached flexibly. The engine features an accessory gearbox for driving fuel, oil and hydraulic pumps and electrical equipment. Starting is electrical by means of an ST2 or ST2-48 starter.

The engine is mounted on a bearer via four attachment points: two trunnions on the right and left sides of the compressor casing below the axis of the engine and two mounting lugs in the upper part of the engine. The engine is attached to fuselage frame 13; when the rear fuselage is detached, the engine is completely exposed.

Control system

Conventional mechanical flight control system with push-pull rods, control cranks and levers.

Roll control is provided by ailerons 1.512m (4ft 11½in) long, with internal aerodynamic balancing. The ailerons are powered by a BU-1 (BU-1A) reversible hydraulic actuator mounted on the front spar of the starboard wing to reduce stick forces. The port aileron has a trim tab. Total aileron area is 1.6m² (17.2ft²), including 0.034m² (0.36ft²) for the trim tab. Aileron deflection is ±18° and trim tab deflection ±15°.

Directional control is provided by a rudder which, like the fin, is built in two sections; the upper and lower sections are single-spar structures connected by a universal joint and suspended on two and three brackets respectively. The rudder is aerodynamically balanced; additionally, both sections have mass balances – 2.6kg (5.73 lb) for the upper section and 5.38kg (11.86 lb) for the lower section. The rudder is controlled manually by means of pedals and push-pull rods, cranks and levers. Rudder area is 0.947m² (10.18ft²); rudder deflection is ±25°.

The elevators are symmetrical single-spar structures with aerodynamical and mass balances. Each elevator is suspended on three brackets. The elevators are manually-controlled by means of push-pull rods, cranks and levers; the port elevator features a trim tab. Elevator area is 0.884m² (9.5ft²); elevator deflection is -32/+16° and trim tab deflection ±10°. Aileron and elevator trim tabs are remotely controlled by UT-6D electric motors transmitting torque through a system of levers and rods.

Fuel system

Internal fuel is carried in two tanks holding a total of 1,400 to 1,415 litres (308 to 311.3 Imperial gallons). The main fuel cell (bag tank) housed in the forward fuselage between frames 9 and 13 holds 1,250 litres (275 Imperial gallons); it is inserted via a removable ventral panel. An integral tank of 150 to 165 litres (33 to 36.3 Imperial gallons) capacity is located in the rear fuselage under the engine jetpipe. The fuel burnoff sequence does not affect CG position.

Two 400-litre (88 Imperial gallons) drop tanks or 600-litre (132 Imperial gallons) slipper tanks can be carried under the wings; the drop tanks are pressurized by engine bleed air. The MiG-17 uses T-1 or TS-1 jet fuel or Western equivalents (JP-4 etc). Refuelling is by gravity via two filler caps immediately aft of the cockpit (offset to port) and on the port side of the aft fuselage.

Hydraulics

The hydraulic system works the landing gear, flaps, airbrakes and the aileron actuator. The hydraulic system includes a hydraulic fluid tank, low-pressure reduction gear, a pump installed on the engine accessory gearbox, a hydraulic accumulator, a filter, safety and return valves, a manometer, hydraulic lines etc Hydraulic pressure is 140 bars (2,000psi) or, on late versions, 125 bars (1,785psi).

Electrics

28.5 V DC main electrical system with a 3kW GSR-3000 generator as the main power source. Radar-equipped interceptors (MiG-17P/PF/PFG/PFU) are equipped with a 6kW GSR-6000 generator. Backup DC power is provided by a 12SAM-25 (28 V, 25 A h) silver-zinc battery in the forward avionics/equipment bay. Electrical system switches are arranged on the side control consoles in the cockpit.

Pneumatic system

Two subsystems (main and emergency). The main pneumatic system actuates the wheel brakes, cannon recharging mechanisms and is responsible for cockpit pressurization. The emergency system is responsible for landing gear and flap emergency extension (in case of hydraulics failure) and emergency braking.

Armament

The MiG-17 and MiG-17F are armed with one 37mm (1.45 calibre) Nudel'man N-37D cannon on the starboard side with 40 rounds and two staggered 23mm (.90 calibre) Nudel'man/Rikhter NR-23 guns on the port side with 80 rounds per gun. Both models utilise recharging by recoil action, which allowed the heavy calibre cannons to have a high rate of fire and be reasonably lightweight. The N-37 weighs 103kg (227lbs) and fires 750 gram (26.475oz) projectiles; rate of fire is 400 rounds per minute and muzzle velocity 690m/sec (2,263ft/sec). The NR-23 weighs 39kg (86lb) and fires 200 gram (7.06oz) projectiles; rate of fire is 800 –

950rpm and muzzle velocity 680m/sec (2,231ft/sec)[1]. The MiG-17P/PF is armed with either one N-37D and two NR-23s or two or three NR-23s with up to 100rpg. All cannons are mounted on a common tray under the forward fuselage which can be lowered quickly by means of a built-in winch for reloading and maintenance. The tray also carries the ammunition boxes and pneumatic charging mechanisms.

The MiG-17PFU is armed with four RS-1-U air-to-air missiles with semi-active radar homing carried on four pylons with APU-4 launch rails and D3-40 shackles. There are no cannons.

In the strike role the MiG-17 and MiG-17F can carry two 50-kg (110-lb), 100-kg (220-lb) or 250-kg (551-lb) bombs on the wing hardpoints instead of the drop tanks. Bomb release is electrically-actuated. Some MiG-17F batches completed to MiG-17AS standard can carry two 212mm 8.34in) S-21 heavy unguided rockets on PU-21 launch rails attached to the standard wing hardpoints or to special pylons installed inboard of these.

The MiG-17 is equipped with an ASP-3NM automatic gunsight; the MiG-17F has an ASP-4NM gunsight linked to an SRD-1 Radal' (SRD-1M Radal'-M) gun ranging radar. An S-13 gun camera mounted on the air intake upper lip records the firing and bombing results. The gun camera can operate independently from the cannons or in conjunction with them. Film capacity is 150 exposures; at a speed of 8 frames per second, the S-13 can shoot continuously for 19 seconds. An FKP-2 camera records a pilot's eye view of the target.

Oxygen system

For operations above 9,000m (29,257ft), oxygen bottles are installed in the forward avionics/equipment bay.

Air conditioning and pressurization system

The MiG-17 has a ventilation-type cockpit pressurized by engine bleed air to a pressure differential of 0.3 bars (4.28psi). Cockpit air pressure is governed by an RD-2ZhM pressure regulator. The cockpit is equipped to work with the PPK-1 G suit. The canopy is sealed by an inflatable rubber hose pressurized to 3 bars (42.8psi).

Fire suppression system

Two 3-litre (0.66 Imperial gallons) fire extinguisher bottles charged with carbon dioxide installed on fuselage frame 13. System operation is manual.

Crew escape system

The MiG-17 is equipped with a cartridge-fired ejection seat. The seat pan is dished to take a ribbon-type parachute. Ejection is accomplished by pulling canopy jettison handles located on both sides of the seat.

MiG-17 Family Specifications

	MiG-17	MiG-17F	MiG-17P	MiG-17PF	MiG-17PFU
Powerplant	VK-1A	VK-1F	VK-1A	VK-1F	VK-1F
Thrust, kgp (lbst):					
dry	2,700 (5,952)	2,600 (5,732)	2,700 (5,952)	2,600 (5,732)	2,600 (5,732)
reheat	–	3,380 (7,451)	–	3,380 (7,451)	3,380 (7,451)
Overall length	11.09m (36' 4½")	11.09m (36' 4½")	11.36m (37' 3¼")	11.36m (37' 3¼")	11.36m (37' 3¼")
Wing span	9.628m (31' 7")	9.628m (31' 7")	9.628m (31' 7")	9.628m (31' 7")	9.628m (31' 7")
Height on ground	3.8m (12' 5½")	3.8m (12' 5½")	3.8m (12' 5½")	3.8m (12' 5½")	3.8m (12' 5½")
Wing area, m² (ft²)	22.6 (243.0)	22.6 (243.0)	22.6 (243.0)	22.6 (243.0)	22.6 (243.0)
Empty weight, kg (lb)	3,798 (8,373)	n/a	n/a	4,151 (9,151)	4,065 (8,961)
Normal TOW, kg (lb)	5,340 (11,772)	5,354 (11,803)	5,550 (12,235)	5,620 (12,389)	5,703 (12,572)
MTOW, kg (lb)	6,072 (13,386)	n/a	6,280 (13,844)	6,552 (14,444)	6,433 (14,182)
Fuel capacity, litres (Imp gals):					
in 'clean' condition	1,435 (315.7)	1,410 (315.7)	1,480 (325.6)	1,395 (306.9)	n/a
with drop tanks	2,235 (491.7)	2,235 (491.7)	2,280 (501.6)	2,195 (482.9)	n/a
Wing loading, kg/m² (lbft²)	236.3 (1,148)	236.9 (1,151)	245.6 (1,193)	248.7 (1,208)	252.3 (1,226)
Top speed, km/h (kts):					
at 4,000m (13,123ft)	n/a	n/a	n/a	n/a	1,107/1,059 (598.37/572.43)
at 5,000m (16,404ft)	1,070 (578.37)	1,130 (610.81)	1,085 (586.48)	1,123 (607.0)	n/a
at 10,000m (32,808ft)	1,030 (556.75)	1,071 (578.91)	1,033 (558.37)	1,060 (572.97)	n/a
Never-exceed speed, km/h (kts)	1,200 (648.64)	1,150 (621.62)	1,200 (648.64)	1,150 (621.62)	n/a
Touchdown speed, km/h (kts)	170 to 190 (92 to 102)	n/a	180 to 200 (97 to 108)	n/a	170 to 190 (92 to 102)
Rate of climb, m/sec (ft/min):					
at 5,000m (16,404ft)	30.5 (6,004)	65.0 (12,795)	27.0 (5,315)	55.0 (10,826)	n/a
at 10,000m (32,808ft)	16.5 (3,248)	38.4 (7,559)	15.0 (2,952)	32.3 (6,358)	n/a
Time to height, min:					
to 5,000m (16,404ft)	3.0	2.1	2.5	2.5	n/a
to 10,000m (32,808ft)	6.7	3.7	6.6	4.5	4.8
to 15,000m (49,212ft)	14.3	7.4	n/a	9.8	n/a
Service ceiling, m (ft):					
in full afterburner	14,700 (48,228)	15,100 (49,540)	14,500 (47,572)	14,450 (47,408)	n/a
at full military power	–	16,470 (54,035)	–	16,300 (53,477)	15,650 (51,345)
Range on internal fuel, km (nm):					
at 5,000m (16,404ft)	700 (378)	670 (362)	780 (421)	690 (373)	n/a
at 10,000m (32,808ft)	1,165 (629)	1,080 (583)	1,290 (692)	1,100 (594)	n/a
Range with drop tanks, km (nm):					
at 5,000m (16,404ft)	1,010 (546)	1,040 (562)	1,140 (616)	1,070 (578)	n/a
at 10,000m (32,808ft)	1,735 (937)	1,670 (902)	1,900 (1,027)	1,730 (935)	1,850 (1,000)
Take-off run, m (ft)	550 (1,804)	590 (1,804)	805 (2,641)	730 to 930 (2,395 to 3,051)	n/a
Landing run, m (ft)	820 to 850 (2,690 to 2,788)	n/a	885 (2,903)	885 (2,903)	n/a

Avionics and equipment

a) navigation equipment: OSP-48 instrumental landing system comprising ARK-5 Amur ADF with omnidirectional aerial and loop aerial, RV-2 Kristall radio altimeter with two aerials on the port wing and the lower forward fuselage, and MRP-48 Dyatel marker beacon receiver. A DGMK-3 remote gyromagnetic compass is installed in the starboard wing.

b) radio equipment: Early-production MiG-17s had an RSIU-3 Klyon two-way VHF radio (RSI-6M receiver and RSI-6K transmitter) in the forward avionics/equipment bay with whip aerial installed on the right side aft of the cockpit. On the MiG-17F and later versions it was replaced by an RSIU-4M, RSIU-4V or R-800 VHF radio.

c) flight instrumentation: KUS-1200 airspeed indicator (ASI), VD-17 altimeter, RV-2 radio altimeter indicator, AGK-476 artificial horizon on early aircraft (replaced by AGI-1 on aircraft built from 1954 onwards), EUP-46 electric turn and bank indicator, VAR-75 vertical speed indicator (VSI), DGMK-3 gyromagnetic compass indicator, M-0,95 Mach meter and ARK-5 ADF indicator.

d) IFF equipment: SRO-1 Bariy-M IFF transponder with dorsal blade aerial on the aft fuselage.

e) radar: MiG-17Fs from c/n 0415351 onwards are equipped with an SRD-1 Radal' gun ranging radar; late batches have the upgraded SRD-1M Radal'-M version. The MiG-17P and early-production MiG-17PFs are equipped with an RP-1 Izumrood-1 aiming radar which ensures target detection at up to 9.5km (5.13nm) in search mode and auto-tracking at approximately 2km (1.08nm) range. Late-production MiG-17PFs have an RP-5 Izumrood-2 radar with a target detection range of 12km (6.48nm). The MiG-17PFU is equipped with an RP-1-U fire control radar for guiding the RS-1-U AAMs.

f) electronic support measures (ESM) equipment: Sirena-2 radar homing and warning system (RHAWS) with aerials on the fin, wing leading edges and wingtips.

g) exterior lighting: BANO-45 port and starboard navigation lights. Retractable LFSV-45 landing light in the port wing root ahead of the mainwheel well. ESKR-46 four-round signal flare launcher incorporated into the starboard side of the lower fin section.

MiG-17 production

The MiG-17 was built in much smaller numbers than the MiG-15 family. *Fresco* production in the USSR and abroad is detailed below.

Kuybyshev aircraft factory No1	392
(named after Iosif V Stalin)	
Gor'kiy aircraft factory No 21	2,424
(named after Sergo Ordzhonikidze)	
Tbilisi aircraft factory No 31	836
(named after Gheorgi Dimitrov)	
Komsomol'sk-on-Amur aircraft factory No126	2,180
(named after the Lenin Young Communist League)	
Novosibirsk aircraft factory No153	2,167
(named after Valeriy P Chkalov)	
Total Soviet production:	7,999
Aero-Vodochody, Czechoslovakia	457
PZL (WSK Mielec), Poland	540
Shenyang aircraft factory (SAIC), China:	
single-seaters	767
JJ-5 (FT-5) trainers	1,061
Total Foreign production:	2,825
GRAND TOTAL:	**10,824**

End Notes

Introduction

1 OKB = **o**pytno-kon**strook**torskoye byu**ro** – experimental design bureau; there were no 'companies' as such in the USSR. The number is a code allocated for security reasons.
2 MMZ = *Moskovskiy mashinostroitel'nyy zavod* – Moscow Machinery Plant number something-or-other. MMZ 'Zenit' or MMZ No155 was the name of Mikoyan's experimental shop.
3 I = *istrebitel'* – fighter. At the time it was still customary for fighter prototypes to be designated by the I- prefix, just as in the pre-war days. A 'personalized' designation using the first two letters of the OKB leader's last name – eg, 'Yak' for Yakovlev – was usually allocated only when the aircraft entered service.
4 *Izdeliye* (product) such and such was a term often used for coding Soviet military hardware items.
5 RD = *reaktivnyy dvigatel'* – jet engine; F = *forseerovannyy* – uprated. The designation *forseerovannyy* usually applied to afterburning turbojets at the time but not in this instance, as the RD-45F was non-afterburning.
6 The VK initials stood for Vladimir Yakovlevich Klimov, suggesting that enough Soviet research had gone into the engine to qualify it as an indigenous design. It was a refined derivative of the RD-45 and a stepping stone to the afterburning VK-1F rated at 3,380 kgp (7,451 lbst). Structural and manufacturing technology improvements produced the VK-1A with a 150 to 200-hr service life.

Chapter One

1 DFS = *Deutsche Forschungsinstitut für Segelflug* – German Gliding Flight Research Institute. The aircraft was also referred to in Russian sources as Siebel 346 since manufacture was contracted to Siebel Flugzeugwerke KG.
2 Initially the MiG-15*bis* had 0.5 m² (5.37ft²) airbrakes. In January 1952 the airbrakes were redesigned to improve manoeuvrability and their area increased to 0.8m² (8.6ft²).
3 ie, *izdeliye* S, *perekhvahtchik* (interceptor), version 1.
4 The c/ns are deciphered as follows: 1.02.005 = Kuyby-

shev aircraft factory No1 named after Iosif V Stalin, Batch 02, 005th aircraft in the batch (up to 120 per batch). On the Kuybyshev (now Samara) production line, MiG-15 batches 1 to 20 were *Fagot-As* and batches 21 to 37 were *Fagot-Bs*.
5 SRO = *samolyotnyy rahdiolokatseeonnyy otvetchik* – aircraft-mounted radar responder (ie, transponder); RPKO = *rahdiopolookompas* – DF; OSP = *oboroodovaniye slepoy posahdki* – blind landing equipment.
6 ARK = *avtomateecheskiy rahdiokompas* – ADF; RV = *rahdiovysotomer* – radio altimeter; MRP = *markernyy rahdiopreeyomnik*. The MRP-48 has also been designated Khrizantema (Chrysanthemum) in some sources.
7 A division of the Ministry of Aircraft Industry. LII is now named after test pilot Mikhail M Gromov.
8 Now called NAZ (*Nizhegorodskiy aviatseeonnyy zavod* – Nizhniy Novgorod aircraft factory) 'Sokol' (Falcon).
9 The c/n is deciphered as follows: 53.21.06.71 = *izdeliye* 53 (factory code for the MiG-15*bis*), factory No 21, Batch 06, 71st aircraft in the batch. Gor'kiy-built MiG-17 c/ns followed the same pattern; here, we have Batch 00. The c/n is stencilled on the fin and rudder and/or the main gear doors.

Chapter Two

1 This became the Moscow Research Institute of Instrument Engineering (MNIIP – *Moskovskiy naoochno-issledovatel'skiy institoot preeborostroyeniya*), aka NPO 'Vega-M', in 1967.
2 Some documents say from 165 litres (36.3 Imperial gallons) to 255 litres (56.1 Imperial gallons).
3 Hence the c/n 54210002 was retained on some airframe parts.
4 All aircraft built in Novosibirsk used a c/n system deciphered as follows: 01.153.02 = Batch 01, Novosibirsk aircraft factory No153 named after Valeriy P Chkalov, 02nd aircraft in the batch. The c/n is stencilled on the fin and rudder and sometimes on the ailerons and outer wings.
5 In Novosibirsk, the *Fresco-A* and the *Fresco-C* had separate batch number sequences.

6 TRS = *tyazholyy reaktivnyy snaryad* – heavy [unguided] rocket.
7 Some documents state the designation as '*izdeliye* SIO' (with no dash).
8 The acronym *Radahl'* is a contraction of *rahdiodal'nomer* – radio rangefinder.
9 ORO = *odinochnoye reaktivnoye oroodiye* – lit. 'single jet gun' (by analogy with recoilless guns).
10 Kuybyshev-built MiG-17s have a different c/n system from the MiG-15s built there. For example, 638 Blue, c/n 1.40.6.038 = Kuybyshev aircraft factory No1, *izdeliye* 40 (factory product code for the MiG-17 *Fresco-A*), Batch 6, 038th aircraft in the batch (up to 100 per batch?). The c/n is stencilled on the gun barrel fairings, fin and rudder, main gear doors and/or the centre fuselage.
11 PZV = *preebor zaryadki vzryvahteley*.
12 ie, the rockets could not be fired when the gear was down.
13 V stands for *variahnt* – version.
14 ie, *izdeliye* S s *oopravlyayemym vo'orouzheniyem* – with movable armament.
15 Called 'automatic radar sight/direction finder' in Russian documents. Some documents state the SN was equipped with a Gamma gun ranging radar developed by NII-17.
16 TKB = *Tool'skoye konstrooktorskoye byuro* – Toola [weapons] design bureau.
17 The designation was re-used in 1975 for a single-seat championship aerobatic aircraft which was built in quantity and won many international competitions.
18 RP = *rahdiopreetsel* – radio sight, in the terminology of the time.
19 This figure turned out to be theoretical; the actual detection range was 9 to 9.5km (4.86 to 5.13nm).
20 Currently NPO Almaz (Diamond). NPO = *naoochno-proizvodstvennoye obyedineniye* – research and production association.
21 The Lavochkin OKB later switched completely to missile design after the La-250 heavy interceptor programme was terminated.

22 K = *kompleks* [*vo'oroozheniya*] – weapons system.
23 According to various sources, originally the non-afterburning variety was known simply as the 'MiG-17 with the Izumrood radar' and the afterburning variety as the MiG-17P (!). Later, both versions were briefly referred to as the MiG-17P before the afterburning variety finally became the MiG-17PF.
24 ARO-57-6 = *avtomateecheskoye reaktivnoye oroodiye kalibra pyat'dyesyat sem' millimetrov na shest' zaryadov* – lit. 'six-round 57mm automatic jet gun'.
25 GKAT = *Gosoodahrstvennyy komitet po aviatseeonnoy tekhnike* – State Committee for Aircraft, as MAP was renamed for a while.
26 RS-1-U = *reaktivnyy snaryad, tip odin, oopravlyayemyy* [*po loochoo*] – rocket, Type 1, with [radar] beam guidance (ie, semi-active radar homing). Similarly, the K-5 weapons system as a whole was redesignated S-1-U (S for *sistema*).
27 KS = *Kometa-snaryad* (Comet missile), NOT *krylahtyy snaryad* (winged missile) as frequently stated; Kometa was the code name of the anti-shipping cruise missile programme. The KS-1 is also referred to as KSS in come documents.
28 FK = *izdeliye* F (ie, MiG-9) [*dlya ispytahniy po programme*] *Kometa* – modified for tests under the Kometa programme. FS = *izdeliye* F-*sereeynoye* (production version).
29 Until the mid-60s, the term *dooblyor* was commonly used in Soviet aviation to mean 'second prototype' which, so to say, doubles for the first prototype; however, this meaning is obviously not applicable in this case.
30 TBAP DD = *tyazhelobombardeerovochnyy aviapolk dahl'nevo deystviya* – long-range heavy bomber regiment; ≅ bomber wing (heavy). On 3rd October 1957 the unit was transformed into the 124th MTAP DD (*minno-torpednyy aviapolk* – long-range minelayer and torpedo-bomber regiment).
31 This aircraft was the first step in the development of the MiG-19.
32 Some documents state the forward fuel cell and aft integral tank held 1,220 litres (268.4 Imperial gallons) and 330 litres (72.6 Imperial gallons) respectively.

Chapter Three
1 The hieroglyph 中 (Chung) is the first part of the country's name in Chinese.
2 The first flight date has also been erroneously reported as 2 August 1956.
3 A different presentation, LiM and LiS, would have been more logical perhaps.
4 The c/ns follow the usual system used in Mielec. 1 is a WSK PZL division code (plant No1 = WSK-Mielec). C is an in-house product code (Lim-5); each type built at Mielec is designated by up to three letters – eg, G = PZL (Antonov) An-2 Colt, AH = PZL M-20 Mewa, AJE = PZL M-28 Skytruck etc 00 is the batch number and 01 the number of aircraft in batch.
Batch zero contained four aircraft, batch 1 contained five, batch 2 had ten, batch 3 had fifteen, and batches 4 and 5 had 20 aircraft each. From batch 6 onwards there were 30 units per batch, though batch 12 had 31 aircraft and batch 19 had just 14.
The c/n is stencilled all over the aircraft (on the forward and aft fuselage, fin, control surfaces, gear doors etc) The split presentation used here is given for the sake of convenience only; actually the number is stencilled all 'lumped together' – eg, 1C1210.
5 Some sources claim the first Lim-5 was manufactured on 25th October 1956.
6 Later renamed ITWL (*Instytut Techniczny Wojsk Lotniczych* – Air Force Technical Institute).
7 This aircraft was subsequently delivered to the East

German Air Force as 925 Red.
8 This is the figure quoted by Polish sources. However, if you add up the aircraft, batch by batch (4 + 5 + 10 + 15 + 2 x 20 + 6 x 30 + 31 + 6 x 30 + 14), you get 479 units. The static test airframe (c/n 1C 01-01) was apparently discounted, but that still makes 478, not 477!
9 Batch 1 contained ten aircraft, batch 2 had fifteen, batches 3 and 4 had 20 aircraft each, batch 5 contained 24 units and batch 6 had 41 aircraft.
10 The suffix denoted *tahač*
(tug) – or possibly [*pro vlekáni*] *terčů*
(for target towing).
11 This was the Polish designation of the TP-19 brake parachute used on the MiG-19 which was in service with the PWL since 1958.
12 In addition to the ten confirmed crashes, there are four 'probables' (aircraft whose fate is unknown).
13 This is not to be confused with the original CM-I project.
14 UB = *ooniversahl'nyy blok* – here, standardised FFAR pod.
15 The first digit denotes landing gear configuration (1 = single mainwheels, 2 = twin mainwheels). The letter denotes the aircraft's role (S = *szturmowy* – strike, R = *rozpoznawczy* – reconnaissance). The remaining digits denote the number and type of external stores.

Chapter Four
1 IAD = *istrebitel'naya aviadiveeziya* – fighter division (≅ fighter group); IAP = *istrebitel'nyy aviapolk* – fighter regiment (≅ fighter wing); GvIAP = *gvardeyskiy istrebitel'nyy aviapolk* – Guards fighter regiment. The Guards units are the elite of the Soviet (Russian) armed forces; this appellation was given for gallantry in combat, thus being an indication that this is a WW2-vintage unit.
2 BAD = *bombardeerovochnaya aviadiveeziya* – bomber division (≅ bomber group).
3 VA = *vozdooshnaya armiya* – Air Army (≅ air force).
4 On the B-47 the co-pilot doubled as the gunner, turning his seat to face aft and fire the tail cannon.
5 The solid red version was also used at one time; known aircraft wearing this colour scheme were coded 17 Yellow, 19 Yellow, 21 Yellow, 27 Yellow, 28 Yellow and 35 Yellow. It is not known which of the two colour schemes came first.
6 Transferred to the 149th IAD in May 1955.
7 The honorary appellation *Baranovichskaya* was given for the 239th IAD's part in liberating the Belorussian town of Baranovichi during the Great Patriotic War. Likewise, the appellation *Novorossiyskiy* was given for the 159th IAP's part in liberating the city of Novorossiysk.
8 *Grooppa sovetskikh voysk v Ghermahnii* – Group of Soviet Forces in Germany; renamed ZGV (*Zahpadnaya groopa voysk* – Western Group of Forces) in 1989.
9 NATO and the Soviet command often used different names for the same East German airbases. In such cases the Soviet name comes first with the NATO name following in parentheses.
10 ie, *otlichnyy samolyot* – excellent aircraft; this title was awarded for excellent maintenance. In the 1970s the inscription was replaced by the current symbol – a stylised aircraft silhouette within a 'Quality Mark' pentagon in red.
11 DOSAAF = *Dobrovol'noye obschchestvo sodeystviya armii, aviahtsii i flotu* – the Voluntary Society for the Support of the Army, Aviation (ie, Air Force) and Navy. In post-Soviet times it was renamed ROSTO (*Rosseeyskoye oboronnoye sportivno-tekhneecheskoye obschchestvo* – Russian Defence (ie, paramilitary) Sports and Technical Society).
12 The Egyptian Air Force also operated the Chinese licence-built version (F-6C) at a later date.
13 The aircraft could have belonged to the 105th Sqn which was reportedly also based at Hatzor.
14 Some sources call it the Gulf of Tongking.

15 Some sources claim that Soviet-built MiG-17Fs were also operated by the VPAF.
16 The first encounter the Americans had with VPAF MiGs was probably on the preceding day when two *Fresco-Cs* attacked a flight of Skyhawks and damaged one of them.
17 A 'Vietnamised' version of the MiG-21PF with improved corrosion protection for operations in the hot and humid South-East Asian climate.
18 He eventually rose to Brigadier General.
19 Royal Thai Air Force Base. The 8th TFW has also been reported as operating from Korat RTAFB.
20 According to US sources, this was shot down by a Talos SAM from a ship mining Haiphong harbour.
21 BuNo 153019 was quoted in ...*And Kill MiGs* (Lou Drendel, © Squadron/Signal Publications 1974). However, this Bureau Number *does not fit any F-4B production block* (cf. *McDonnell Douglas Aircraft Since 1920*, René J Francillon, © Putnam Books 1979)!
22 Soviet sources claim a figure of 51 B-52s shot down!
23 The MiG-17's small canopy with limited headroom meant that its pilots could not use modern 'bone dome' helmets – unlike, eg, MiG-21 drivers.
24 Some sources claim that the first Sidewinder missed and the MiG was shot down by the *last* missile.
25 Another Pan African Airways DC-4 was claimed destroyed at Benin City, but the aircraft was actually already a hulk, being written off in a landing accident some time before and reduced to spares.
26 The aircraft was nominally owned by Syrianair but in all probability operated by the Syrian Air Force.
27 Some sources name him Lt Khadam.
28 According to other reports, Sudan had F-4s (MiG-17 *Fresco-As*), not F-5s; see operators section.
29 There have been unconfirmed reports of Iraqi MiG-17PFs taking part in the Gulf War in 1988.

Chapter Five
1 SAP = *smeshannyy aviapolk* – composite air regiment.
2 N = *noseetel'* – lit. 'carrier' (in this case, of nuclear munitions); also referred to as IL-28A (*ahtomnyy* – 'atomic', ie, nuclear-capable).
3 Available sources say two aircraft were delivered; however, *three* CzAF MiG-17Fs have been reported.
4 S = *stihací* [*letoun*] – fighter.
5 Marxwalde reverted to its original name, Neuhardenberg, following German reunification in 1990.
6 JG 2 was named after the famous Soviet cosmonaut who was the first man in space; JG 3 after another Soviet cosmonaut who died on 24th April 1967 when his spacecraft's heat shield failed during reentry, and JG 7 after the East German president of the early 1950s.
7 Formerly *Flugzeugwerke Dresden* (Dresden Aircraft Factory), a manufacturer of VEB-14s (licence-built Ilyushin IL-14P *Crates*). The East German aircraft industry was killed off by the government in 1961 as 'uneconomical'.
8 A German book on the LSK/LV stated the unit number as JBG 37. However, the fleet list section in the same book uses JBG 31 throughout and this is corroborated by other German publications. The unit was named after the first Czech president.
9 ODRAP = *otdel'nyy dal'niy razvedyvatel'nyy aviapolk* – independent long-range reconnaissance regiment.
10 *Not* the notorious Liberation Tigers of Tamil Eelam (LTTE) – they have been around since 1983.

Chapter Six
1 The rounds for the N-37 and NR-23 weigh 1,300g (45.89oz) and 340g (12oz) respectively.

The flight line at a Soviet airbase with at least eleven red-coded MiG-17s; the pilots are already in their seats and 'ready to roll'. The second aircraft in the row, 33 Red, is a Komsomol'sk-on-Amur built example (c/n 2194).
Yefim Gordon archive

The MiG-17 in Colour

01 Red, an early-production MiG-17 on display at the Russian Air Force Museum, Monino. Yefim Gordon

MiG-17 '55 Red' preserved in the Museum of the Kubinka AB garrison. Yefim Gordon

39 Red (originally 139 Red, c/n 54211399), a late-production Fresco-A displayed in the Great Patriotic War Museum, Poklonnaya Gora, Moscow. This aircraft was operated by the DOSAAF in the closing stage of its flying career. Yefim Gordon

This rare colour shot of a MiG-17PF illustrates the enlarged centrebody radome of the RP-5 Izumrood-2 radar fitted to late-production aircraft. Sergey and Dmitriy Komissarov collection

This MiG-17M operated by the Russian Air Force Flight Test Centre (GLITs) in Akhtoobinsk has unusually few 'bumps and bulges'; note the antenna fairing on the air intake splitter. Yefim Gordon

This MiG-17M preserved at the North Fleet Air Arm Museum in Safonovo is a converted MiG-17AS fighter-bomber. Unusually, it lacks the large ventral fairing but has a fintip antenna fairing and a strake-like fairing ahead of the fin. Yefim Gordon

31092 Red, a rather weathered production J-5 in standard natural metal finish, is towed by a Soviet-built GAZ-66 4x4 army truck.
Yefim Gordon archive

Flanked by an incomplete USAF F-4 Phantom and an Aero L-39 Albatros trainer, this unmarked MiG-17F serialled 413 Red sits in the backyard of the Auto- und Technik Museum, Sinsheim; this is probably an ex-Polish Air Force Lim-5 (c/n 1C 04-13). Yefim Gordon

Lim-6bis '105 Red' started life as a Lim-5M (c/n 1F 01-05). It is now preserved at the Muzeum Lotnictwa i Astronautyki, Kraków.
Yefim Gordon

Flying in diamond nine formation, the Kubinka team's MiG-17s show the new solid red colour scheme. Yefim Gordon archive

Two Albanian Air Force/1875th Regiment F-5s, including 4-10 (c/n 7707?), seen over the canopy of an F-6 (MiG-19S) at Kucovë AB near Berat. Key Publishing Group

22 Red, a Soviet-built early-production Bulgarian AF MiG-17PF, preserved at Graf Ignatiev AB. Keith Dexter

A quartet of 'August 1' JJ-5s in diamond formation over the rugged scenery of China. Yefim Gordon archive

506 White displays the early version of the team's colour scheme (parts of the airframe are natural metal rather than white). AIR International

This JJ-5 formerly operated by the 'August 1' display team resides at the Datangshan museum. The non-standard wraparound windshield is noteworthy. F C W Käsmann

A Force Aérienne Congolaise MiG-17 with the old-style insignia. *Air Forces Monthly*

This camouflaged East German Air Force Lim-5 fighter-bomber retrofitted with pylons for MARS-2 FFAR pods (c/n 1C 08-20) is on display at the Luftwaffenmuseum Berlin-Gatow. 905 Red was the last of the type overhauled by FWD. Yefim Gordon

Wearing the fake serial '091 Red', this East German Air Force Lim-5P (MiG-17PF) is also preserved at the Luftwaffenmuseum Berlin-Gatow; its true identity is unknown. Yefim Gordon

A three-quarters rear view of Lim-5P '091 Red' at the Luftwaffenmuseum Berlin-Gatow.
Yefim Gordon

A pair of No 1 FCU FT-5s in different colour schemes pose for the camera over the rugged mountains of Pakistan. *Koku-Fan*

Lim-6M '618 Red' (c/n 1D 06-18) displayed at the Muzeum Lotnictwa i Astronautyki, Kraków. The ventral camera fairing is not readily visible in this view. Yefim Gordon

This rear view of 105 Red at the Muzeum Lotnictwa i Astronautyki, Kraków, shows the brake parachute container and faired radio altimeter aerials of the Lim-6bis. Yefim Gordon

Sri Lanka Air Force Fresco-As in a hangar. RART

CTF 701, the first of two Sri Lanka Air Force FT-5s. The titles on the fuselage are in Sinhalese on the starboard side and in English on the port side. *Air Forces Monthly*

A rare colour shot of Soviet Air Force Fresco-As on a dirt strip, probably during an exercise. Unusually, the aircraft are painted light grey overall, making an interesting comparison with the natural metal drop tanks; the rudders are not black but deflected fully to port, the shadow making them appear darker than the rest of the aircraft. Yefim Gordon archive

Top left: **The three NR-23 cannons of the MiG-17PF.** Yefim Gordon

Top right: **The aft fuselage and tail unit of the MiG-17F/PF.** Yefim Gordon

Centre left: **This view illustrates the Fresco's cranked wing trailing edge and triple wing fences.** Yefim Gordon

Centre right: **The main landing gear of the MiG-17.** Yefim Gordon

Above left: **The convergent-divergent nozzle of the VK-1F's s afterburner.** Yefim Gordon

Above right: **Close-up of the wing pylon and MARS-2 FFAR pod on Lim-5 '905 Red'. Note that the pod is also camouflaged and the sharp tip of the pylon is painted red to warn ground personnel and minimise the risk of injury.** Yefim Gordon

Right: **The bulbous radomes of the Lim-5P's RP-5 radar are readily apparent in this view. The stencil on the nose reads 'Filler for de-icing liquid'.** Yefim Gordon

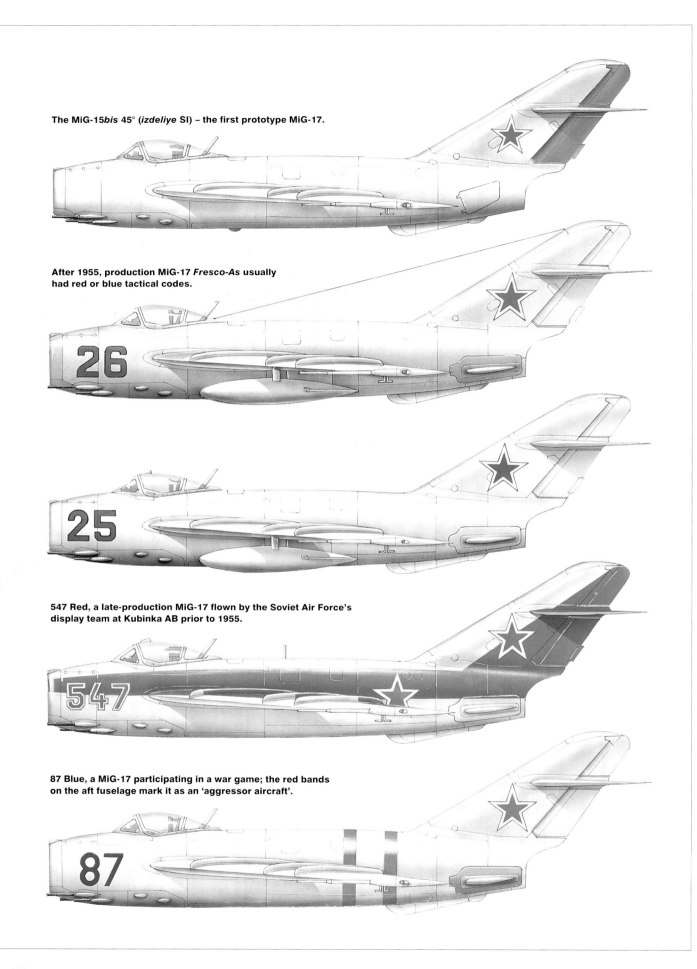

The MiG-15*bis* 45° (*izdeliye* SI) – the first prototype MiG-17.

After 1955, production MiG-17 *Fresco-As* usually
had red or blue tactical codes.

547 Red, a late-production MiG-17 flown by the Soviet Air Force's
display team at Kubinka AB prior to 1955.

87 Blue, a MiG-17 participating in a war game; the red bands
on the aft fuselage mark it as an 'aggressor aircraft'.

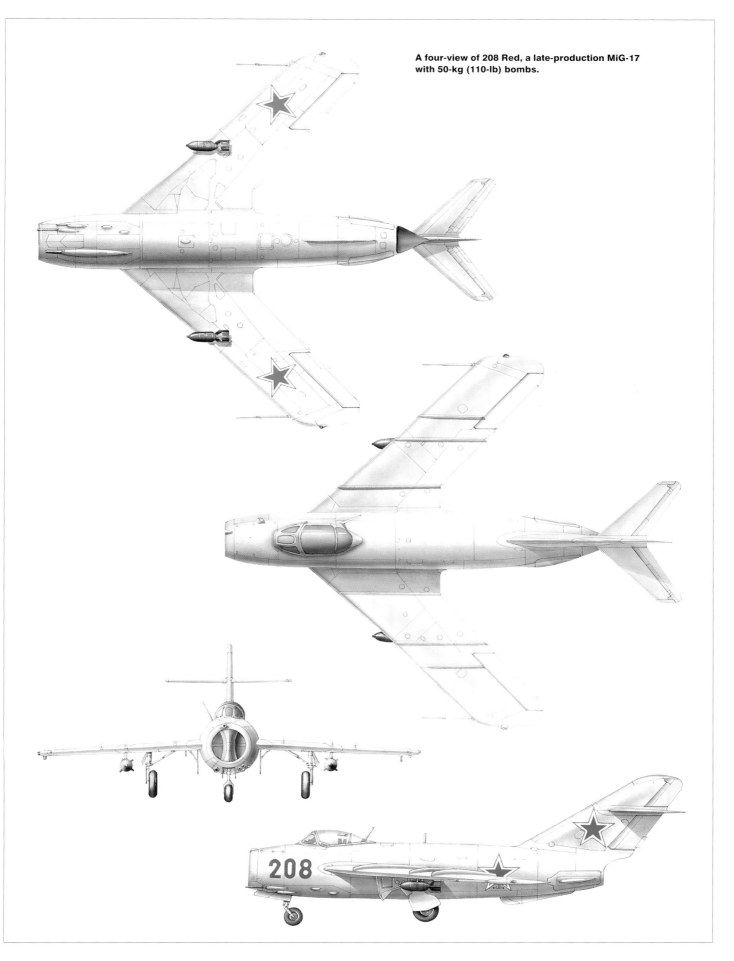

A four-view of 208 Red, a late-production MiG-17
with 50-kg (110-lb) bombs.

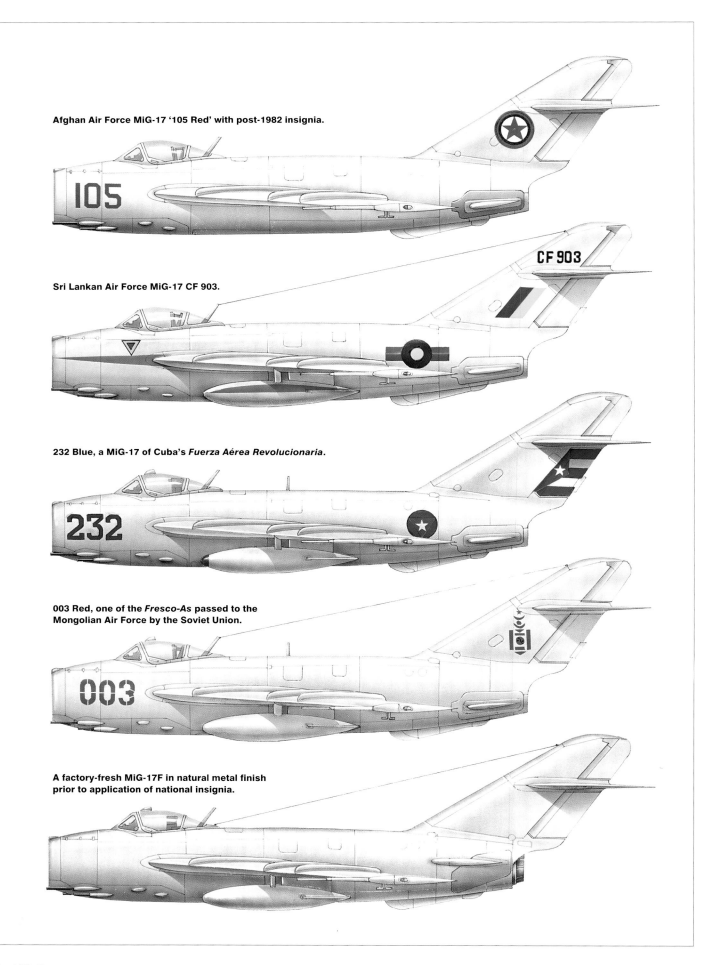

Afghan Air Force MiG-17 '105 Red' with post-1982 insignia.

Sri Lankan Air Force MiG-17 CF 903.

232 Blue, a MiG-17 of Cuba's *Fuerza Aérea Revolucionaria*.

003 Red, one of the *Fresco-As* passed to the Mongolian Air Force by the Soviet Union.

A factory-fresh MiG-17F in natural metal finish prior to application of national insignia.

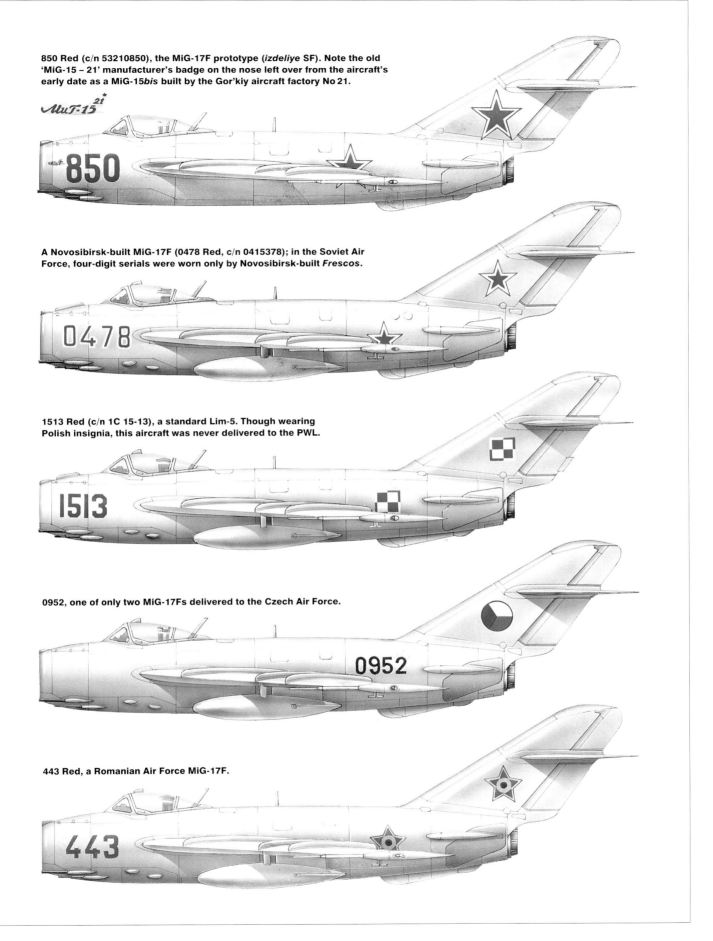

850 Red (c/n 53210850), the MiG-17F prototype (*izdeliye* SF). Note the old 'MiG-15 – 21' manufacturer's badge on the nose left over from the aircraft's early date as a MiG-15*bis* built by the Gor'kiy aircraft factory No 21.

A Novosibirsk-built MiG-17F (0478 Red, c/n 0415378); in the Soviet Air Force, four-digit serials were worn only by Novosibirsk-built *Frescos*.

1513 Red (c/n 1C 15-13), a standard Lim-5. Though wearing Polish insignia, this aircraft was never delivered to the PWL.

0952, one of only two MiG-17Fs delivered to the Czech Air Force.

443 Red, a Romanian Air Force MiG-17F.

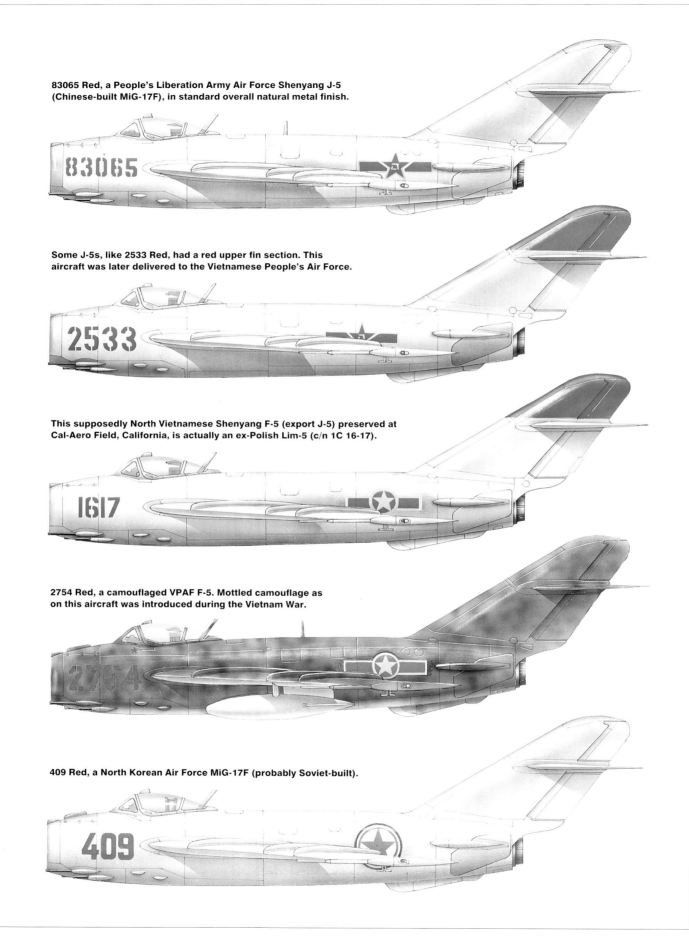

83065 Red, a People's Liberation Army Air Force Shenyang J-5 (Chinese-built MiG-17F), in standard overall natural metal finish.

Some J-5s, like 2533 Red, had a red upper fin section. This aircraft was later delivered to the Vietnamese People's Air Force.

This supposedly North Vietnamese Shenyang F-5 (export J-5) preserved at Cal-Aero Field, California, is actually an ex-Polish Lim-5 (c/n 1C 16-17).

2754 Red, a camouflaged VPAF F-5. Mottled camouflage as on this aircraft was introduced during the Vietnam War.

409 Red, a North Korean Air Force MiG-17F (probably Soviet-built).

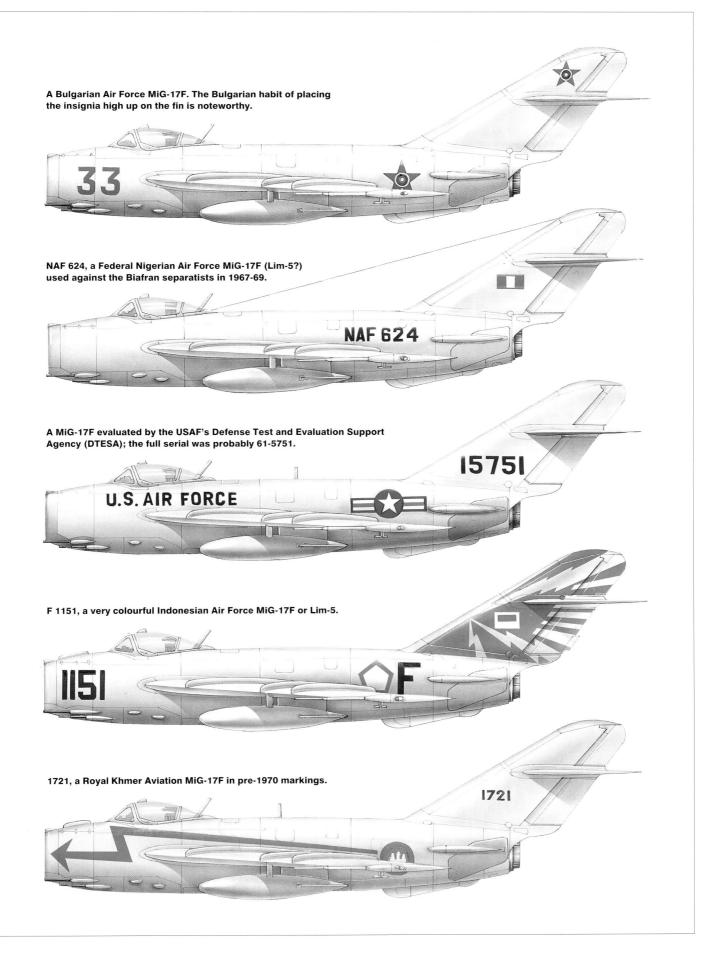

A Bulgarian Air Force MiG-17F. The Bulgarian habit of placing the insignia high up on the fin is noteworthy.

NAF 624, a Federal Nigerian Air Force MiG-17F (Lim-5?) used against the Biafran separatists in 1967-69.

A MiG-17F evaluated by the USAF's Defense Test and Evaluation Support Agency (DTESA); the full serial was probably 61-5751.

F 1151, a very colourful Indonesian Air Force MiG-17F or Lim-5.

1721, a Royal Khmer Aviation MiG-17F in pre-1970 markings.

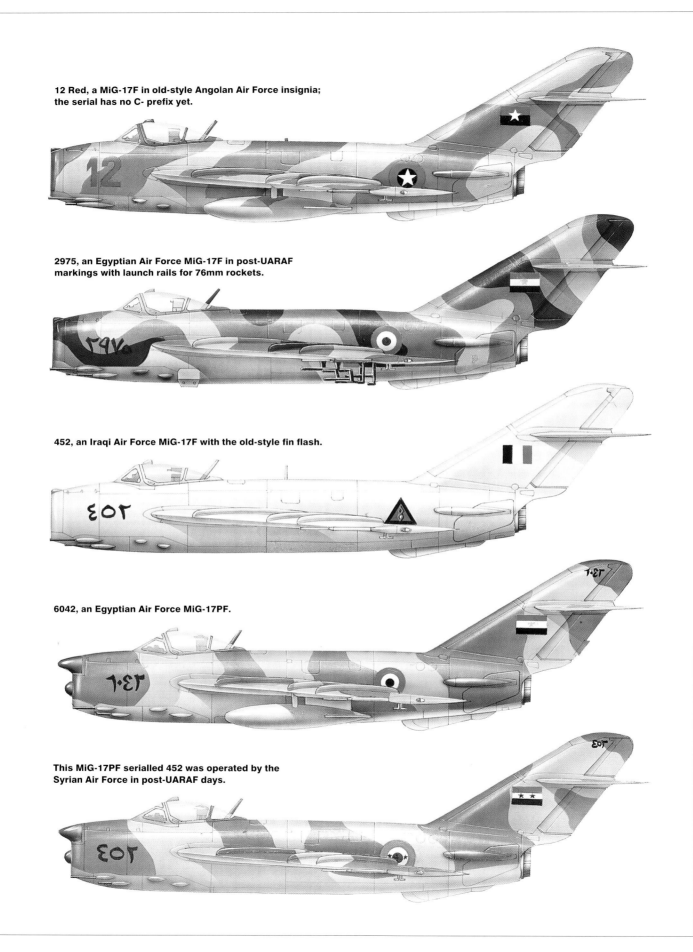

12 Red, a MiG-17F in old-style Angolan Air Force insignia; the serial has no C- prefix yet.

2975, an Egyptian Air Force MiG-17F in post-UARAF markings with launch rails for 76mm rockets.

452, an Iraqi Air Force MiG-17F with the old-style fin flash.

6042, an Egyptian Air Force MiG-17PF.

This MiG-17PF serialled 452 was operated by the Syrian Air Force in post-UARAF days.

A four-view of a production Soviet Air Force MiG-17PFU with RS-1-U AAMs.

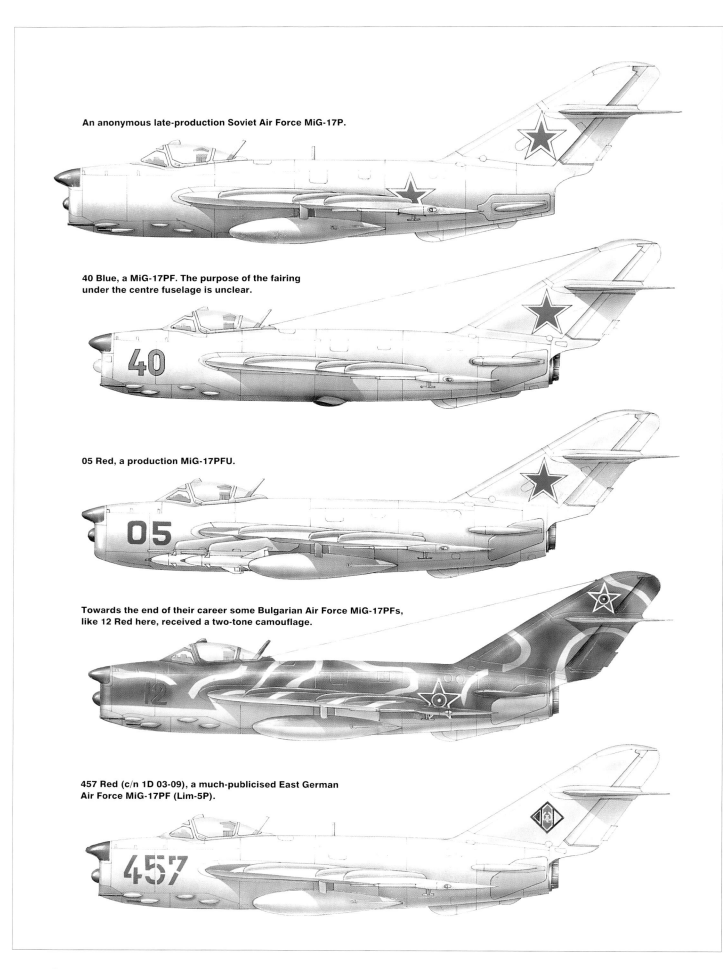

An anonymous late-production Soviet Air Force MiG-17P.

40 Blue, a MiG-17PF. The purpose of the fairing under the centre fuselage is unclear.

05 Red, a production MiG-17PFU.

Towards the end of their career some Bulgarian Air Force MiG-17PFs, like 12 Red here, received a two-tone camouflage.

457 Red (c/n 1D 03-09), a much-publicised East German Air Force MiG-17PF (Lim-5P).

While there is information about a Polish Air Force Lim-6M serialled 971 Red, the serial is obviously bogus since the last Lim-5P built (the basis for Lim-6M conversions) was 641 Red – batch 6, 41st aircraft in the batch.

Ex-Polish Air Force 511 Red (c/n 1D 05-11), a Lim-6M operated by the USAF/DTESA from 1988 and October 1992 for threat simulation purposes.

Bangladesh Air Force Shenyang FT-5 724 (c/n 1724).

Some FT-5s operated by the Pakistan Air Force's No1 Fighter Conversion Unit (FCU) at Mianwali AB, like 55-1136, were gloss white overall.

55-1208 illustrates another typical colour scheme worn by the FCU's FT-5s.

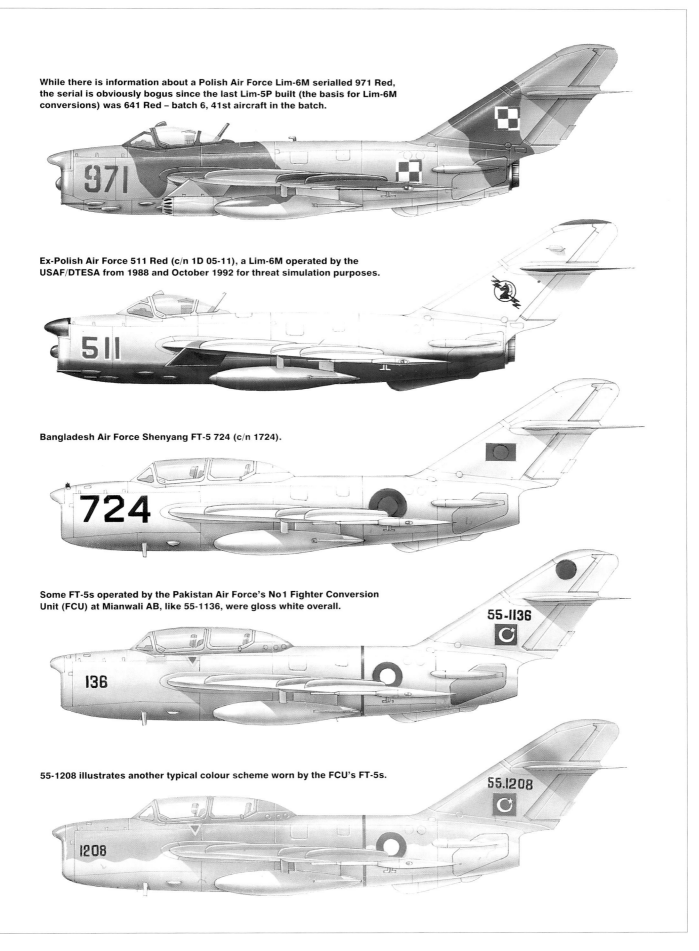

MiG-17 Family Drawings

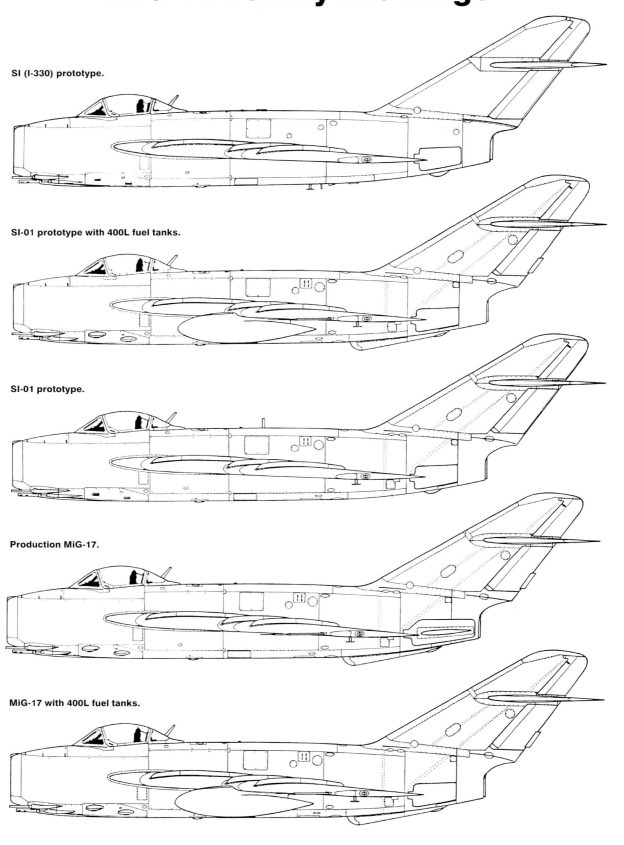

SI (I-330) prototype.

SI-01 prototype with 400L fuel tanks.

SI-01 prototype.

Production MiG-17.

MiG-17 with 400L fuel tanks.

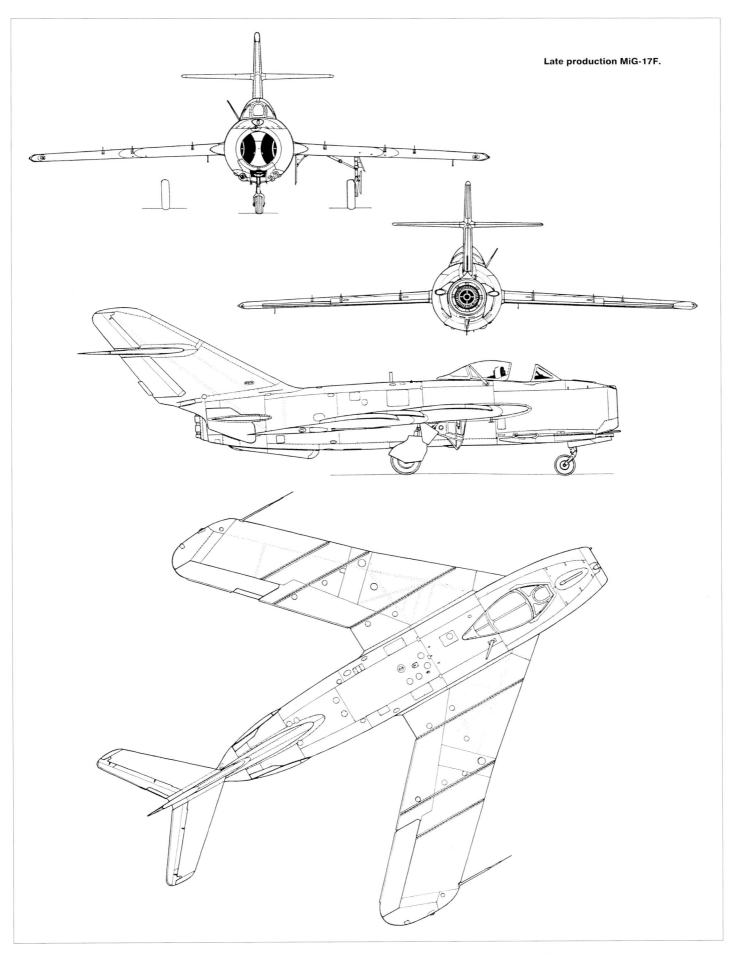

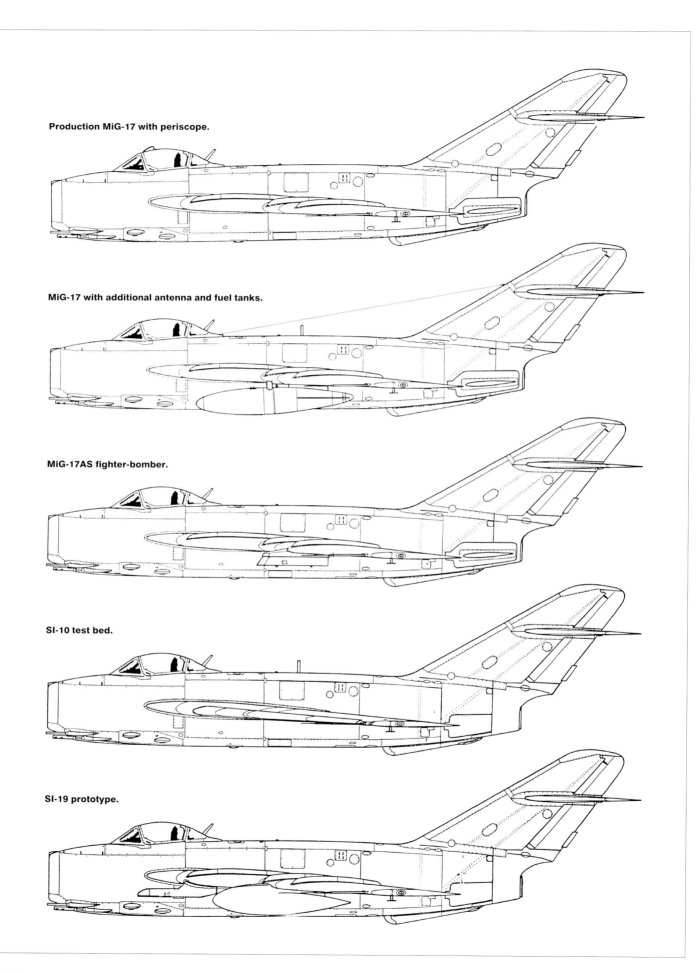

Production MiG-17 with periscope.

MiG-17 with additional antenna and fuel tanks.

MiG-17AS fighter-bomber.

SI-10 test bed.

SI-19 prototype.

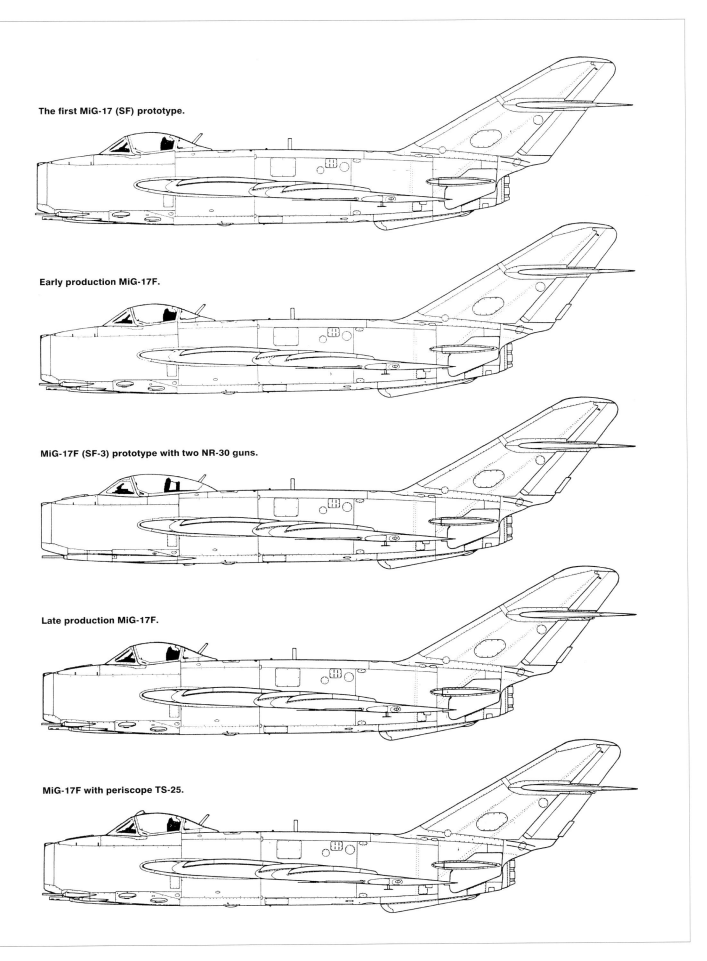

The first MiG-17 (SF) prototype.

Early production MiG-17F.

MiG-17F (SF-3) prototype with two NR-30 guns.

Late production MiG-17F.

MiG-17F with periscope TS-25.

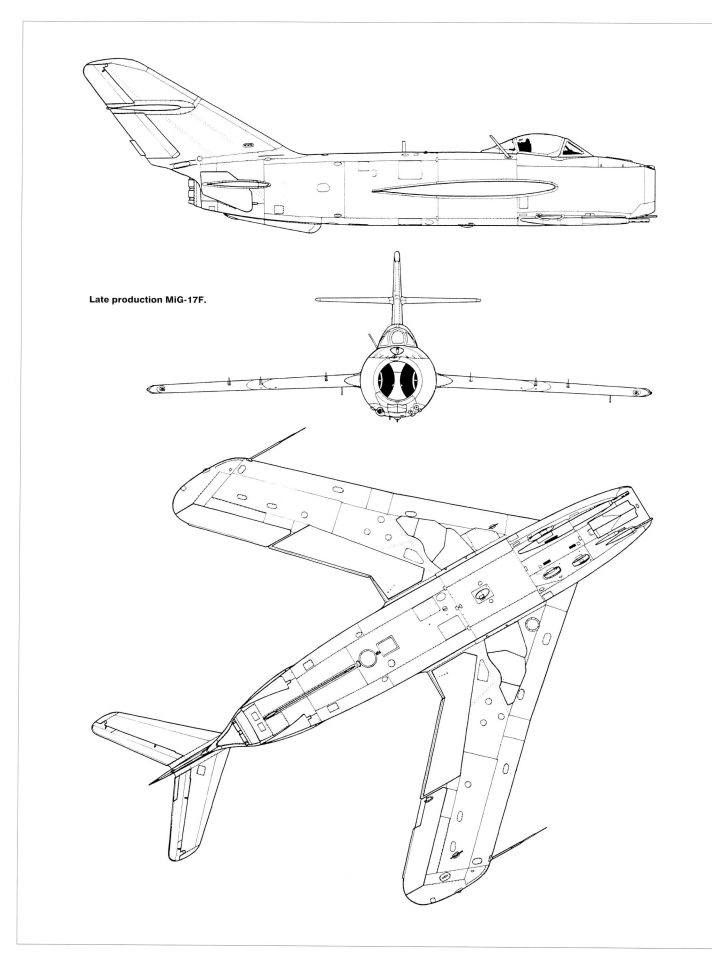

Late production MiG-17F.

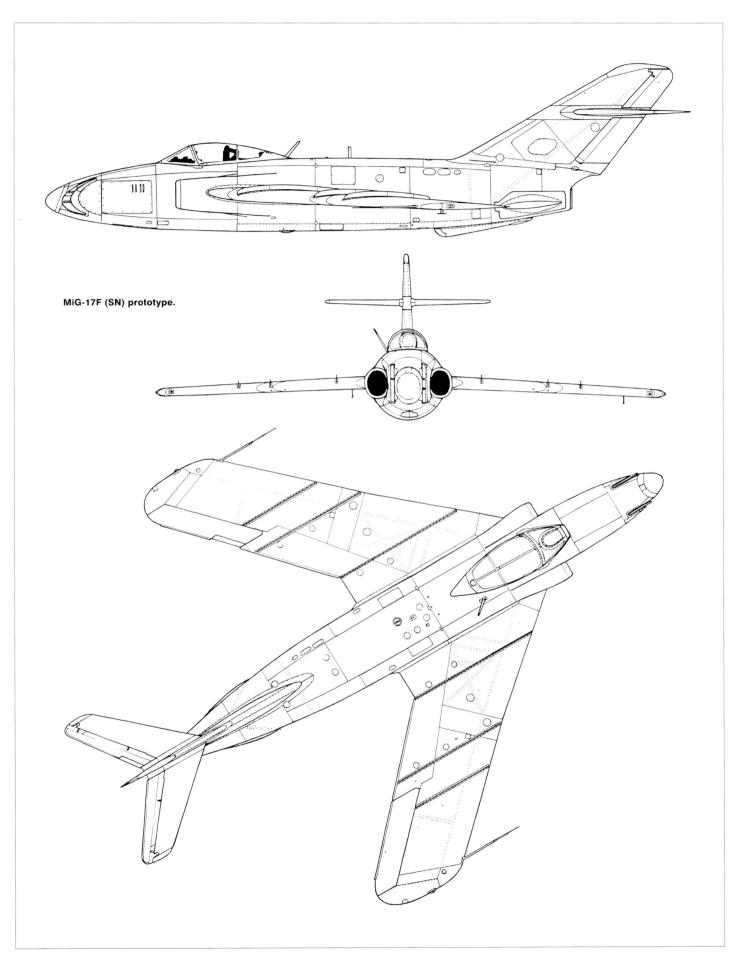

MiG-17F (SN) prototype.

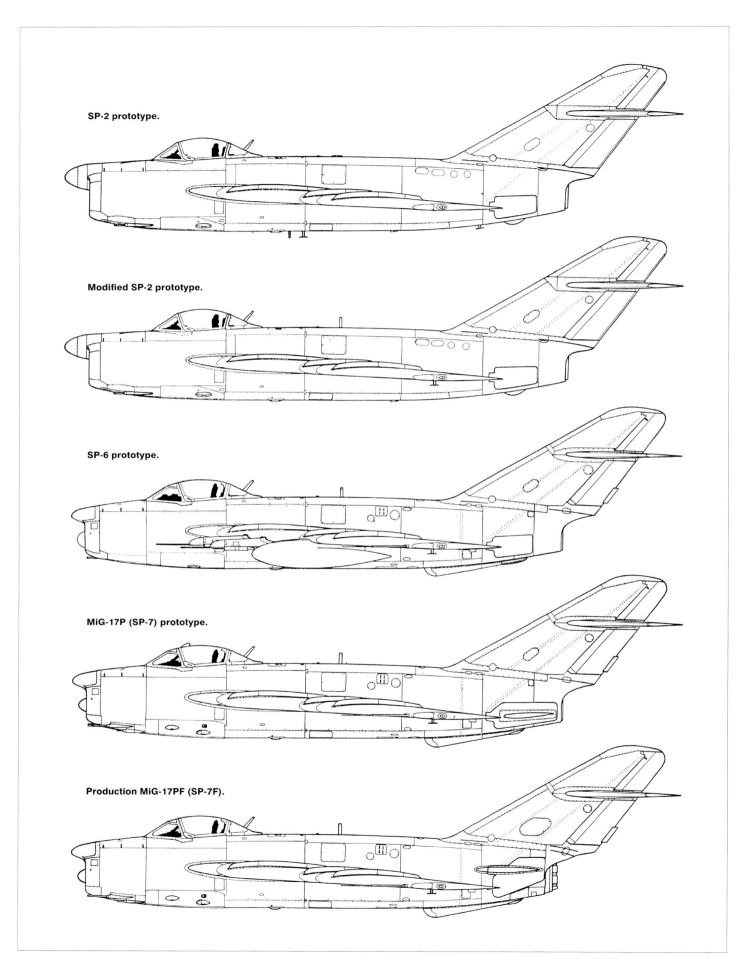

SP-2 prototype.

Modified SP-2 prototype.

SP-6 prototype.

MiG-17P (SP-7) prototype.

Production MiG-17PF (SP-7F).

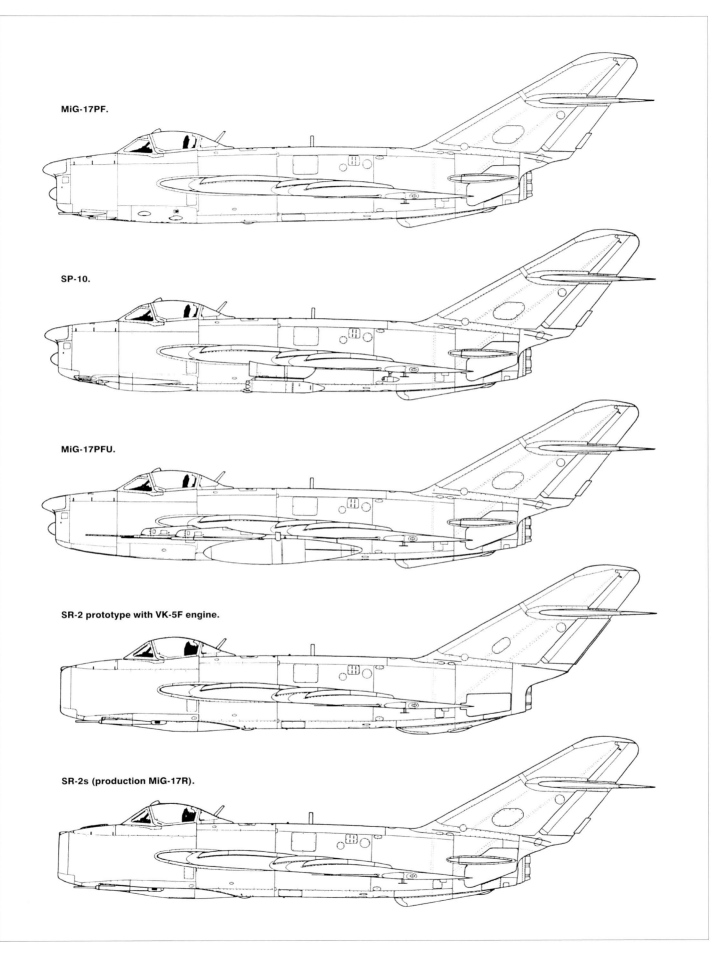

MiG-17PF.

SP-10.

MiG-17PFU.

SR-2 prototype with VK-5F engine.

SR-2s (production MiG-17R).

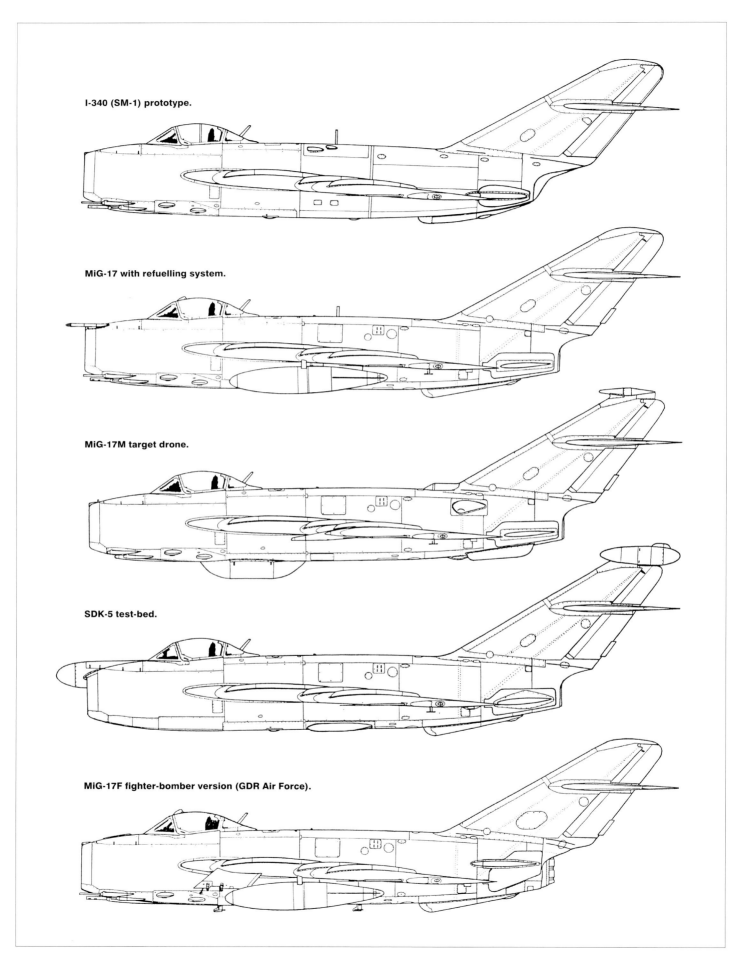

I-340 (SM-1) prototype.

MiG-17 with refuelling system.

MiG-17M target drone.

SDK-5 test-bed.

MiG-17F fighter-bomber version (GDR Air Force).

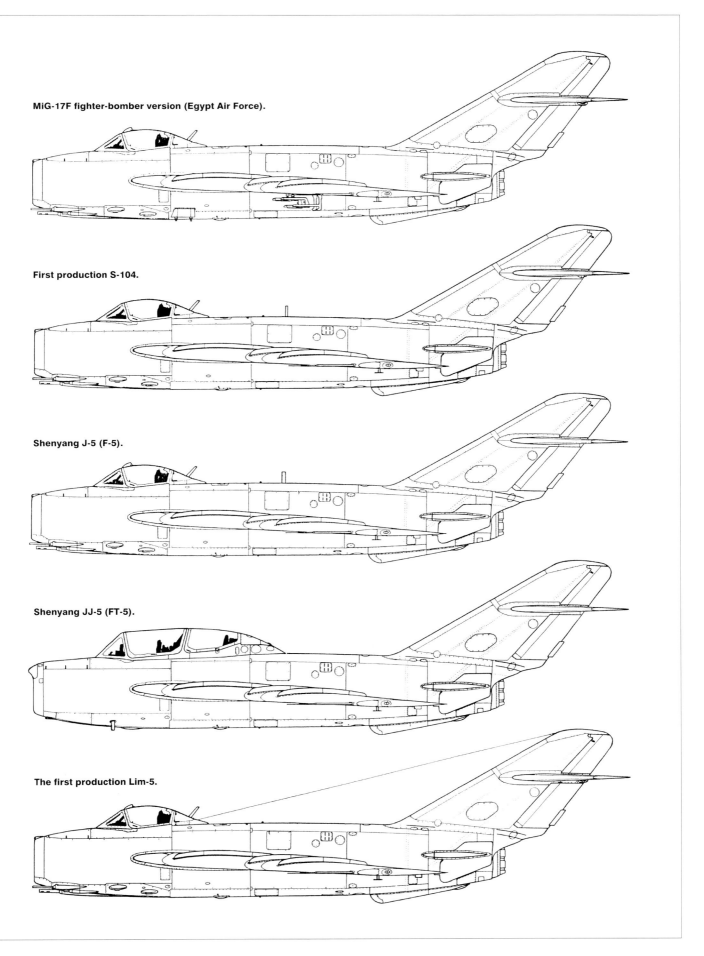

MiG-17F fighter-bomber version (Egypt Air Force).

First production S-104.

Shenyang J-5 (F-5).

Shenyang JJ-5 (FT-5).

The first production Lim-5.

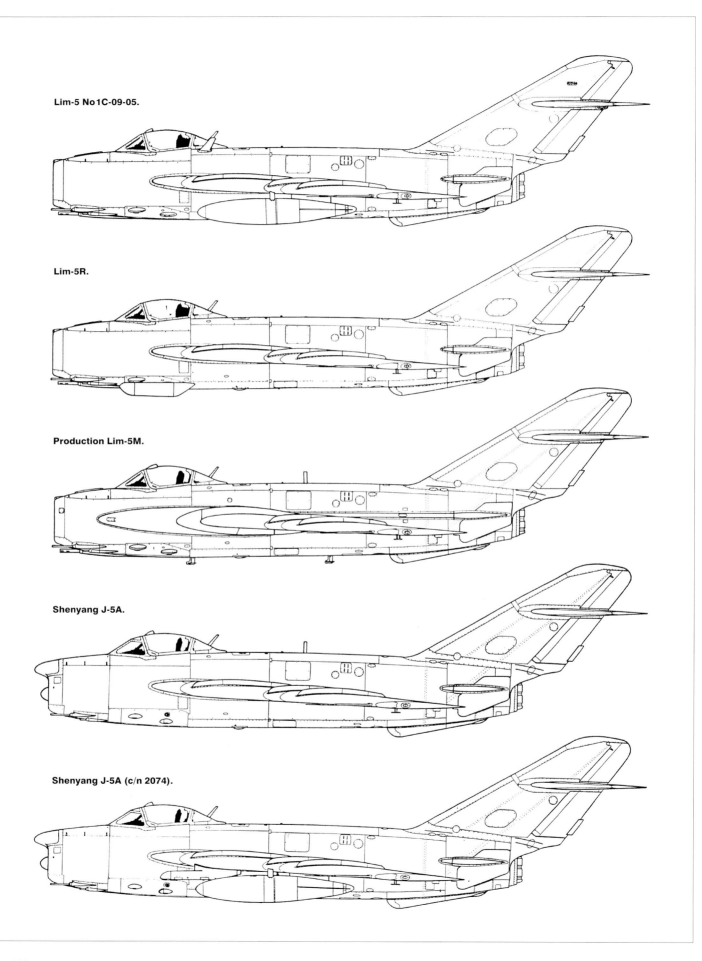

Lim-5 No1C-09-05.

Lim-5R.

Production Lim-5M.

Shenyang J-5A.

Shenyang J-5A (c/n 2074).

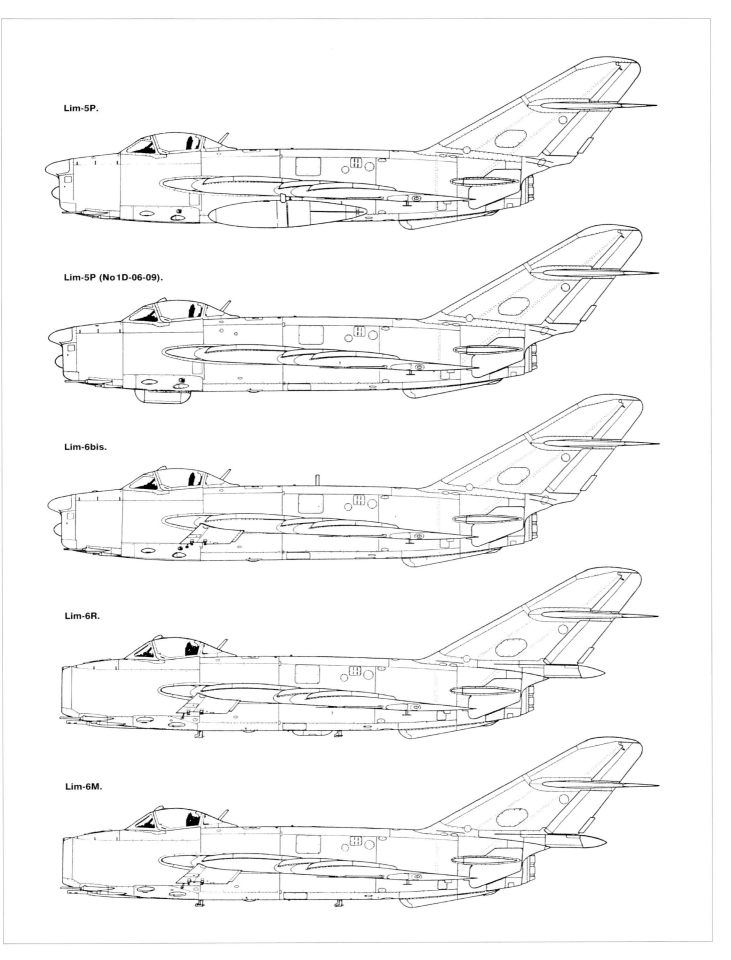

Lim-5P.

Lim-5P (No1D-06-09).

Lim-6bis.

Lim-6R.

Lim-6M.

Red Star Volume 1
SUKHOI S-37 & MIKOYAN MFI
Yefim Gordon

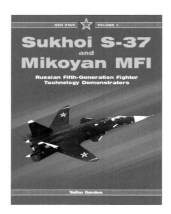

Conceived as an answer to the American ATF programme, the Mikoyan MFI (better known as the 1.42 or 1.44) and the Sukhoi S-37 Berkoot were developed as technology demonstrators. Both design bureaux used an approach that was quite different from Western fifth-generation fighter philosophy. This gives a detailed account of how these enigmatic aircraft were designed, built and flown. It includes structural descriptions of both types.

Sbk, 280 x 215 mm, 96pp, plus 8pp colour foldout, 12 b/w and 174 colour photos, drawings and colour artworks
1 85780 120 2   **£18.95/US $27.95**

Red Star Volume 2
FLANKERS: The New Generation
Yefim Gordon

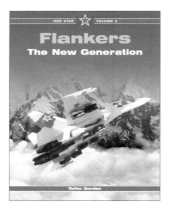

The multi-role Su-30 and Su-35 and thrust-vectoring Su-37 are described in detail, along with the 'big head' Su-23FN/Su-34 tactical bomber, the Su-27K (Su-33) shipborne fighter and its two-seat combat trainer derivative, the Su-27KUB. The book also describes the customised versions developed for foreign customers – the Su-30KI (Su-27KI), the Su-30MKI for India, the Su-30MKK for China and the latest Su-35UB.

Softback, 280 x 215 mm, 128 pages 252 colour photographs, plus 14 pages of colour artworks
1 85780 121 0   **£18.95/US $27.95**

Red Star Volume 3
POLIKARPOV'S I-16 FIGHTER
Yefim Gordon and Keith Dexter

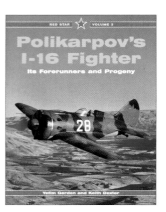

Often dismissed because it did not fare well against its more modern adversaries in the Second World War, Nikolay Polikarpov's I-16 was nevertheless an outstanding fighter – among other things, because it was the world's first monoplane fighter with a retractable undercarriage. Its capabilities were demonstrated effectively during the Spanish Civil War. Covers every variant, from development, unbuilt projects and the later designs that evolved from it.

Sbk, 280 x 215 mm, 128 pages, 185 b/w photographs, 17 pages of colour artworks, plus line drawings
1 85780 131 8   **£18.99/US $27.95**

SOVIET X-PLANES
Yefim Gordon & Bill Gunston

A detailed review of Soviet experimental aircraft from the early 1900s through to the latest Russian prototypes of today.

The book is the first to collect the stories of the more important Soviet experimental aircraft into one volume. Working from original sources the authors have produced an outstanding reference which although concentrating on hardware also includes many unflown projects. About 150 types are described, each with relevant data, and including many three-view drawings.

Hardback, 282 x 213mm, 240 pages 355 b/w, 50 colour photos; 200 dwgs
1 85780 099 0   **£29.95/US $44.95**

Aerofax
MiG-21 'FISHBED'
Most widely used Supersonic Fighter
Yefim Gordon and Bill Gunston

The ubiquitous MiG-21 is unquestionably one of the greatest fighters of the post-Second World War era. It was Russia's first operational Mach 2-capable interceptor, and a stepping stone for many nations to enter the age of supersonic air combat. Access to the files of the MiG design bureau and other previously inaccessible sources reveal the secrets of the fighter that has flown and fought in more countries than any other supersonic jet.

Softback, 280 x 216 mm, 144 pages 335 b/w and 46 col illusts, plus colour artwork and scale plans.
1 85780 042 7   **£17.95/US $27.95**

Aerofax
MIKOYAN-GUREVICH MiG-15
Yefim Gordon

In this Aerofax, compiled from a wealth of first-hand Russian sources, there is a comprehensive history of every evolution of the Soviet Union's swept-wing fighter and its service. Notably in this volume, there are tables listing intricate details of many individual aircraft, a concept which would have been unthinkable in any publications only a few years ago.

There is extensive and detailed photo coverage, again from Russian sources, almost all of which is previously unseen.

Softback, 280 x 215 mm, 160 pages 214 b/w and 21 colour photographs, 7pp col sideviews, 18pp b/w drawings
1 85780 105 9   **£17.95/US $29.95**

Aerofax
YAKOVLEV Yak-25/26/27/28
Yakovlev's Tactical Twinjets
Yefim Gordon

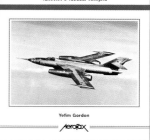

During the 1950s and 1960s the Soviet design bureau Yakovlev was responsible for a series of swept-wing twin-engined jet combat aircraft, known in the west under various names including *Firebar*, *Flashlight*, *Mandrake*, *Mangrove*, *Brewer* and *Maestro*. All the various models are covered in this Aerofax – as usual with a mass of new information, detail and illustrations from original Russian sources.

Softback, 280 x 215 mm, 128 pages 202 b/w and 41 colour photographs, plus drawings and 21 colour side-views
1 85780 125 3   **£17.99/US $27.95**